AF342140

strokes of genius | 8

THE BEST OF DRAWING
expressive texture

edited by
RACHEL RUBIN WOLF

NORTH LIGHT BOOKS
CINCINNATI, OHIO
artistsnetwork.com

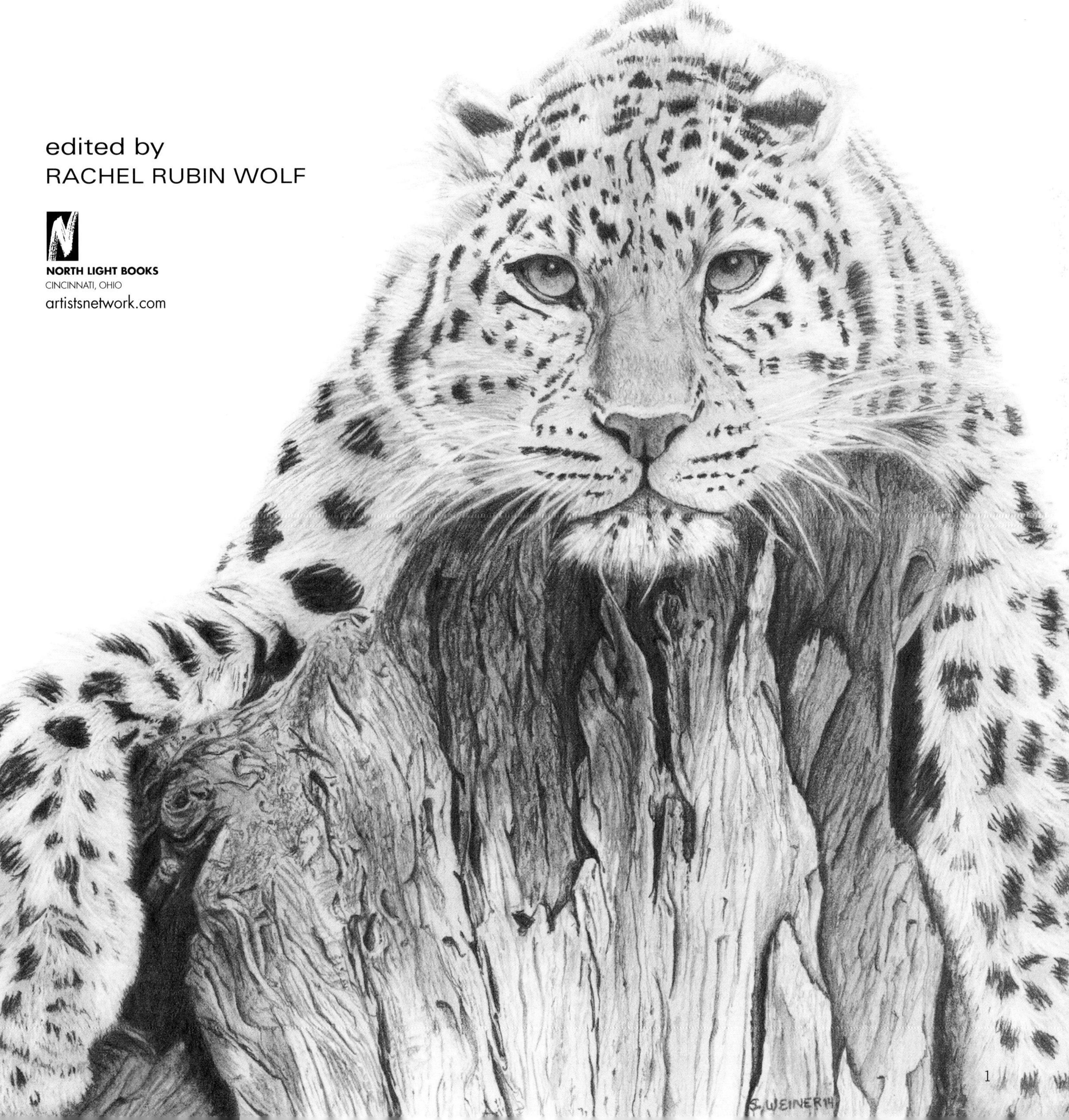

Contents

Introduction 5

Contributors 138

Index 142

About the Editor 143

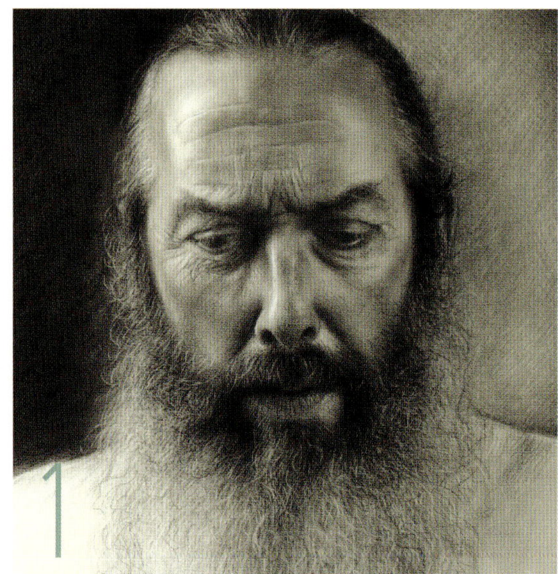

Fabulous Faces 6

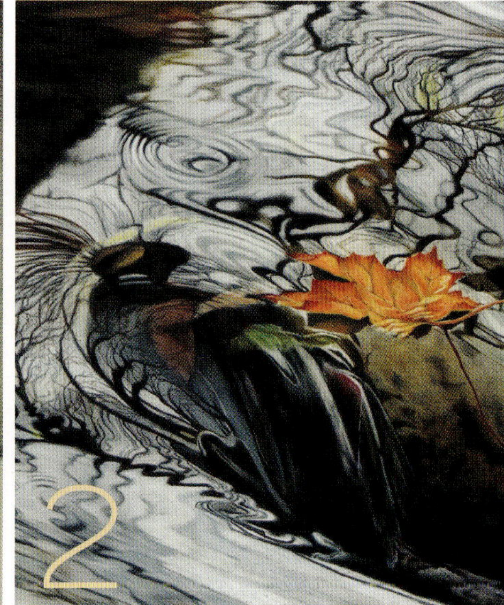

Scenes from Town &
Country 34

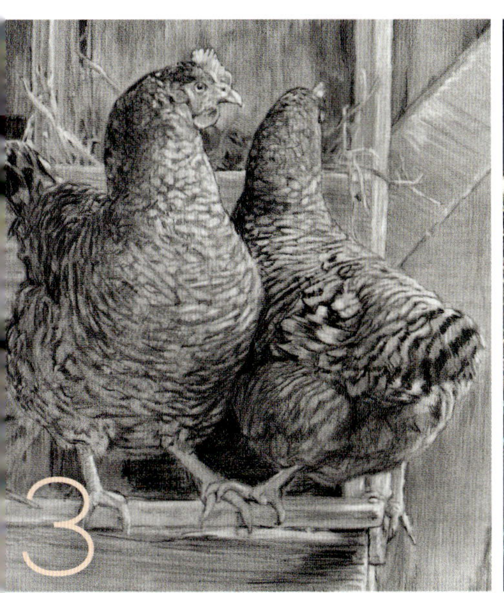

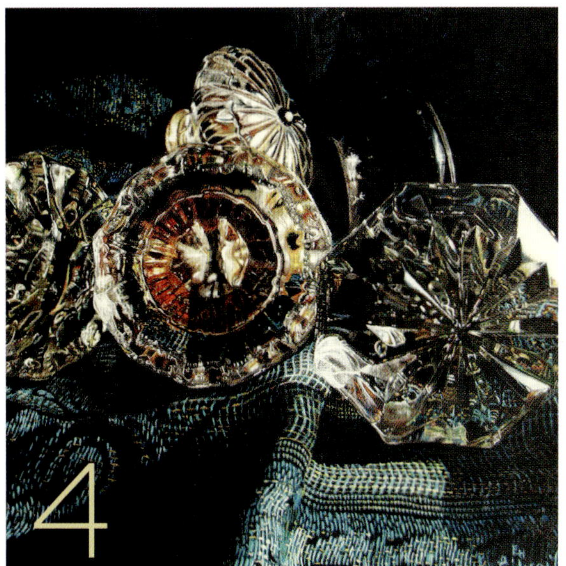

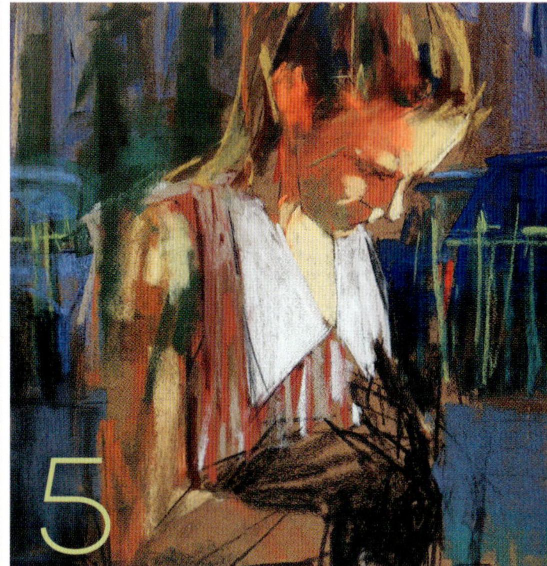

Animals: Home, Farm & Wild   58

The Still Life   88

The Human Spirit   108

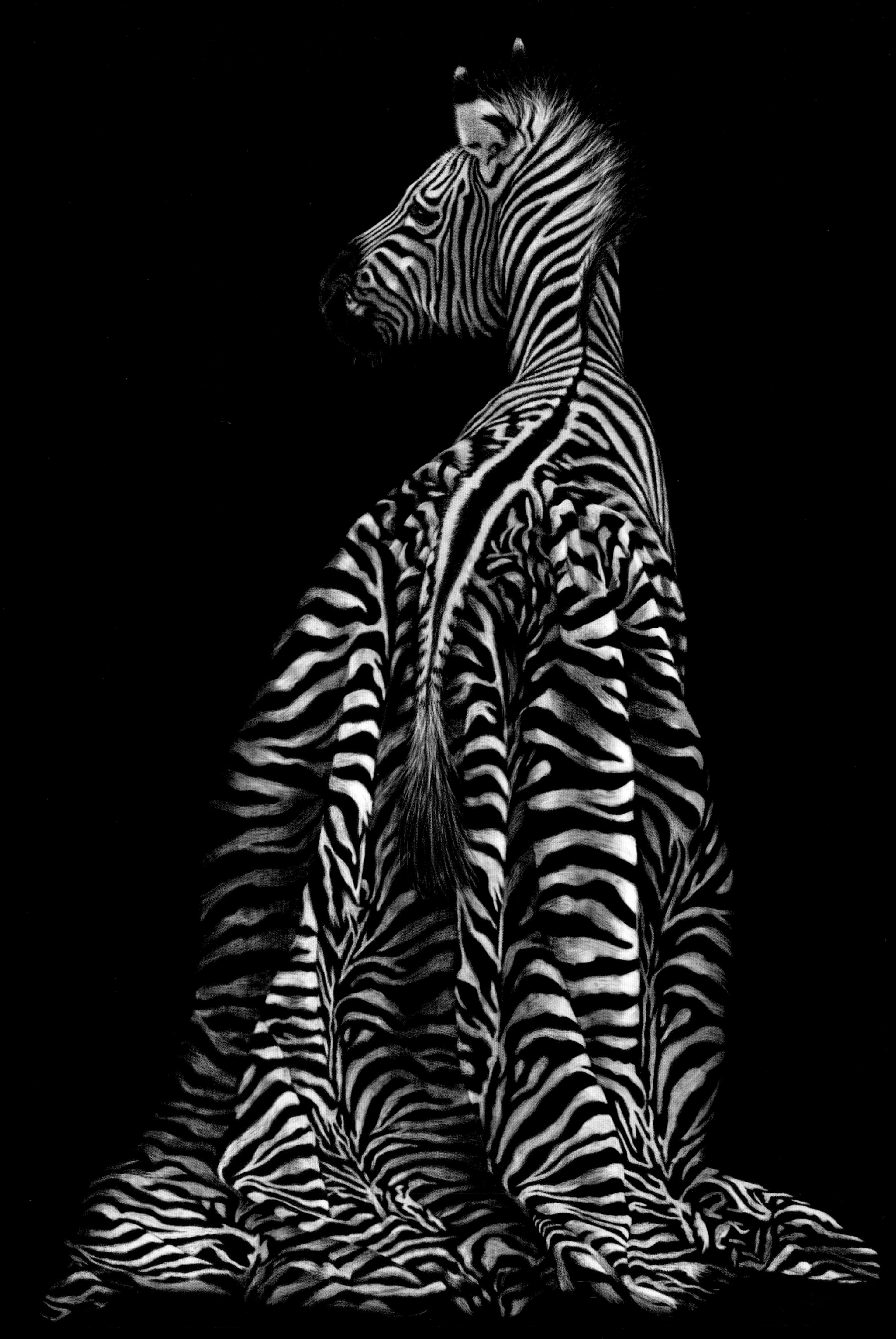

Introduction

To many artists, texture is where the fun comes in! Though often a key aspect of the finished piece, it is added after the work of building the foundation. "With a strong composition, texture is the icing on the cake," is Bill Shoemaker's way of saying this. The diverse range of drawing materials and techniques allows for endless possibilities for textural elements as exhibited in the collection of drawings in *Strokes of Genius 8*. These include replicating natural or man-made textures, creating imagined textures, or interpreting emotions in a textural way. Texture can be defined as: surface quality, feel, grain, character, finish, weave, personality, nature, makeup, appearance. We can even create textures that are not there or could not exist— witness Karen Neal's drawing on the facing page.

Texture can tell a story. "I think of texture as beauty marks," says Christine Swann. "There is something so beautiful about a deliberate, descriptive mark when it clearly tells the story." Further, "A sensitive scribble with a pencil can make magic," according to Deb Hoeffner.

How does texture happen? To James W Voshell: "The illusion of texture is created by a light source raking across the surface particulars of a subject." Steve Wilda continues this thought: "In creating texture it's important to observe the surface, substance, lighting and shadows."

For Steven Rockwell, sounding rapturous as a wine connoisseur, "Texture is a spice that when mixed in one's drawing can develop deep rich complexities, subtle apparitions and brave bursts of interest." Summing it up, Mandy Boursicot says, "Texture is the finishing touch and the crowning glory of excellent drawing."

Rachel

—Rachel Rubin Wolf

◄ **DO MY STRIPES LOOK BIG IN THIS?**
Karen Neal
Scratchboard
36" × 24" (91cm × 61cm)

This is my favorite piece so far because of its quirkiness! Scratchboard is a subtractive medium that involves the use of abrasive tools to directly remove the top layer of black India ink to expose a secondary layer of white kaolin clay. I use tools such as tattoo needles, fiberglass brush and no. 11 craft knife blades. These sharp instruments produce meticulous strokes.

"Art makes the impossible possible." —KAREN NEAL

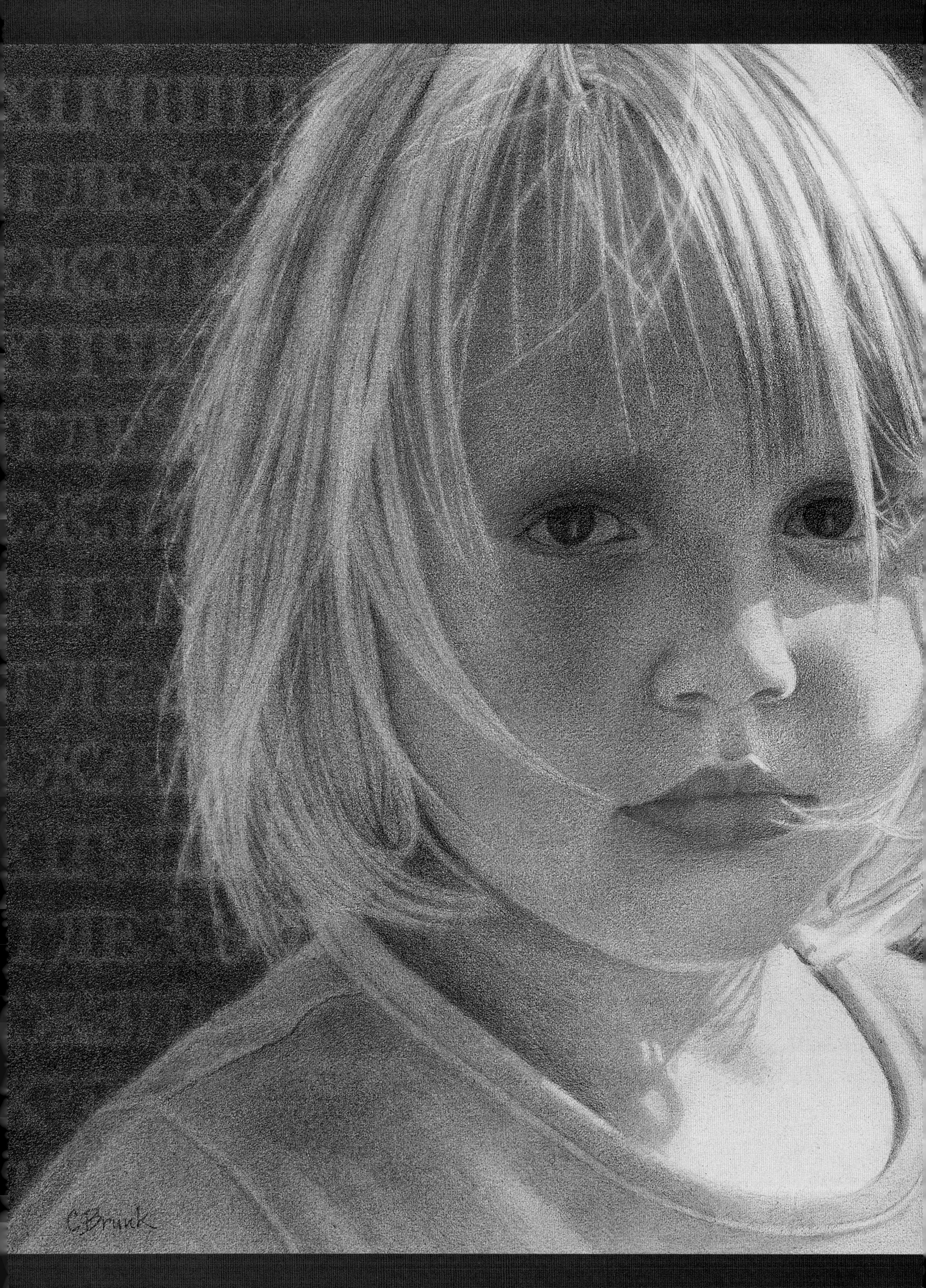

CBrink

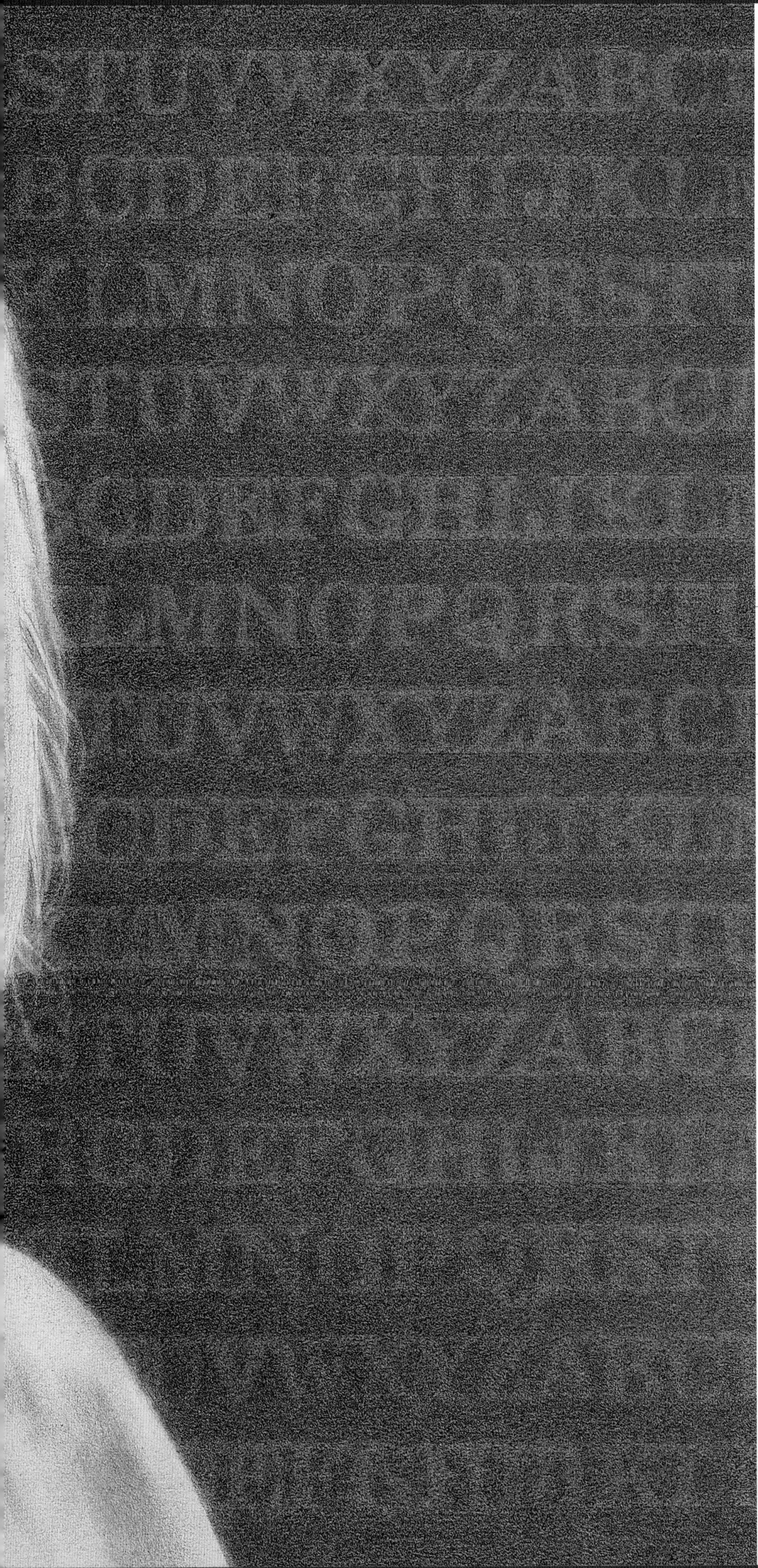

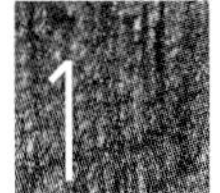

1

Fabulous Faces

In recent graphite portraits, my focus has been on integrating textural and patterned elements in a way that both aesthetically and metaphorically enhance the compositions. To create meaningful backgrounds I've incorporated elements that relate to the subject's history or areas of special interest. In this portrait of Sophie, a Russian adoptee, I've combined repeated, similar patterns of the Cyrillic and English alphabets to complement and contrast with the soft textures of her face and to represent her transition from one culture to another.

On a family vacation I took a picture of my son. It was a lucky moment: His eyes were a lot more telling than posed smiles. I aimed to depict the intensity of his gaze, the look of adolescence seen in the thoughtfulness and contemplation of that moment. Colored pencil drawing requires the use of smooth paper. Here I deviate from the norm and draw on pastel paper instead. The unfilled spaces of the colored, slightly textured paper mix optically with the colored pencils, revealing the texture of skin and hair. I work on details with very sharp Caran d'Ache Pablo pencils and shade everything else using soft, permanent Caran d'Ache Luminance and some Lightfast Premier Prismacolors.

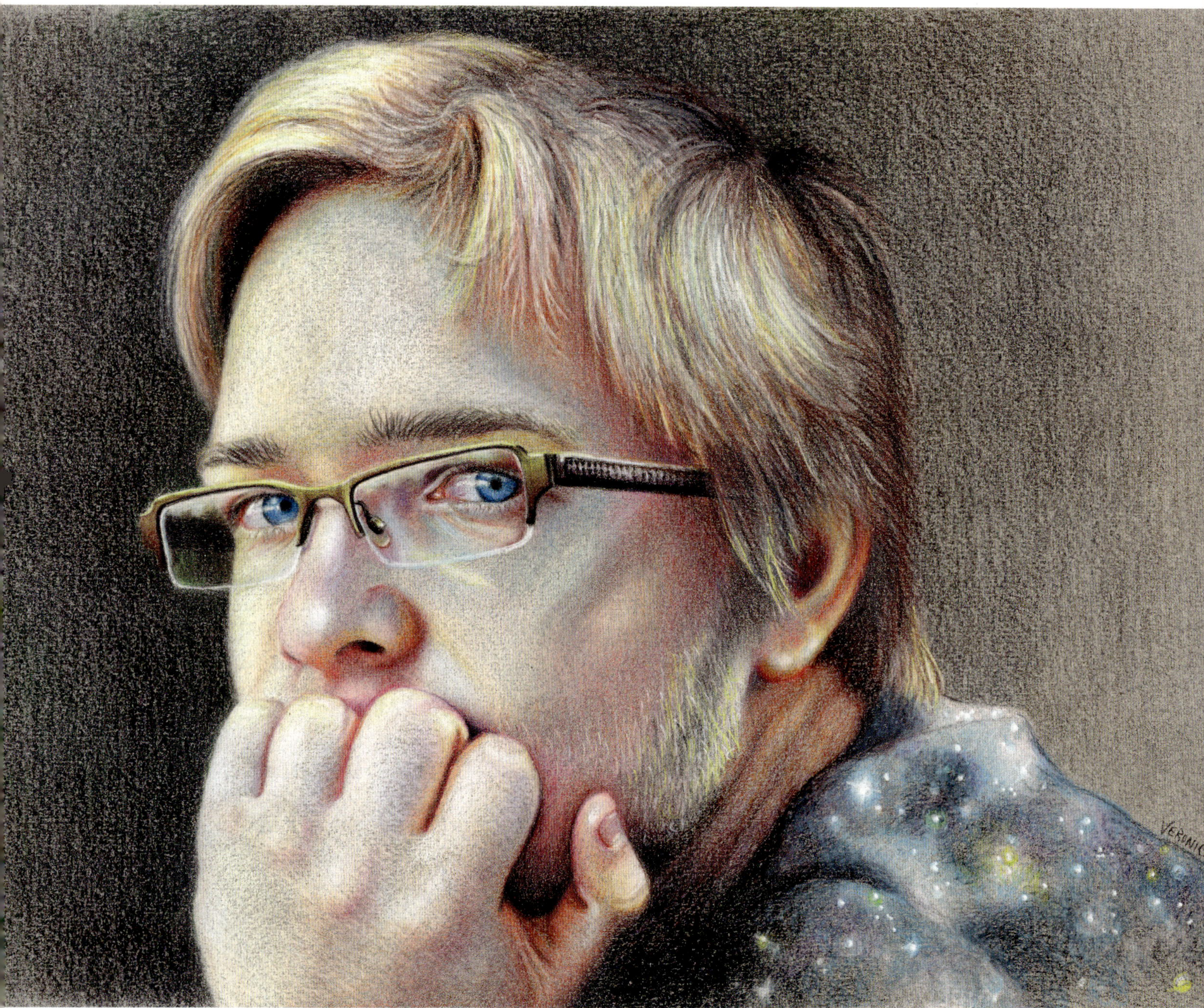

I was struck by this image taken at a local multicultural festival of an Italian singer; it depicted so many different surfaces—skin, a bristly moustache, metal, glass and cloth. I painted my heavily textured red mat board with black India ink, leaving some of the red to show through. The surface tooth allowed me to apply many layers of colored pencil while the underlying texture emphasized the weathered skin. A year or so later, one of my students showed a friend this image on my website. That friend turned out to be the daughter of the gentleman in the painting, who then bought it as a gift for him!

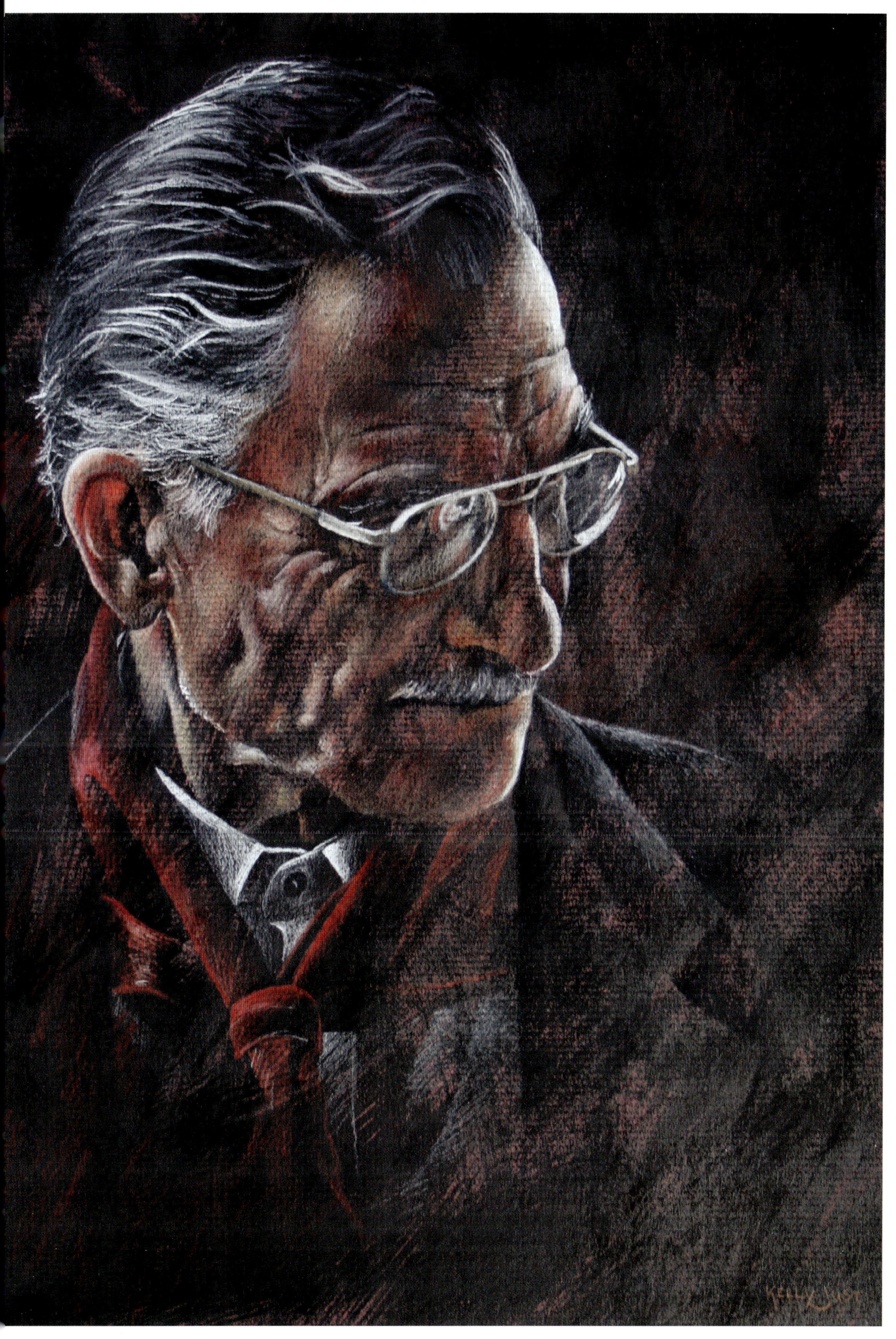

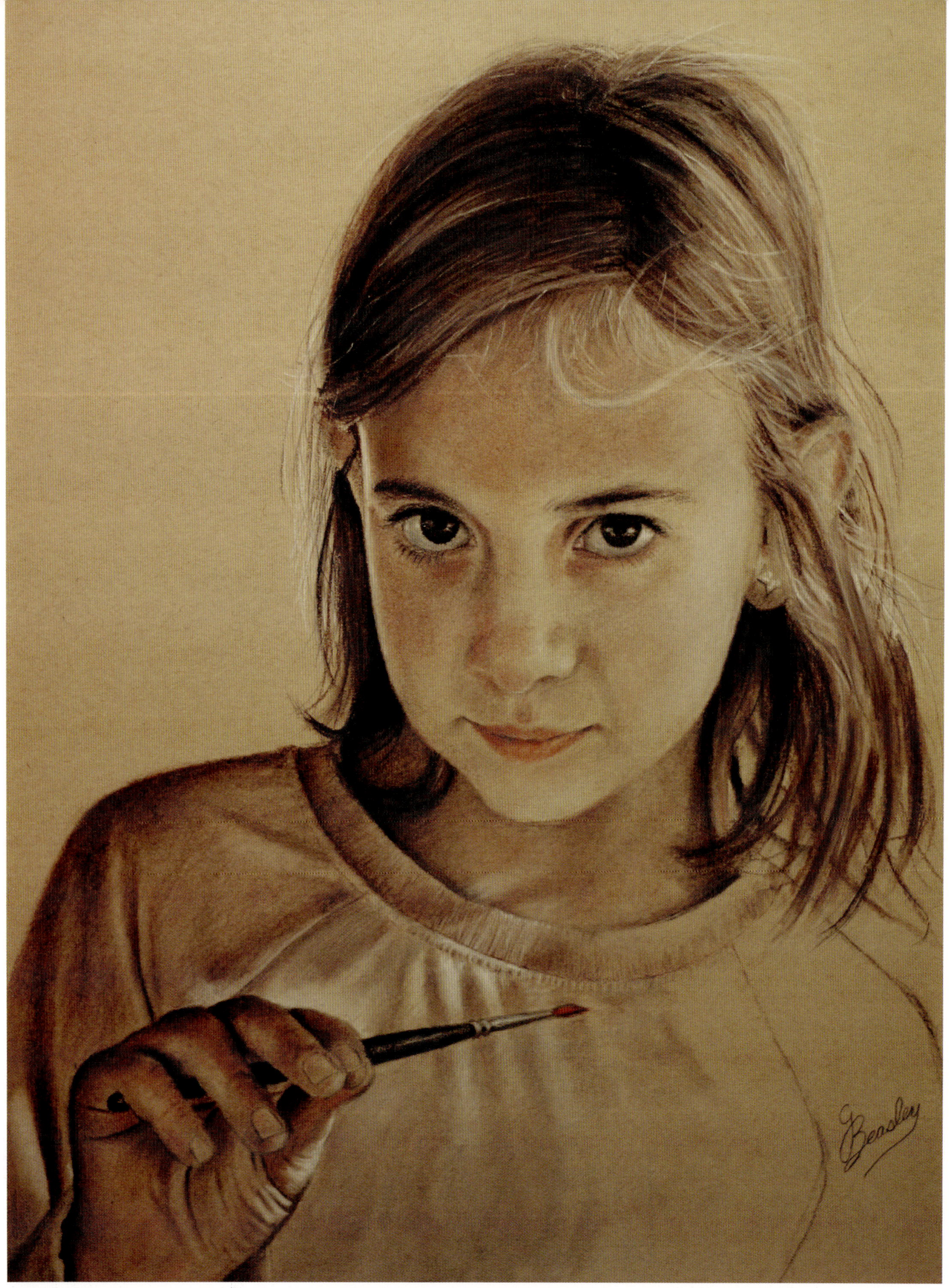

▲ EMERGING YOUNG ARTIST
Glenn Beasley
Multicolored chalk and graphite on
Strathmore toned paper
14" × 11" (36cm × 28cm)

After studying many reference photos of Scarlet, I realized that I needed to select materials for an approach that would best personify this young artist. The natural grain, medium tooth and visible toned texture of the Strathmore paper allowed for the blending of red, white and sepia chalks, along with graphite and charcoal, to produce a work that is neither monotone nor fully rendered in color but has a soft-filter effect. This best represents the young artist that is not quite fully formed or saturated in vivid colors, but her talent and persona are emerging for all to see.

▼ NO EXCUSES
Olga Nielsen
Pastel on Canson Mi-Teintes
toned paper
14" × 11" (36cm × 28cm)

No Excuses was done from life during a three-hour session at the Drawing Marathon at the Delaware College of Art and Design, where I teach. I love to draw from life, and it was very enjoyable to capture the play of light and shadows on the face of the spirited young model and to capture the subtle textural differences of her cheeks, lips and eyes. I started with a light touch using sharpened NuPastel sticks, working out the proportions and expression of her lovely animated face. Next I added soft Unison pastels for middle values and lights, using the tone of pastel paper for cool shadows. The details were finished with Koh-I-Noor Gioconda soft pastel pencils.

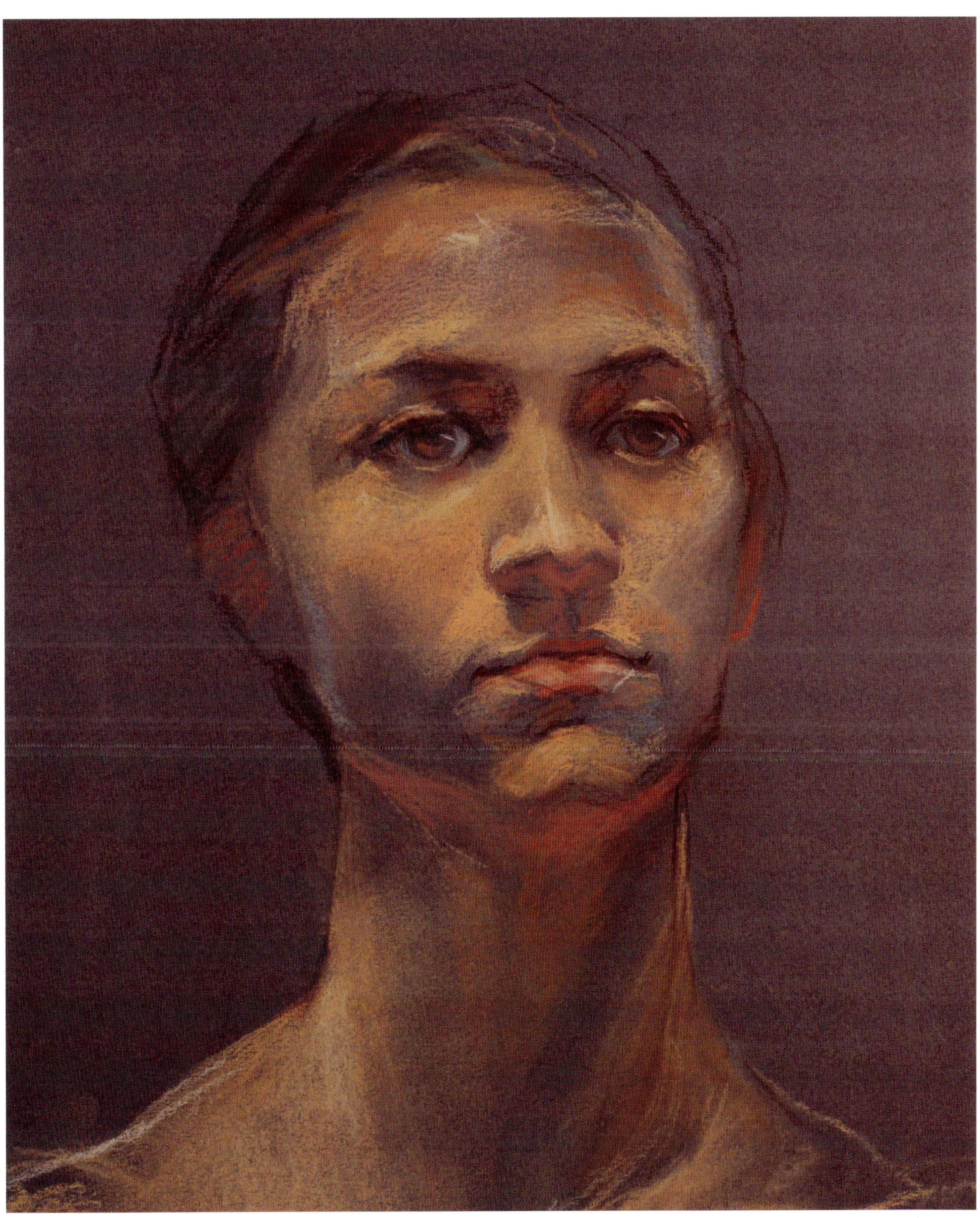

"Different textures in a portrait give it richness and life." —OLGA NIELSEN

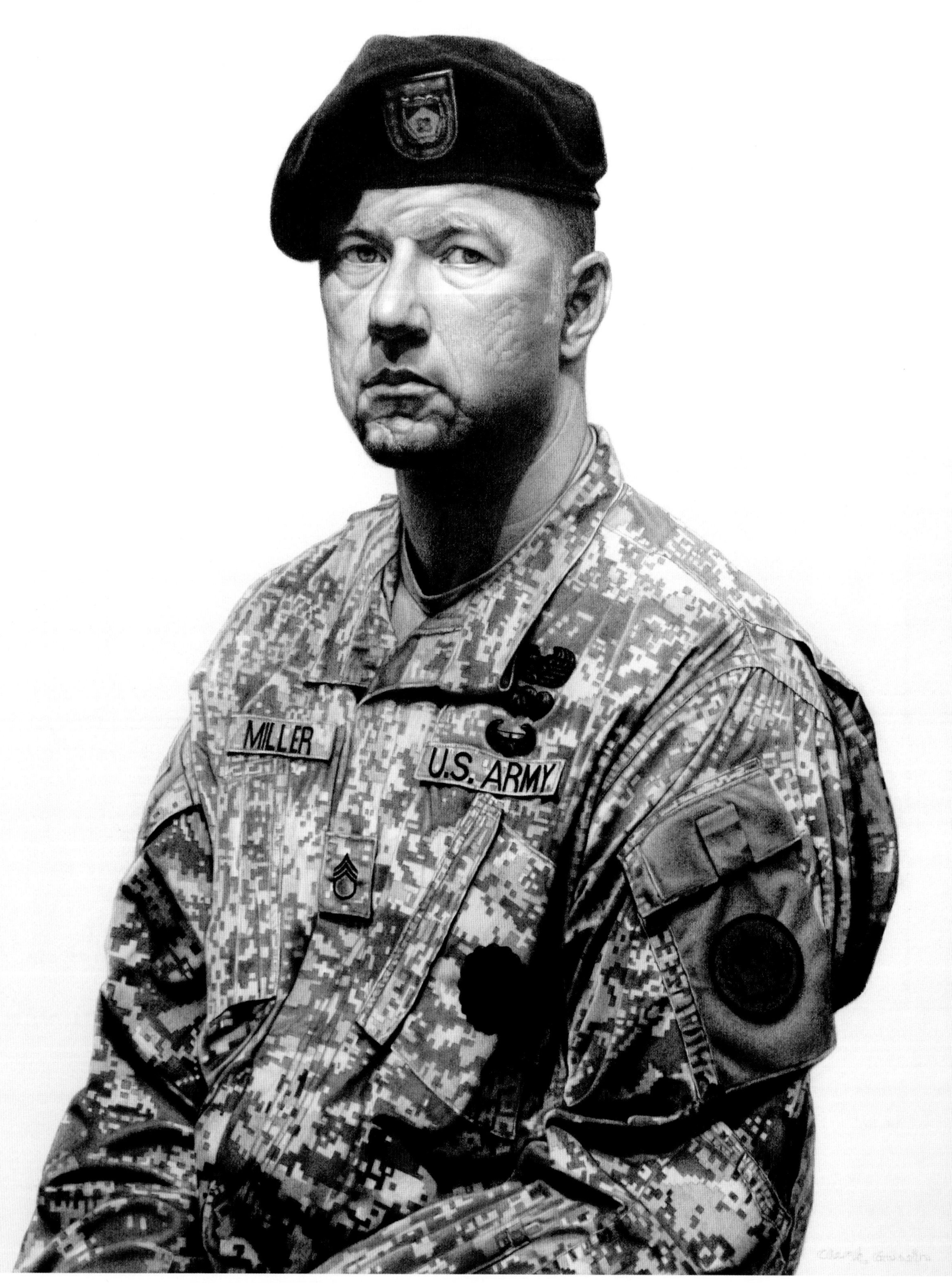

MILLER
U.S. ARMY

The more I got to know my son-in-law, a career combat soldier, the more I was compelled to make his portrait. I traveled to Texas for a formal sitting where I was able to control the pose, the lighting and the mood. After choosing the desired pose from the photography session I was excited by the challenge to render the textures and crypsis (i.e., camouflage pattern) of his uniform, and hopefully capture the hard years etched on his face and resonating from his gaze. It took me three months to complete rendering and modeling. The value transitions of the surface textures were achieved using General's charcoal pencils and charcoal powder applied with stumps and tortillons.

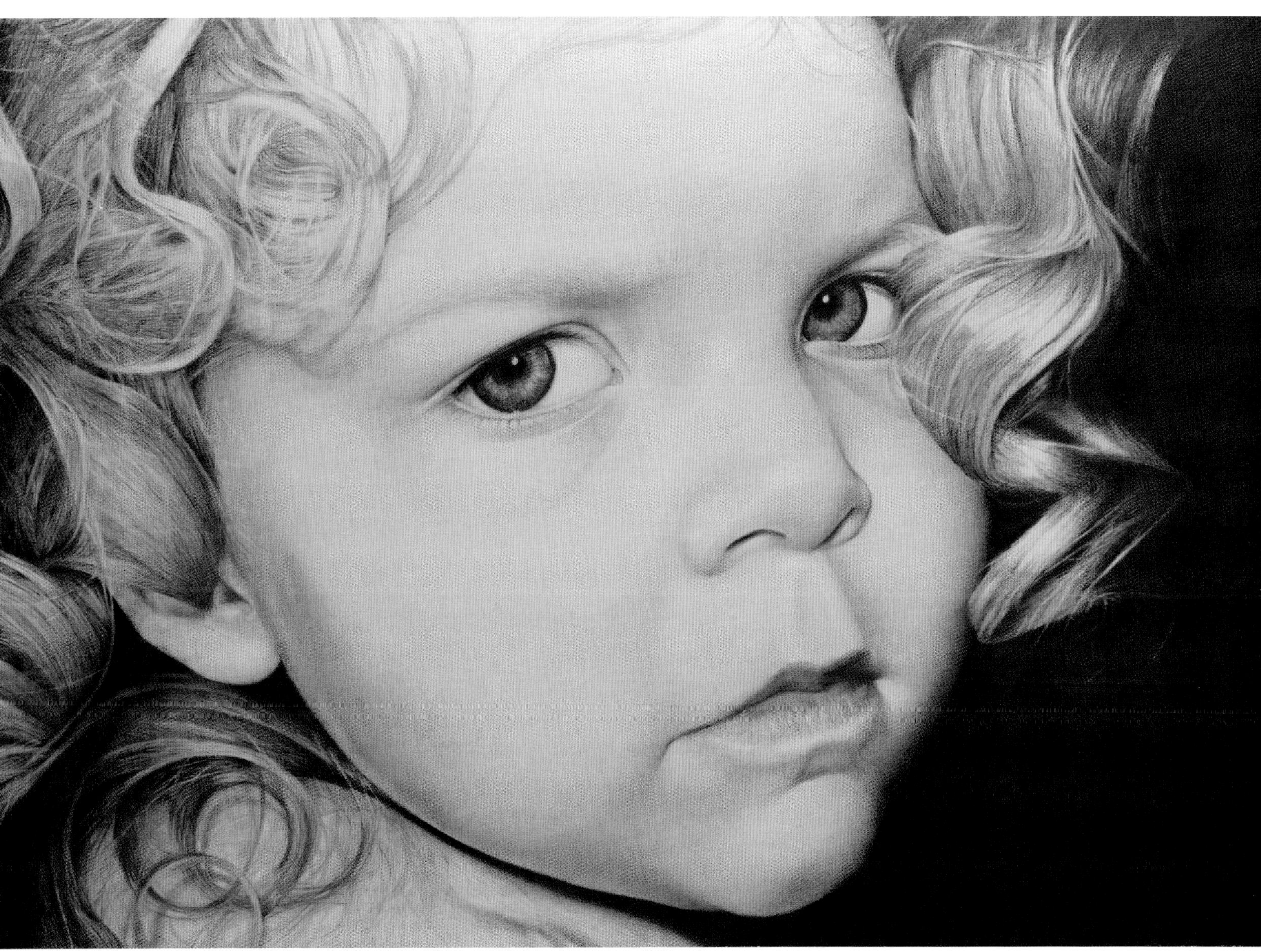

I lightly draw a grid directly onto the bristol board, then transfer from a copy of the photograph I'm working from. I then begin to build up the values, gradually working from light to dark. I use a combination of cross-hatching and a smooth shading/blending technique. I do not blend with smearing or rubbing, but mostly use a buildup of pencil marks, carefully controlling the pressure. The artist must give the viewer an illusion of the tactile texture, relying on the light that falls on the surface. By carefully controlling value contrasts and details, this illusion can be successful. But it is a technique that requires time and patience.

While having a bite to eat, I was watching people at the picnic benches. A small distance away an older gentleman was eating. I watched him on and off, then all at once the sun came out and shined through his straw hat leaving specks of light on his face. I grabbed my camera and took several pictures as he changed positions. I combined pictures for *The Straw Hat* composition. I work with many types of colored pencils, depending on the effect I want to achieve, but I always use the Magic Eraser. This eraser removes a lot of the pigment, so many layers have to be put down. But it also pushes the pigment into the nooks and crannies of the paper.

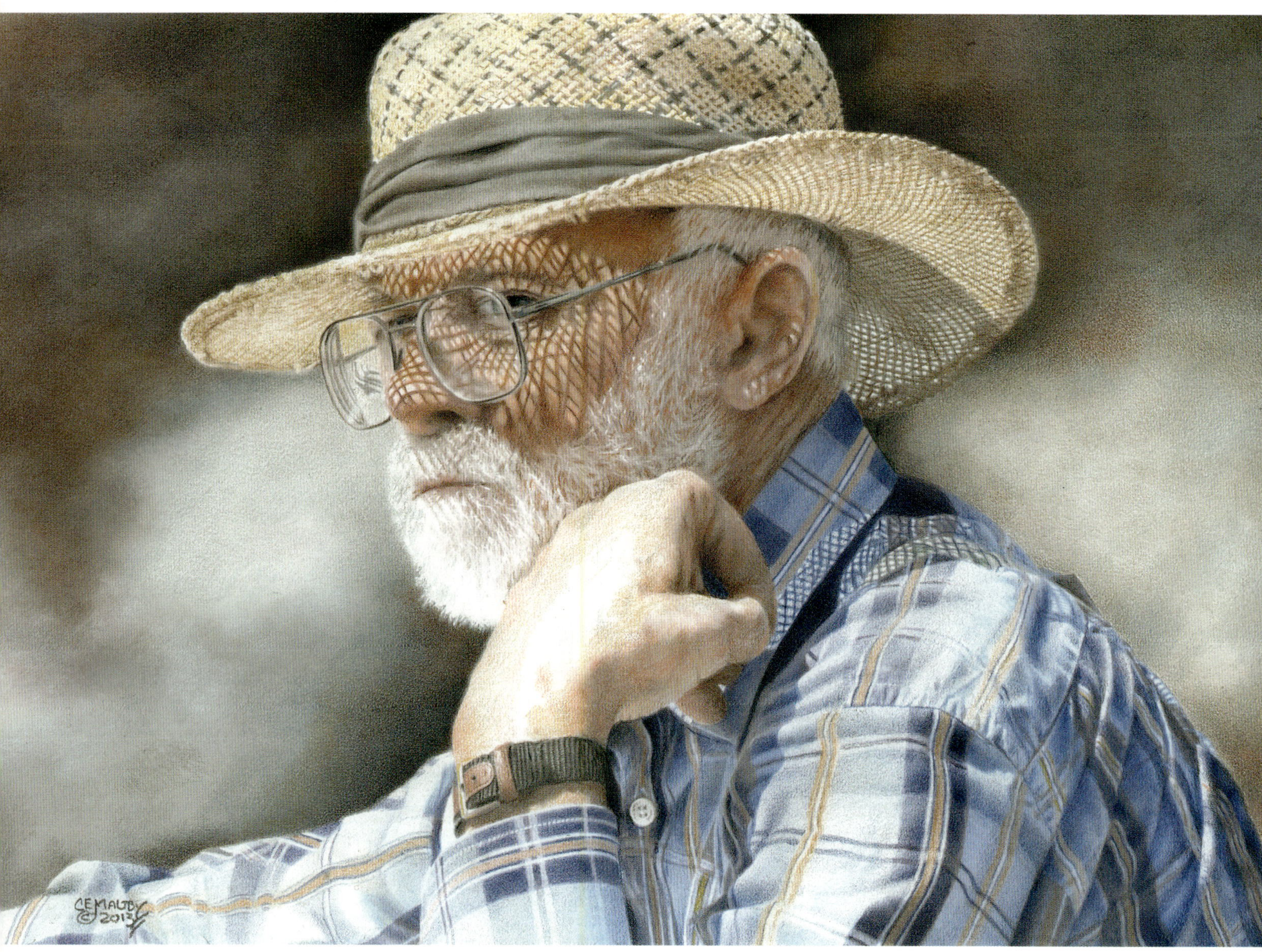

This drawing started life as an idea for an oil painting, then it developed its own credibility so I ran with it. The subject is an old friend and renowned painter, Peter Wileman. I felt it was important to reflect his character through the texture and landscape of his face as affected by light from a nearby window. I developed the basic drawing from my own photographic studies, drawing with Derwent Burnt Carmine and white, then bringing in the warm and cool halftones on either side of his face with Luminance Burnt Sienna, along with pinks and grays.

"Texture is best conveyed by carefully positioned light, just like a raking light across a landscape." —DAVID SANDELL

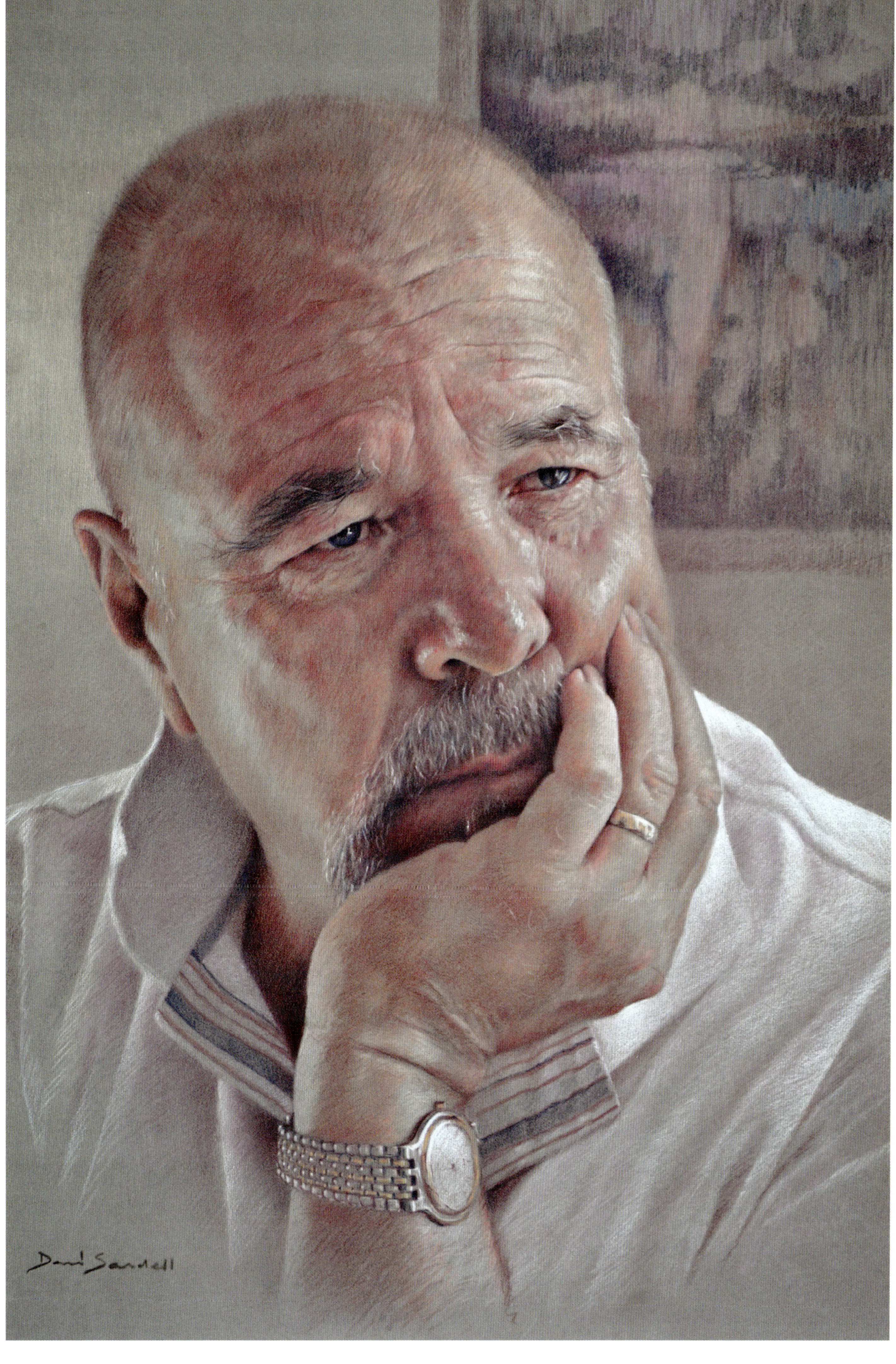
David Sandell

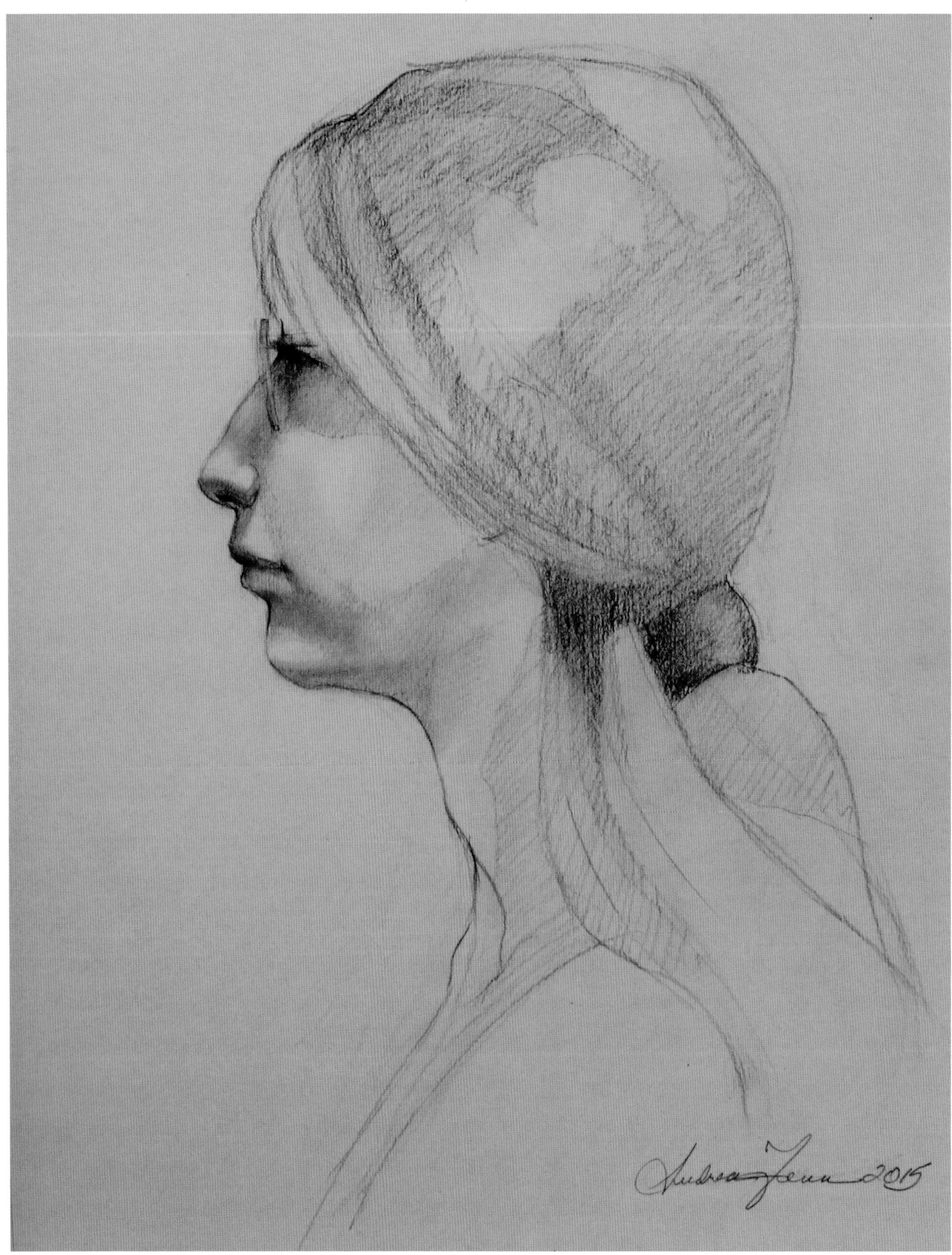

▲ ANDREA
Andrea Fenn
Graphite and charcoal on Strathmore
14" × 11" (36cm × 28cm)

I like Oscar Wilde's quote: "Every portrait that is painted with feeling is a portrait of the artist, not of the sitter." My first love in art is portraiture. This drawing was completed during a short pose model session. The model's name eluded me after the session was over, and she remained nameless until two people who know me well said they thought the piece was a self-portrait. She has since been dubbed *Andrea*. Mr. Wilde would be pleased.

This portrait was drawn from life using a combination of vine charcoal and charcoal pencils. I begin by establishing the overall big shapes with vine charcoal and switch to charcoal pencils for the finer and darker detail. The white pastel is added last as I develop form in the light side. Working on toned paper is an efficient and traditional way to establish a full value drawing using the tone of the paper for much of the middle value. I attempt to keep the shadow side flatter and more shape-oriented. Most of the finely developed texture and modeling occur in the light side.

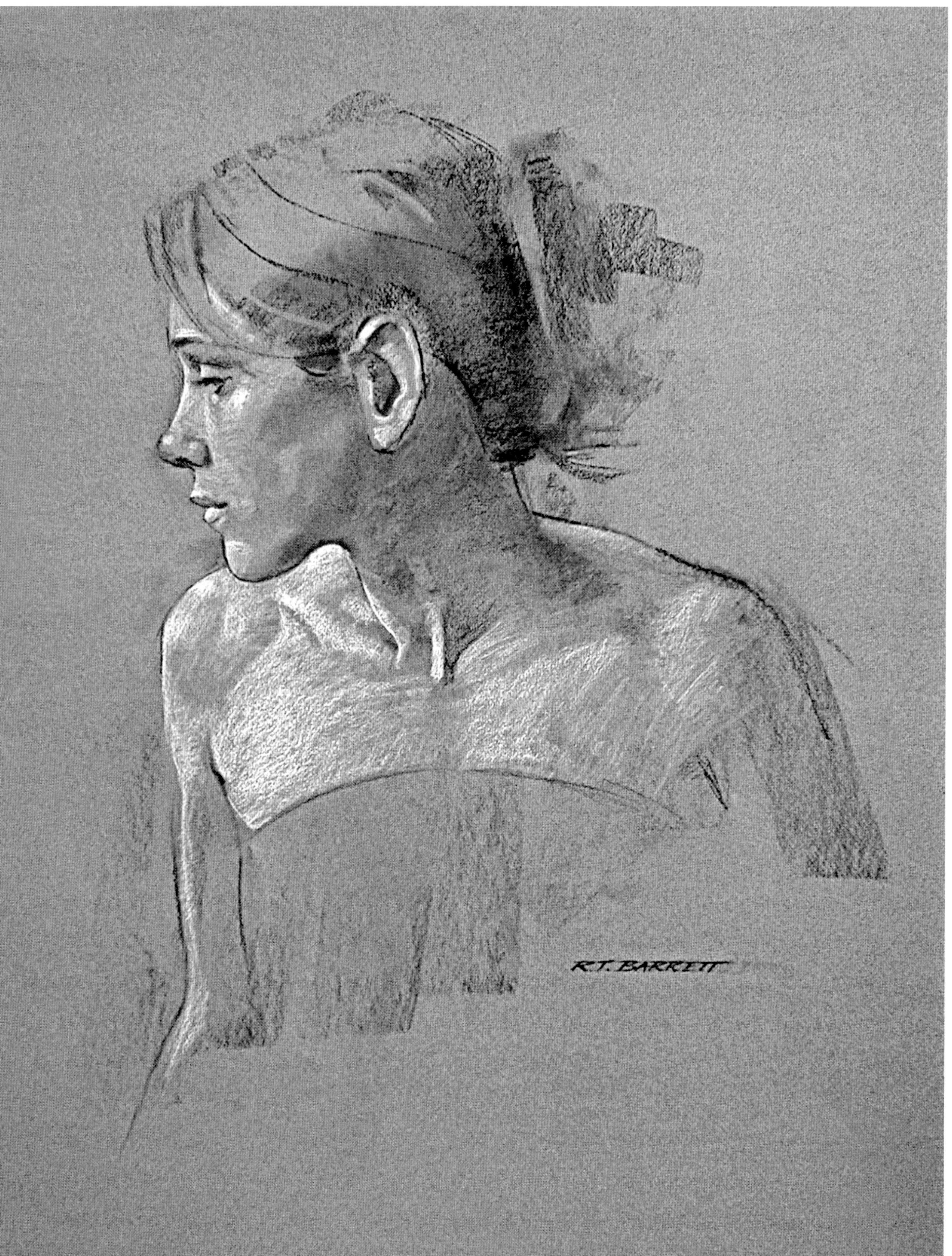

▼ **LIZZIE**
Robert T. Barrett
Charcoal heightened with white pastel on toned paper
25" × 19" (64cm × 48cm)

Using reference photos allowed me ample time for experimentation with this portrait. Feeling dissatisfied with my initial results, I grabbed a Prismacolor Magic Rub eraser and made random strokes with its edge. When I stepped back I saw that the erasure marks had serendipitously framed the face, which I was then inspired to further refine. The juxtaposition of the loose textural background and the tightly rendered visage brings a heightened emotional quality to this piece and leaves room for the viewer's imagination.

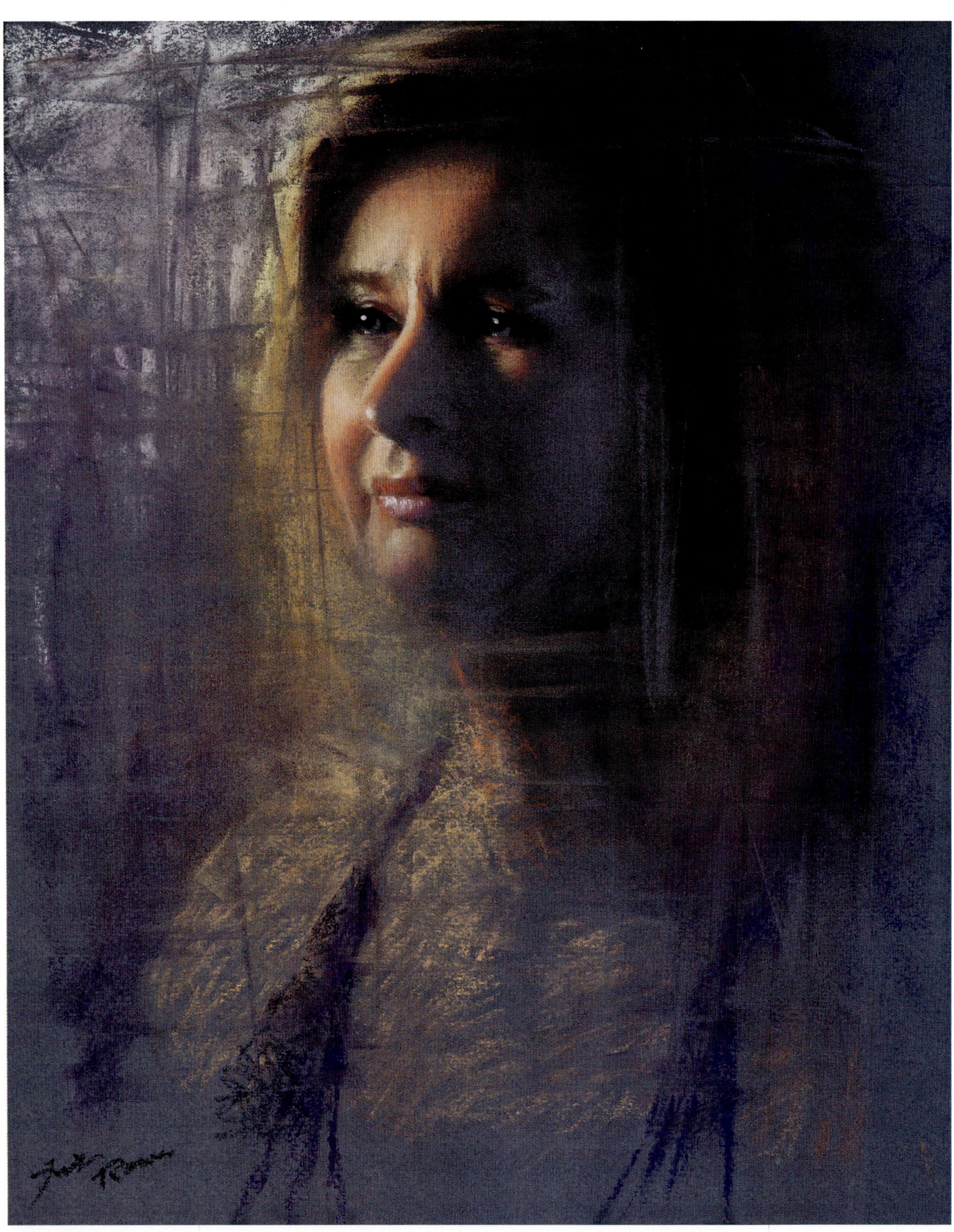

"In a portrait, loose textural strokes can convey a sense of anticipation about how the subject's life will unfold." —JENNIFER ROWE

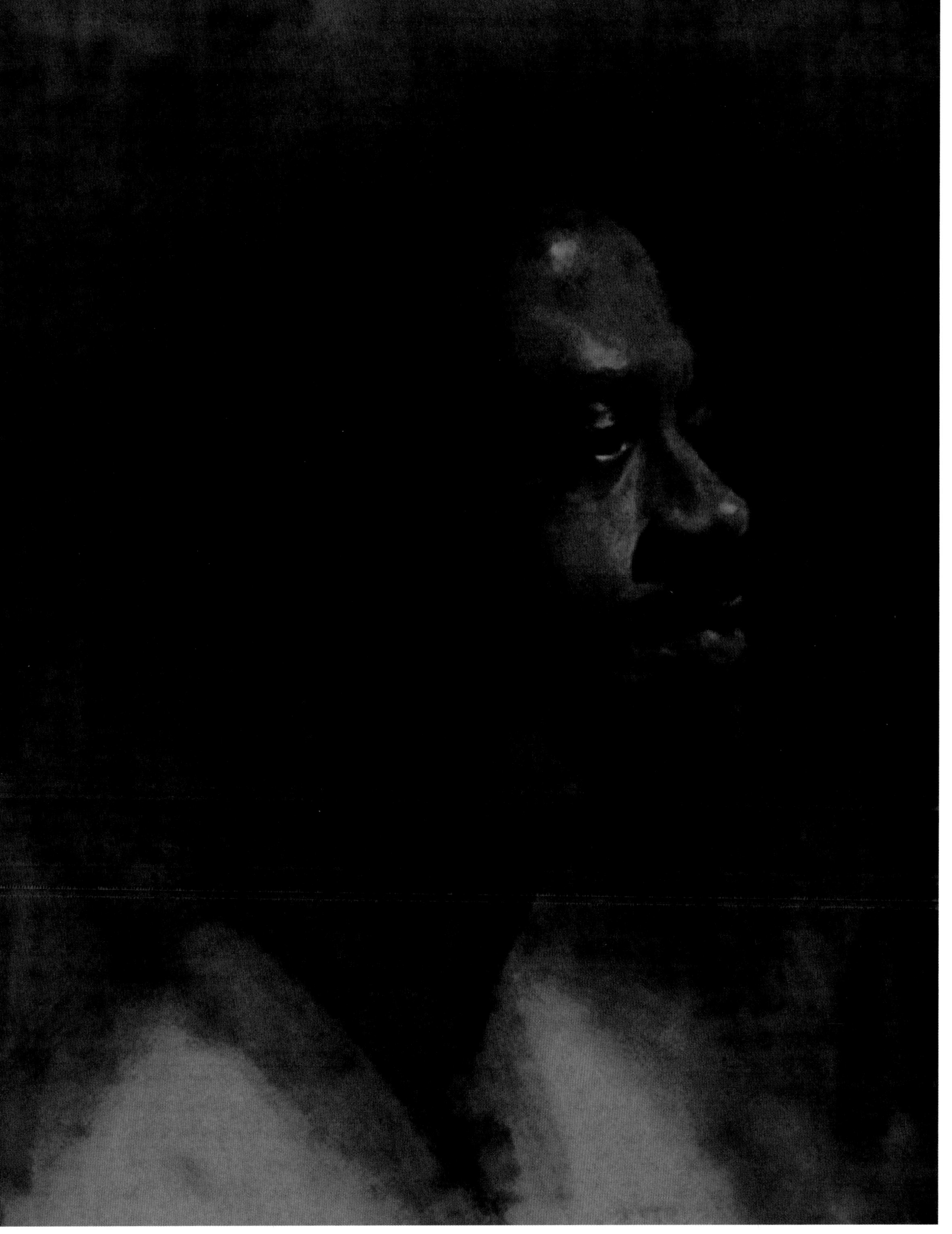

I did this portrait of New York model Kevin as a kind of creative experiment. First I painted Kevin from life, using a monochromatic palette of Terra Rosa and Venetian Red, both by Vasari, on a gray-toned panel. Next I photographed both the painting and Kevin in black and white, and finally I created this drawing from those sources. My primary intention was to first gain a solid structural understanding of my subject and then hope that it translated into a solid piece.

▲ KEVIN
Chris Page
Black PanPastel and General's black and white
charcoal pencils on Strathmore gray-toned paper
12" × 11" (30cm × 28cm)

Thoughts portrays my mother's partner and caregiver for over twenty years. His appearance often reminds me of philosophers or biblical characters, and that is how I wanted to depict him in this portrait. I work from photography so I can capture fleeting moments and expressions. I used a combination of soft pastel and pencil in both the underdrawing and final drawing stages, adding highlights and hair and skin texture with putty rubber, an eraser stick and a few touches of white pastel pencil. I merely hinted at certain areas so as not to overwork it and lose the vitality.

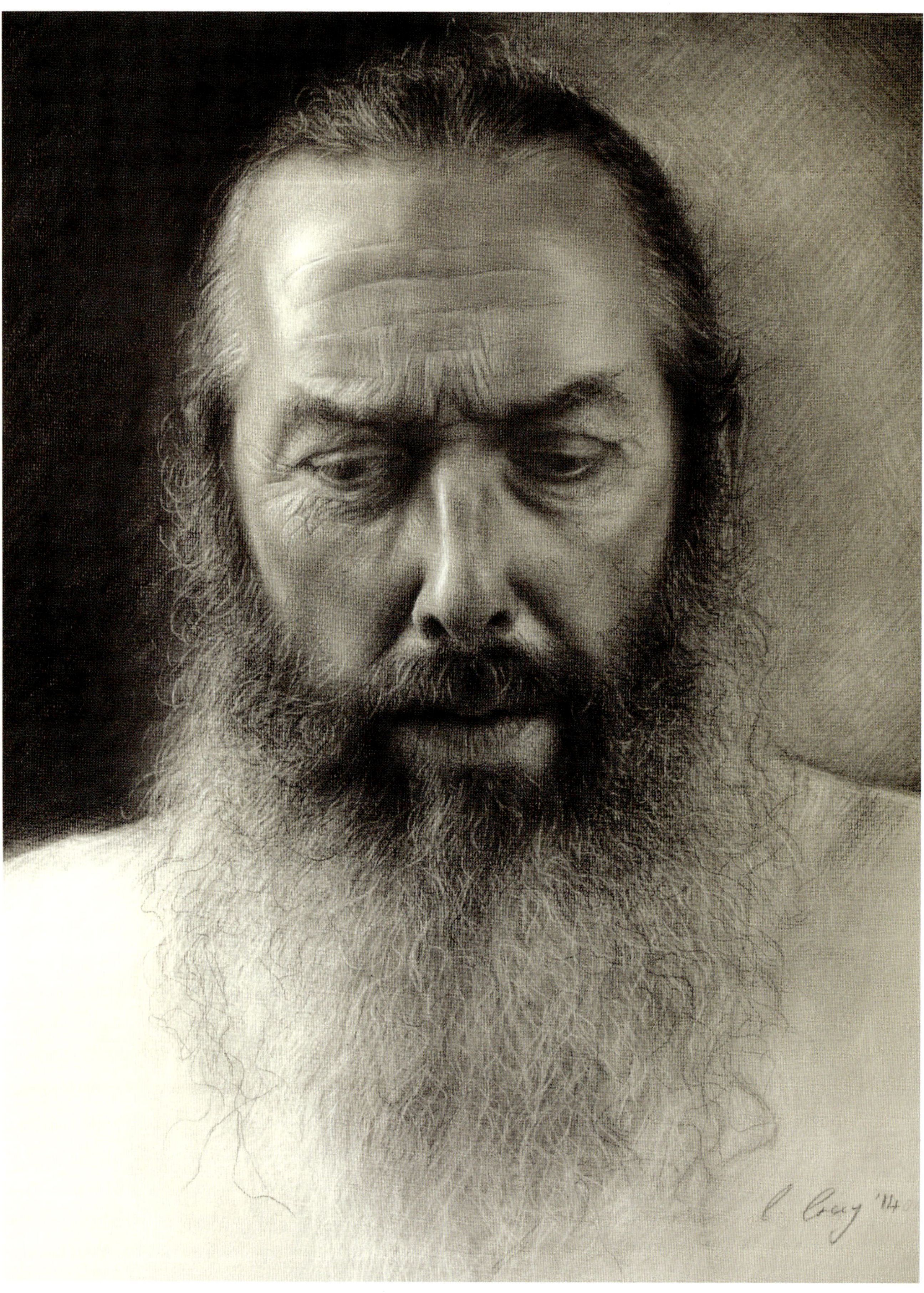

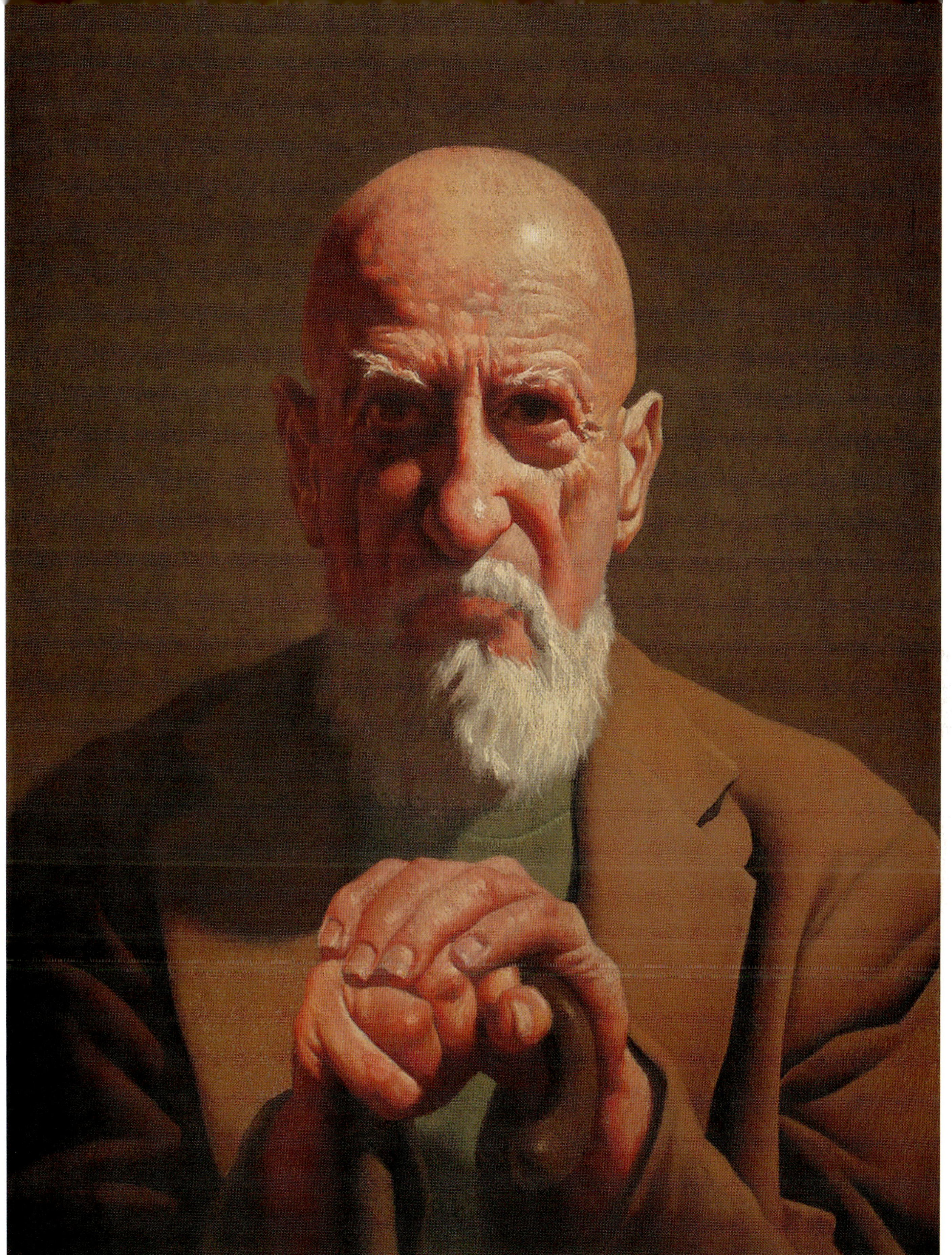

This pastel painting depicts an elderly gentleman who sometimes modeled for my classes and workshops at the Academy of Art University in San Francisco. The anatomical structure of his head and the texture of his wrinkled skin were fascinating to draw. My photo references for this piece did not include the hands, so I used my own hands with an old cane. I began with a detailed charcoal underdrawing on gray Canson paper and then began layering with NuPastels and Rembrandt pastels, carefully selecting hues that would capture the strong warm light. I kept cast-shadow edges sharp while allowing round turning forms to have softer edges. Controlling the edges in this way helps to create a sense of dimension and solidity.

▲ STALWART
Douglas Malone
Pastel on gray Canson paper
25" × 19" (64cm × 48cm)

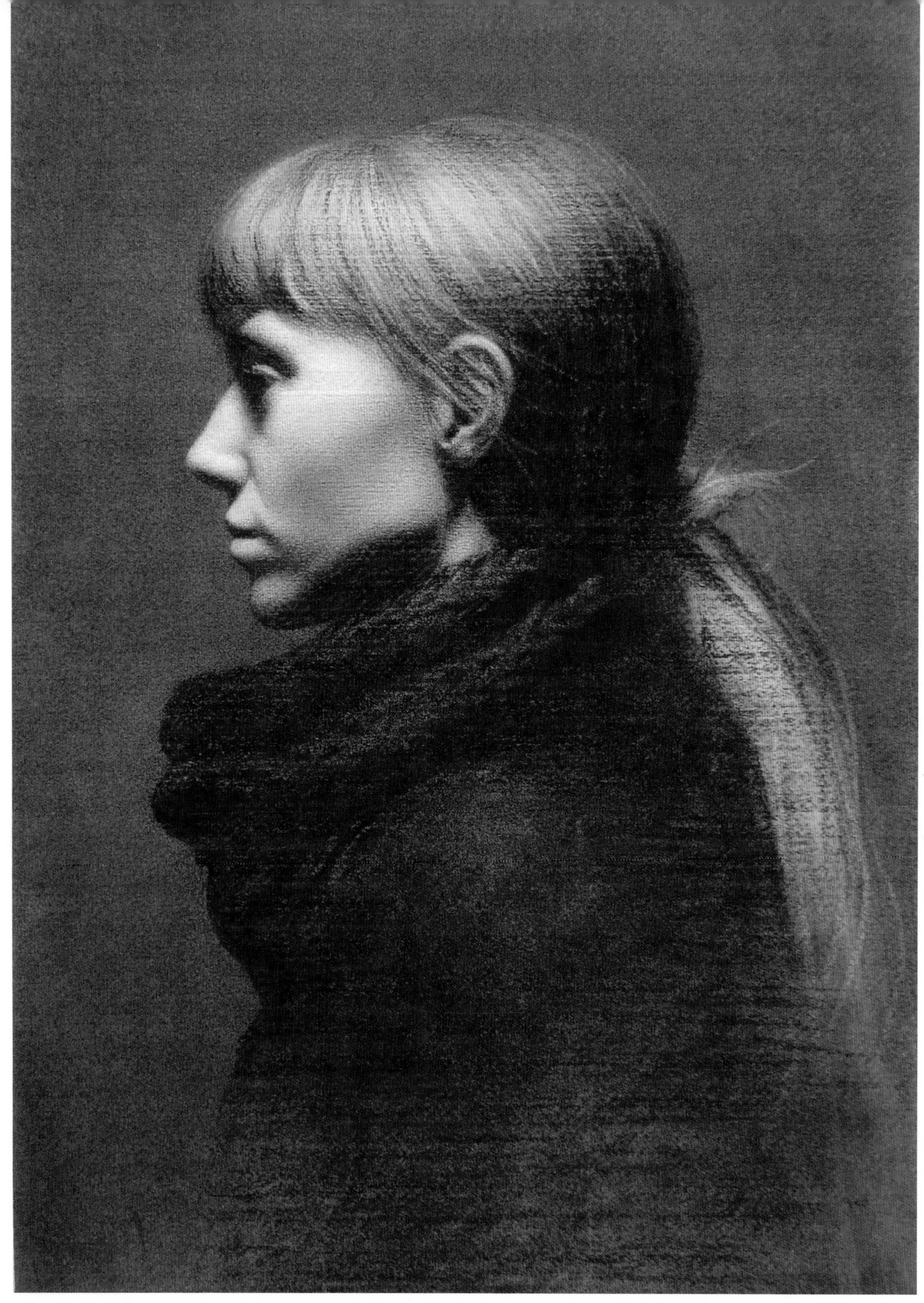

This is part of a drawing series of my friends and acquaintances. The background noise has been stripped away to draw attention to form and texture. In these quiet drawings I focus on my subjects and investigate the poignant humanity of daily life. The texture of the paper accentuates the drawn texture. Smooth areas like Laurie's skin are juxtaposed with looser strokes in the hair and sweater. I prefer to work from life but also use reference photographs. I find preliminary sketches from life essential to keeping my work looking fresh.

I was moved by this beautiful woman and her sweet child while I was studying in Belgium. To achieve the textural dimensions of the hair, I built up layer after layer of graphite starting with an HB pencil, then gradually building layers of values up to an 8B pencil. Using a clay-coated paper similar to what is used in silverpoint, I am able to carve out nuanced highlights with a razor blade. This also provides a true three-dimensional quality by having some of the drawing in relief. When I draw I think about moving the lines and values in such a way that I am actually sculpting the form rather than making a two-dimensional linear representation.

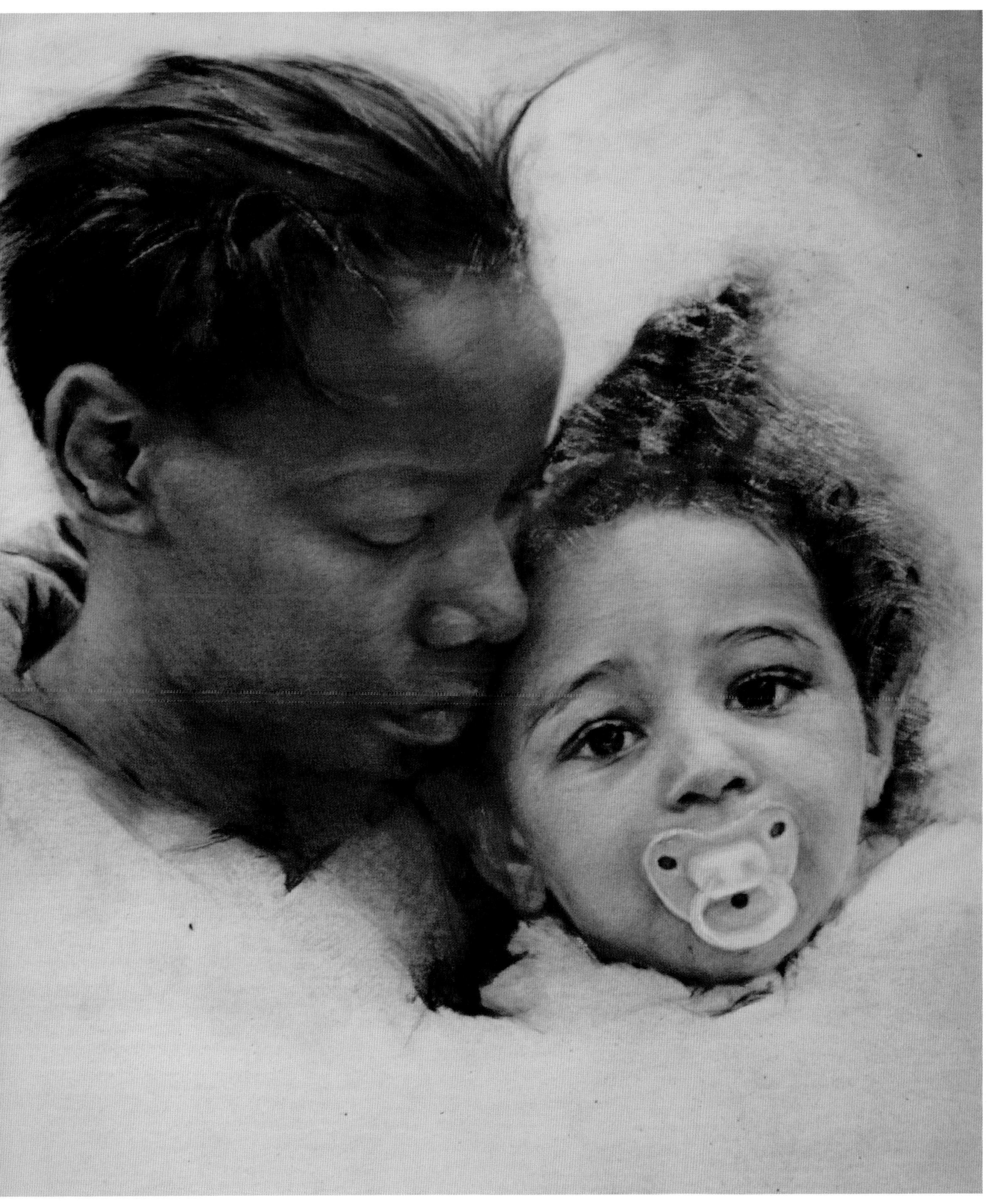

Walking in downtown Houston, Texas, I came across a man with tattered clothing perched on a concrete bench with a large duffle bag beside him. The lines in his face told a thousand stories. He gazed at me with gentle eyes, so I approached him. After a long conversation about his life, I asked permission to photograph him for my *Faces of Humanity* series. I started the drawing with the eyes—the single most important detail to convey emotion. The gel pen added a depth to the beard and highlights to the thread in his knitted hat. I left the background simple to represent how his surroundings were insignificant compared to his own physical requirements to merely survive.

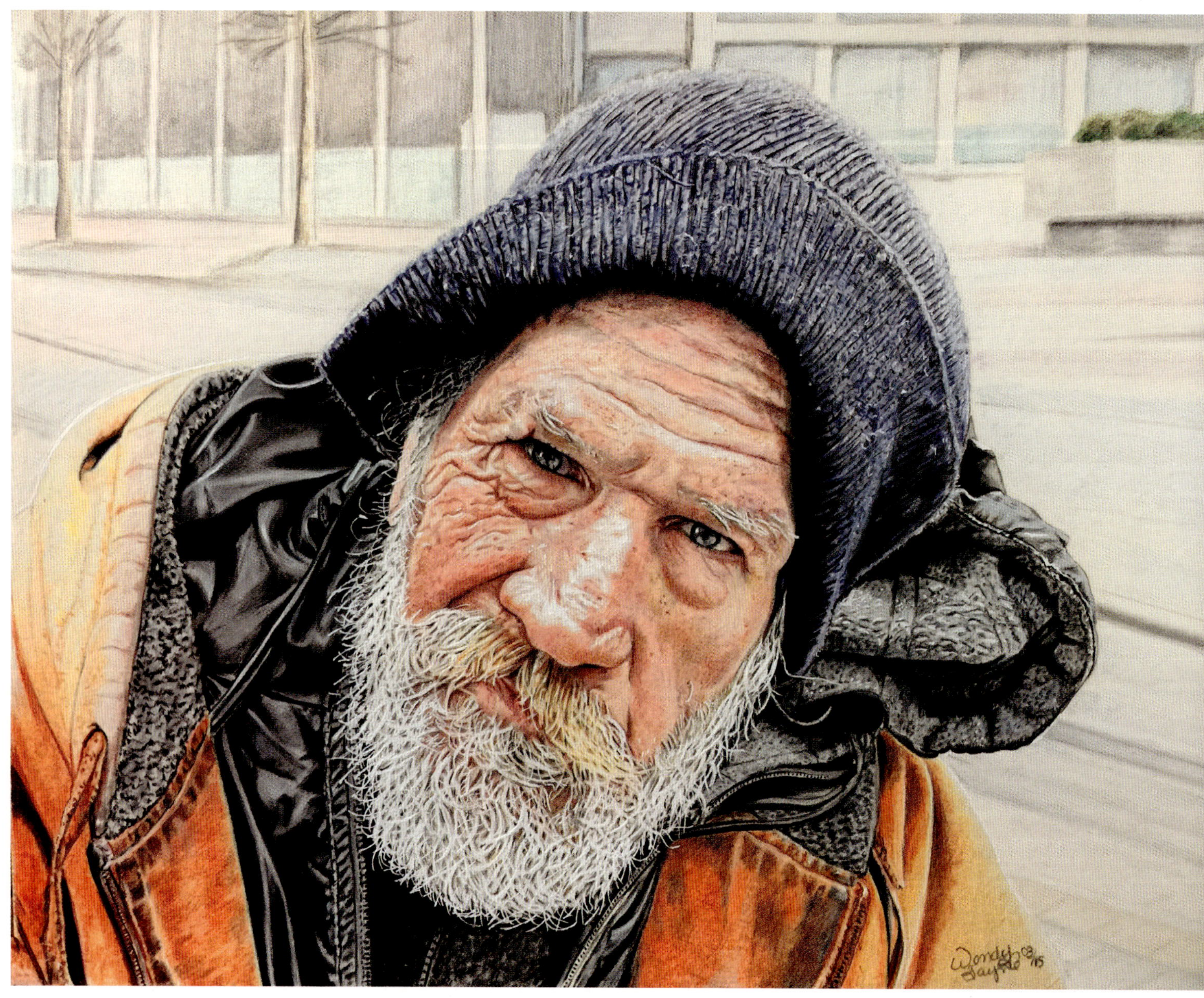

I first met Ady as one of my daughter's dance students. In time, a loving bond formed and I became her honorary grandpa. My inspiration for this portrait was Ady's bubbly disposition. She displayed that expressive smile when her dad called her name after noticing my camera was pointed her way. Black sanded paper and various brands of soft pastels were used to vignette the composition. I used small strokes of warm white highlights to create the water droplets on her skin and in her hair that gleamed in the midday sun. A warm palette was utilized for her skin tones, shadows and highlights to equal her colorful personality.

"It is helpful to know your portrait subjects well in order to capture the depth of their character." —MIKE BARRET KOLASINSKI

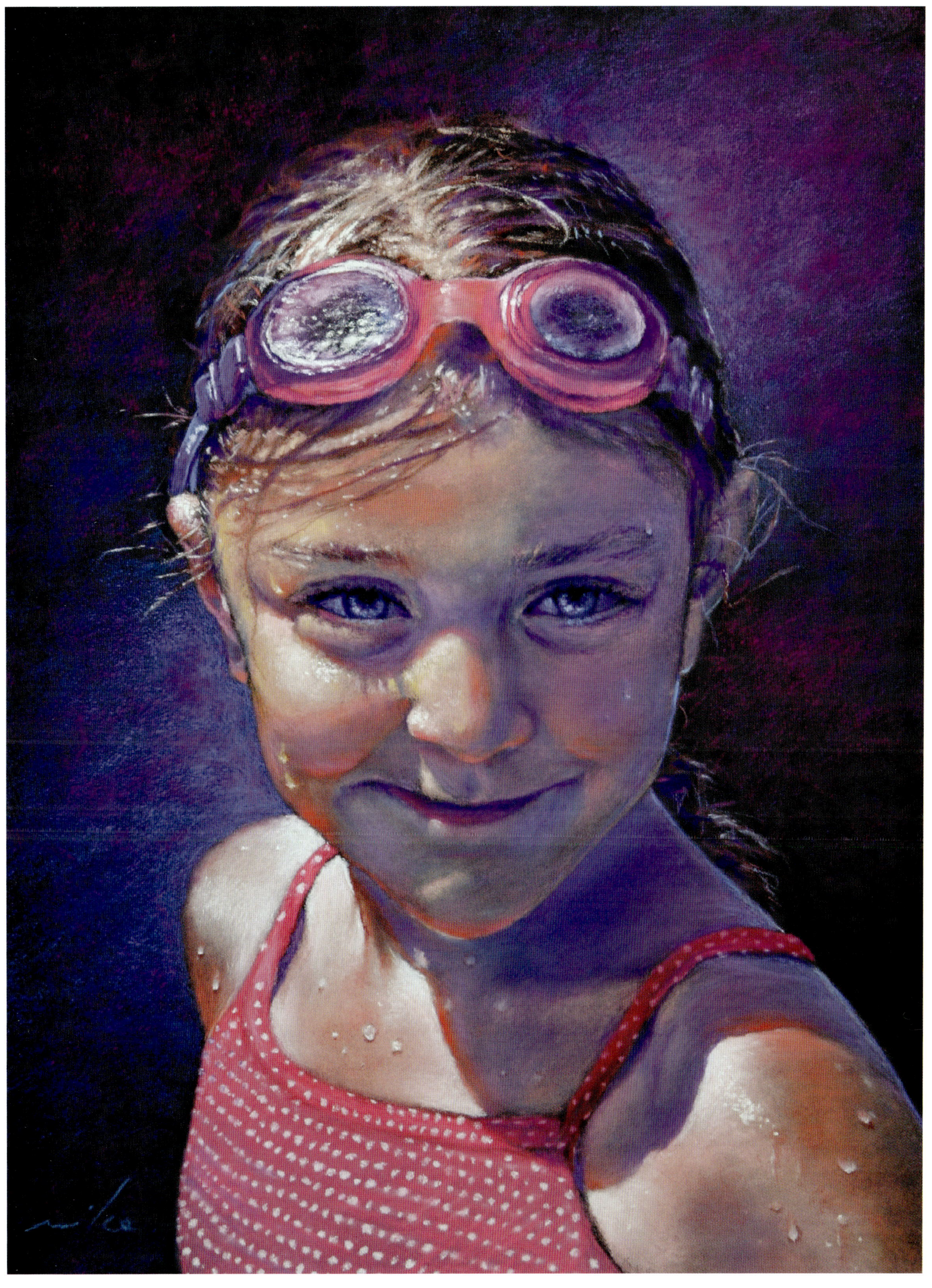

Defense Mechanisms is from a recent
series where I turned my focus towards
my animation students. This unique
subculture contrasts with traditional
societal norms. Contrasting textures,
then, become a visual metaphor for
this feature of the sitter. The oval format
unifies as it repeats the ovals in the
image, but contrasts by the fact that
the sitter is not the customary subject
of an oval format. Even the space
above the figure was intentional, sug-
gesting that the subject is not fitting
into our frame of reference.

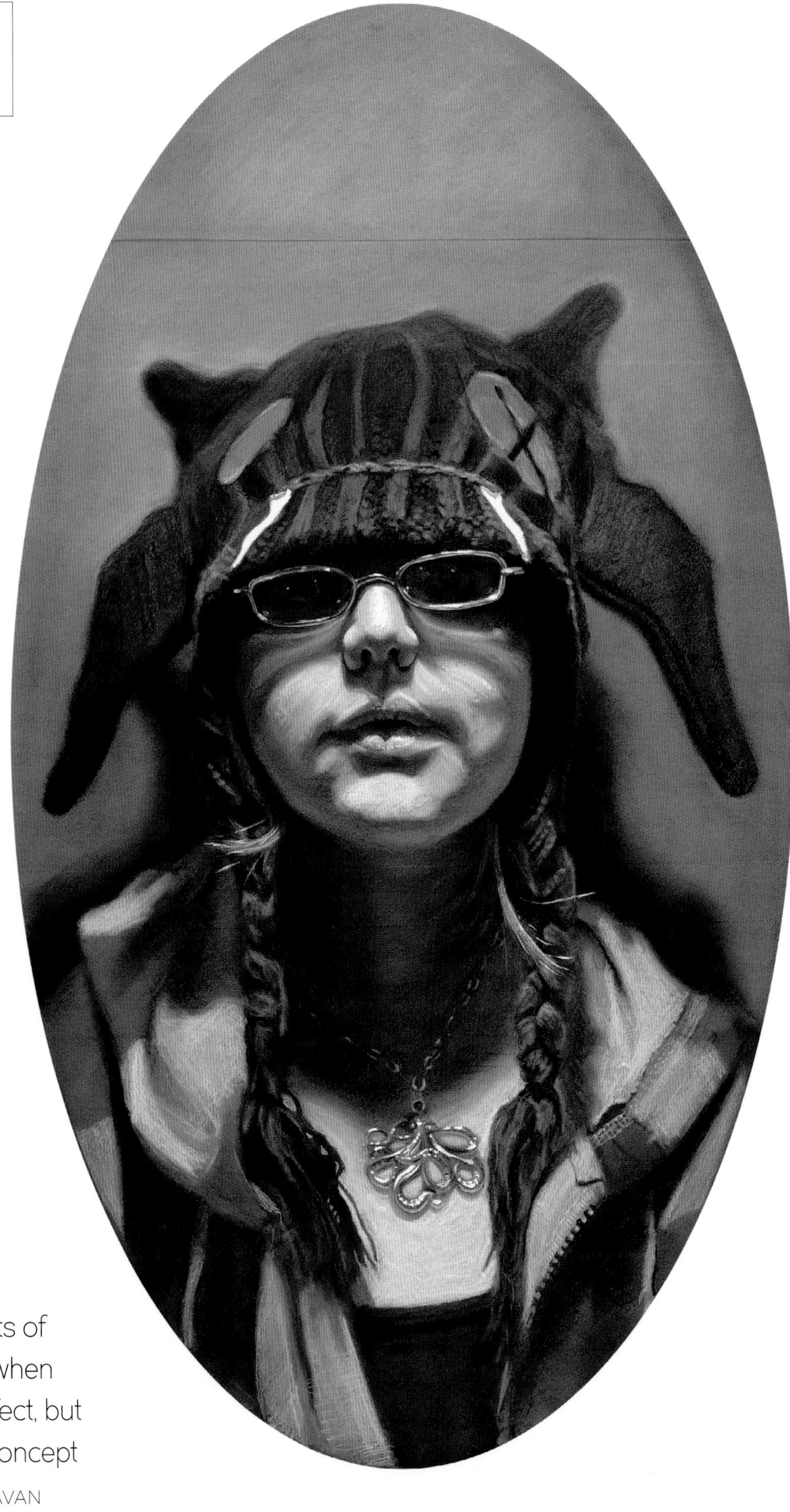

"Texture, like other elements of
design, is most powerful when
used, not just for visual effect, but
also in the service of the concept
of the work." —MARK A. HANAVAN

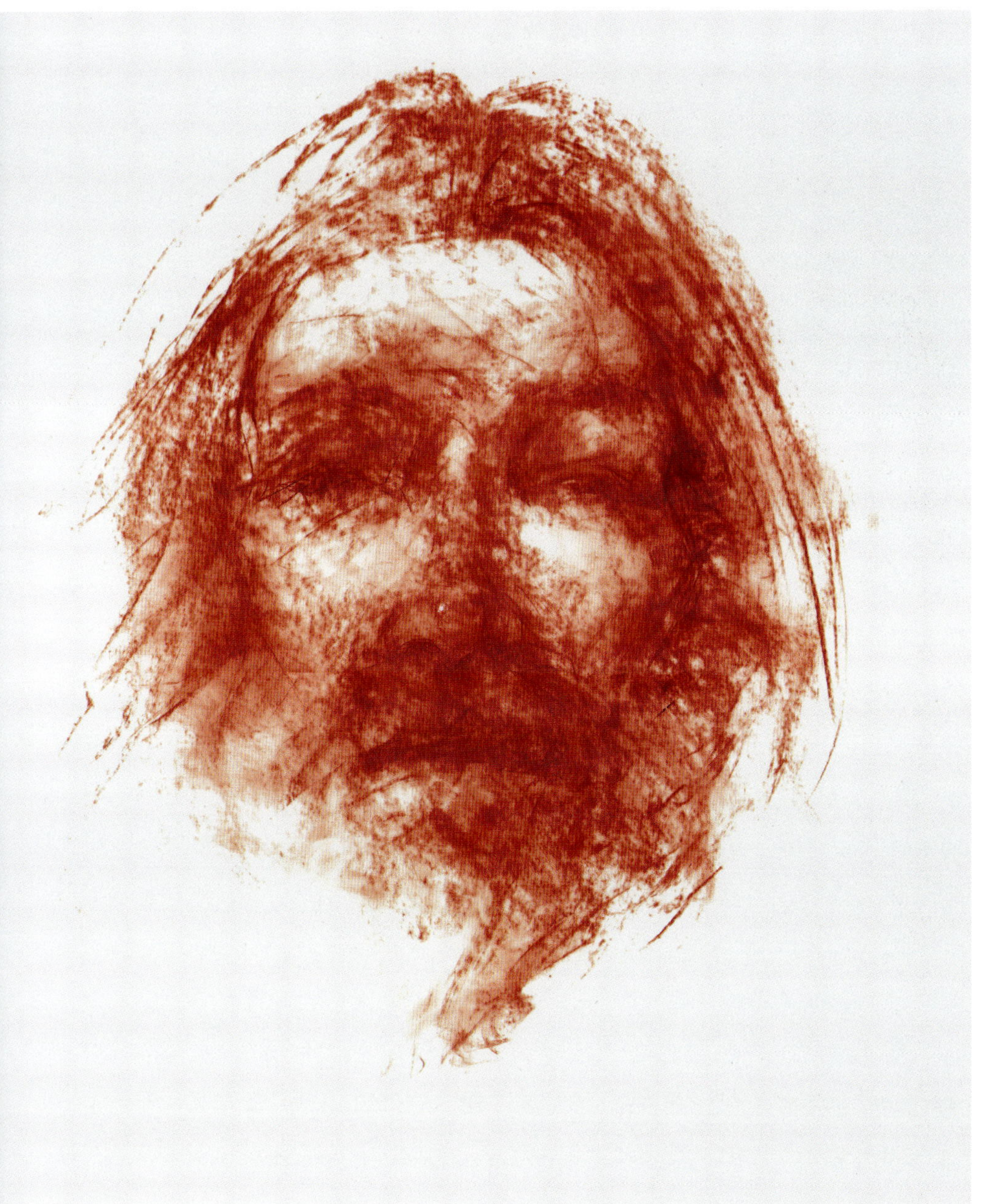

Drawing portraits from life, I seek to portray our shared humanity. I start with no pre-conceived notion of the finished portrait. An interplay of random marks, textural strokes and empty spaces lets the viewer inside—with the intention of revealing a glimpse of the soul. I like Mylar because it is receptive to different kinds of strokes without dictating any textures of its own.

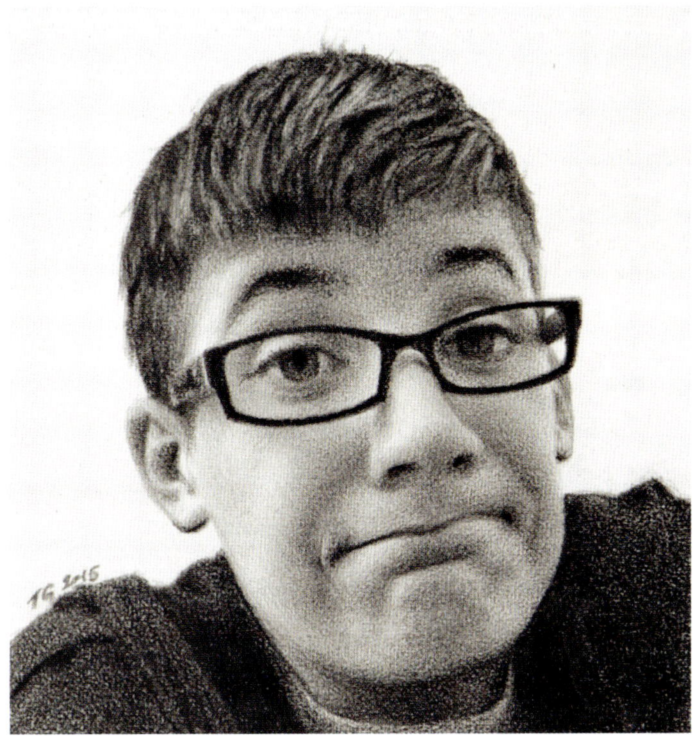

I drew *Sanctum* from an older photograph of my stepson, Galen. I wanted to challenge myself by getting as much detail, texture and attitude on as small a surface as I could. I built up the values using a regular mechanical pencil with an HB 0.5mm lead and a very light touch. The darkest values were done with a 9B grade pencil. As I sometimes do, I closely cropped the image and left the background white to draw all the attention to that sweet face.

Composing this drawing was an attempt to portray an image surrounded by an illusive texture that would resemble a dream-like environment. Graphite as a medium plays a part in interpreting these effects. Using my own photography enables me to attain a depiction of the selected subject in various backgrounds and lighting.

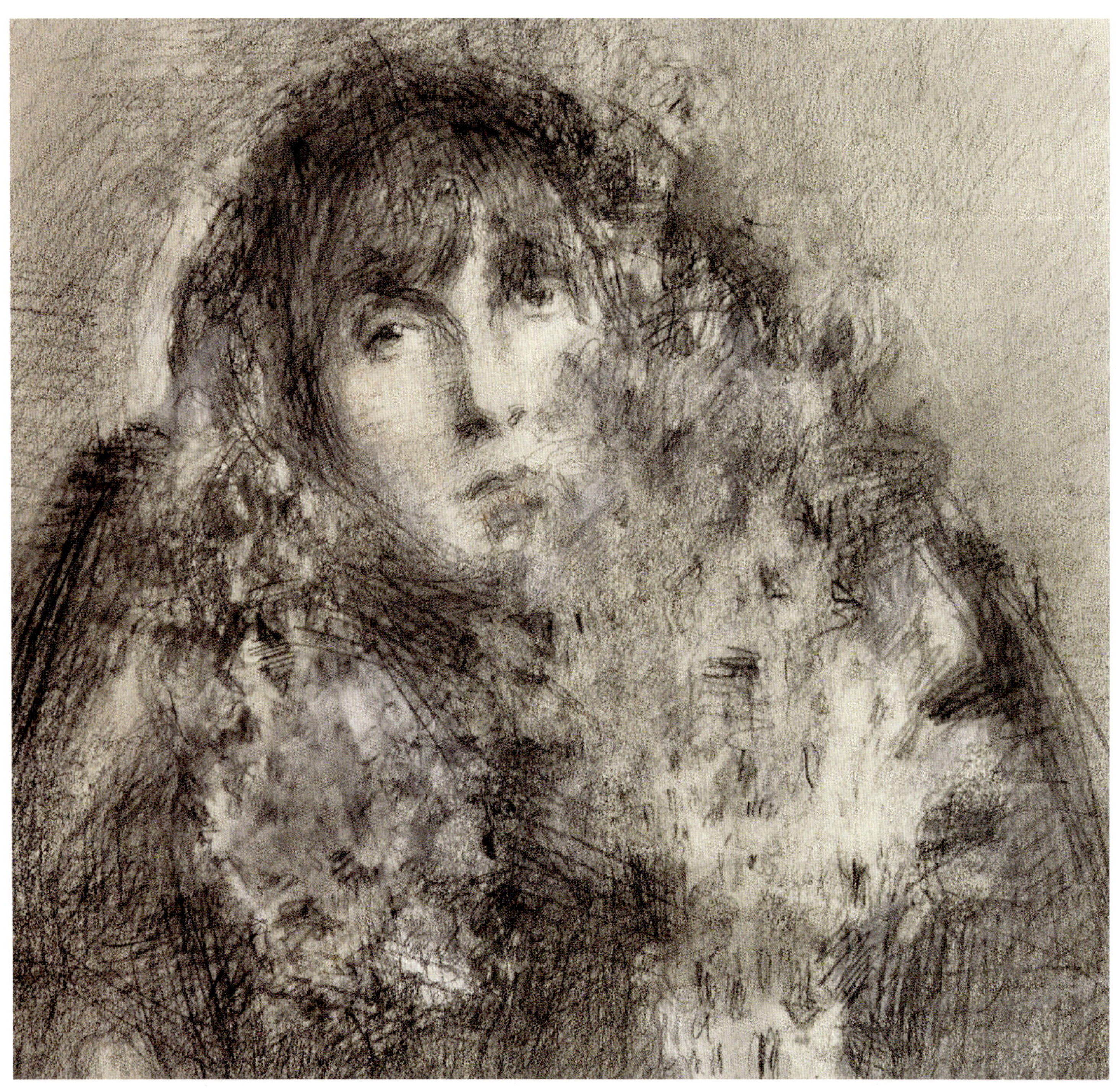

Fran is one of my best friends and a practicing artist here in Kent, Ohio. At age 87, she works on her art every day. I've taken quite a few digital images of her over the years and decided to create a portrait of her in my expressive style. I kept it as a surprise for a special occasion. I started with a very detailed line drawing focusing on shapes and contours. From there I started to block in the colors with a controlled scribble until the surface of the board was covered. From this point on my mark-making gets spontaneous and I strive to use as many types of lines as possible. The overlapping lines and vivid colors create dynamic textures that capture the essence of this beautiful woman.

"Texture is ultimately mark-making and it is critical that you find your own way of doing it." —JOHN P. SMOLKO

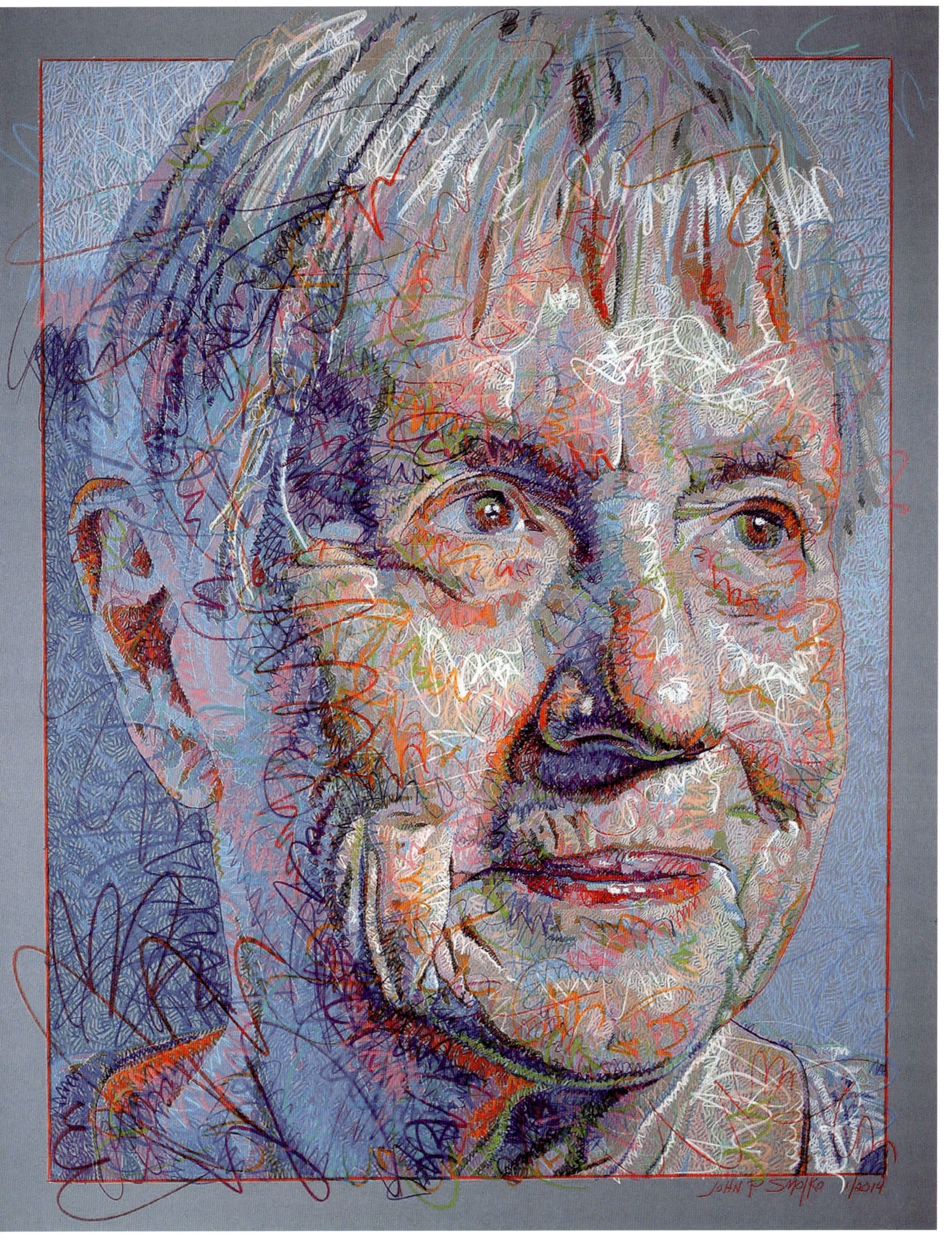

John P. Smolko 1/2014

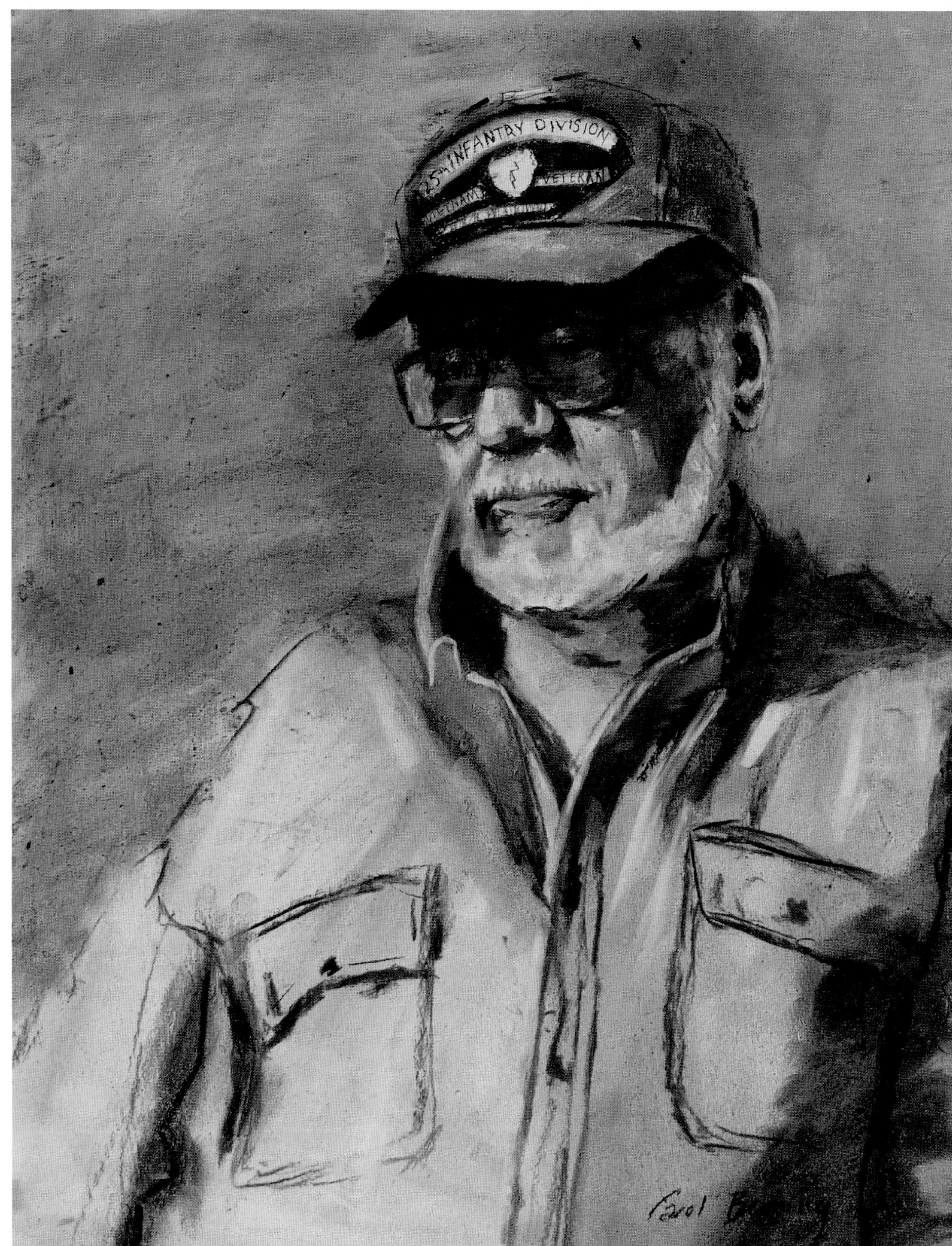

▼ **MY HUBBY, VIETNAM VETERAN**
Carol N. Berning
Vine and Nitram Charcoal on MDF board
20" × 16" (51cm × 41cm)

My husband and I met and married more than forty years ago after his return from Vietnam as an infantry officer. I recently asked him to pose for photographs wearing a cap that bore the 25th Infantry Division patch. I had covered the board with three coats of gesso, and this gessoed surface gave me the roughness that I sought in his clothing and gesture. Using sides and sharpened points of charcoal sticks, as well as a kneaded eraser, I created lost and found edges, soft passages and hard lines. I wanted the starkness of charcoal, along with his pensive gaze, his face half-covered in shadow, to symbolize his memories of war-time experiences and the impact the war has had on his life.

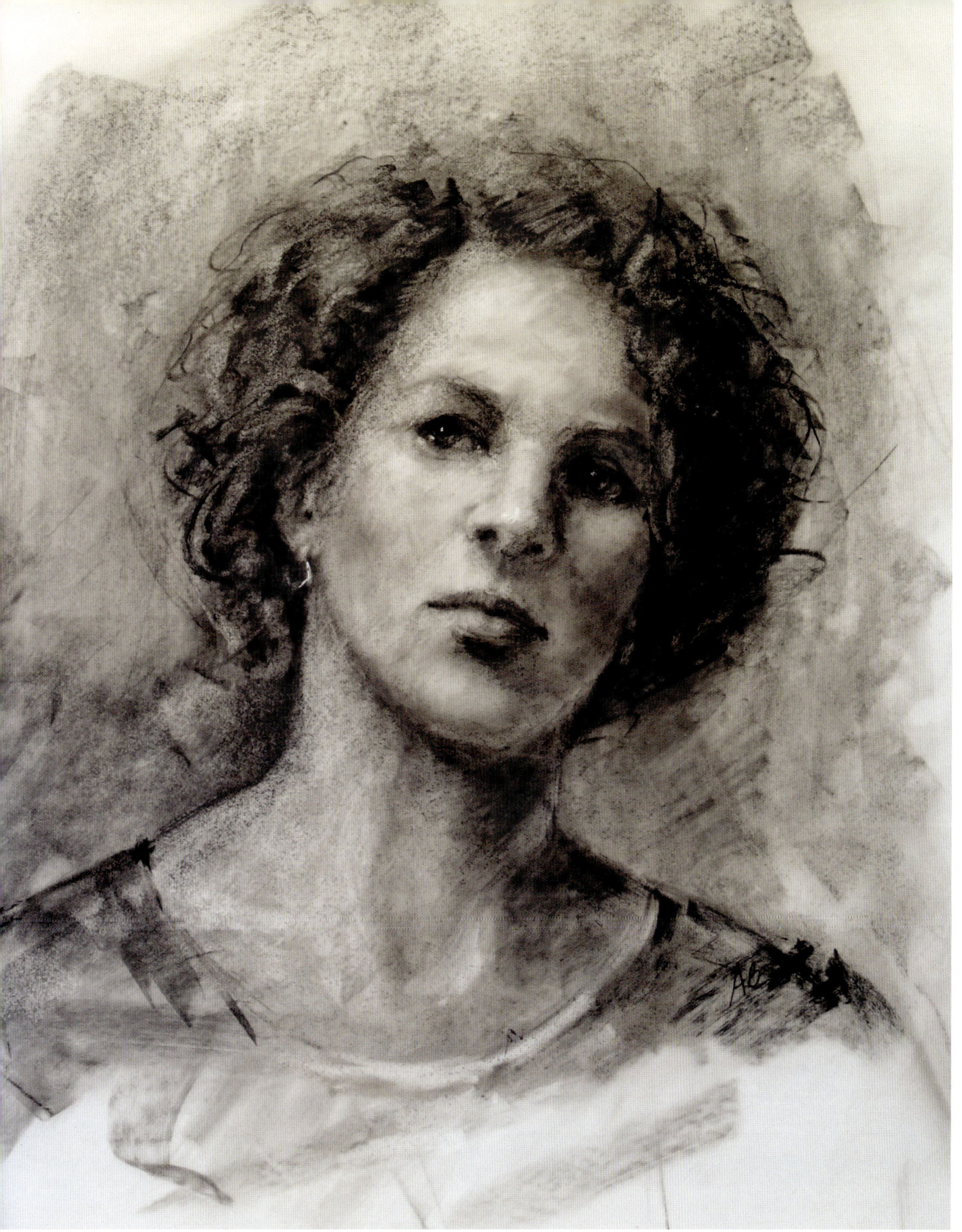

Doing a self-portrait presents both opportunity and challenge as the model is at the same time well known and elusive. In this self-portrait on Mylar, using a mirror to guide me, I began by drawing myself at the easel. Then, putting the mirror aside, I applied layers of charcoal, smudging and erasing as necessary, and finally spraying with a fixative. Mylar allows the charcoal to be easily wiped away and added again; it has the feeling of sculpting the form. The addition of a fixative works against this soft modeling, creating small pools of charcoal and a rough texture. Interestingly, the final portrait was an accurate depiction of myself at a younger age.

▲ **IN RETROSPECT**
August Burns
Charcoal on Mylar
14" × 11" (36cm × 28cm)

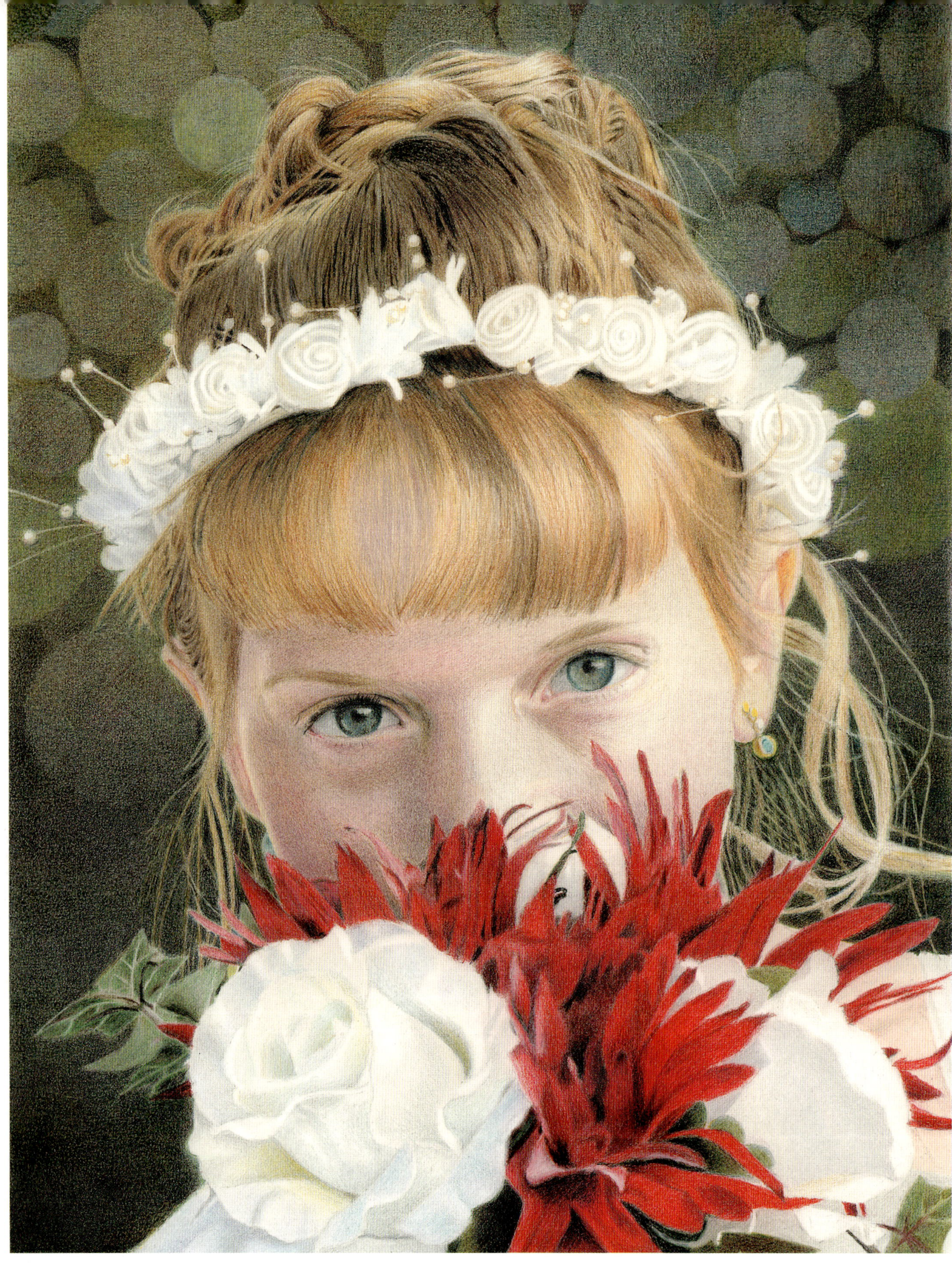

▲ FLOWER GIRL
Robert M. Richard
Colored pencil on 4-ply smooth bristol
14½" × 11" (37cm × 28cm)

There are fleeting moments when people express spontaneous emotions that are universally compelling. It's often necessary to use photos to capture this—especially with children. What drew me to create Rhianon's portrait was the intensity and mystery of her gaze over the flowers. When this drawing was almost complete I put it aside for a long time because it needed … something. There are times when one must take a leap of faith. So, after considerable distance and thought, I went for it! A major push of contrast in the values and textures. More punch to match the intensity in the eyes.

"An important part of getting the textures right is getting the values right." —ROBERT M. RICHARD

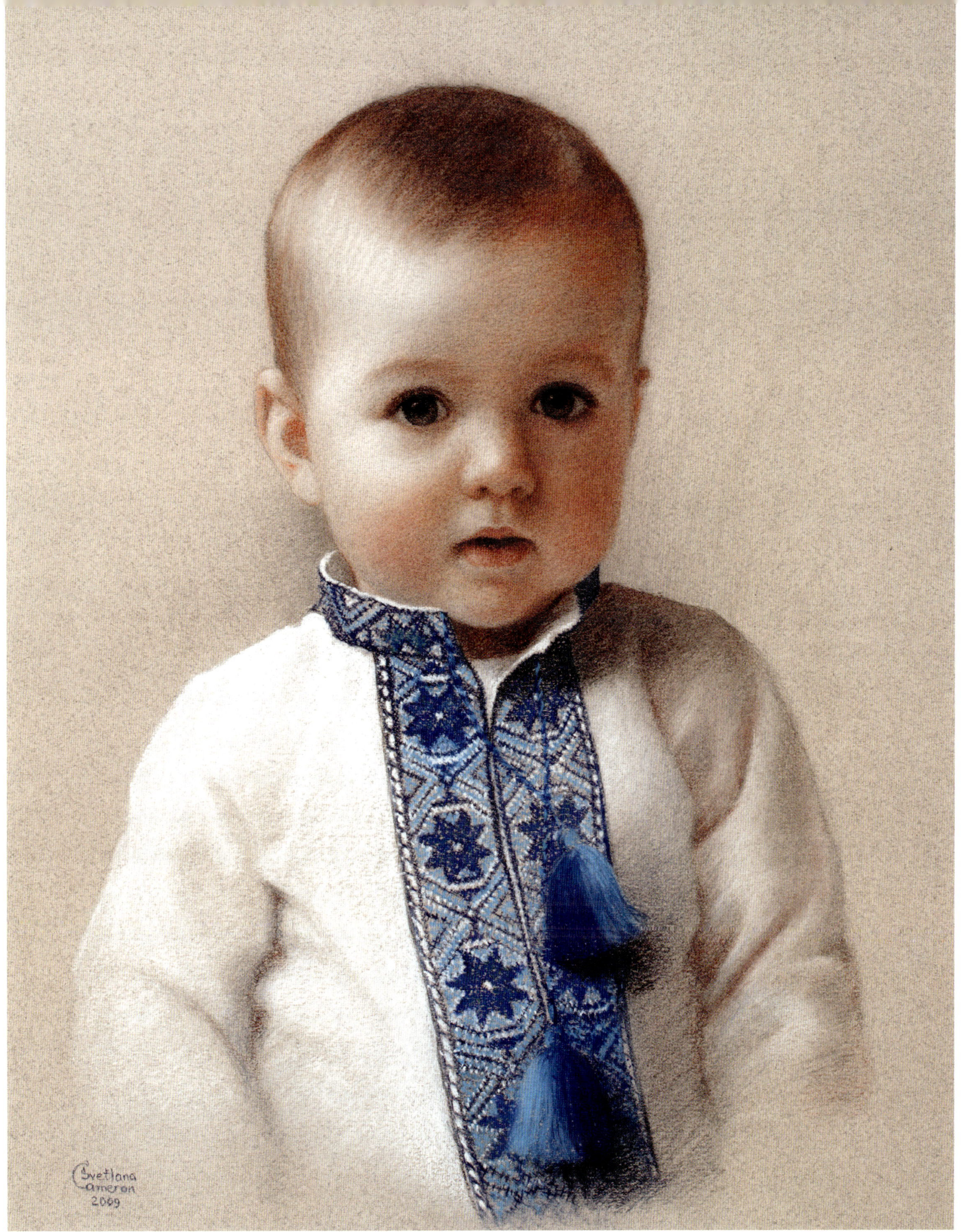

The embroidery in this drawing is more than just a decorative element. Not long before the portrait was created Daniel's mother took him to Ukraine, her country of origin, where the boy wore this traditional shirt during his christening ceremony. First I lightly drew the whole image in charcoal on warm gray paper for proportions and values. I added red and white Conté to the flesh areas and carefully blended them for delicate, translucent skin tones. I switched to white pastel for the fabric and three shades of blue to render the embroidered pattern. I kept the shirt in my studio and captured the fabric and the embroidered pattern entirely from life.

▲ **DANIEL**
Svetlana Cameron
Conté and pastel on Canson Mi-Teintes paper
16" × 12" (41cm × 30cm)

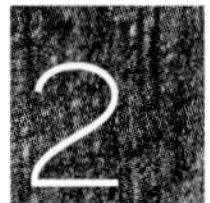

Scenes from Town & Country

▶ **SILENCE #2**
Kathleen McDonnell
Pastel on Wallis pastel board
18" × 24" (46cm × 61cm)

Living in a rural area I am able to observe
the many moods of the landscape. On
one of my morning walks the fog was
so dense that it was hard to see beyond
the immediate trees and the silence was
overwhelmingly beautiful. My idea was to
re-create that stunning quiet by contrasting the smooth texture of the snow with
the linear textures of the background
trees. Dabs of cool white pastel, long linear
strokes, the broad side of my pastel as well
as the sharpened point of a hard pastel
created the textures of the pastel painting
with a very limited palette of warm and
cool grays.

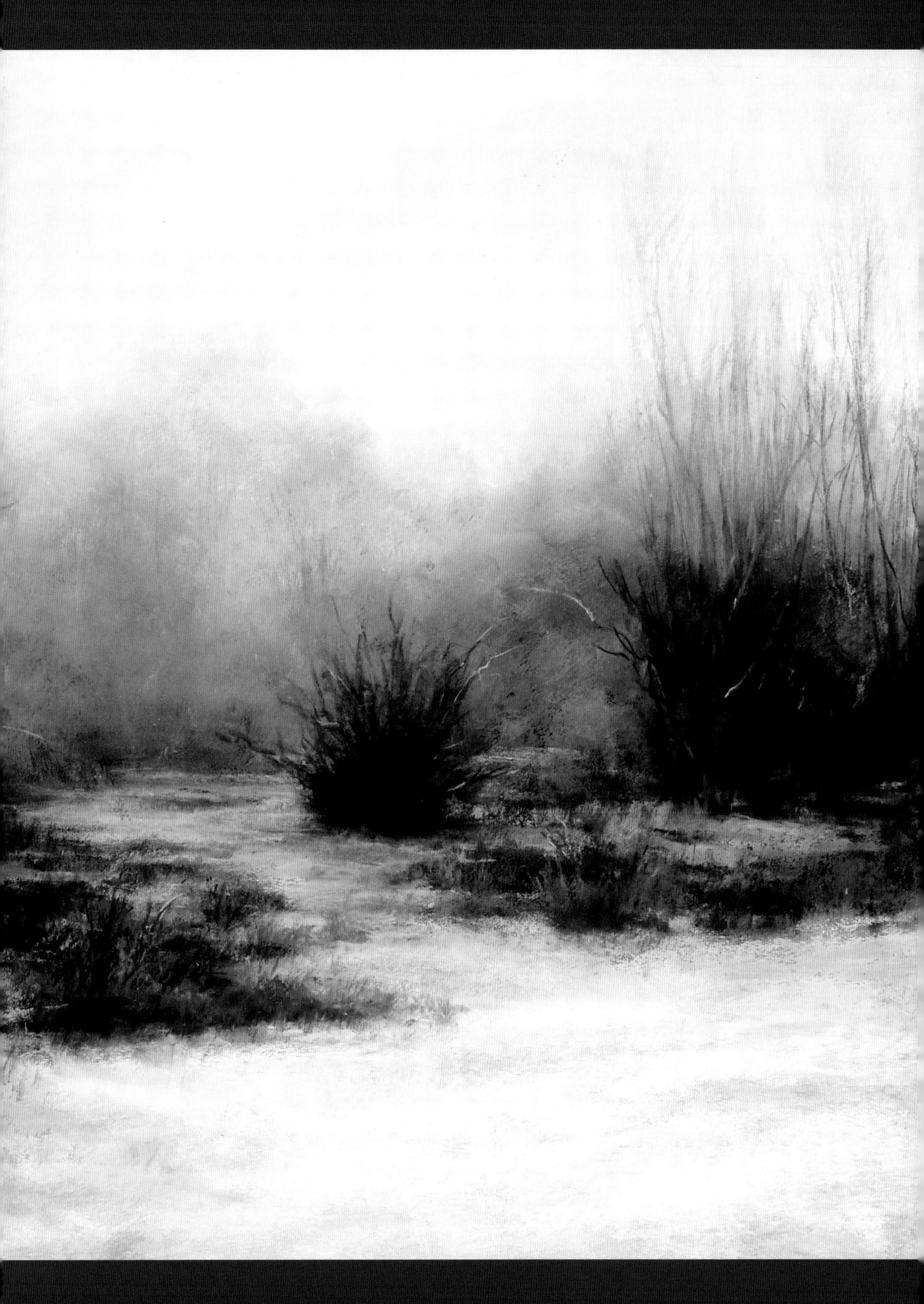

▼ SOUTH GRAND ISLAND BRIDGE
Chris Breier
Ink on Arches rough watercolor paper
8" × 10" (20cm × 25cm)

I completed this drawing in my studio by working from my own reference photos. The strategy I used was to capture the details with line work and use transparent washes for the shading. The basic shapes were quickly sketched out with a disposable technical pen. When I was satisfied with the accuracy of the drawing, I began adding the bold lines. I improvised a crude dip pen from a wood stick by sharpening the end of it to a chisel point, which helped me to create the ragged, sketchy lines that I was looking for.

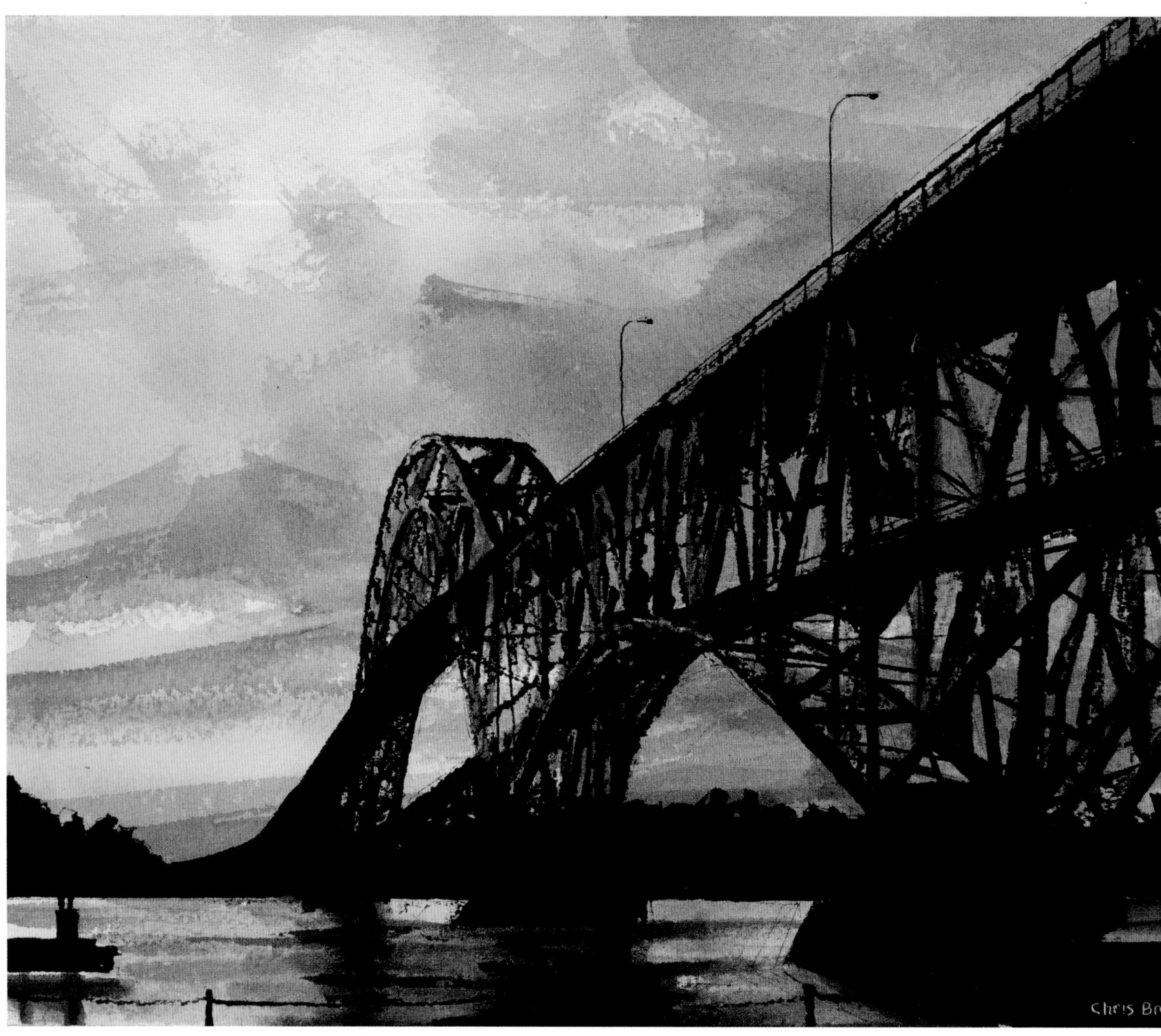

"Experiment with unconventional drawing tools to create interesting textures."

—CHRIS BREIER

▶ BASILICA
Chris Breier
Ink on rough Arches watercolor paper
10" × 8" (25cm × 20cm)

This basilica is located in Lackawanna, New York. Inspired by the churches of Europe, it was completed in 1929 and it contains hundreds of paintings and sculptures. While the accuracy of a drawing is important to me, I find it is texture that brings a drawing to life. Most drawing mediums can't be used to build up actual texture, so I often use techniques that capitalize on the texture of the paper. The irregular edges of the clouds and some of the subtle textures of the church were created by drybrushing transparent ink onto rough watercolor paper.

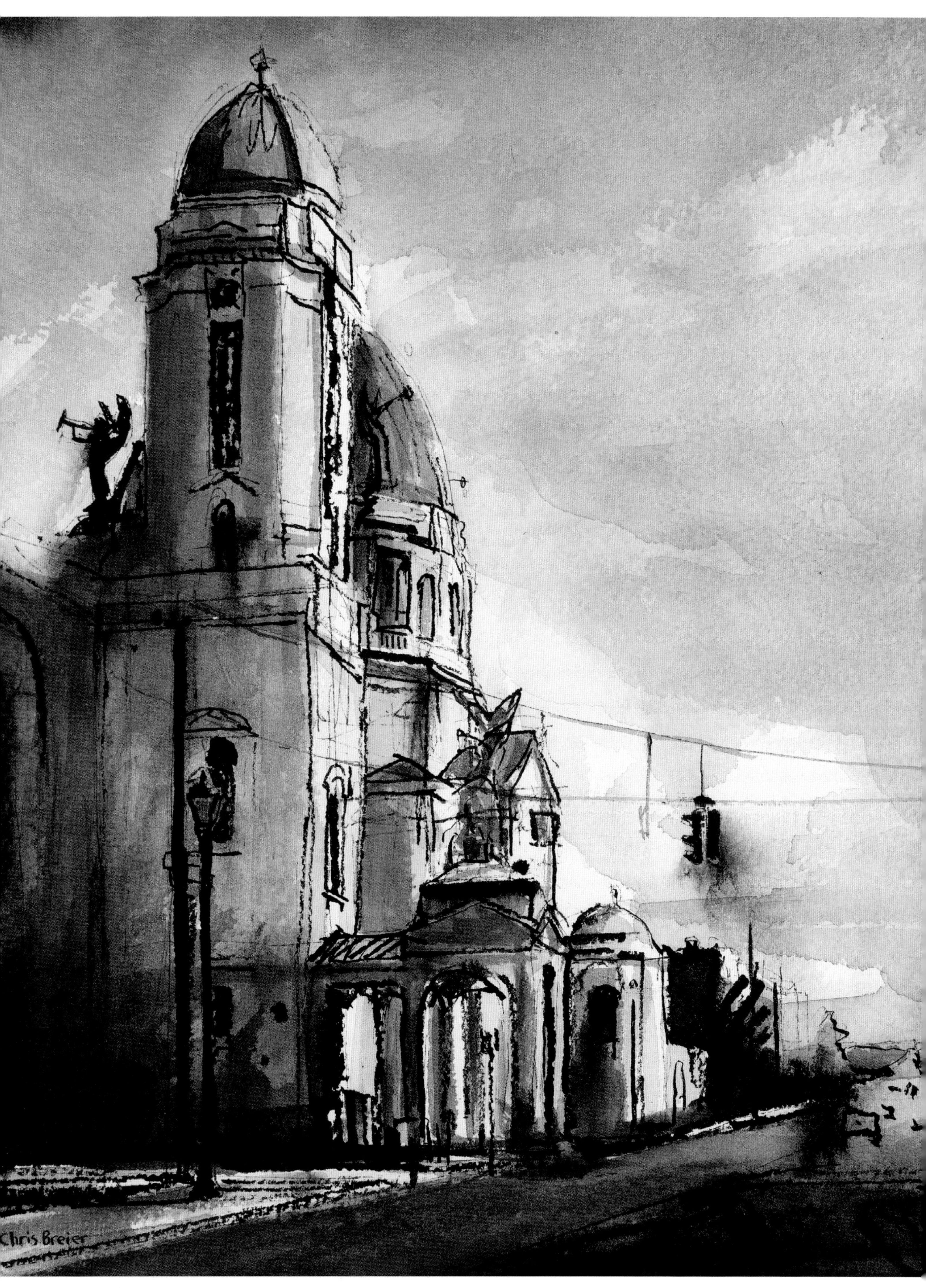

Chris Breier

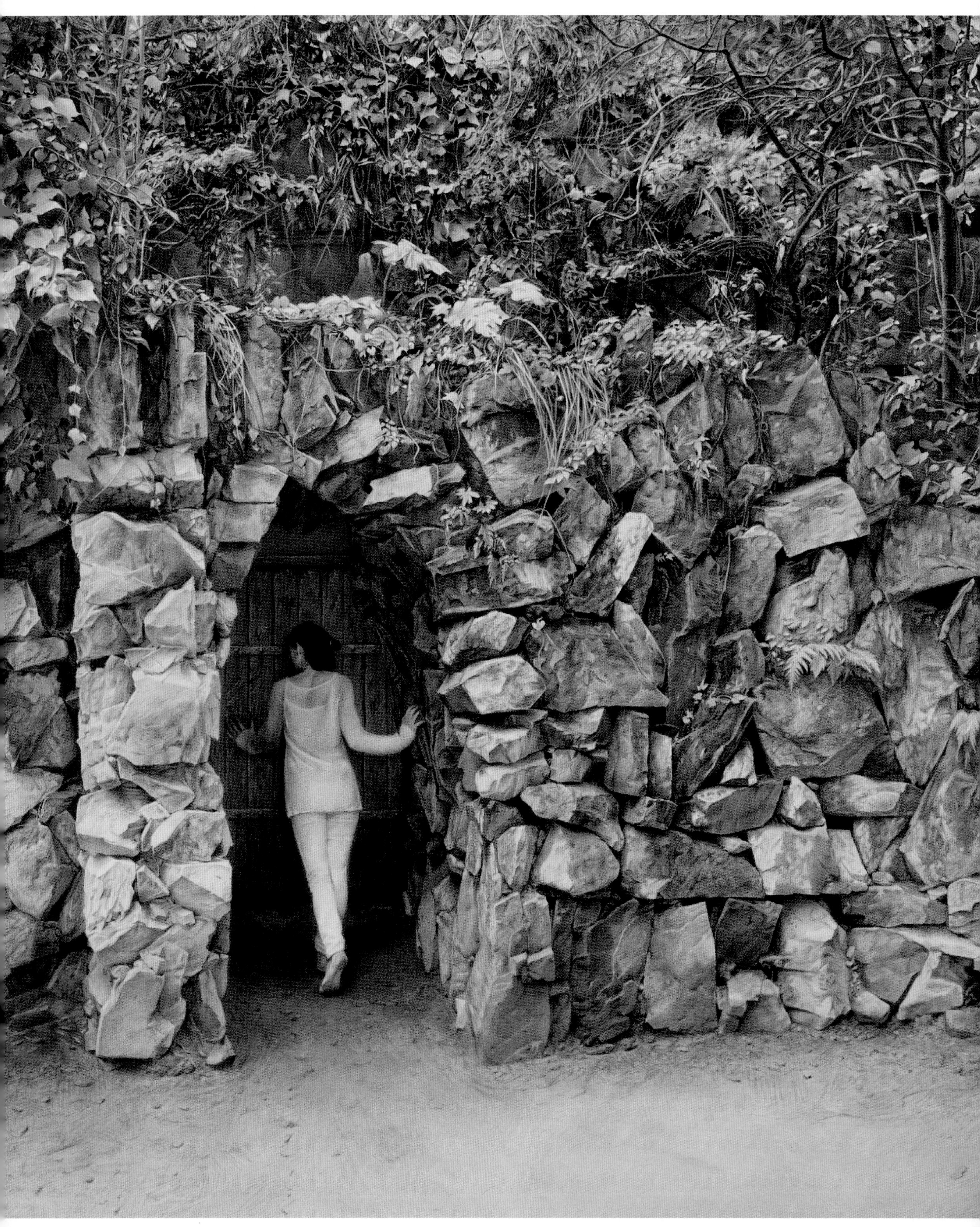

Minotaur is a diptych. The drawing shown here is part 1 of the diptych. It was drawn from photo and imagination in my studio in Berkeley, based on a real location in my town, Argentona, in Spain. This drawing is entirely done with graphite, most of it applied by pencil, some of it in powder form. Texture is a key element: rocks, leaves, branches, wood … all of them creating a huge wall standing between our heroine and her journey, a journey we all face in our everyday lives, a journey that takes us to face the monster within and, hopefully, succeed in our daily battle against it. I like to think patience is the main medium used in this piece since the drawing took over 300 hours.

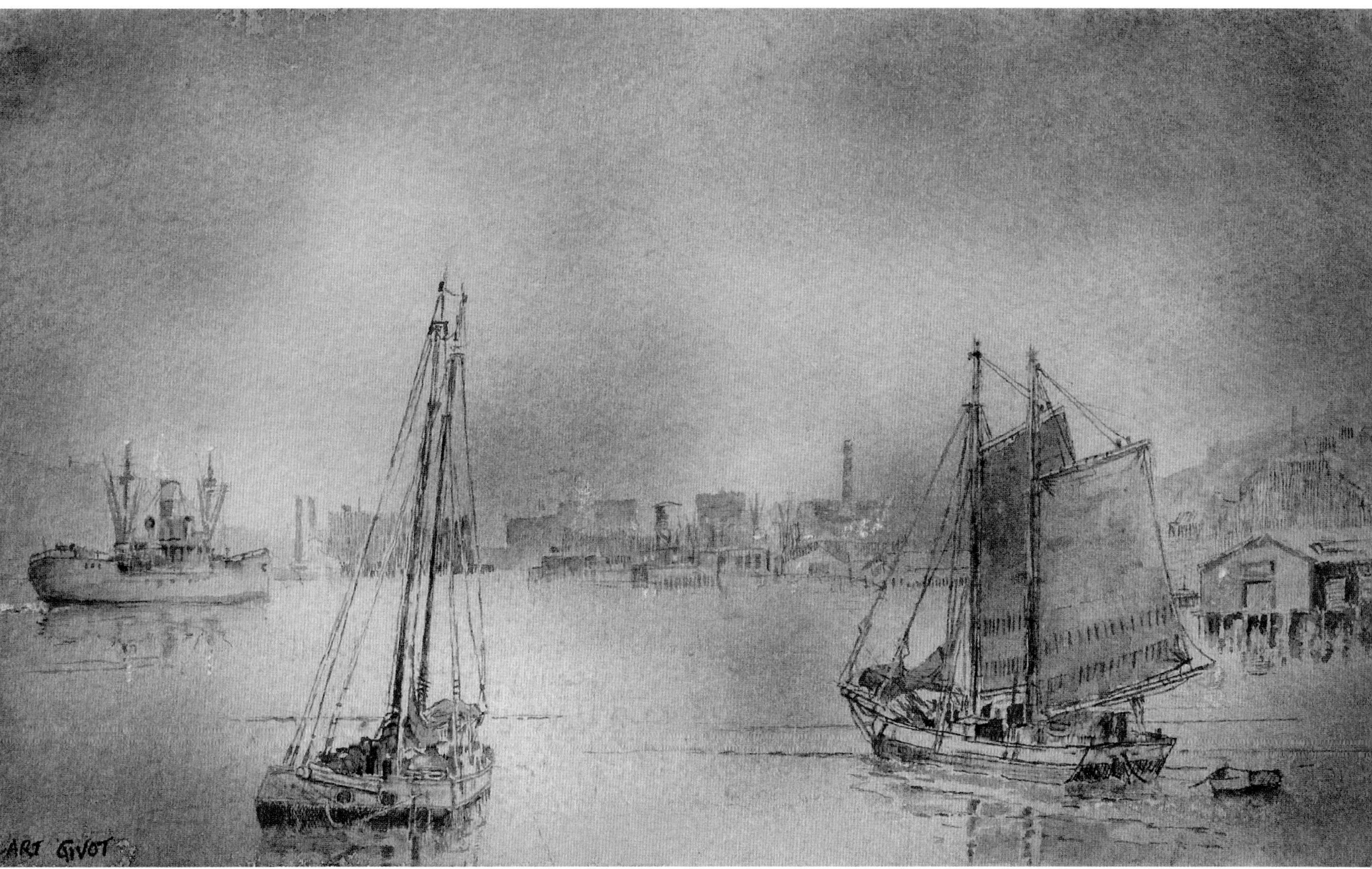

Having a desire to do an ink drawing on tinted paper but having no tinted paper, I decided to "self" tint. I used a scrap of 300-lb. (640gsm) cold-pressed watercolor paper. The tint is a wash of Payne's Gray with Prussian, Cobalt and French Ultramarine Blues. The lighter areas are a combination of yellows. The ink is a walnut ink I make myself. An ink eraser knife was used to pick out the highlights. Hopefully I have conveyed the feeling and velvety texture of fog, of heavy wet canvas and the fine mist.

This type of ornamental grass, Miscanthus, is an invasive plant that should not be in your garden. Yet I was completely taken by the expressive gesture and movement of this stalk, and I brought it home to my studio. Usually when I draw a botanical piece, I spend a lot of time doing a detailed graphite drawing that I transfer to my final surface. But this time I couldn't wait, and immediately began drawing in strokes of colored pencil on green-tinted paper. My goal was to capture the contrasting textures of the fluffy seed plumes and the arching sharp-edged, thin leaves.

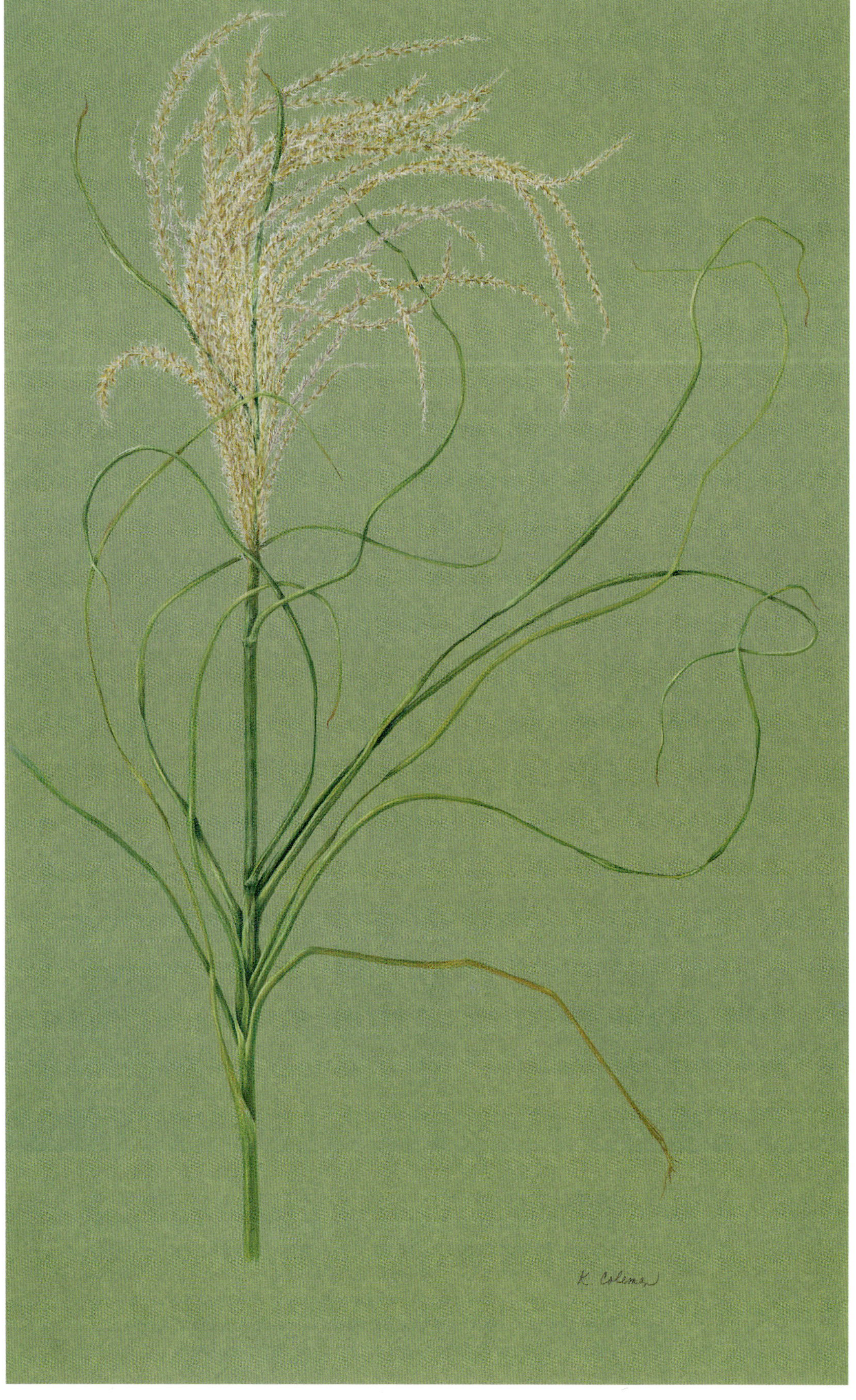

"Sometimes you just have to let go and be free to let the subject guide the strokes of your hand." —KAREN COLEMAN

I started painting the grandeur of Arizona desert 15 years ago and revel in the intricate color palette and unique topography of the region, especially the huge saguaro cactus. This was a live sketch done in the parking lot of a big hotel in Ventana Canyon, just north of Tucson. The 9B woodless graphite pencil on paper allows me to develop the soft gray midtones that provide the light source. The drama of this subject is created with the middle values that build up to surround the highlights. The darkest darks then provide what I refer to as the "anchor values," completing the full range of values. The subtle texture of the paper and the soft graphite allow me to develop images like this in five minutes or less.

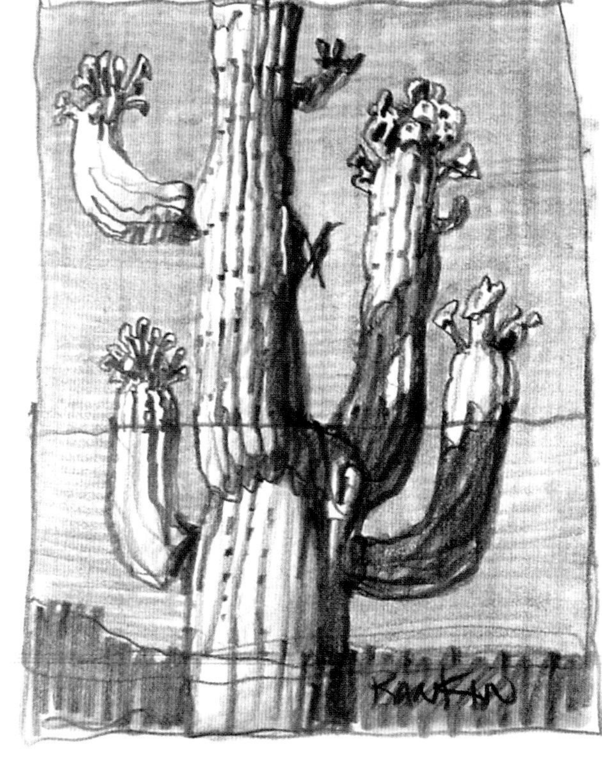

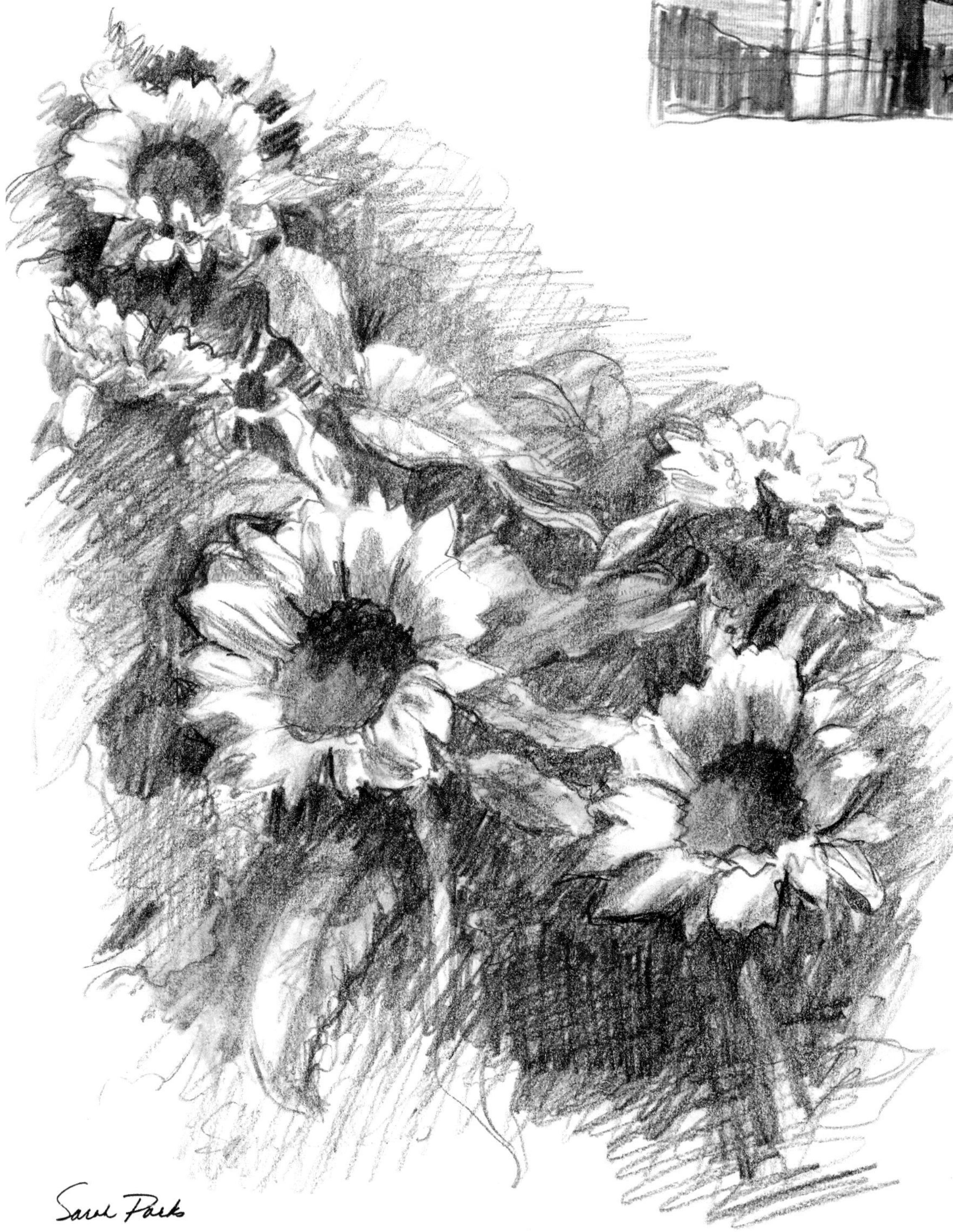

I was in California at a garden center, and amidst all the vibrant flowers one particular spray of sunflowers forming an interesting diagonal line caught my eye. The bright morning sun provided a terrific interplay of light and dark, and the petals cast gorgeous shadows. To reflect the boldness of these flowers I chose to minimize blending and used white paper, which allowed me to leave the highlights unshaded. Except for the focal point, I left the composition less developed with a loose rendering of hatching.

This is from an ongoing series of drawings. Beginning with some circular element, the composition is developed by adding and subtracting elements, lines, values and textures until an interesting image emerges. Various techniques including incising, abrading and scraping are employed in addition to smudging and erasing the surface to create textures. Textures, both real and implied, are significant to each of the works. Value is also key in developing the visual impact of the drawing. This drawing also relies on calligraphic linework and the use of carbon mixed with water to create additional textural interest.

▼ **COSMIC IRRELEVANCE**
Jac Tilton
Carbon and charcoal on 140-lb. (300gsm) paper
20" × 24" (51cm × 61cm)

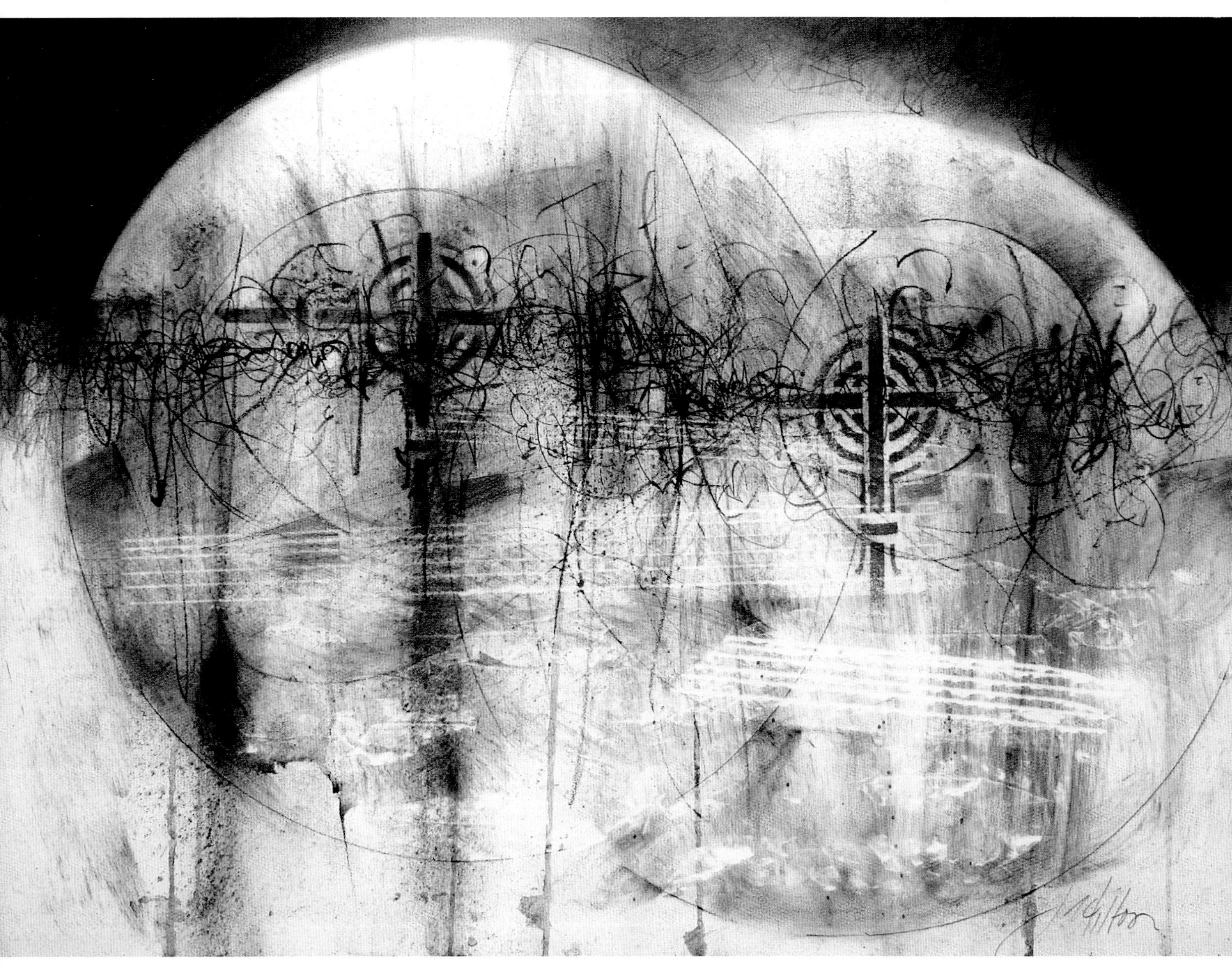

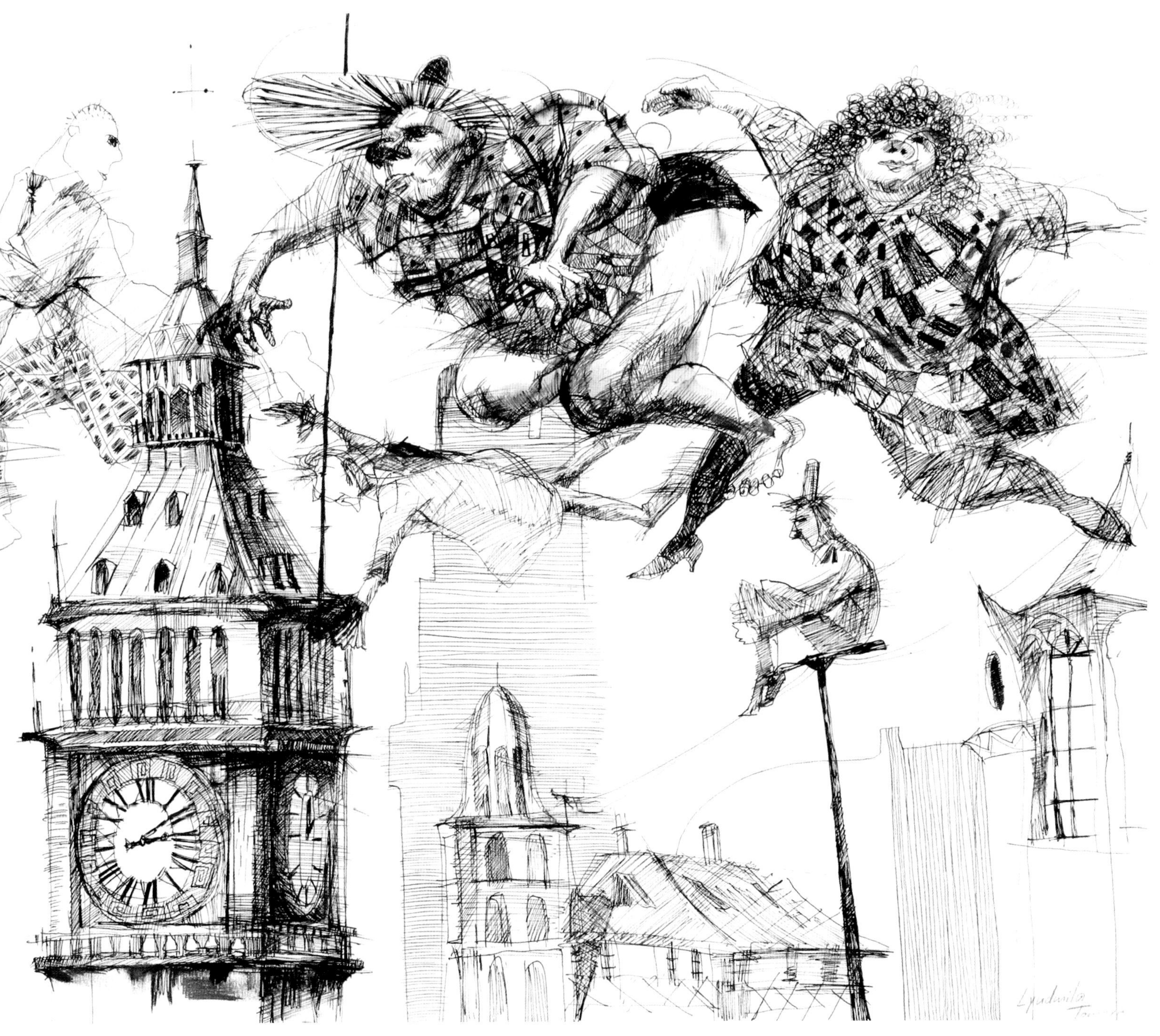

Careless Nation is a drawing created completely from my imagination. I used my favorite pen-and-ink technique of dipping the pen in an ink bottle and sketching the images freely without a preliminary pencil drawing. My goal was to surprise myself, alla prima style, without the restrictions of a preconceived idea. The free drawing, crosshatching and scribbling were intended to express free-flowing movement. I built seemingly chaotic crosshatching in random layers of various textures to further complement the concept of a careless or carefree nation. To my delight, I ended up with a satirical piece with a subtle political statement.

▲ **CARELESS NATION**
Lyudmila Tomova
Dip pen and ink on paper
14" × 17" (36cm × 43cm)

▼ BEYOND ALL BOUNDARIES
Dianna Wallace Soisson
Prismacolor pencils on Stonehenge paper
14" × 31" (36cm × 79cm)

My creations begin through the lens of a camera. Through this lens I capture the scenes that inspire me with their beauty, light, shadows and textures. The flawless beauty of nature is my focus. My instruments are simple; through them I aim to capture the essence of life. My tools are UArt paper, Prismacolor pencils, a heated drawing board and, at times, brush and solvent. After sketching my subject, I begin layering the colors. The heated board enables the wax pencils to blend so seamlessly that it creates an appearance of fluent and polished water. To enhance the smoothness and intensity I sometimes use a light brush of solvent.

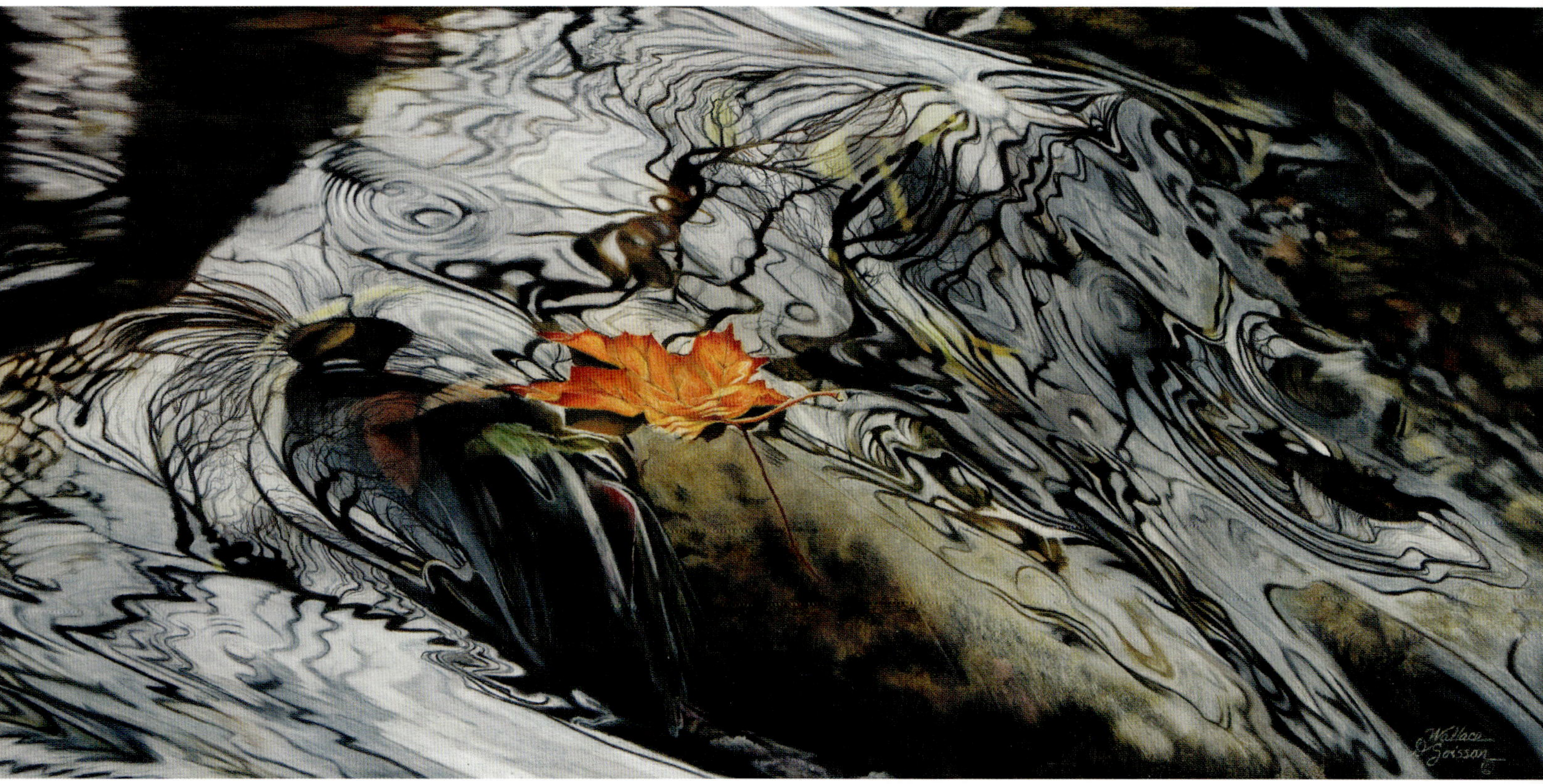

I am fascinated by weathered structures that are vanishing from our landscape. Capturing them in a work of art helps keep them in view. Pastels are a perfect medium for subjects with rough texture, especially on sanded paper. Altering the pressure, direction and stroke allows me to represent a wide variety of textures. Rather than blending, I layer colors and leave visible marks. I selected this image of a porch in Rockland, Maine, because I loved the texture of the peeling paint and the colors of the evening light. I rendered the peeled paint rather quickly, often leaving my initial marks even if they were not what I had originally intended.

▶ PORCH LIGHT
Helen Kleczynski
Soft pastel on Wallis Belgian Mist
24" × 17" (61cm × 43cm)

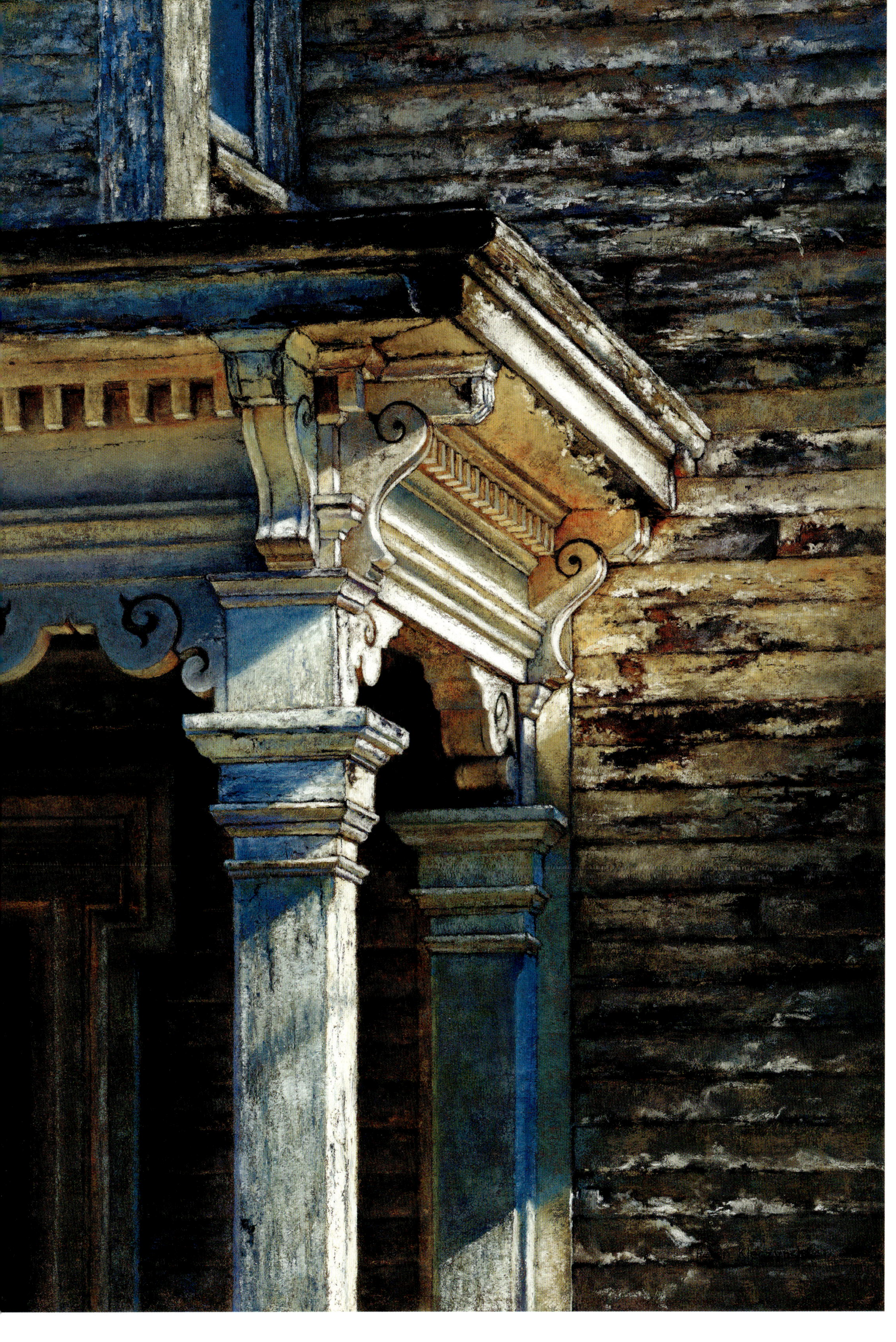

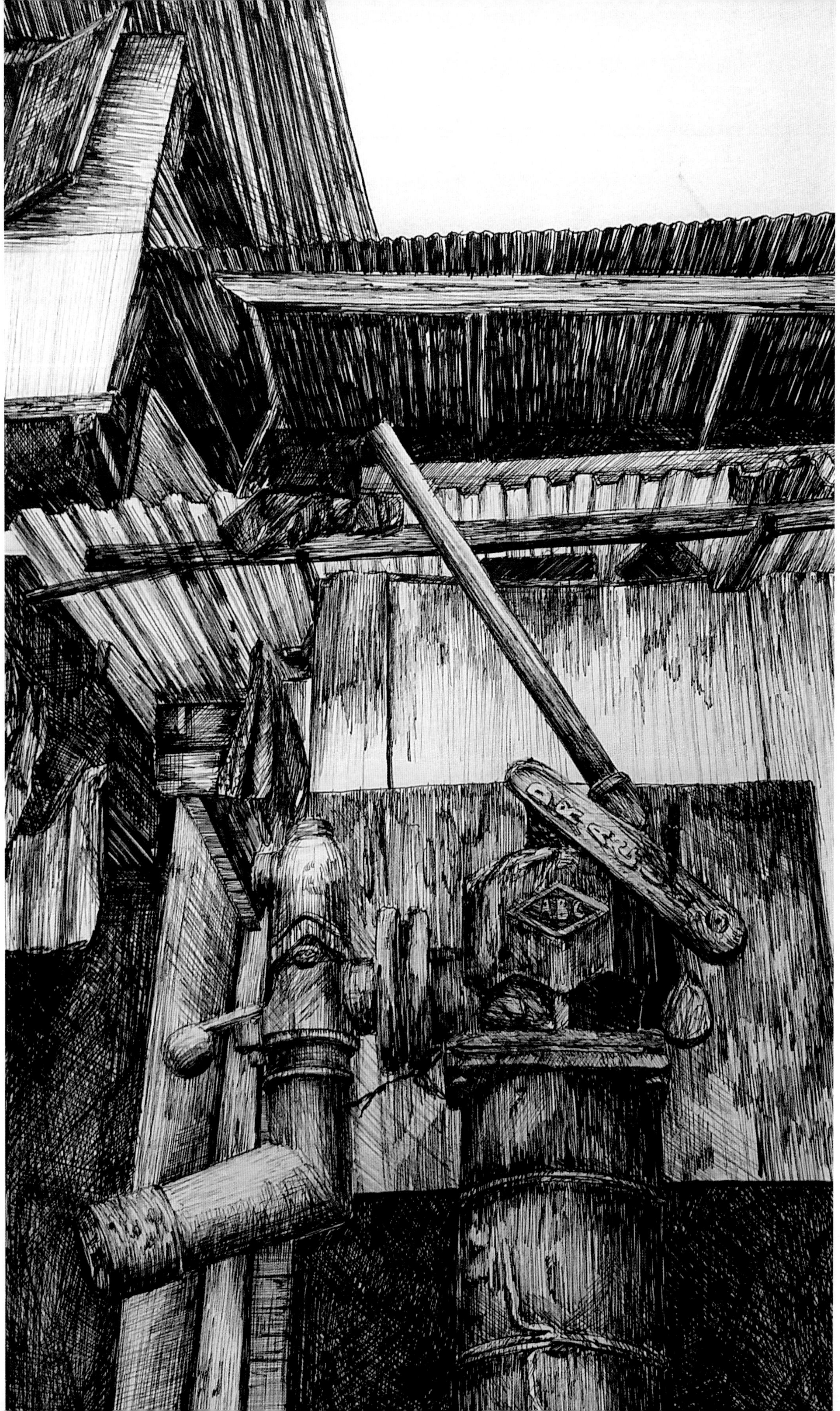

I live in Jakarta, Indonesia. There is a small, traditional area behind my school we call Kampung. The houses are compact and the spaces between them are confined, which allowed me the wonderful opportunity to explore the element of space. Space is communicated through linear perspective, overlapping, and atmospheric perspective. I worked from my original photos of Kampung. The use of pen and ink created strong textures and more definite negative spaces that emphasized the ruralness of Kampung.

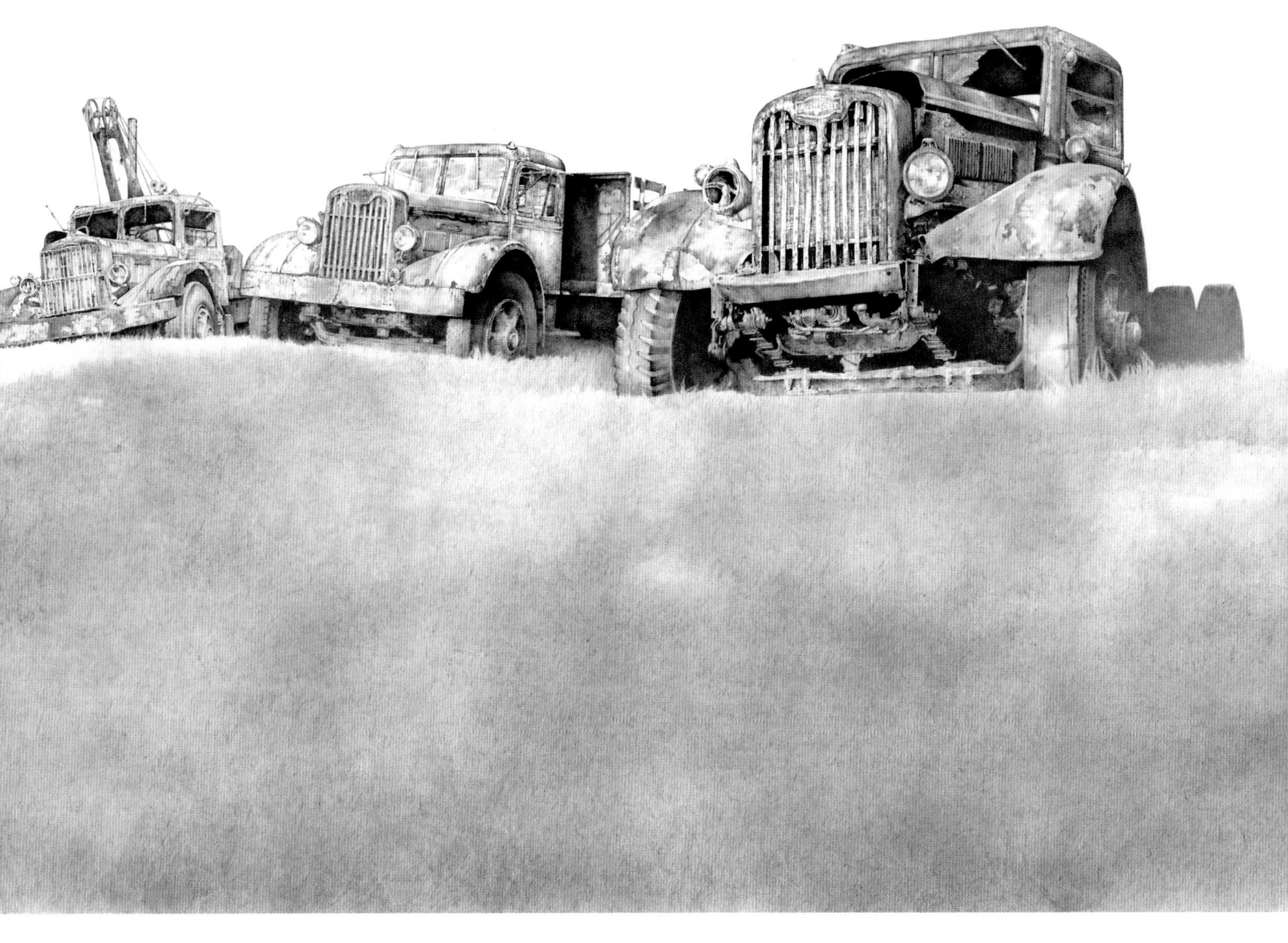

As I caught sight of these vehicles in a grassy field, they immediately reminded me of daunting, muscular gents at the ocean's shore. The drawing's title came to me then, before the first pencil stroke. When I returned to take more reference photos, to my astonishment there on the door, barely legible, was the name "L.E. Beach." Textures from the decades of weathering showed beautiful imperfections like rust and broken windshields. The variety of flaws and unique tire treads add to each truck's individuality. I chose a low angle to accentuate their intimidating quality, contrasted with the delicacy of the expanse of field below them. To balance the picture, an existing metal crane remains behind the truck, far left.

"In creating texture it's important to observe the surface, substance, lighting and shadows." —STEVE WILDA

A visual language of line work, hatching and stippling expresses the myriad textures: natural landscape against the architectonics of the historical warehouses, the spidery cables of the bridge and the pristine glass cube encasing the heritage carousel in the midground. The complex diversity of steel, glass and masonry façades of the background skyscrapers is rendered by simple repetitive patterning of horizontal or vertical lines.

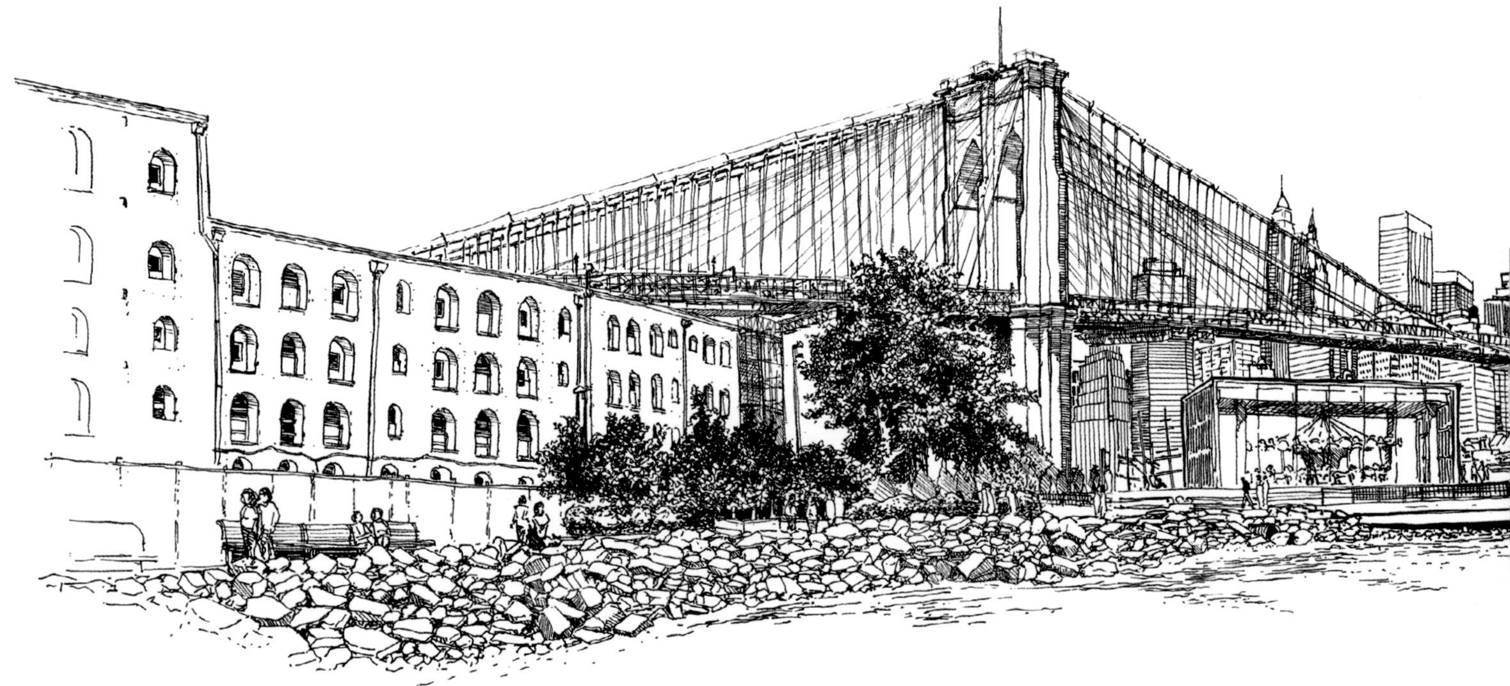

"Detailed drawings in pen require confidence and a mindset that is not preoccupied with how long it will take or how many sittings may be required." —STUART MEYER-PLATH

Gathering reference in the field, I'm drawn to strong textural presence: rocks, trees, vegetation and the way light and shadow play off those textures. Here I really wanted to focus on the character of the rocks—cold, hard, weathered. Therefore, I grayed down the softer distant hillside vegetation and the three deer, creating a much stronger visual separation between foreground and background, and allowing those softer textures to blend into a subtle stage set in front of which the rocks become the stars.

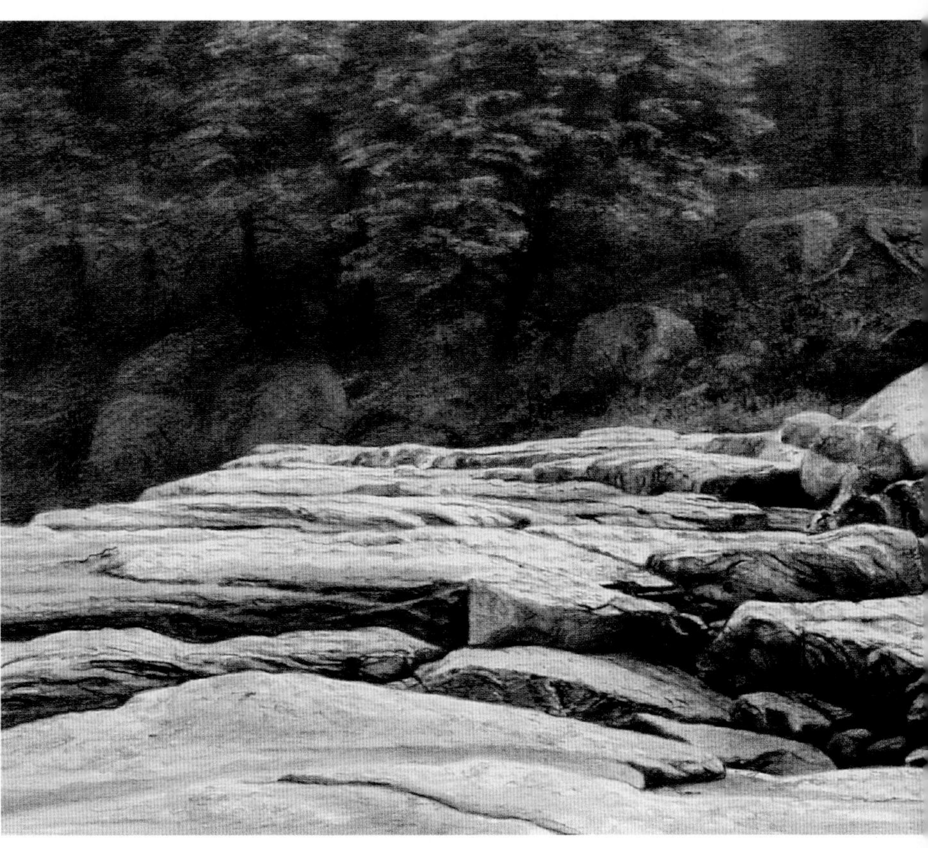

This work was done in-studio from a live plant—the way I always do botanical illustration. Colored pencil is an ideal way to achieve nature's textures like shiny leaves, velvety petals, and rough tree bark. After laying down several layers, I apply baby oil lightly with a brush to blend the colors and smooth the strokes. This technique works very well to achieve a smooth and shiny texture. The philodendron is at the entrance of my new studio, and this was my way to celebrate my art space.

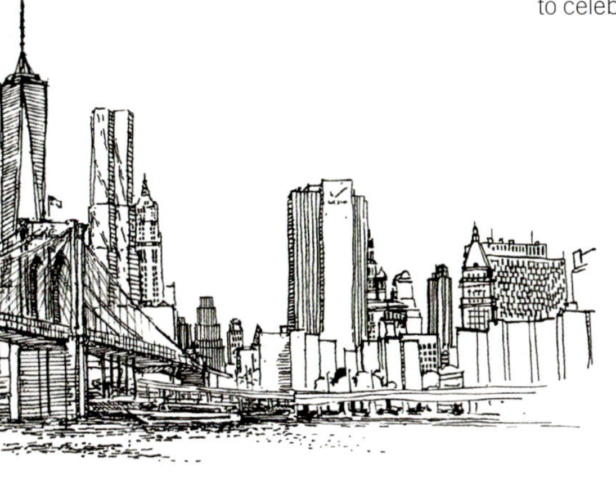

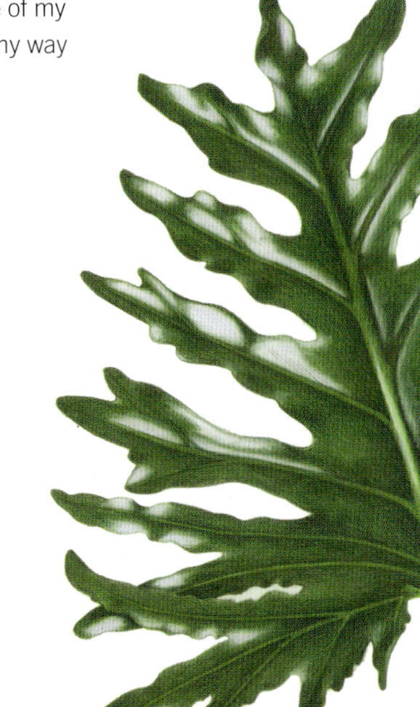

▼ **PHILODENDRON**
Cristina Baltayian
Prismacolor and Caran d'Ache colored pencil
on bristol vellum paper
14" × 11" (36cm × 28cm)

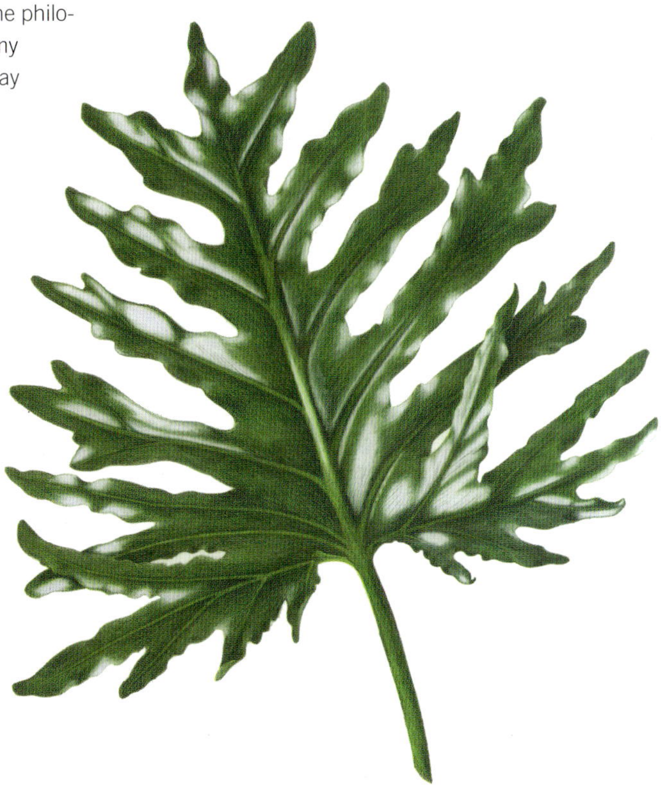

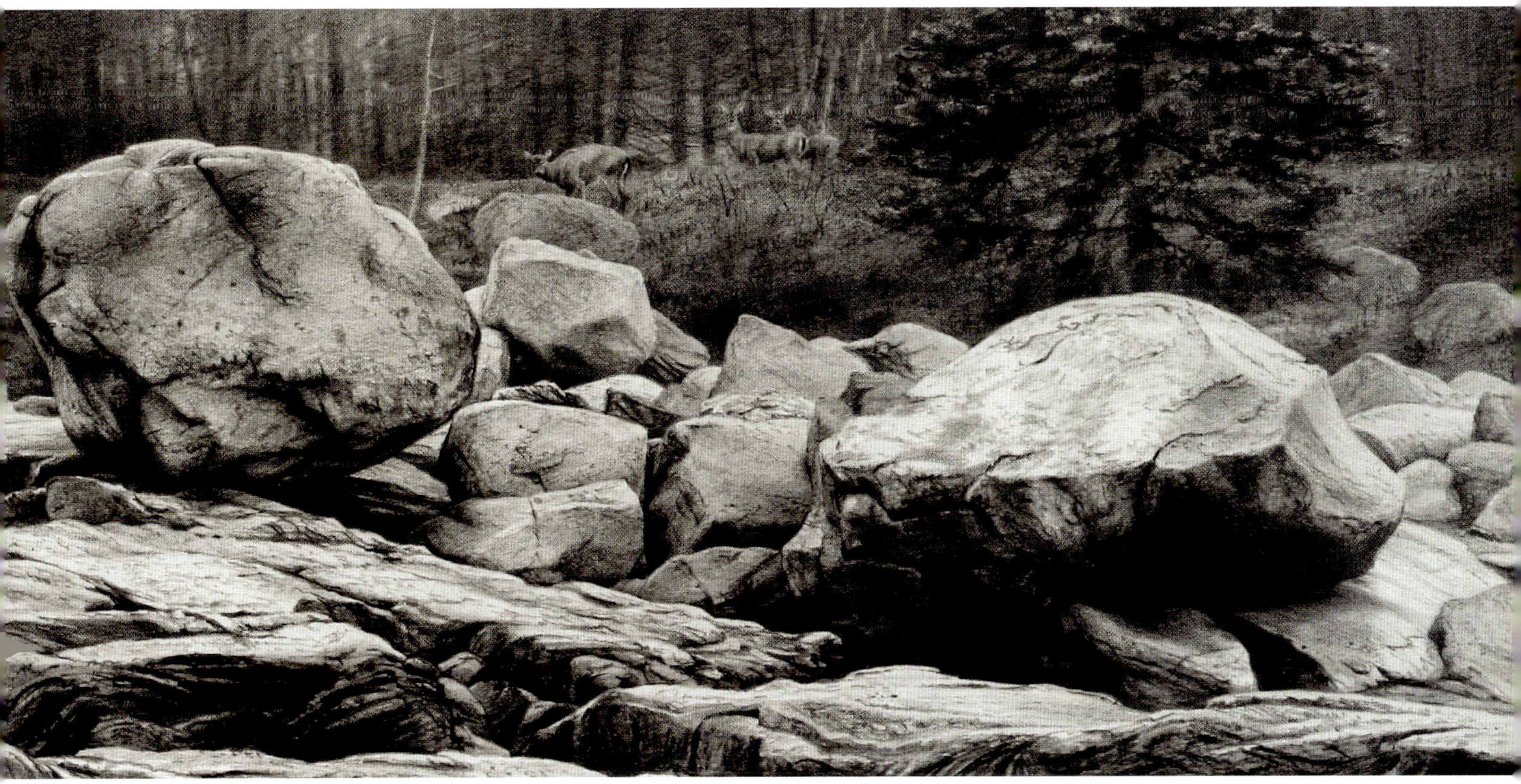

My childhood thrill of seeing the moving world from a car window continues. The textures of experience—twilight, drops of rain on the windscreen, the arrested motion at the traffic light in the evening rush to get home—are expressed in this piece. On gessoed Gator board I applied an imprimatura of watery black paint to create three rough horizontal planes reflecting near, medium, far distance. I allowed the serendipitous reaction of paint on the rough surface to suggest something of the energy of the intersection. Then with deliberate marks of pastel, I carved into the space the forms of the vehicles and lights. In the landscape of black and grays the red holds a shock and a stillness that encourages individual interpretation.

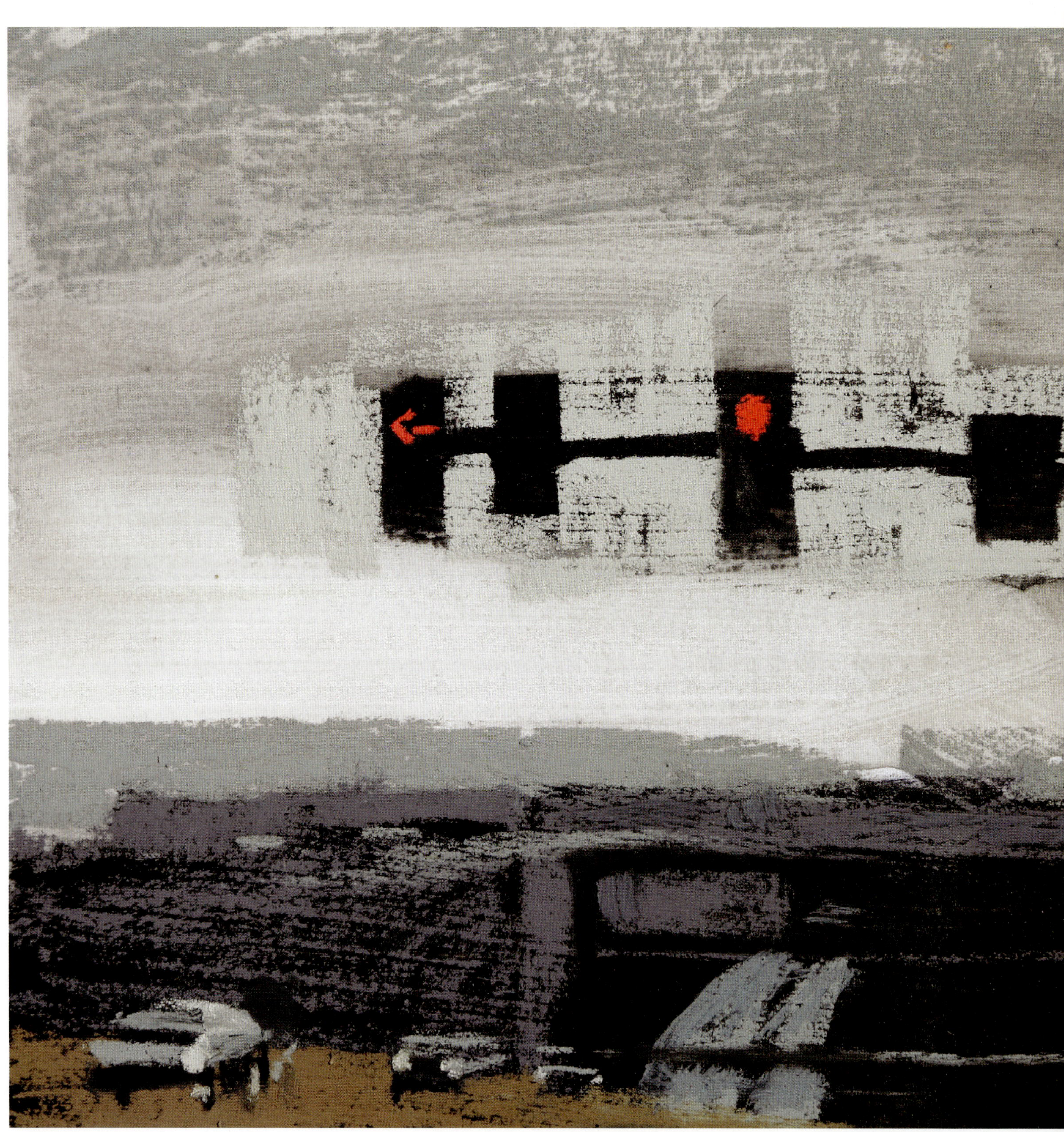

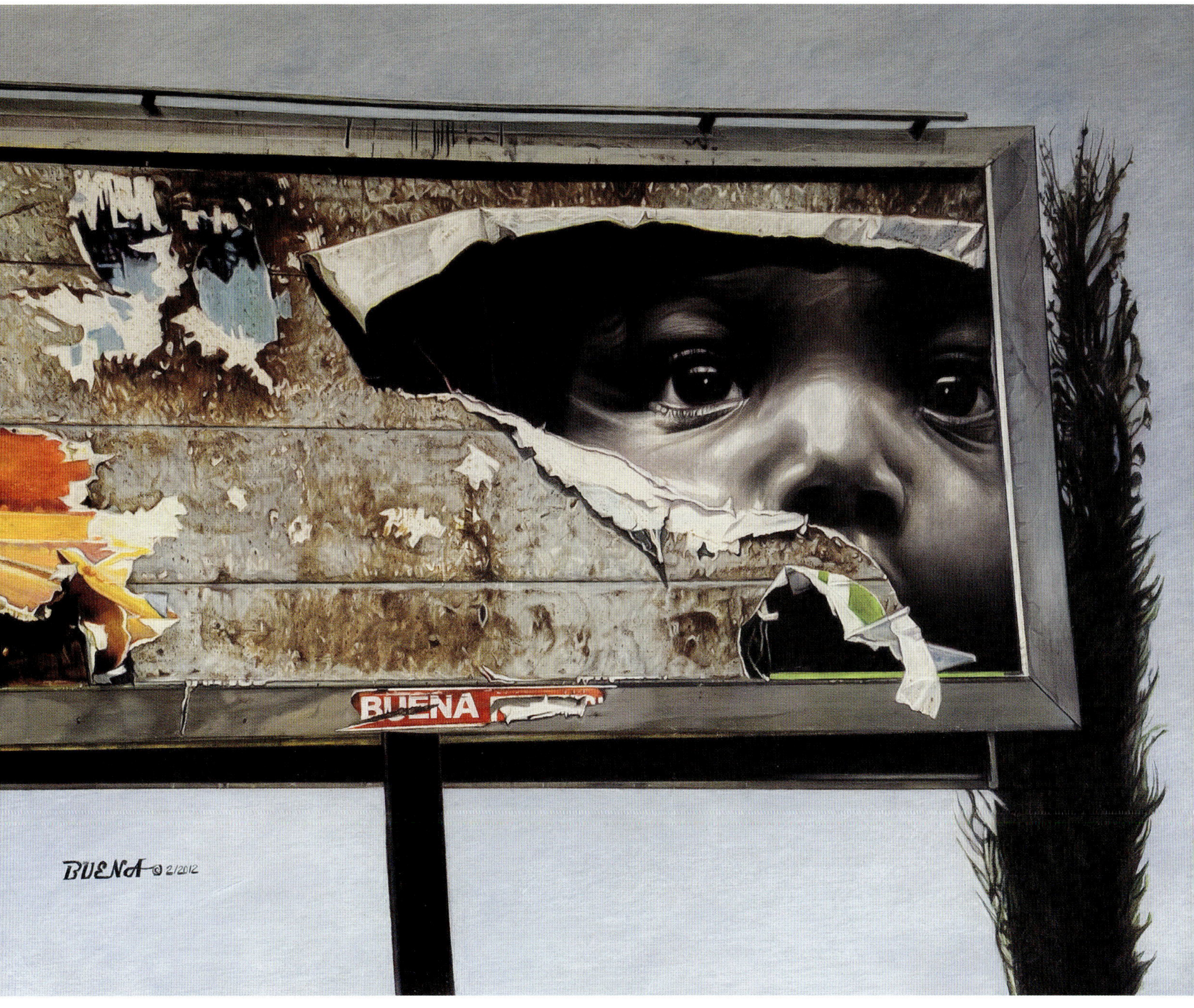

I find beauty in the textures and altered messages generated by the natural deconstruction of neglected billboards, which most others consider eyesores. The original message is often stripped away by the natural process of time. With artistic license my intent is to present a new thought-provoking message for the viewer to consider and personally interpret. Rendering the child's face mainly with black and white lends an emotional impact to the subject, while the tree in the background jolts us into another plane. At the bottom of the steel frame where company signage is normally depicted, my name, BUENA, is rendered in the torn paper area.

▲ HOW 'EYE' WONDER
Buena G. Johnson
Colored pencil on museum board
31" × 37" (79cm × 94cm)

The dynamics of light, shadow and texture bring this realistic rural landscape to life. The highest contrast of light and dark is concentrated in the front corner of the old barn, the drawing's focal point, where the ivy and stone foundation meet. The technique used for the barn boards is a two-step process. The details are put down with a 2B .5mm mechanical pencil. Then a flat chisel-point pencil of harder 2H lead is burnished on top of the details. This creates an even middle tone without losing the details underneath.

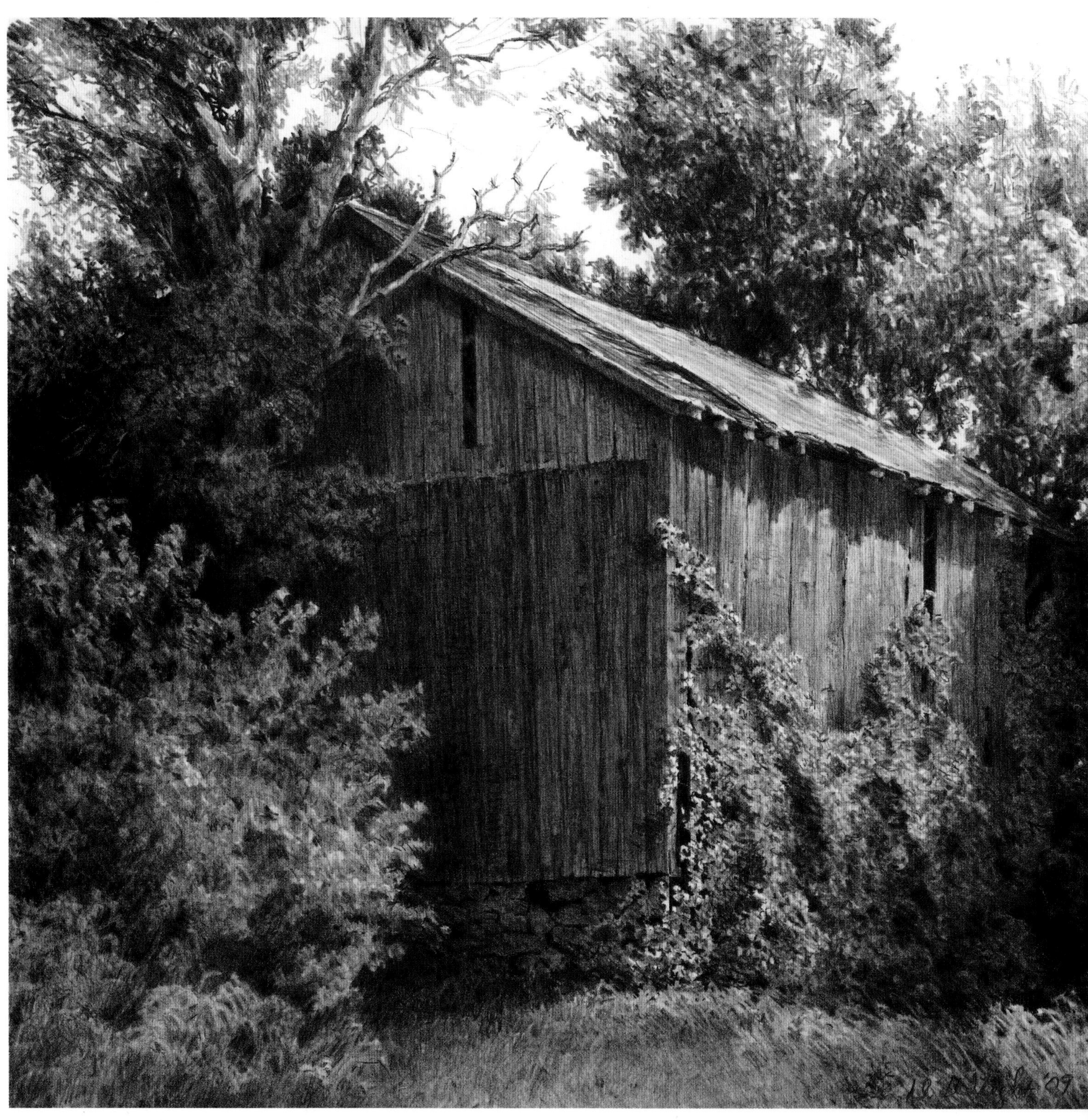

I found this wonderful coast live oak tree at Point Reyes National Seashore. It had so much going on: variations in bark and colors, mosses and lichens, holes and hollows, branches full of light. Together, these textures tell its story of survival, from winter storms to harsh drought. In the Garden of Eden there were a Tree of Life and a Tree of Knowledge. If there had been a Tree of Character, I think it would look like this. I've been seeking other special trees since.

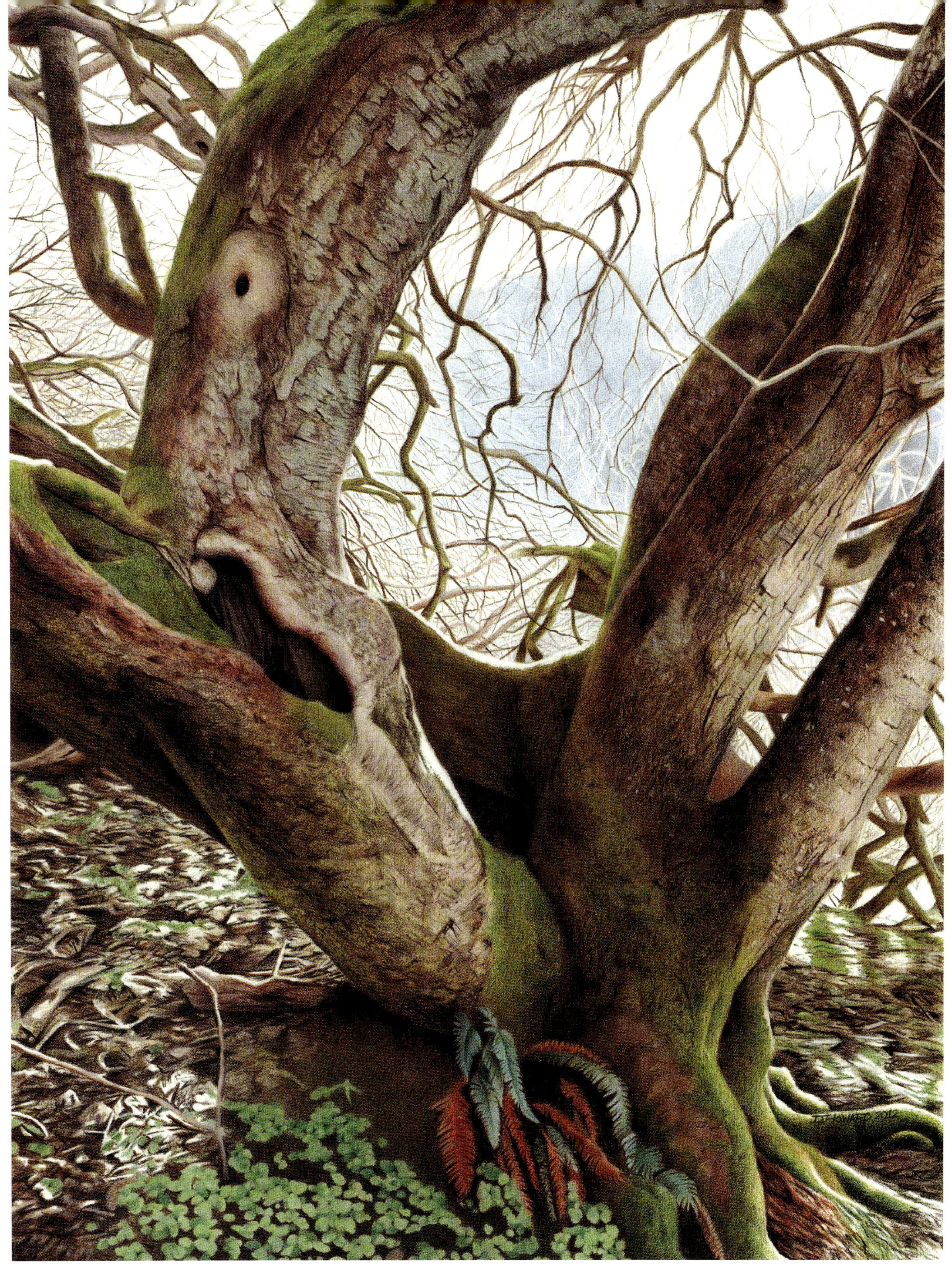

"Most people miss textural details in their daily lives, but notice them in artwork—your opportunity to reopen their eyes to their world." —DENISE J. HOWARD

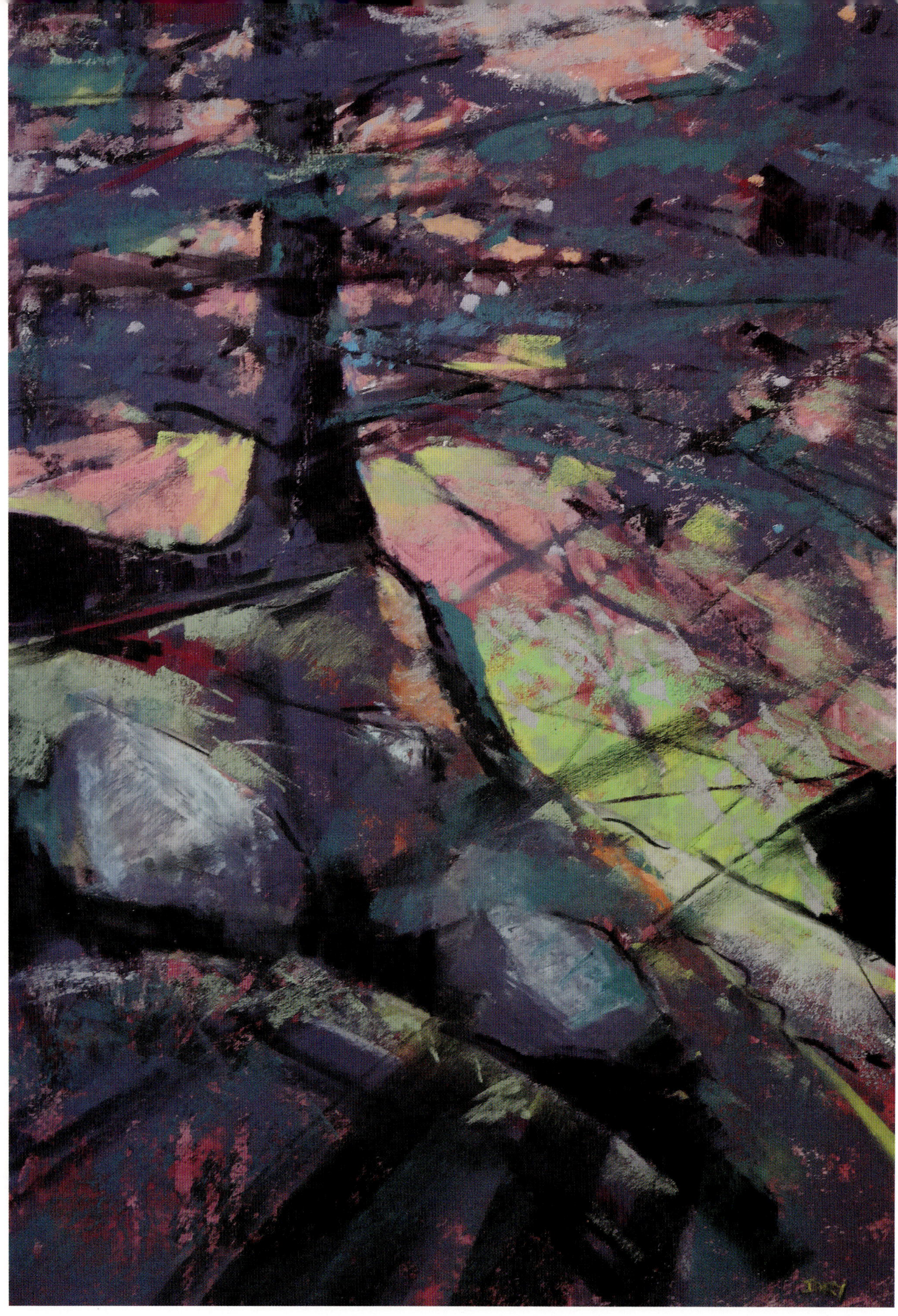

▲ **LOTS A COLOR**
Jory Mason
Assorted soft pastels on UArt 500 sanded paper
15" × 11" (38cm × 28cm)

I have painted this tree three times. Each time I try to move farther away from what I see and into the feeling of the scene. Living in New England, we have an abundance of green, so I enjoy exploring unexpected colors. In order to get the overall texture, I did a mostly hot pink pastel underpainting, then set it with alcohol. I lightly scumbled a few colors on top of this, letting the rough surface and some of the under layers of color show through. My current goal is to try to stop painting before it is completely finished. This is helping me maintain some of its original energy without it looking overworked.

In this piece I am interested in expressing to the viewer the colors and textures of nature. The vast sky above the clash of waves and stone evokes the eternal cycles of nature, in which we all play a fleeting part.

The main focus of *Timeless* is the water, as it is the most dynamic element. The most important thing to creating a believable sense of motion is to get the structure right. Waves have an anatomy that will create patterns of foam and white water, which must be laid in correctly.

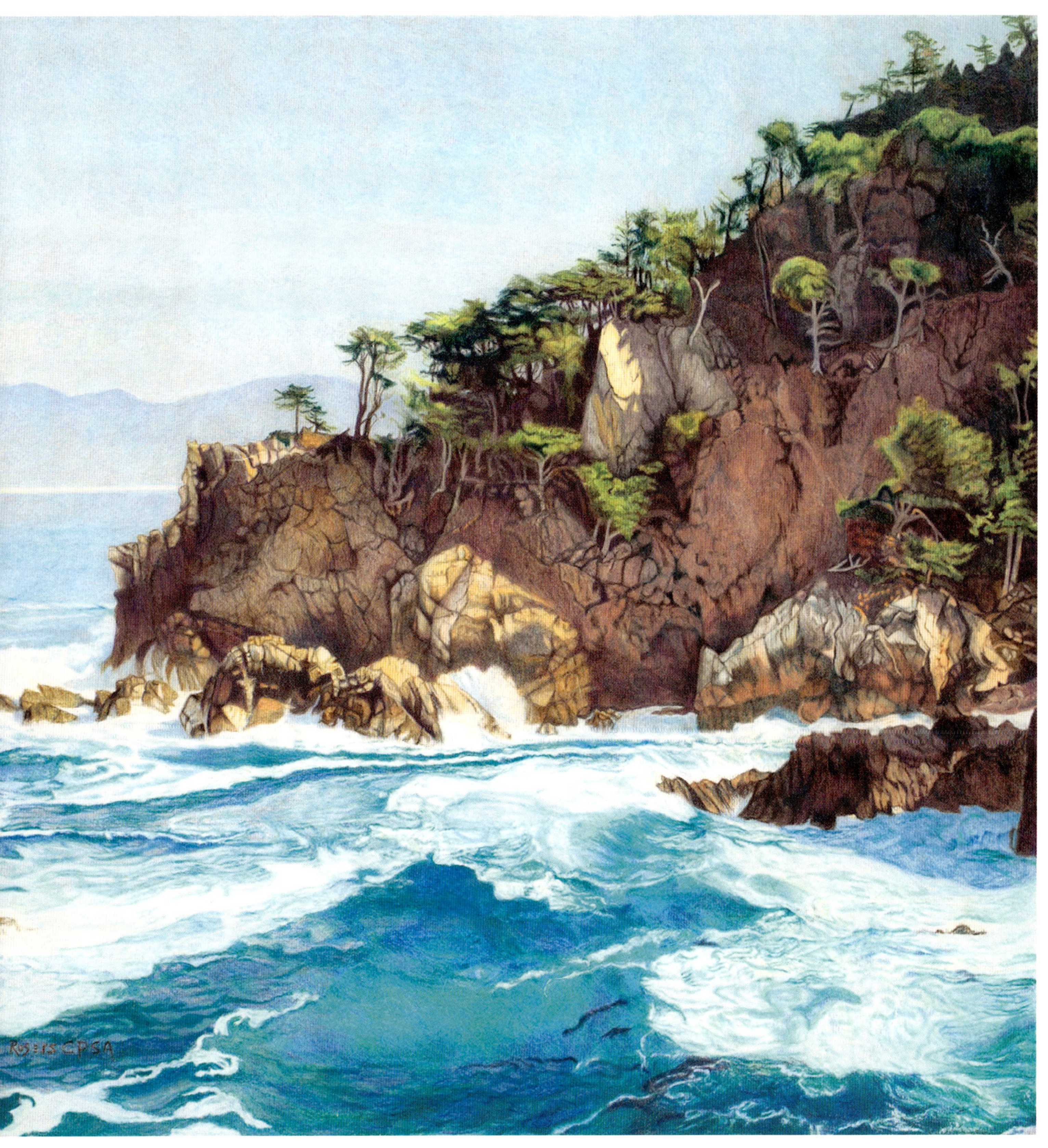

"Watch for color changes in water as it reflects the light above and the objects nearby."
—BARBARA ROGERS

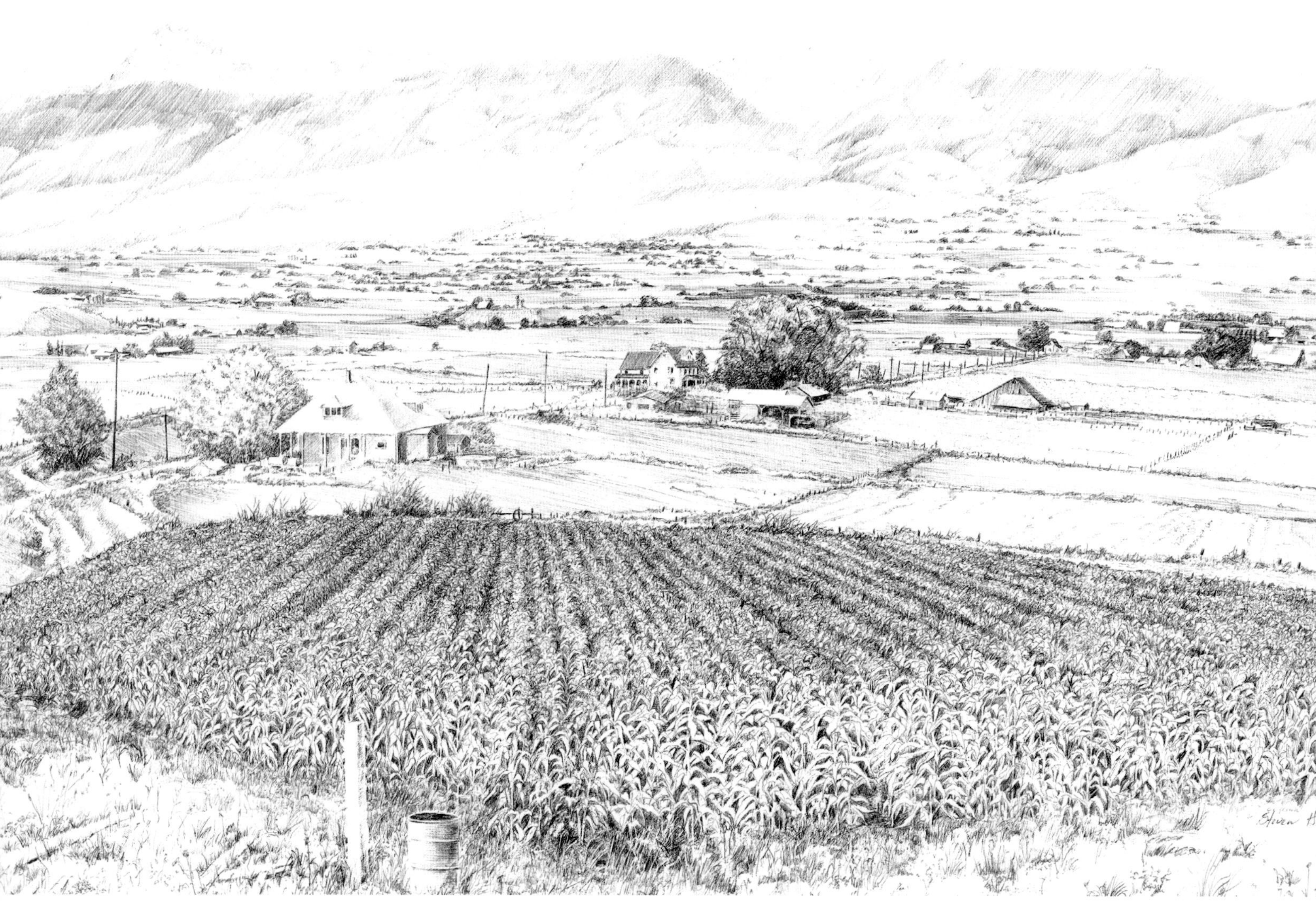

In the southern French town of Rocamadour, all the architecture not only seems to spring from the surrounding rocky cliffs and hillsides of the landscape, it literally does! Beautiful stone houses, chapels, storefronts—many from the 1400s—grow up from, hang down from and cling to the overhanging rock faces, creating a remarkable dialogue between the man-made and the natural worlds. So I wanted to tell this story as a dialogue between light and dark, shade and shadow. I am essentially a watercolorist, but this story seemed to speak most clearly as a study in black and white. Everything about the built environment here is informed by the stony earth from which it springs. So a gritty, earthy, heavily textured paper seemed just right.

▶ FRENCH COTTAGE
Thomas W. Schaller
Graphite on 140-lb. (300gsm) rough Arches watercolor paper
14" × 10" (36cm × 25cm)

▲ KITTITAS VALLEY
Steven R. Hill
Ballpoint pen on watercolor paper
19" × 29" (48cm × 74cm)

Kittitas Valley was created en plein air over the course of one week, using only a ballpoint pen on watercolor paper at an old family farmstead near Ellensburg, Washington. As I experimented, I discovered that I could create an abundance of rich textural effects by simply applying layers of light-pressure strokes with the ball point to build into the darker values. I was fascinated that the real effect of light on the landscape could be captured with such simplicity, reminding me of silverpoint etching.

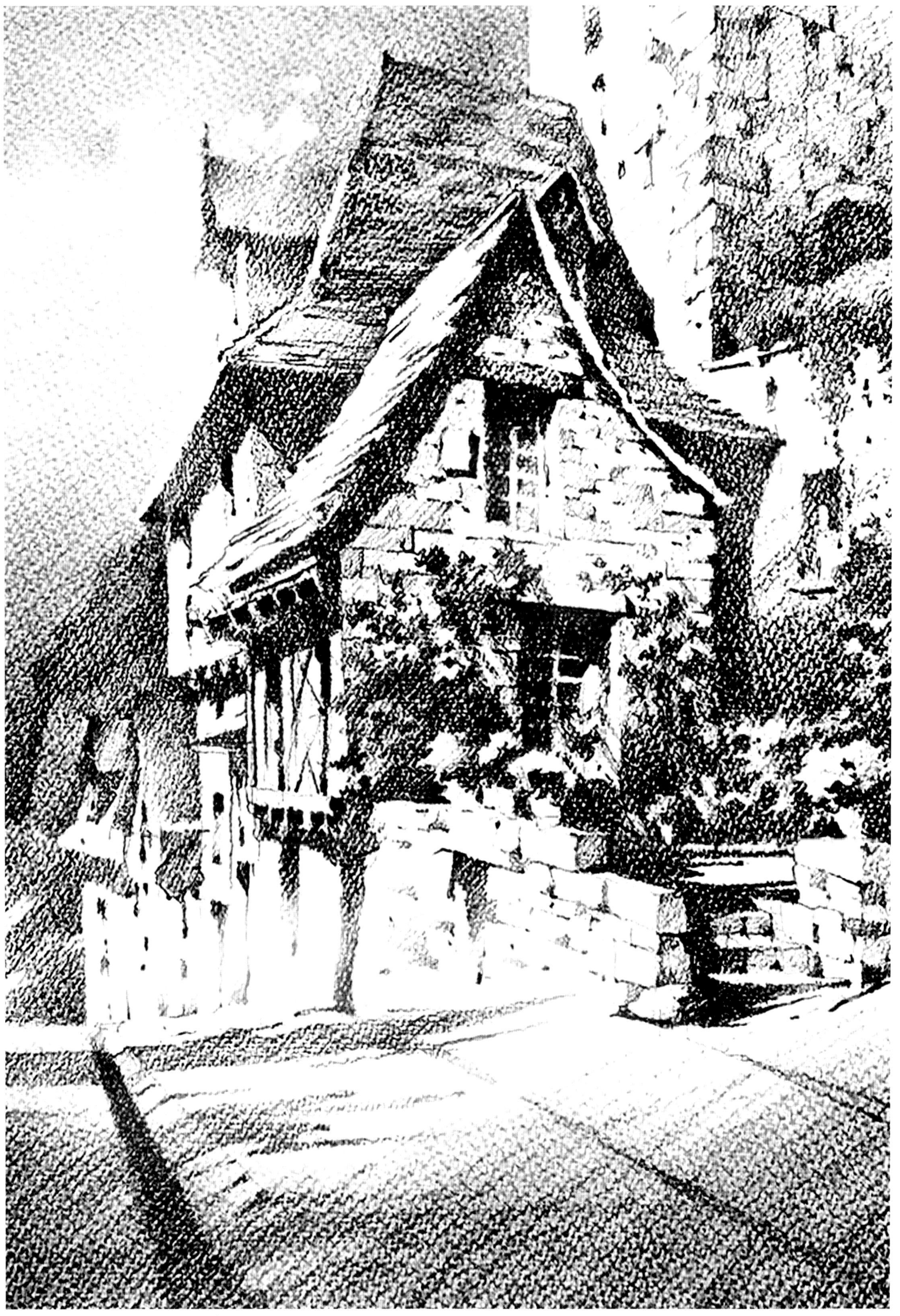

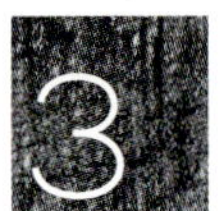

Animals: Home, Farm & Wild

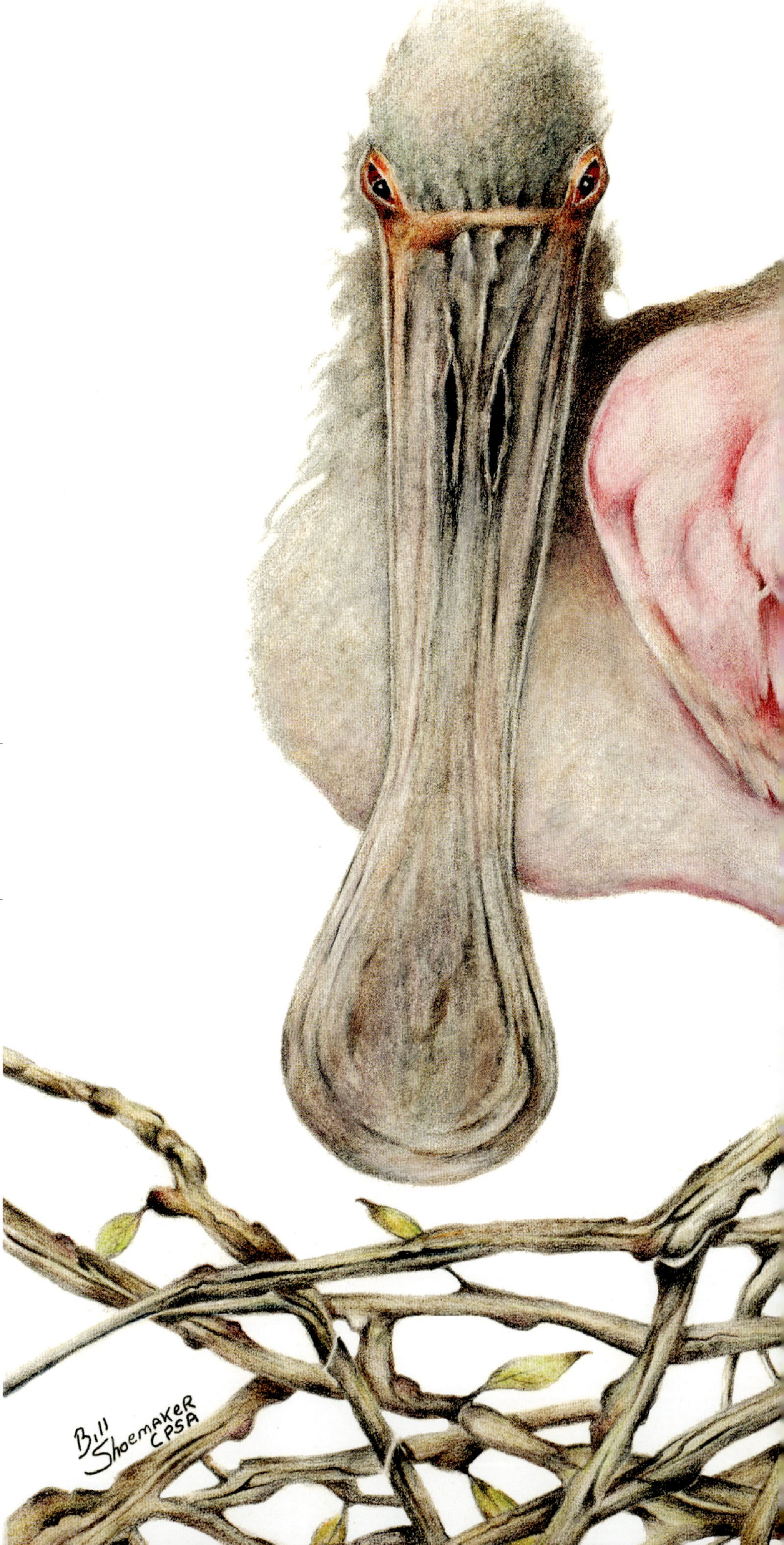

► **LADY IN PINK**
Bill Shoemaker
Prismacolor and Caran d' Ache Luminance
colored pencils on Arches 140-lb. (300gsm)
hot-pressed watercolor paper
11½" × 14" (29cm × 36cm)

I am a studio artist who works from photographs. *Lady in Pink* started at a local rookery where I took hundreds of photos. The network of branches in the foreground was developed by my close observation of nature. The damselfly was an afterthought that added to the composition. I always work out my composition ahead of time to avoid any bumps in the road ahead. Sometimes the negative parts of a picture can be more powerful than the focal point.

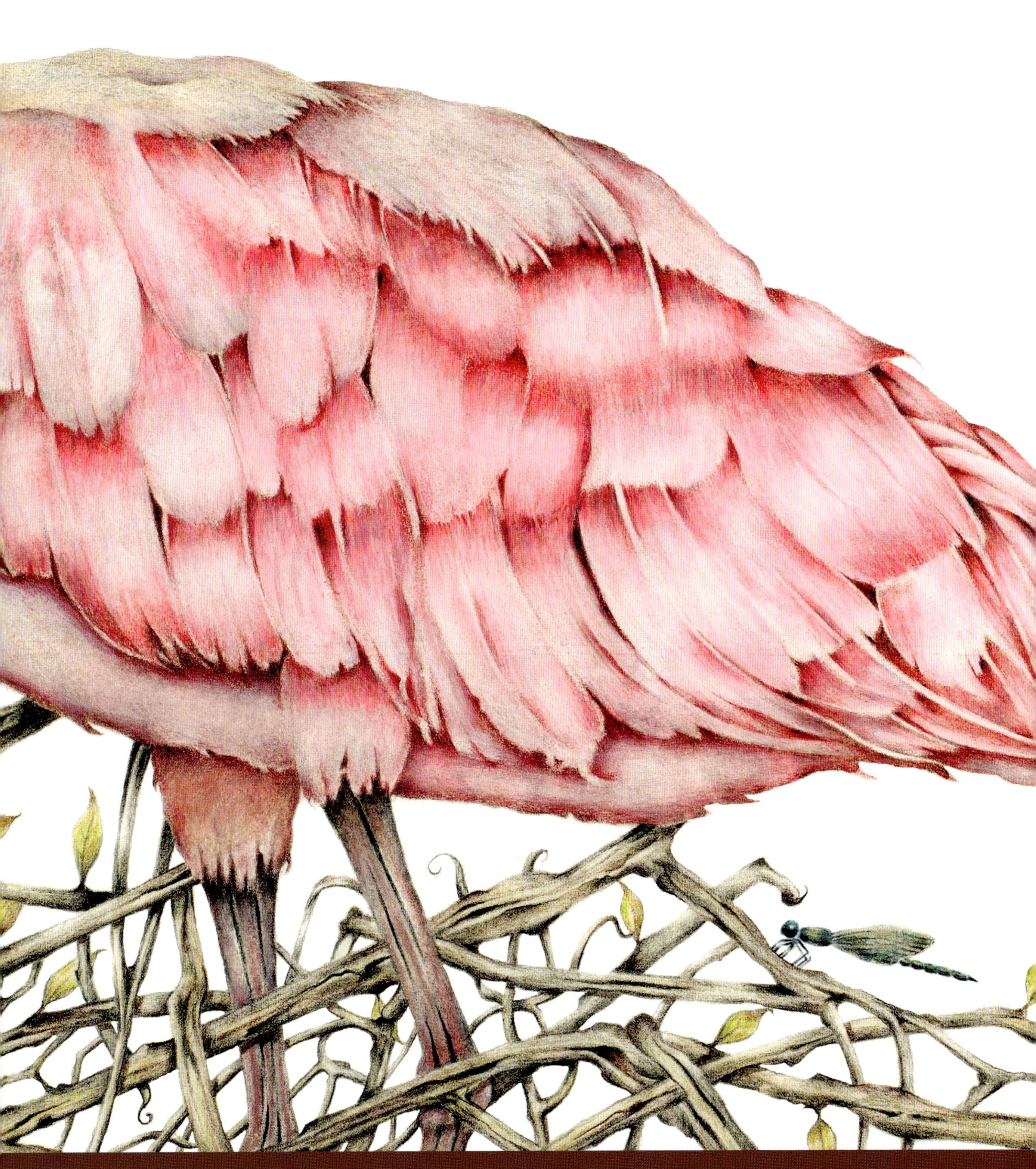

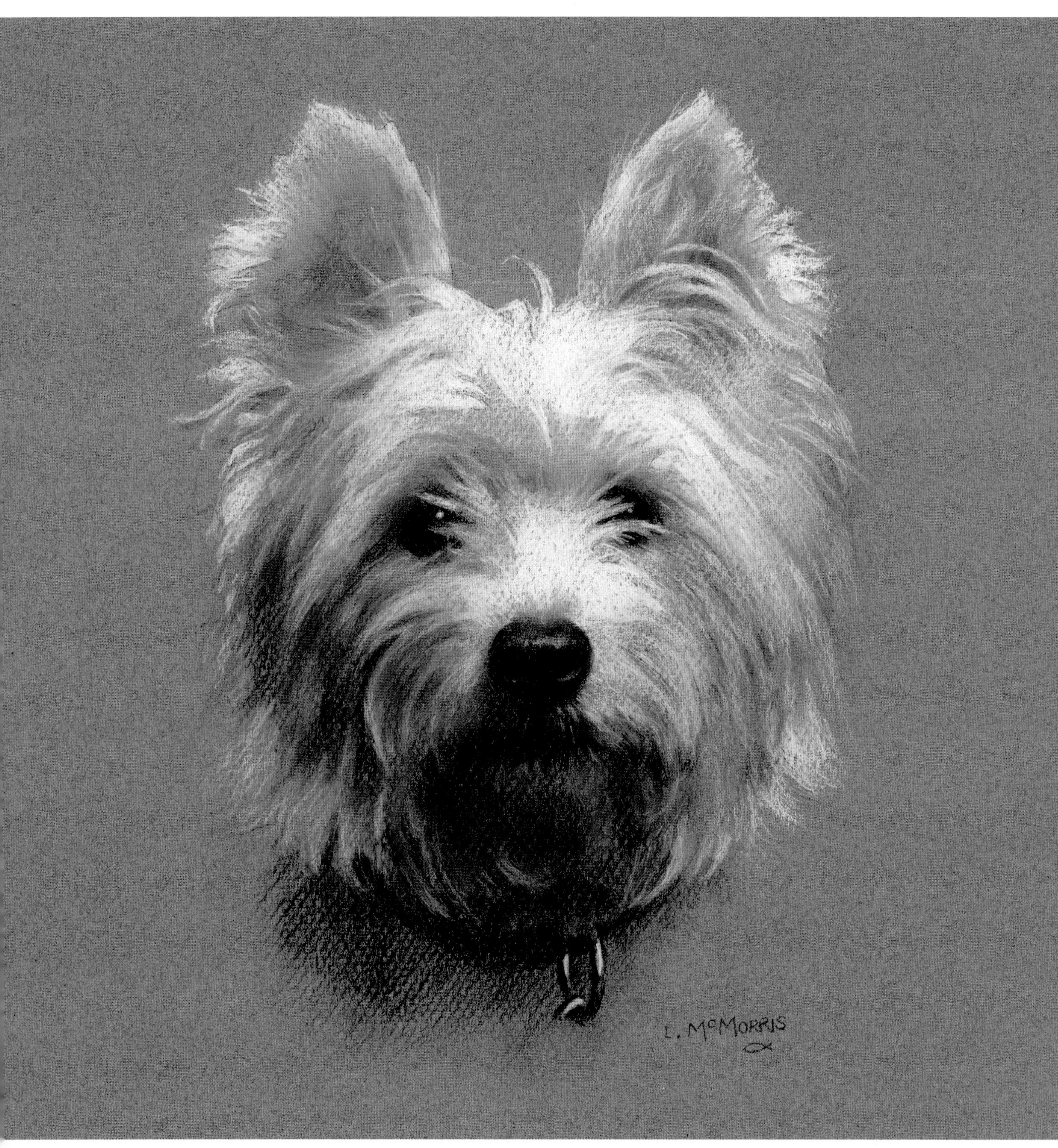

▲ WESTIE I: 'SOOOO ... WHAT'S UP?'
Lynda L. McMorris
Black and white colored pencils on warm gray-toned Canson Mi-Teintes fine art paper
14" × 11" (36cm × 28cm)

This is a portrait of a feisty little West Highland terrier named Ruby. My goal was to create an interesting drawing by using basically three values: white, black and the gray of the paper, with just a bit of blending of the white and black pencils. These produced a range of textures from furry ears to bright shining eyes, moist black nose and shiny metal collar ring. I simplified the white fur areas to emphasize the light, giving her head dimension. The center of interest is her eyes and nose that stand out because of their high contrast.

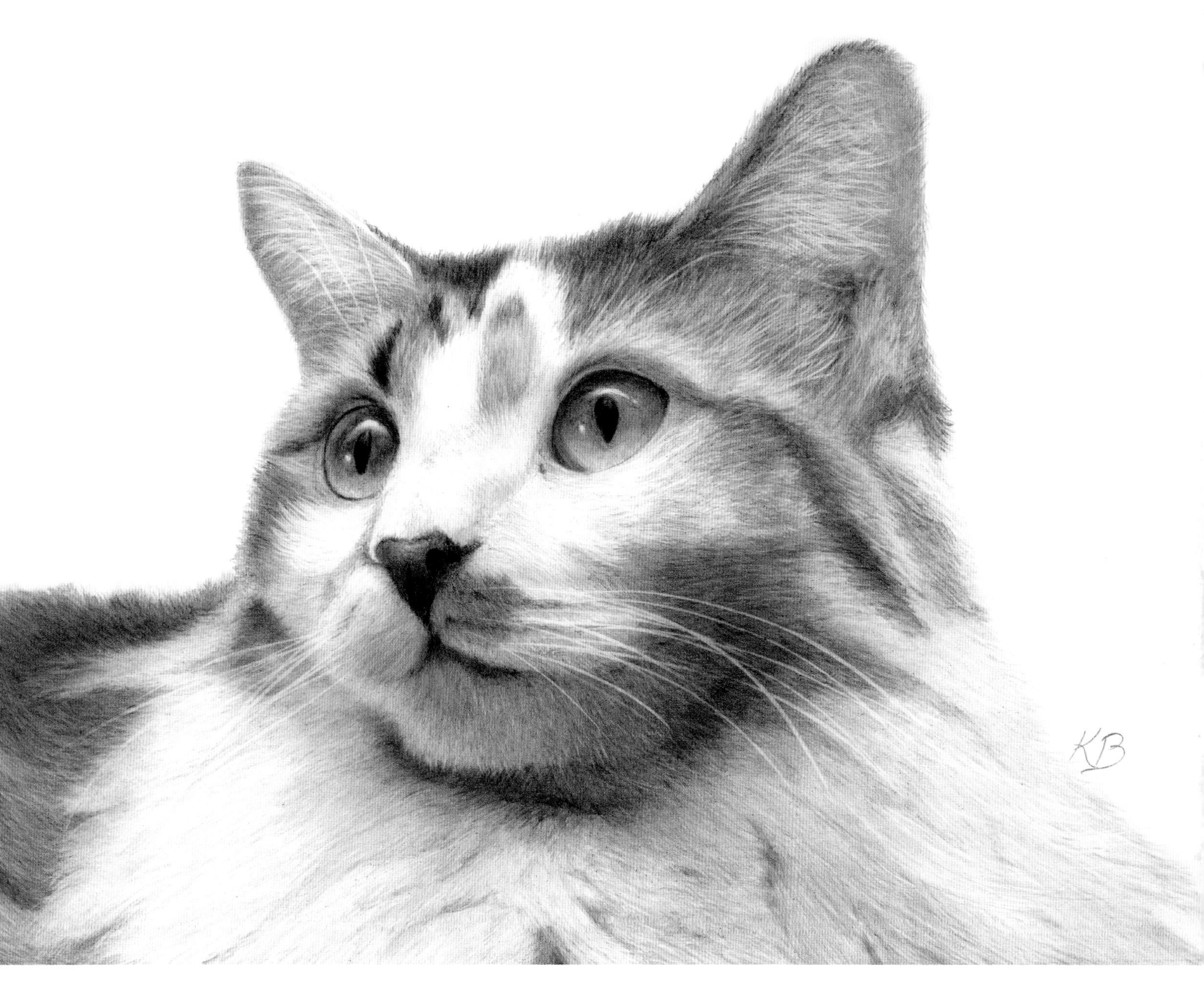

Cassie is a beautiful, long-haired calico cat, the softest cat I have ever felt. I wanted to replicate that texture in pencil. I first put a layer of graphite on the paper that is about the same value as the fur. Then I use a stick eraser with the tip cut off parallel to the end of the tube so it has straight edges. I erase individual hairs and blend them into the main mass of hair. I almost never use a sharp pencil but much prefer a dull tip. This portrait took over 100 hours to complete.

▲ CASSIE
Ken Brown
Graphite on smooth Strathmore bristol paper
10" × 13" (25cm × 33cm)

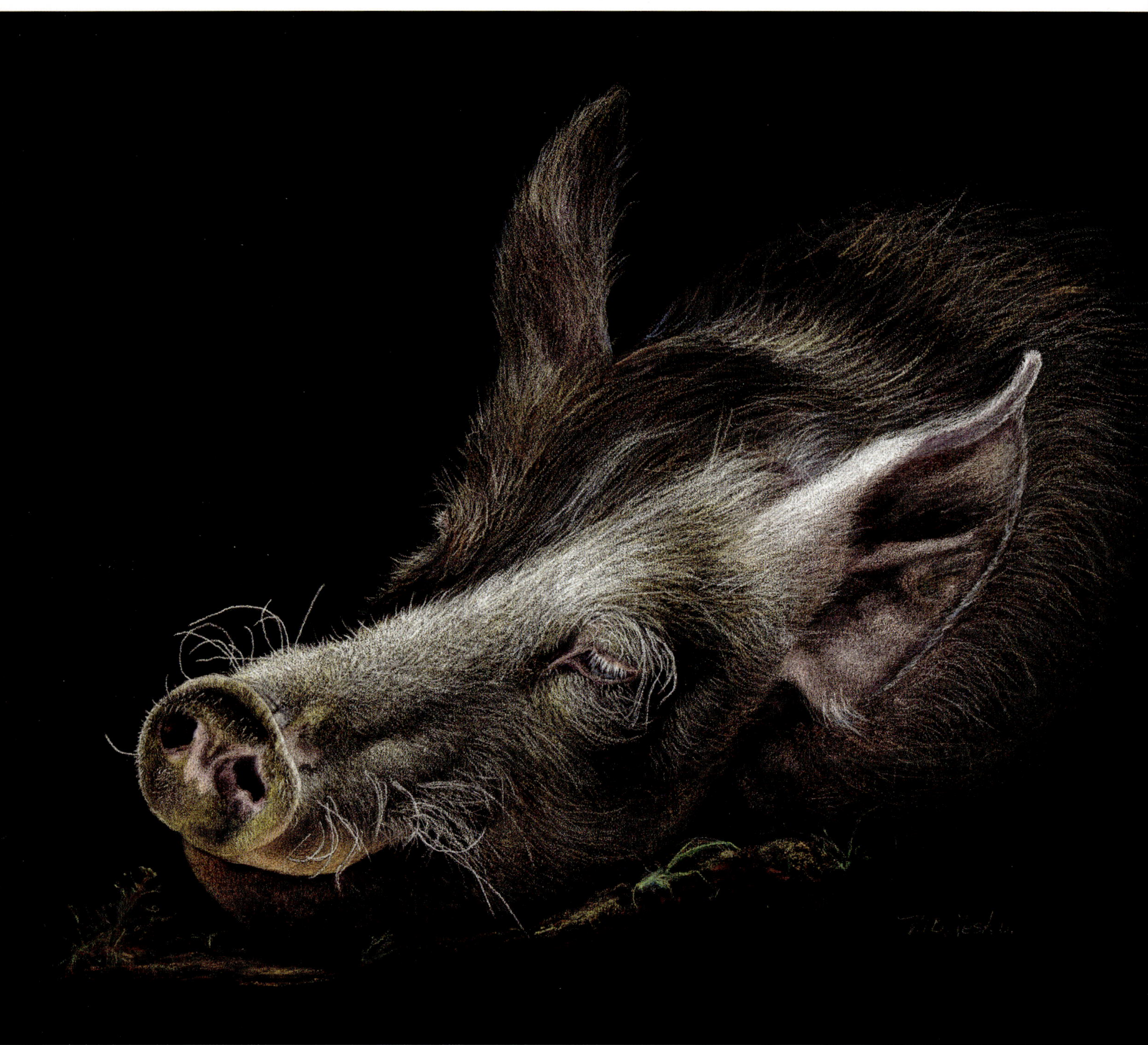

This drawing of a hog with his bristles and prickly hair shining in the late afternoon light was the perfect subject to draw on black sanded board. I worked in my studio from photographs taken at a northeast Pennsylvania hog farm. This particular hog was a large and very cooperative subject; the smile on his face was pure contentment. Colored pencil on black sanded board is perfect for creating the illusion of texture. The sanded surface adds a few bumps and ridges for the hog's skin but also allows lightly applied layers of color to create softness in areas such as the eyes, ears and skin. Every animal has a unique body surface and creating those textures realistically is my goal and challenge.

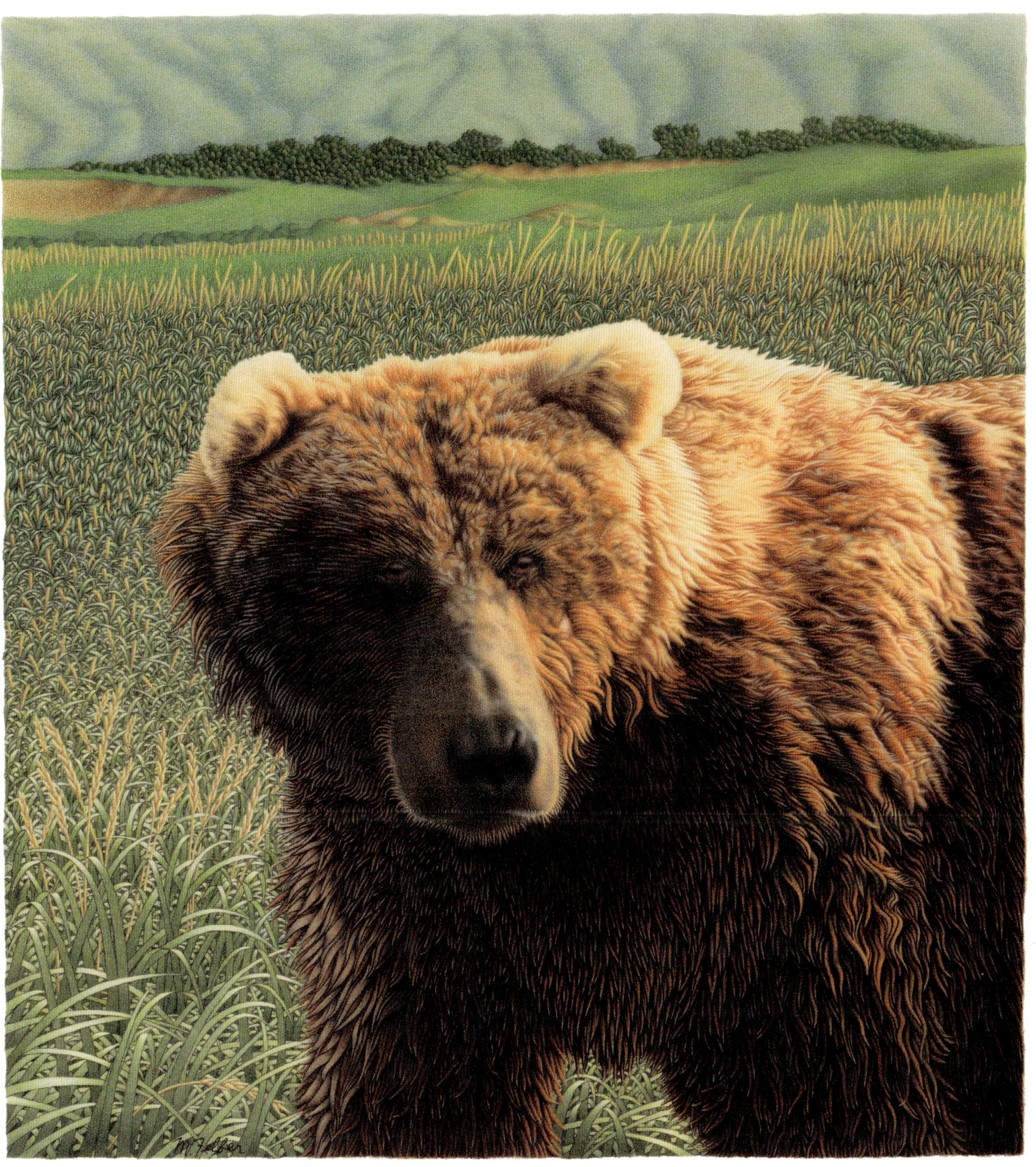

Native Americans traditionally address a brown bear as "Grandfather" as a sign of respect. I observed this dominant male during two trips to Katmai National Park, Alaska. I start with a line drawing, block out the basic colors with watercolor and then complete the shading with colored pencil. The viewer is close enough to see this massive bear as a unique individual. He seemed very relaxed, but the wound on his cheek and the scar on his nose were evidence of his fights. The fur of the upper body and head is fluffier than the legs, as he had just walked through a stream.

▲ GRANDFATHER
Michael J. Felber
Derwent colored pencil over watercolor on coquille paper
12" × 11" (30cm × 28cm)

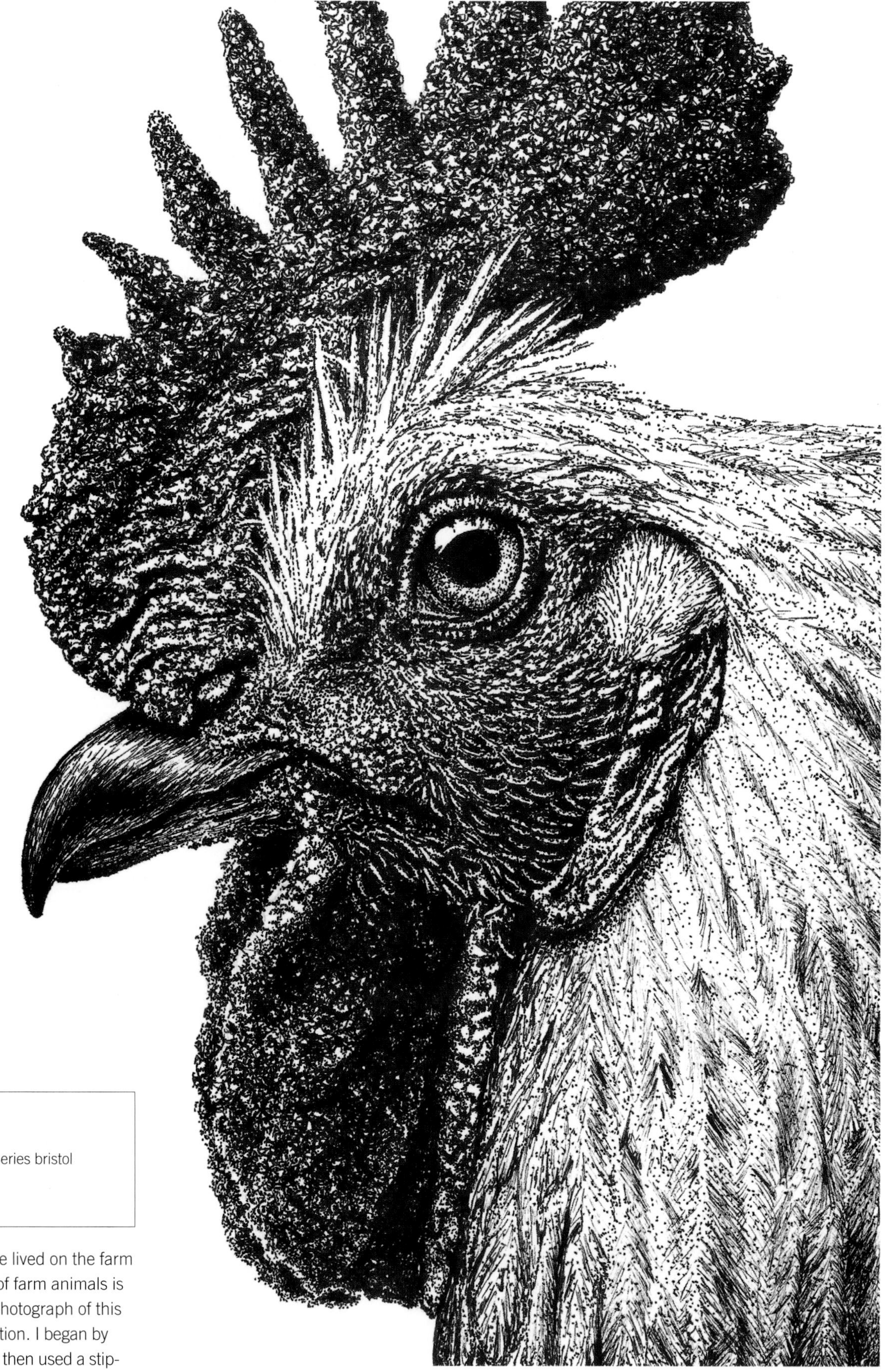

Generations of my family have lived on the farm
where I now live, so the love of farm animals is
deeply rooted in my soul. A photograph of this
proud rooster was my inspiration. I began by
making a graphite outline and then used a stippling technique along with lines and squiggles to
achieve the textural elements and bold contrast
needed for this realistic interpretation. Sakura
Pigma Micron pens, primarily size 005, but
also 01 and 03 with their rich, black ink, were
my tools.

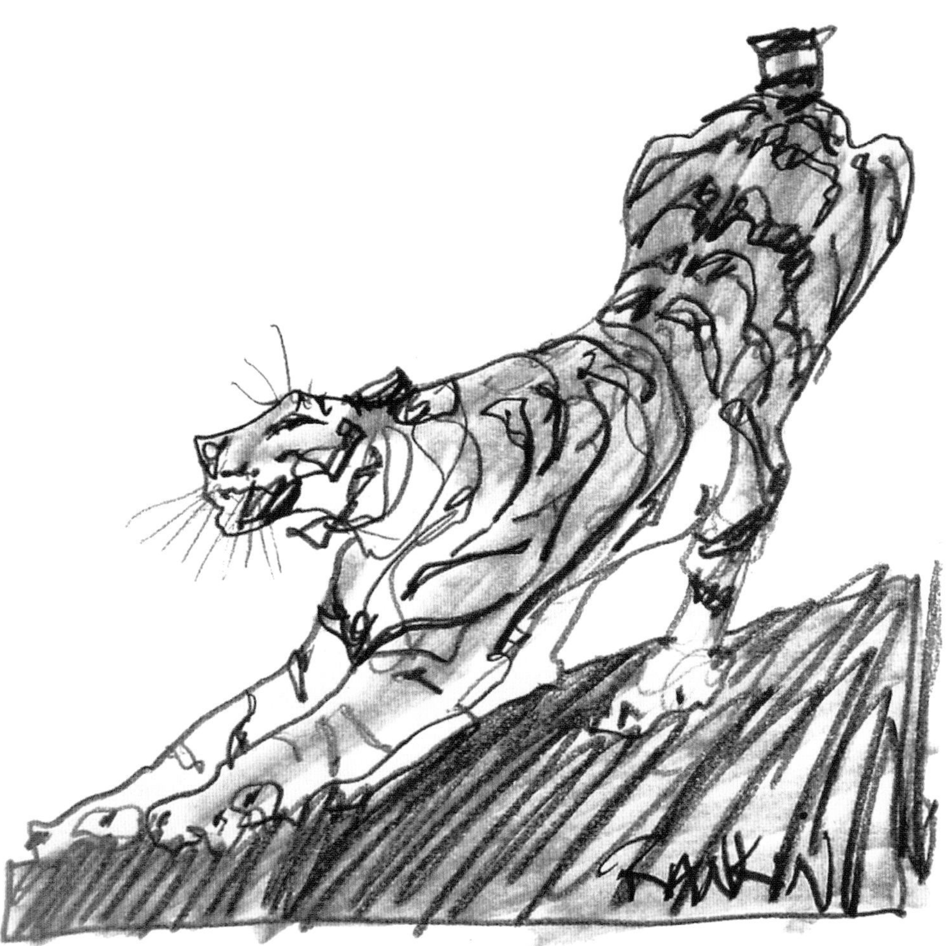

◀ **STRETCHING TIGER – BANDHAVGARH, INDIA**
David Rankin
9B woodless graphite on sketchbook paper
8" × 10" (20cm × 25cm)

It was about 110° F (43° C) in the steamy jungles of India's famous Bandhavgarh National Park tiger reserve, and we had been on elephant-back all morning following a large male tiger up a steep nullah (a dry river bed). We came upon him sound asleep in the rocks. The elephant's movements in the dense bamboo forest woke the tiger abruptly. He wasn't happy, but as he awoke he reached out his huge paws, and, arching his whole spine upwards with his tail reaching toward the sky, he engaged in this prolonged whole-body stretch that must have felt great. But he did this right as I was changing batteries in my camera! Later that evening, I remembered this dynamic pose, and re-created it from memory.

▶ **GREYLAG GOOSE STUDY – KASHMIR, INDIA**
David Rankin
9B woodless graphite on sketchbook paper
10" × 8" (25cm × 20cm)

Although I now also sketch on my Apple iPad, for twenty years I've used a 9B woodless graphite pencil on traditional sketchbook paper. My sketches are studies of form, light and posture. The added half-tone, created by smudging the graphite, provides the light source. This sketch is an example of "live sketching." For sixteen years I spent summers in Kashmir. A farmer I knew had this large beautiful pet greylag goose who posed for me proudly.

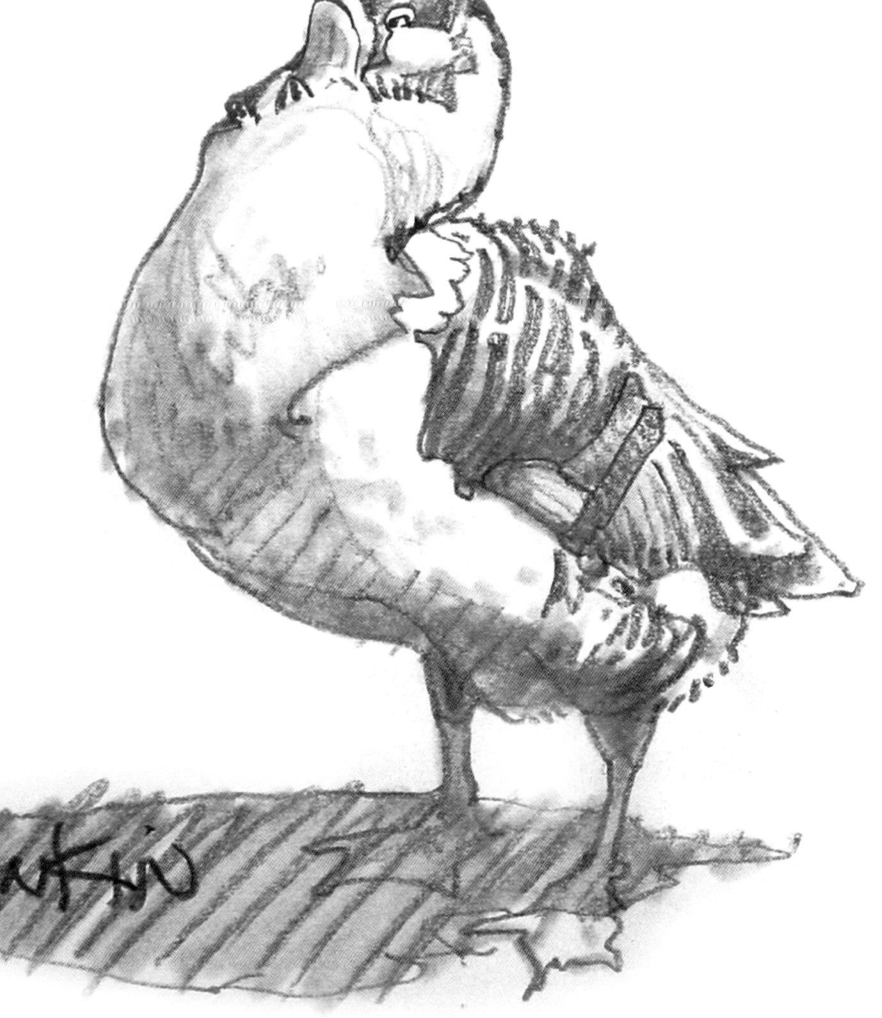

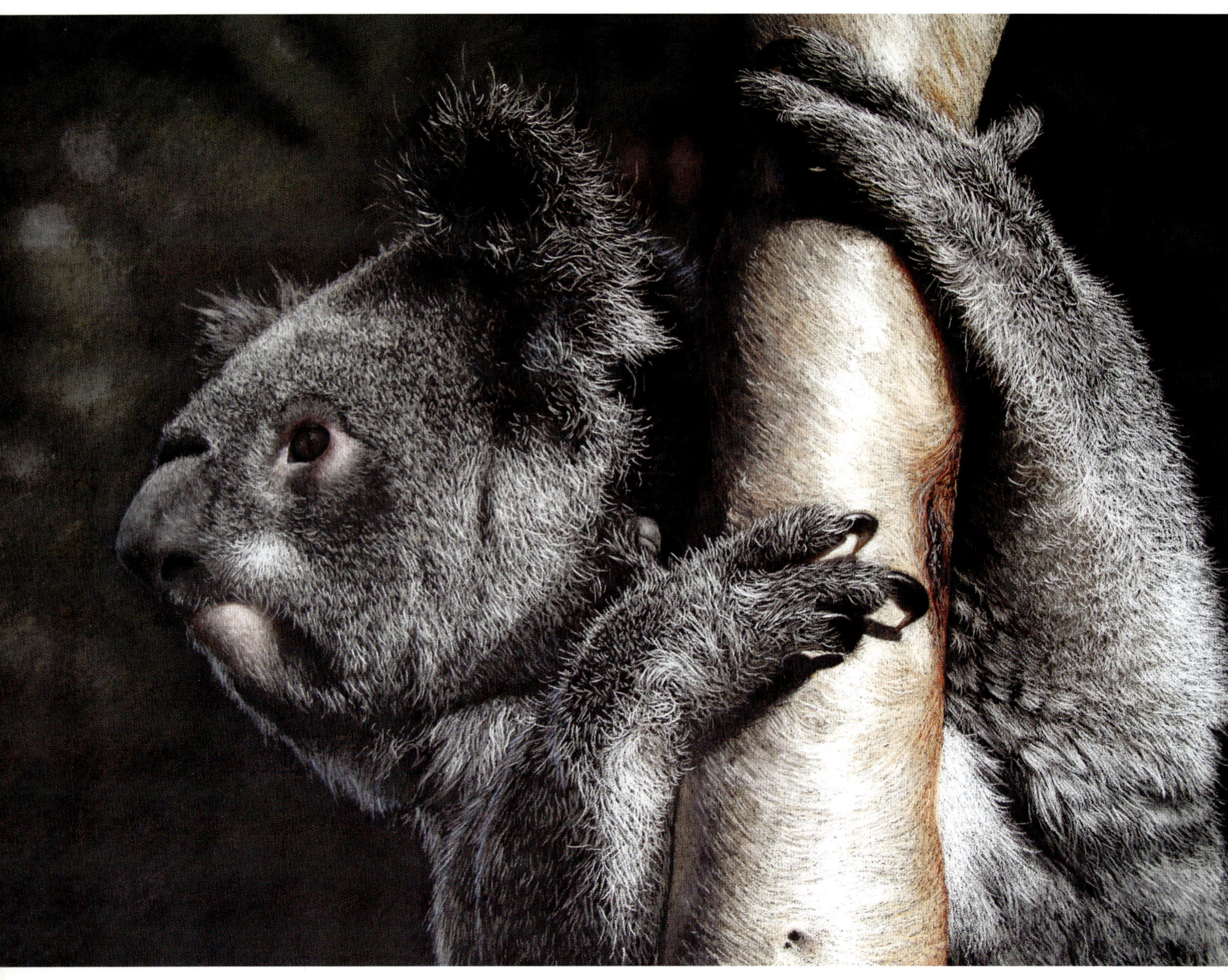

▶ READING THE MENU
Catherine Lidden
Pastel pencil on Mi-Teintes Tex
12" × 17" (30cm × 43cm)

This koala was photographed at Taronga Zoo in Sydney. I wanted to show the contrasting appearance of the fur and the smooth branch. Pastel pencils are ideal for portraying textural qualities, from the rough feel of some furs, bark or rock, to the smooth or glassy surfaces of eyes, claws and horn. Mostly, as in this koala, I use a visual texture using light and shadow to provide the illusion of texture, but sometimes I use the sanded surface itself to create the texture. This works well for anything of a rough or granular nature. I also use a smooth paper such as Colourfix Suede or PastelMat if the subject dictates it.

April Fools was one of a series of twelve images I did to celebrate the year of the horse in the Chinese calendar that were done on the same sized surface, with similar materials, predominantly black and white with a hint of color. But this is obviously a donkey, not a horse, hence the title. By scratching through the surface I was able to create unusual surface qualities. I enjoyed using texture to create the images for this series and found that focusing on one art element (texture) brought a sense of uniformity and coherence to the entire show.

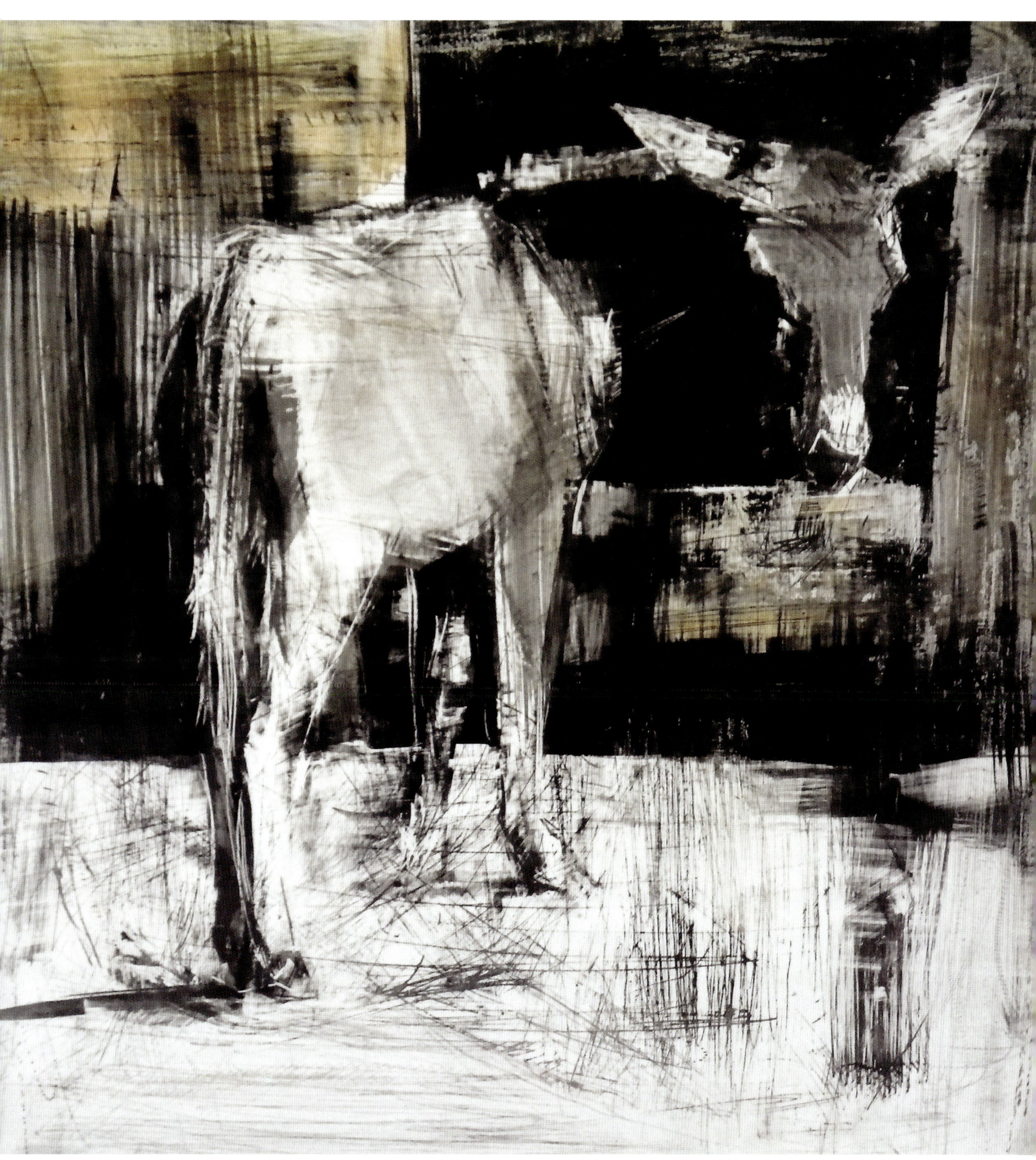

▼ APRIL FOOLS
Dawn Emerson
Black sumi ink and watercolor on
Ampersand Claybord
12" × 12" (30cm × 30cm)

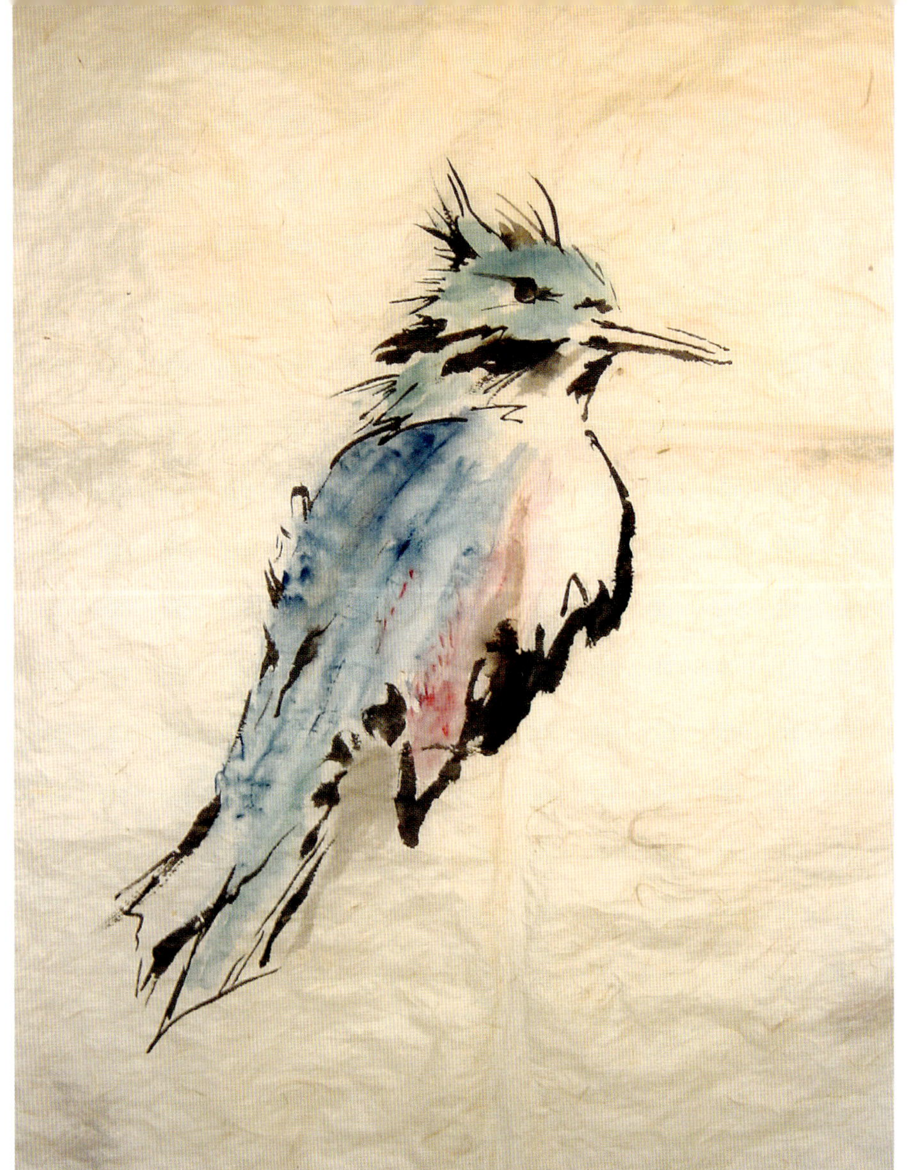

► **CHRISTMAS KING**
Aaron A. Lade
Watercolor and India ink on rice paper
27" × 14" (69cm × 36cm)

I love the effects of incorporating India ink with watercolor. This combination gives me the bold expression and contrast I'm looking for while letting the viewer fill in many of the details. The rice paper adds just a hint of dimension. My paintings tend to be emotional events for me—I love them or hate them. My work is best when I let go, sacrifice detail and let the water and brush do the work.

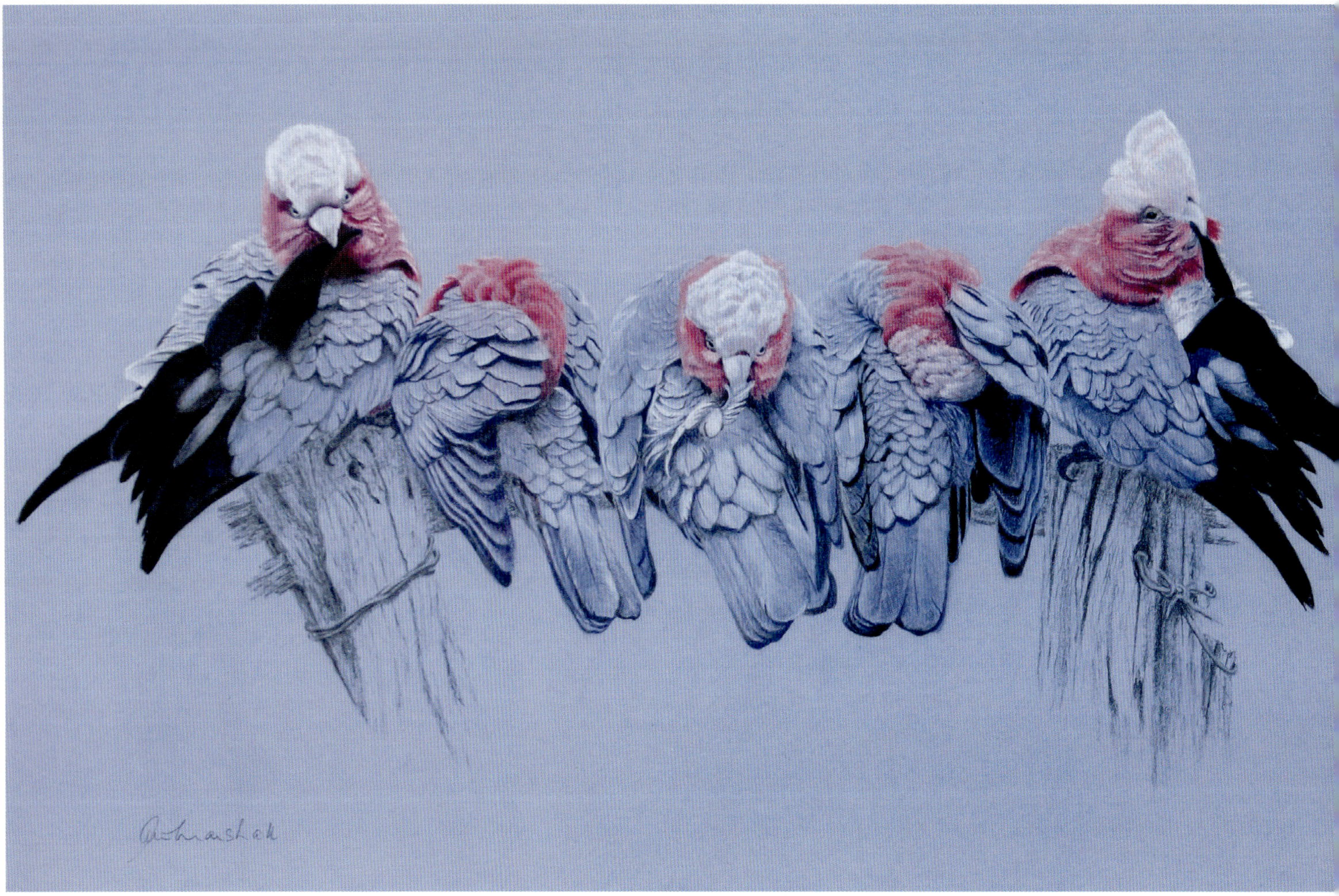

Krill are tiny translucent shrimp-like creatures that populate the cold waters around Antarctica. I've tried to capture the transparency of this small animal with colored pencil. For the thin lines of the hairs and legs, with which it moves in the dark ocean, I used an extra hard Prismacolor Verithin pencil. I love to draw animals that are generally seen as somewhat creepy but are nonetheless beautiful in their strangeness.

These colorful galah cockatoos come to feed in my garden in Australia every morning. They then sit in a row on the fence in the sunshine, busily preening themselves, all with varying attitudes, making a great linear composition. Colored pencils are a perfect way to describe the feathers with just enough detail to create the overall textural form. I deliberately left plenty of negative space to keep the focus on the birds and their crowding onto the rural perch, a sight frequently seen in this part of the world.

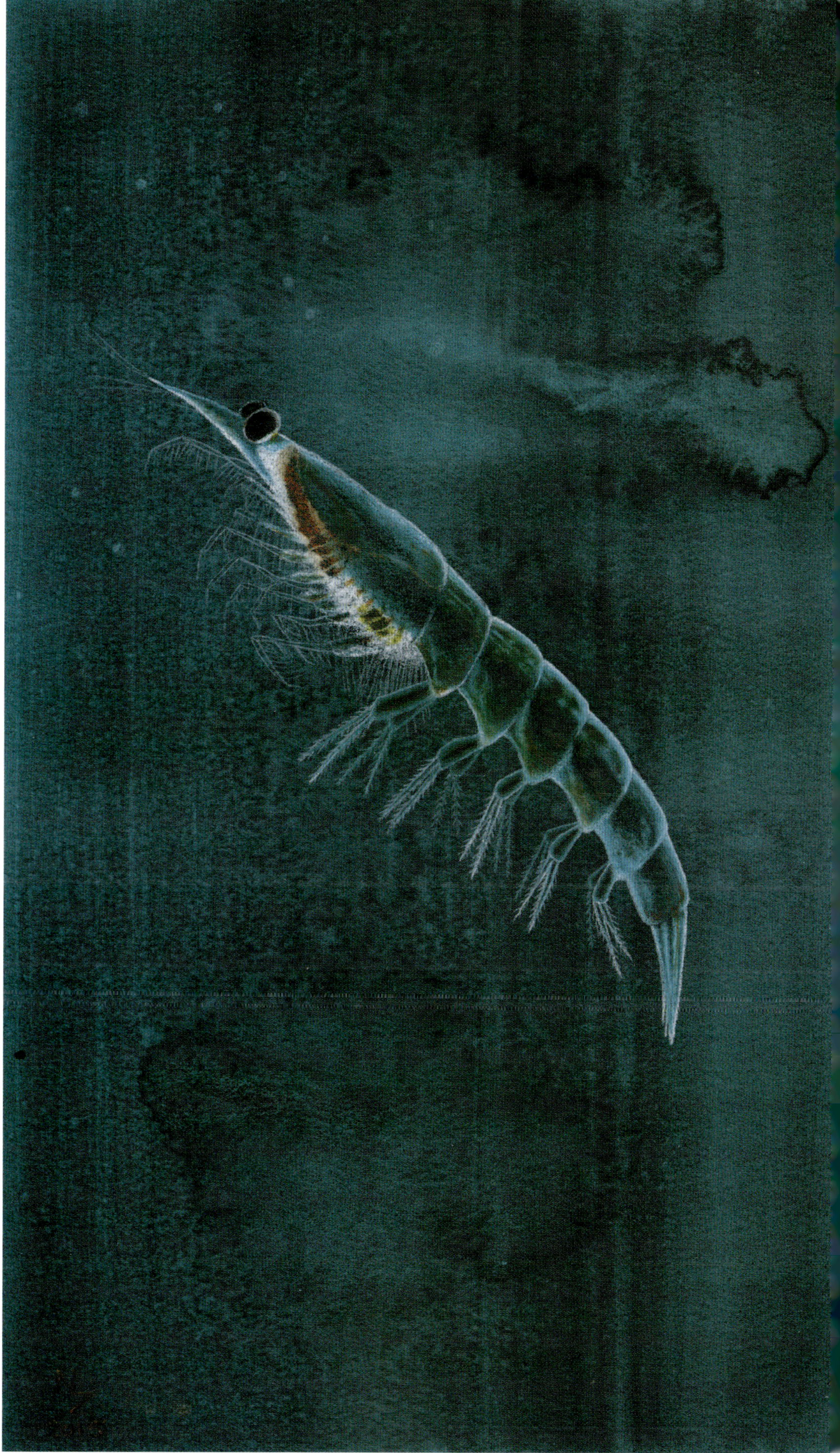

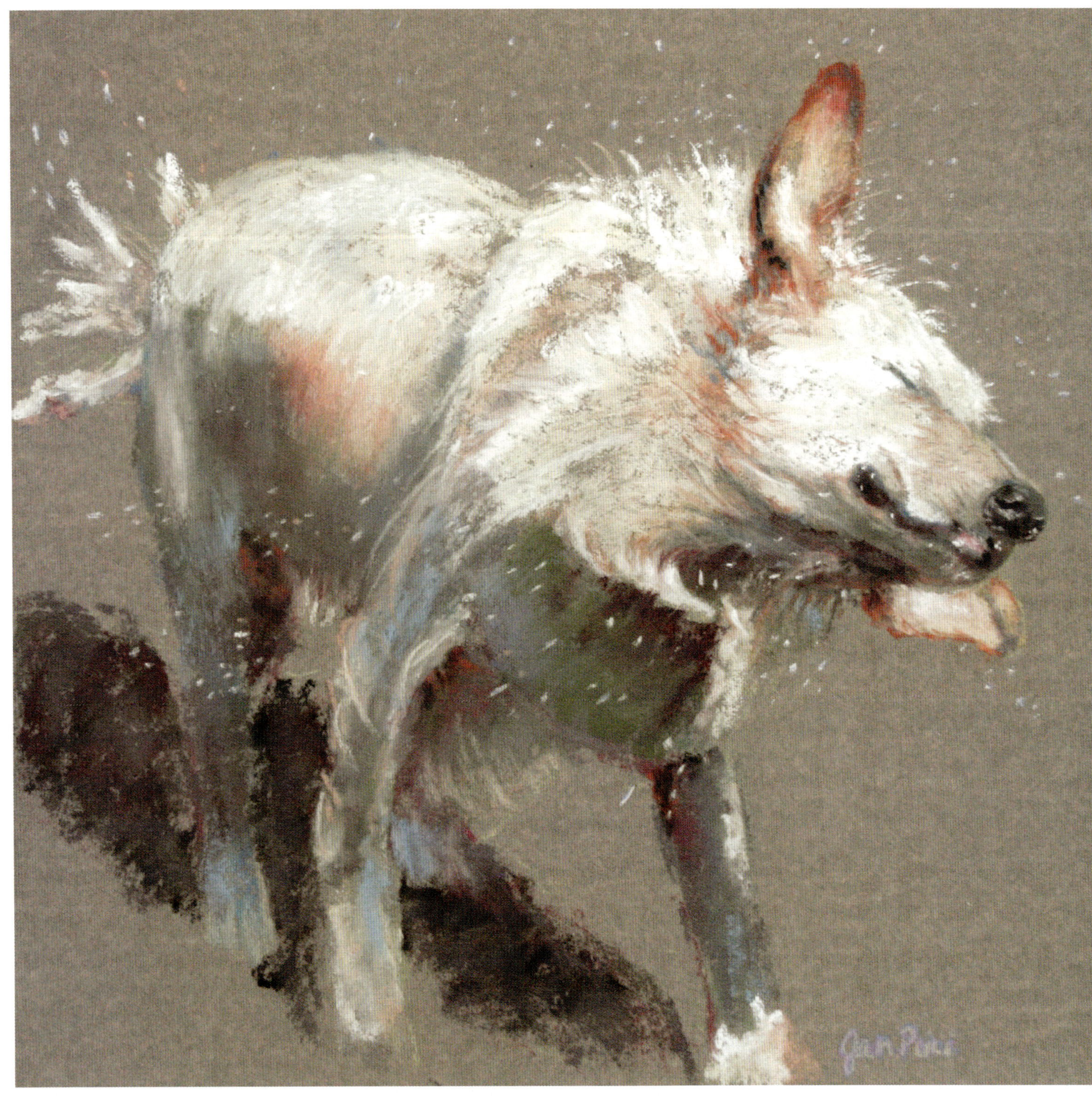

▲ SHAKE IT OFF
Jan Pini
Soft pastel on Wallis Belgian Mist paper
8" × 8½" (20cm × 22cm)

Shake It Off is a painting of my golden retriever Mindy, who loves to swim. I took many, many photos of her shaking off water, trying to capture the action of her in motion with fur, ears, lips and water flying in all directions. I decided to do this painting as a pastel vignette, letting the beautiful Kitty Wallis Belgian Mist sanded paper show. My favorite medium is soft pastel and I use several brands, including Girault, Sennelier and Terry Ludwig. It was great fun trying to capture the texture of her fur and the water droplets.

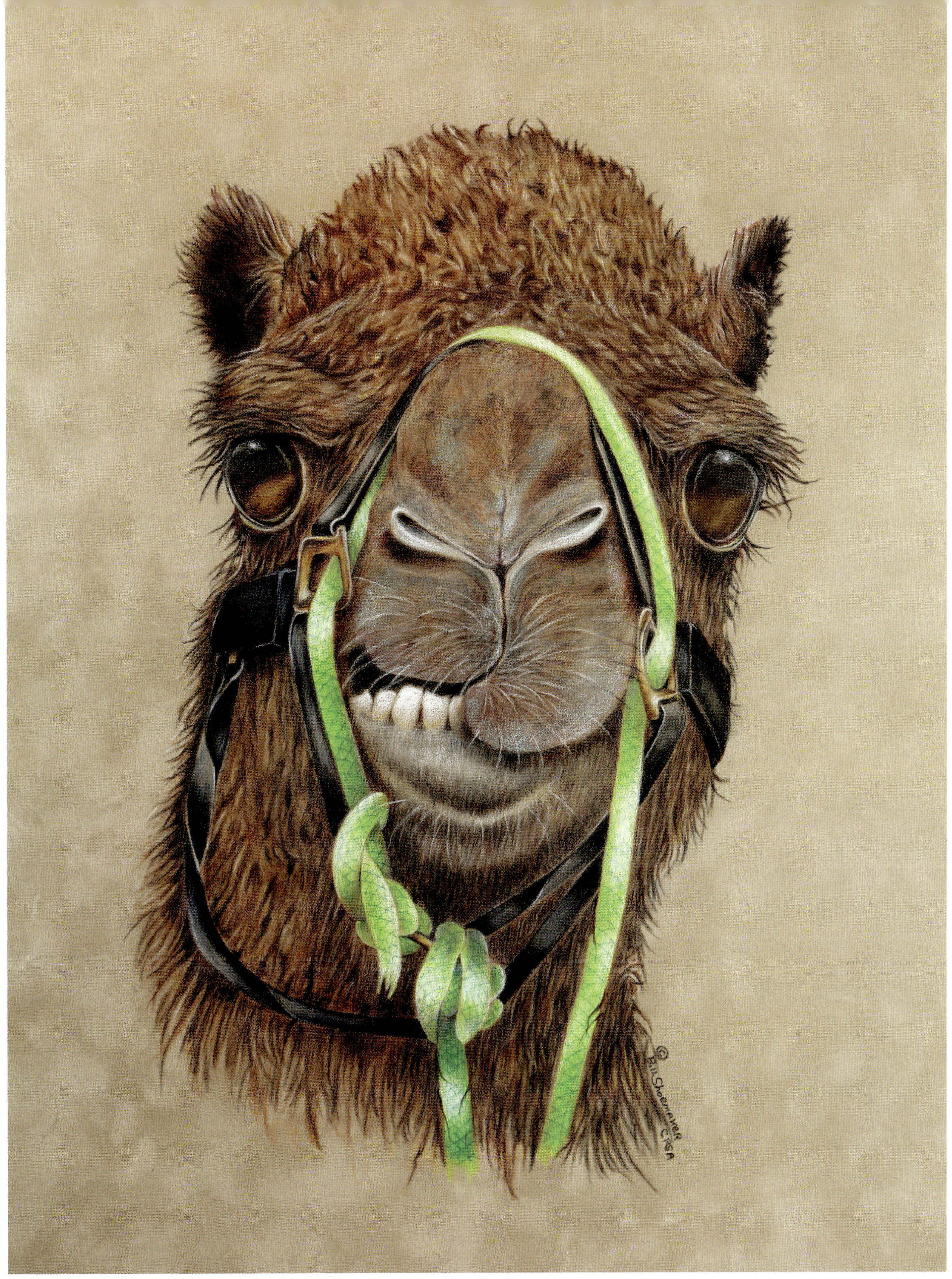

When I saw this camel at a local fair, I knew I had to draw him. He had an offbeat personality that was hard to describe. Developing his character through preliminary sketches, I transferred my drawing onto suede mat board and began the colored pencil work. Suede and sanded surfaces are two of my favorite supports when working with colored pencil as colors blend easily. I have always enjoyed naming my artwork, but this was no problem.

"Texture enhances personality." —BILL SHOEMAKER

▲ **DID YOU FLOSS TODAY?**
Bill Shoemaker
Prismacolor and Caran d'Ache Luminance colored pencils on archival suede mat board
16" × 11" (41cm × 28cm)

In *Deer, Golden Meadow* I wanted to capture different qualities of textures: the graceful delicate appearance of deer and the quality of the surface they are standing on. Deer are ideal subjects for pastel with its wonderful softness. I applied pastel in varying directions using thick and thin layers, pure and overlapping color coats, narrow lines as well as broad strokes. Being expressive with the color and the way it was applied gave me freedom to play and experiment.

"Whatever your subject is, expressiveness is the key element for conveying its magical qualities." —YAEL MAIMON

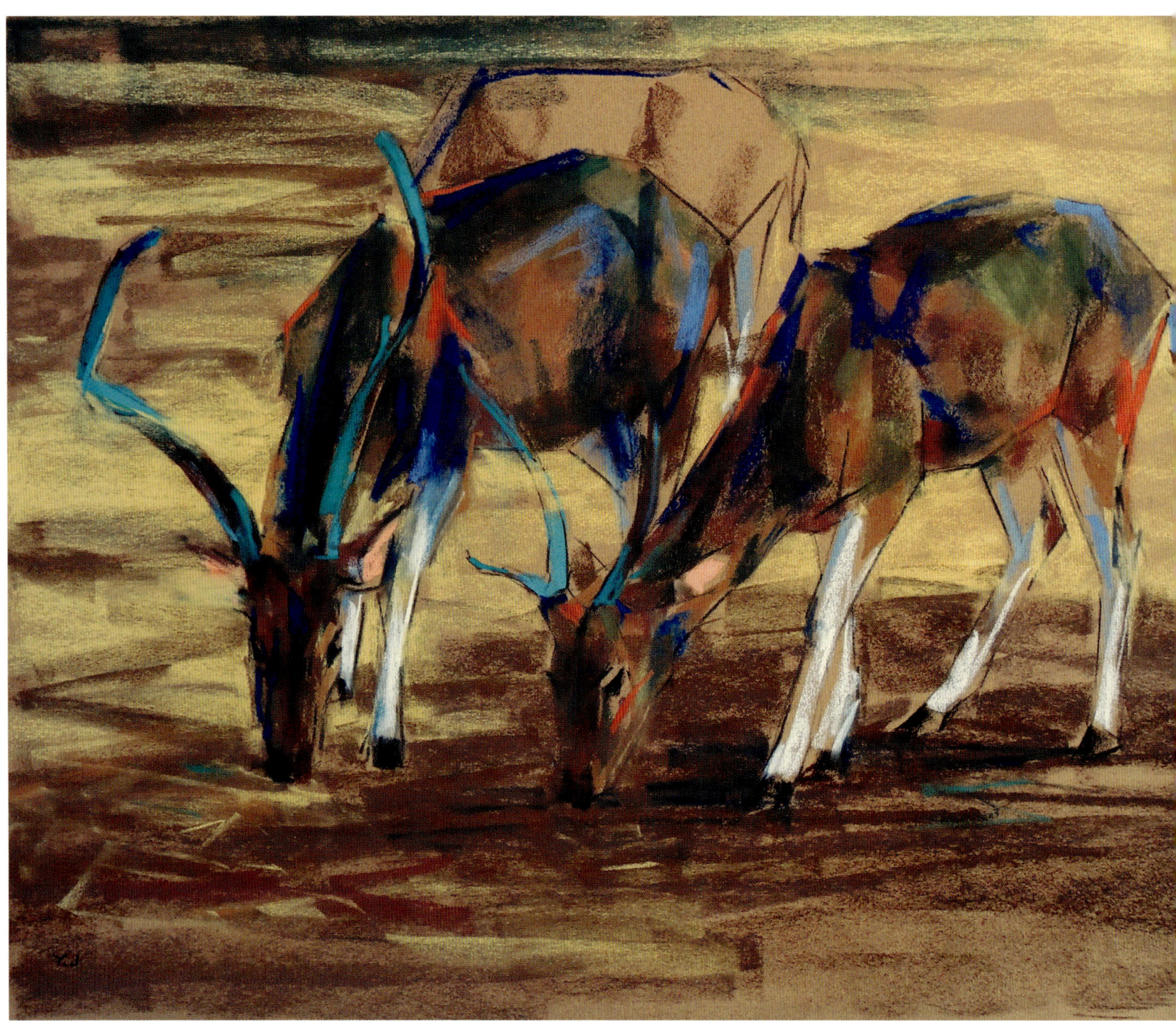

This butcher-bird sits on my fence outside the studio. I've been feeding him for a couple of years. This year he started leaving me gifts: a bit of shell, stone or twig; I reimagined him giving me a flower. The challenge was to visually portray the soft texture of the feathers using my sketches and photographs. I drew him in colored pencils, then burnished the softer feathers with white colored pencil. The black background was painted last.

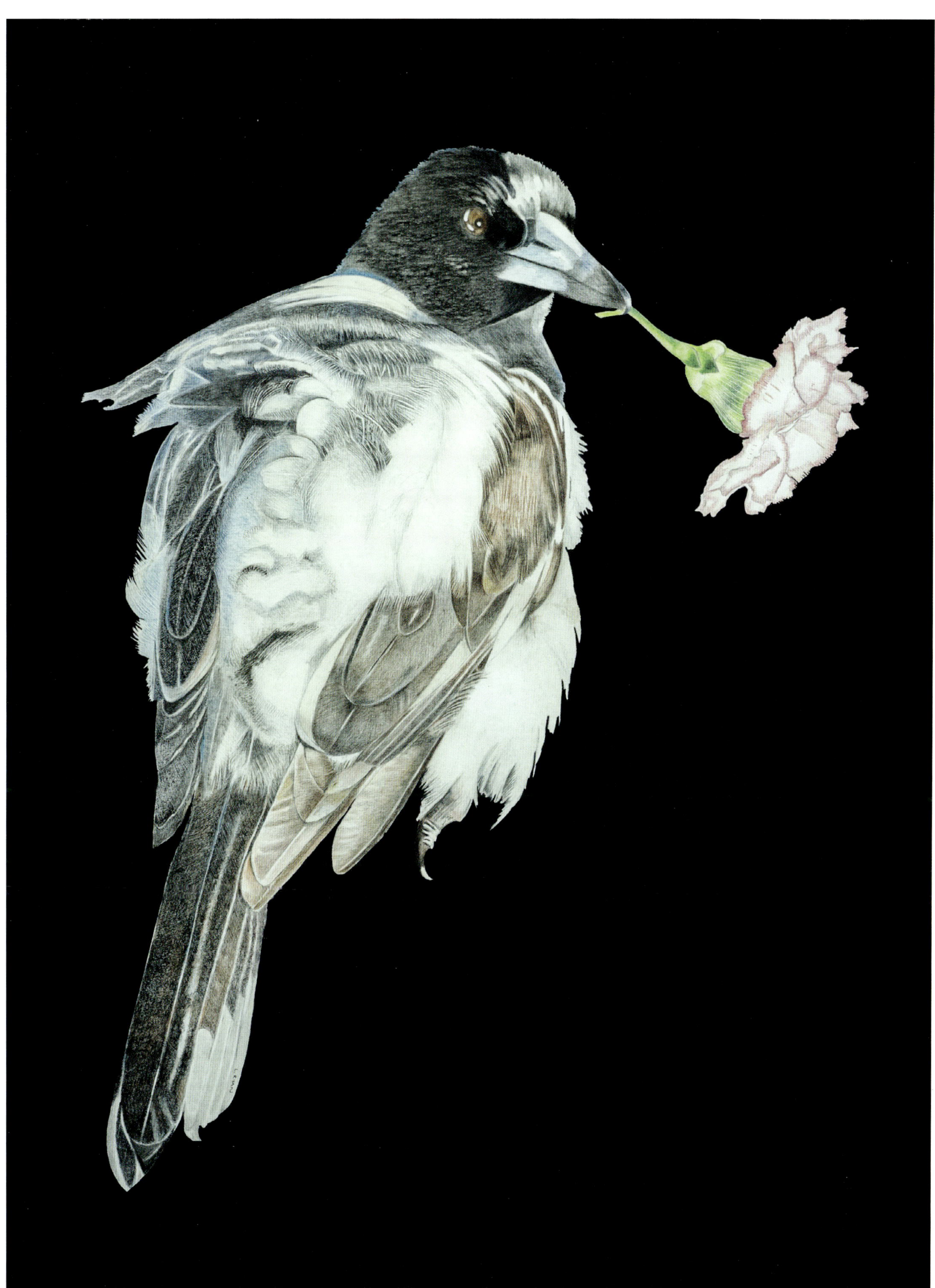

"You know you have achieved texture in your drawing when viewers reach out to touch it."

—LESLEY RYAN

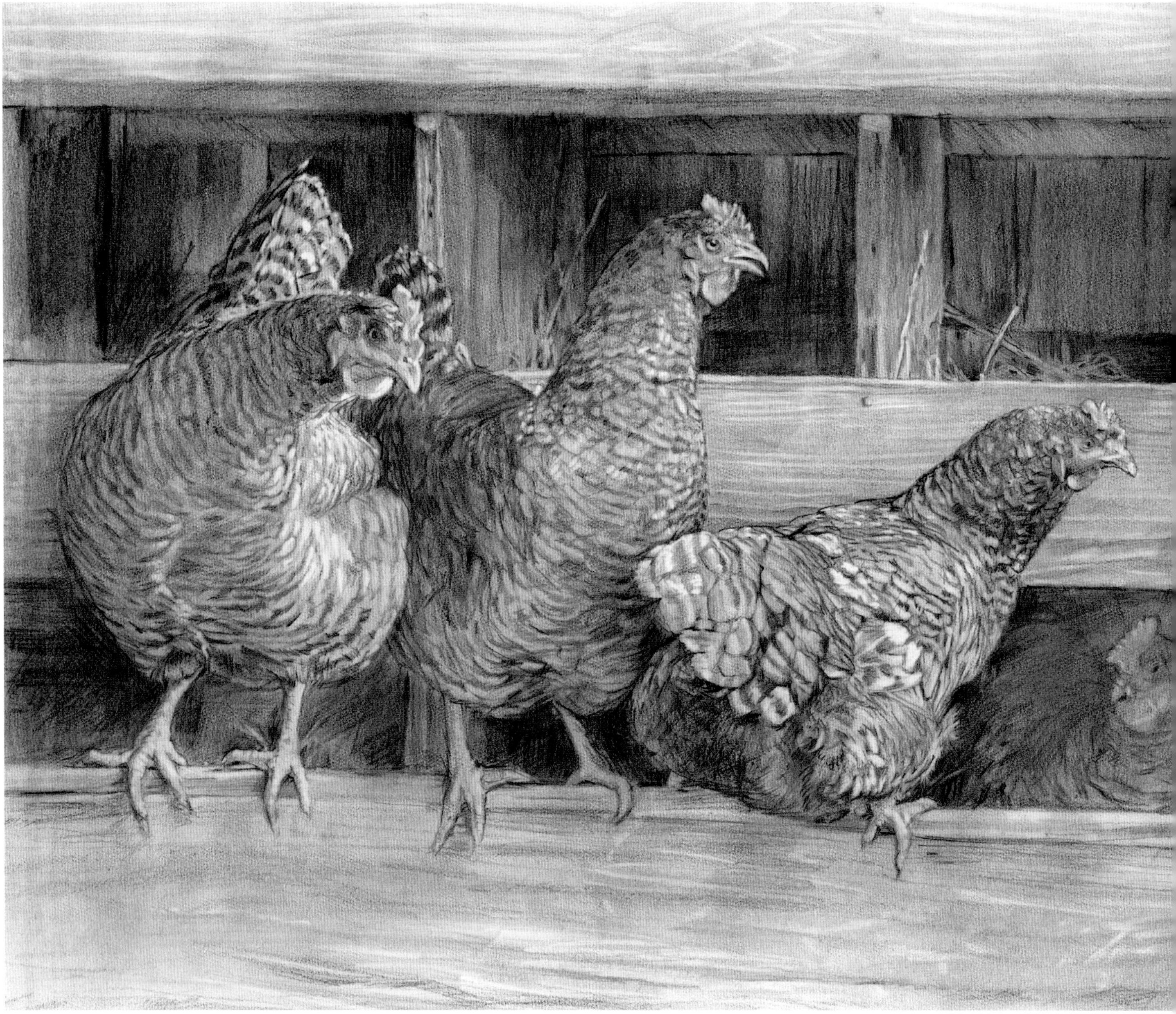

When I moved my art studio from the inner city to an old barn in the countryside, I was greeted by a variety of resident wildlife including a number of black rat snakes on persistent rodent patrol. These impressive reptiles, as they lived out their seasonal growth cycles, often left me gifts of their shed skins, translucent paper-like structures. Using a strong light source and a classical gridding system, I was able to achieve this intricate textural illusion in over 200 hours of controlled pencil work.

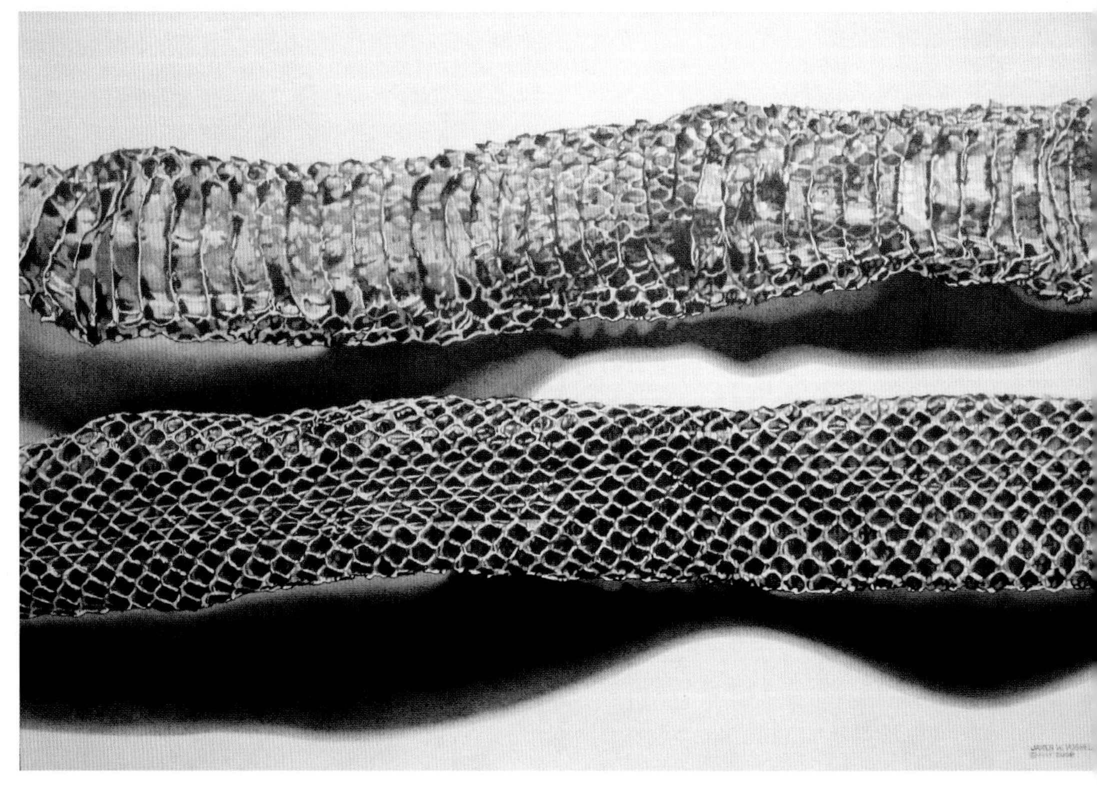

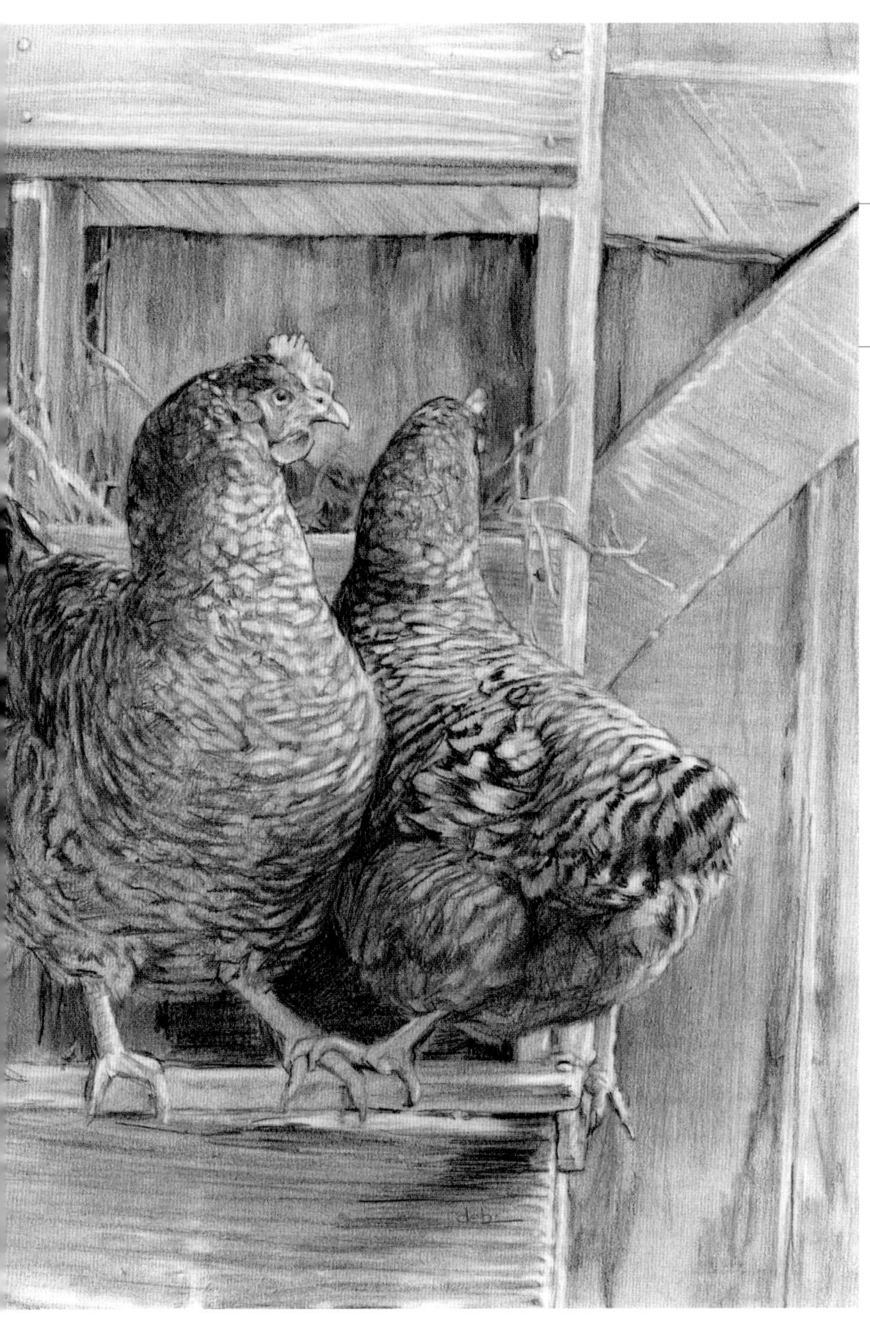

◀ **IN THE HENHOUSE**
Deb Hoeffner
Graphite pencil on Bainbridge cold-pressed board
12½" × 24½" (32cm × 62cm)

The personalities, patterns and positions of these barred Plymouth Rock chickens were a fascinating challenge in textures and values. I start with a light touch using an HB pencil. Then the textures are built up using a slow process of many scribbled layers of graphite softened by smudging with a tissue. I then draw with an electric eraser and a kneaded eraser for the lights, using only the white of the paper. In the last stage a soft 4B pencil is used for a few dark accents.

▶ **SERGEANT STUDY**
Karie O'Donnell
Graphite on 300-lb. (640gsm)
Fabriano paper
9" × 16" (23cm × 41cm)

This portrays a young goose (the sergeant) patrolling the grounds at Boston's Fort Warren on Georges Island. The texture of the warm, downy feathers against the hard granite of this Civil War-era structure intrigued me, and I took several reference photos. Using Photoshop, I zoomed in on the unseen details. This is where I draw from, adding layers of texture to give the bird life under my pencil.

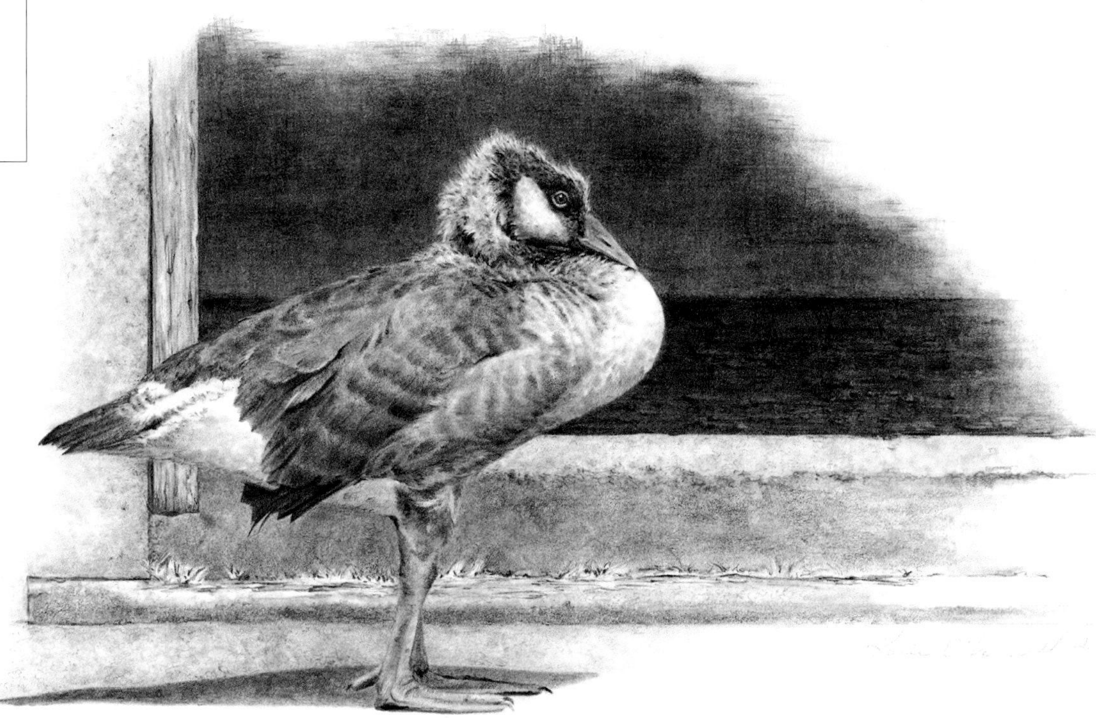

I couldn't but laugh at my cousin's newly arrived goat kids' friendly exuberance. While I snapped photos, I knew traditional scratchboard—white lines carved into black background—would be my choice for capturing the kids' facial expressions. The key to rendering expressive texture in any drawing medium is effective mark-making. Instead of adjusting shadows (highlights in scratchboard) with textbook crosshatching, every mark should simultaneously describe the subjects' texture, define edges and contours, and build up shadows and highlights.

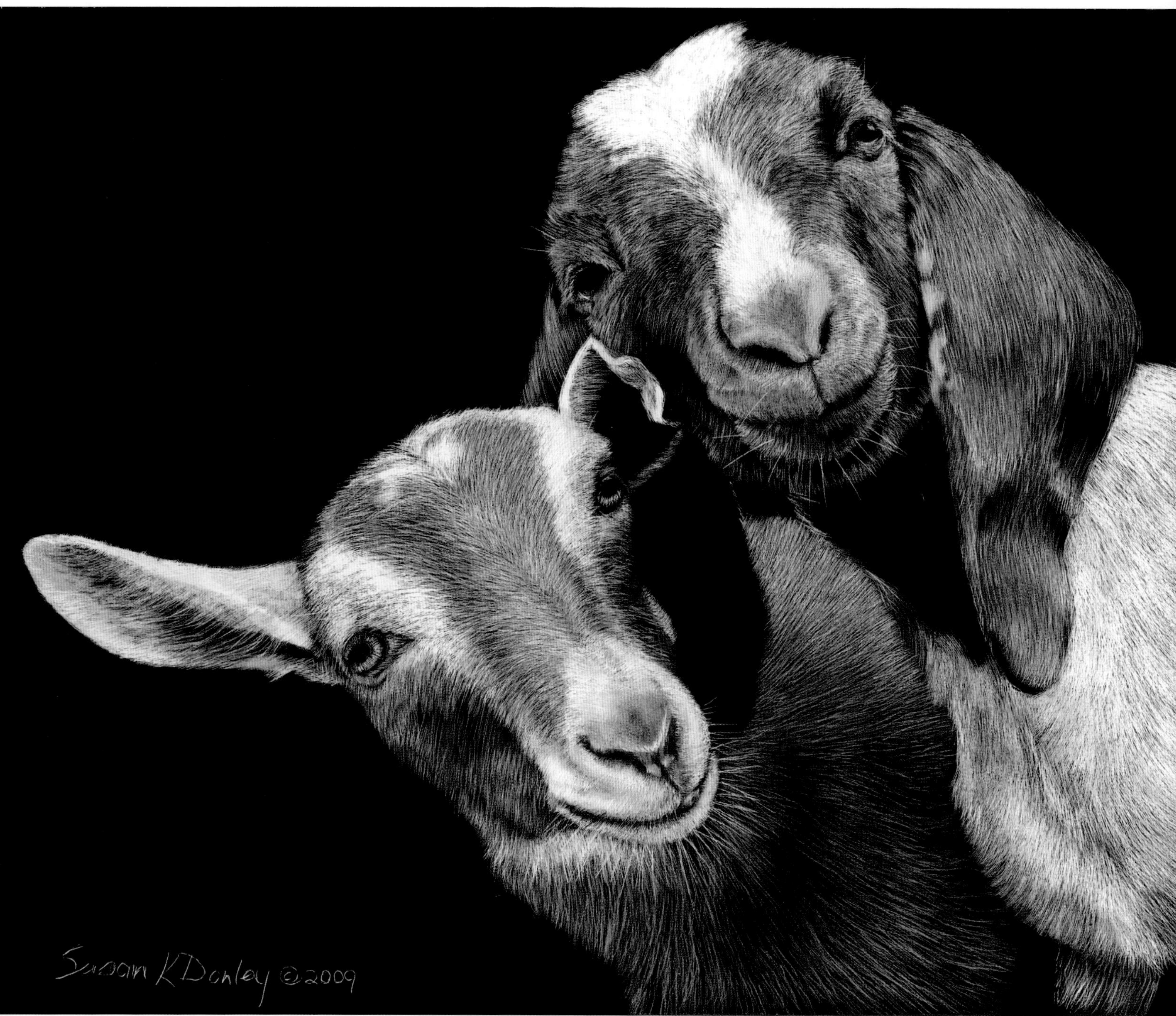

While I was taking photos at a friend's farm, this young cow appeared and batted her long eyelashes at me. I knew I had to draw her! Her face was covered in whiskers, with many cowlicks sending her hair this way and that. Along with her flirty personality, my goal was to capture these lines and textures contrasted with the soft, out-of-focus and foreshortened body to give it a feeling of depth. Also I wanted to convey the sunny backlighting that made her ears glow a bit. My process is slow; I use a light touch with very sharp colored pencils, which gives me a slightly grainy texture on the Mi-Teintes paper.

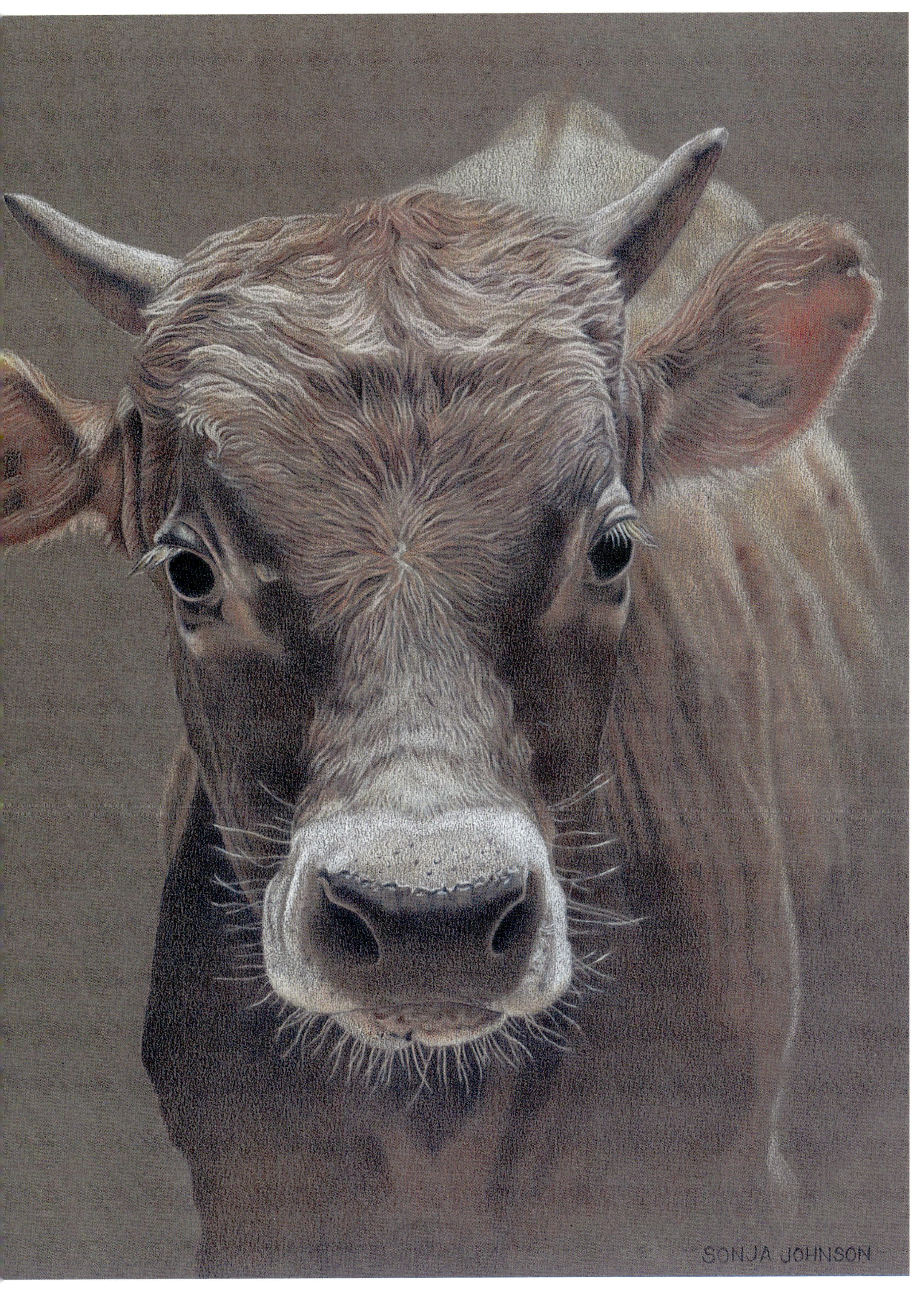

SONJA JOHNSON

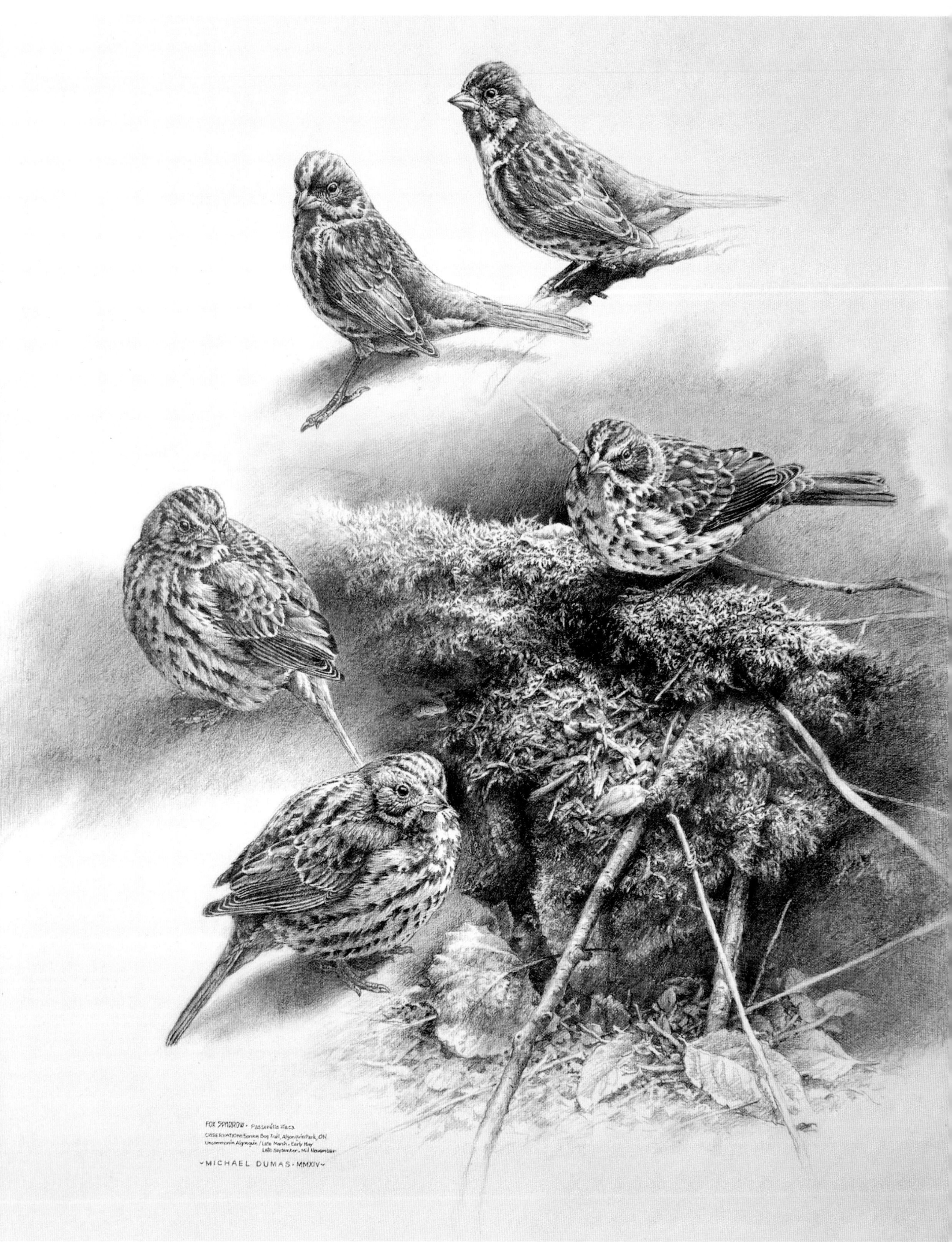

FOX SPARROW · Passerella iliaca
OBSERVATION: Spruce Bog Trail, Algonquin Park, ON
Uncommon in Algonquin / Late March · Early May
Late September · Mid November
~MICHAEL DUMAS· MMXIV~

◀ **FOX SPARROW STUDY**
Michael Dumas
Graphite on canvas
20" × 16" (51cm × 41cm)

For *Fox Sparrow Study* I worked from life drawings, photographs, a specimen and objects from the field. I applied multiple layers of acrylic gesso to fine-weave portrait canvas that I hand-sanded smooth. The two birds at the top and the one at the far left were drawn using H and HB graphite pencils. I wanted the rest of the surface somewhat gritty in texture, so I diluted acrylic gesso to the consistency of skim milk and washed it on. Once dry, the surface took on a pronounced sharp tooth. A very light sanding seamlessly blended the graduated edge, which runs around the left-most bird. Using HB and 2B graphite for the two birds and vegetation in this toothy area enhanced the underlying grain and enriched the darks. Several layers of final varnish spray provided a durable, protective finish.

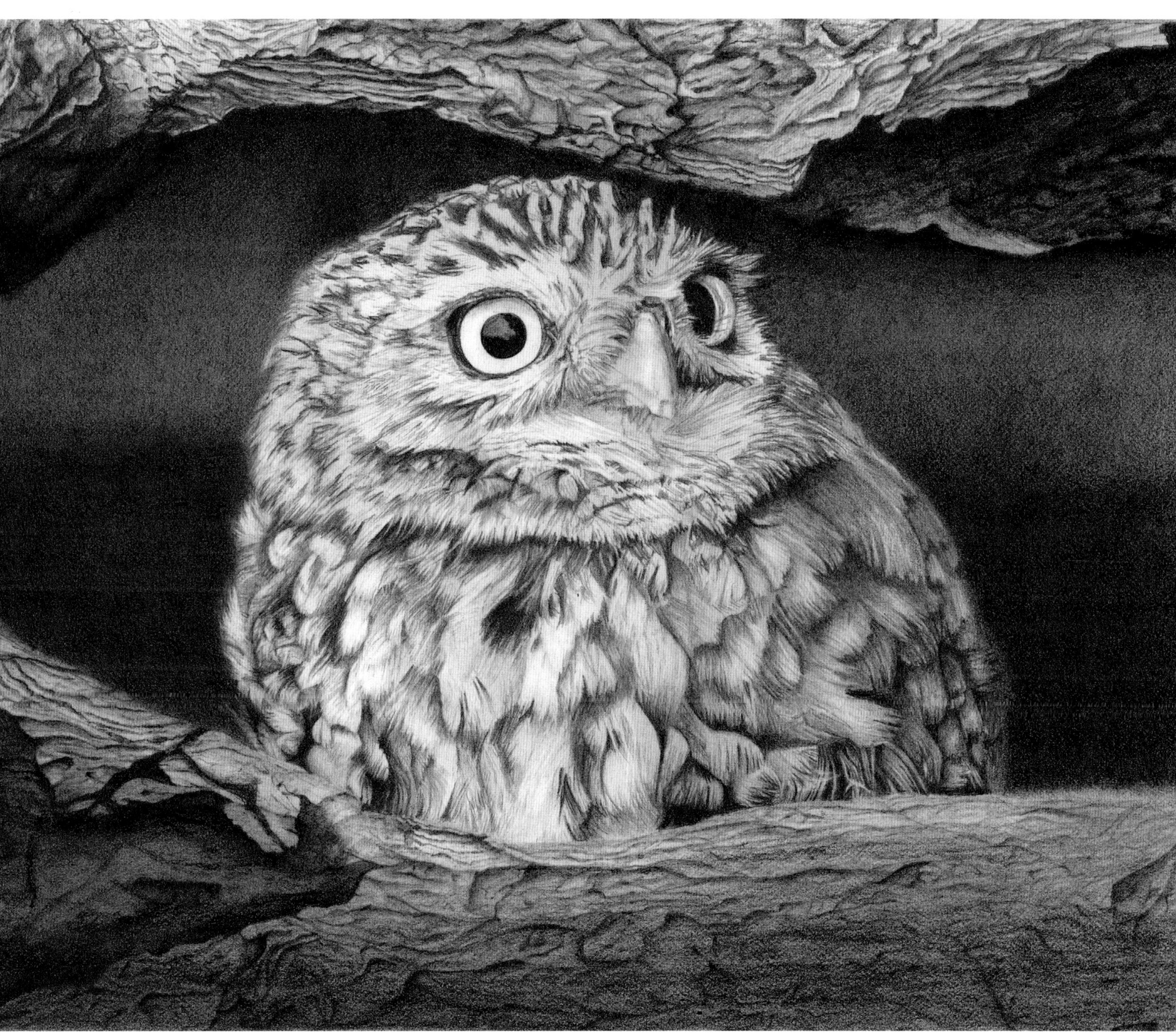

A photo taken by Chris Allsebrook inspired this drawing. I wanted to capture the essence of the subject, eliminating extraneous details and creating missing elements. The highly textured wood required quite a bit of invention to make up for photo distortion and to create more depth in the front of the drawing. Despite the contrasting textures of the wood and fur, I wanted to keep the focus on the eyes, so I lightened the value of the top half of the interior of the owl's home.

▲ **VIGILANCE**
Sandra Weiner
Graphite on bristol board
8" × 10" (20cm × 25cm)

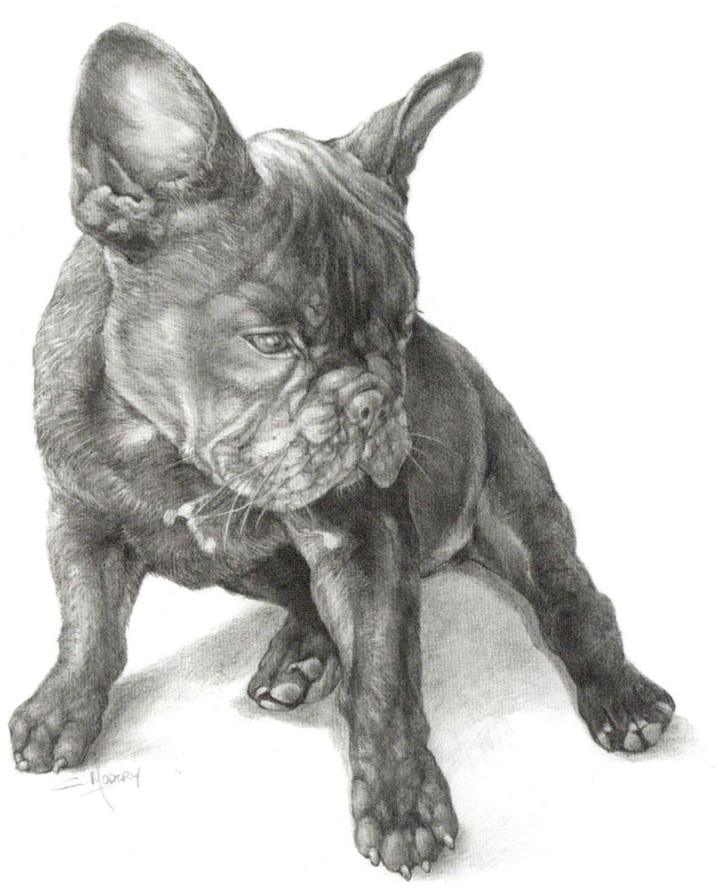

I find inspiration from contradictions: gentle vs. rough, pretty vs. ugly. Including the strongly disliked brown marmorated stink bug in the drawing of an irresistible French bulldog puppy just seemed right and added a bit of whimsy. I began by blocking in form, then layered in shadows and added gentle directional strokes to create the soft fur-like texture. My goal was to keep the drawing simple and innocent.

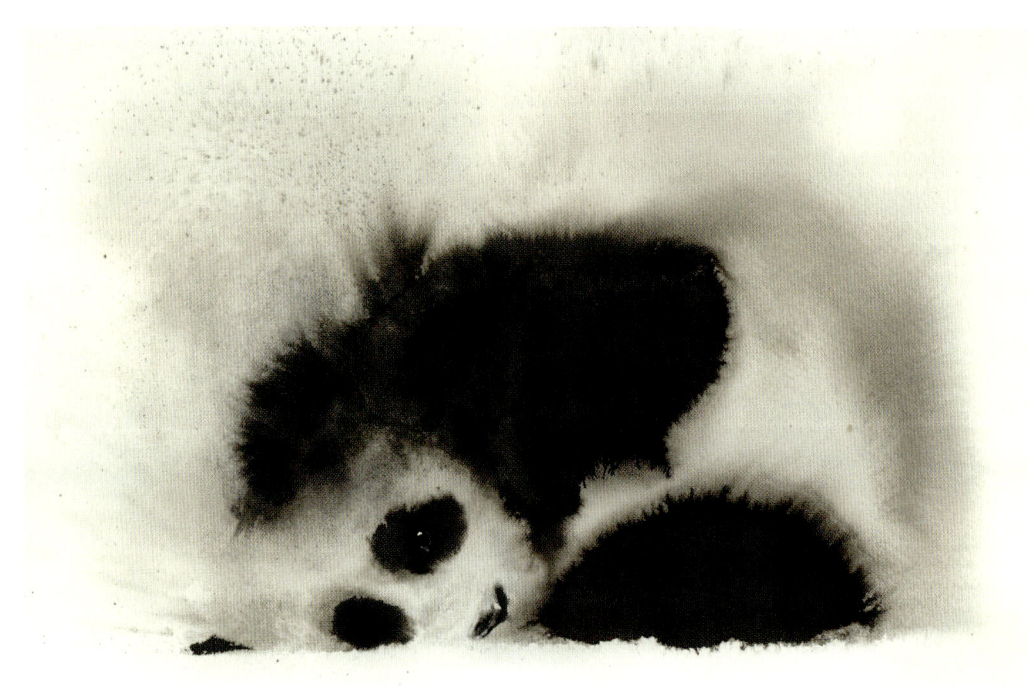

The panda is one of the most adorable animals in existence. Finished with minimal brushstrokes, every single stroke was planned and placed carefully in order to portray the feathery effect, allowing the watercolor and ink to flow freely with the gentle guidance of the brush.

"The essence of painting character is not in the number of strokes, but rather the quality and motive behind each stroke."

—ZE ZE LAI

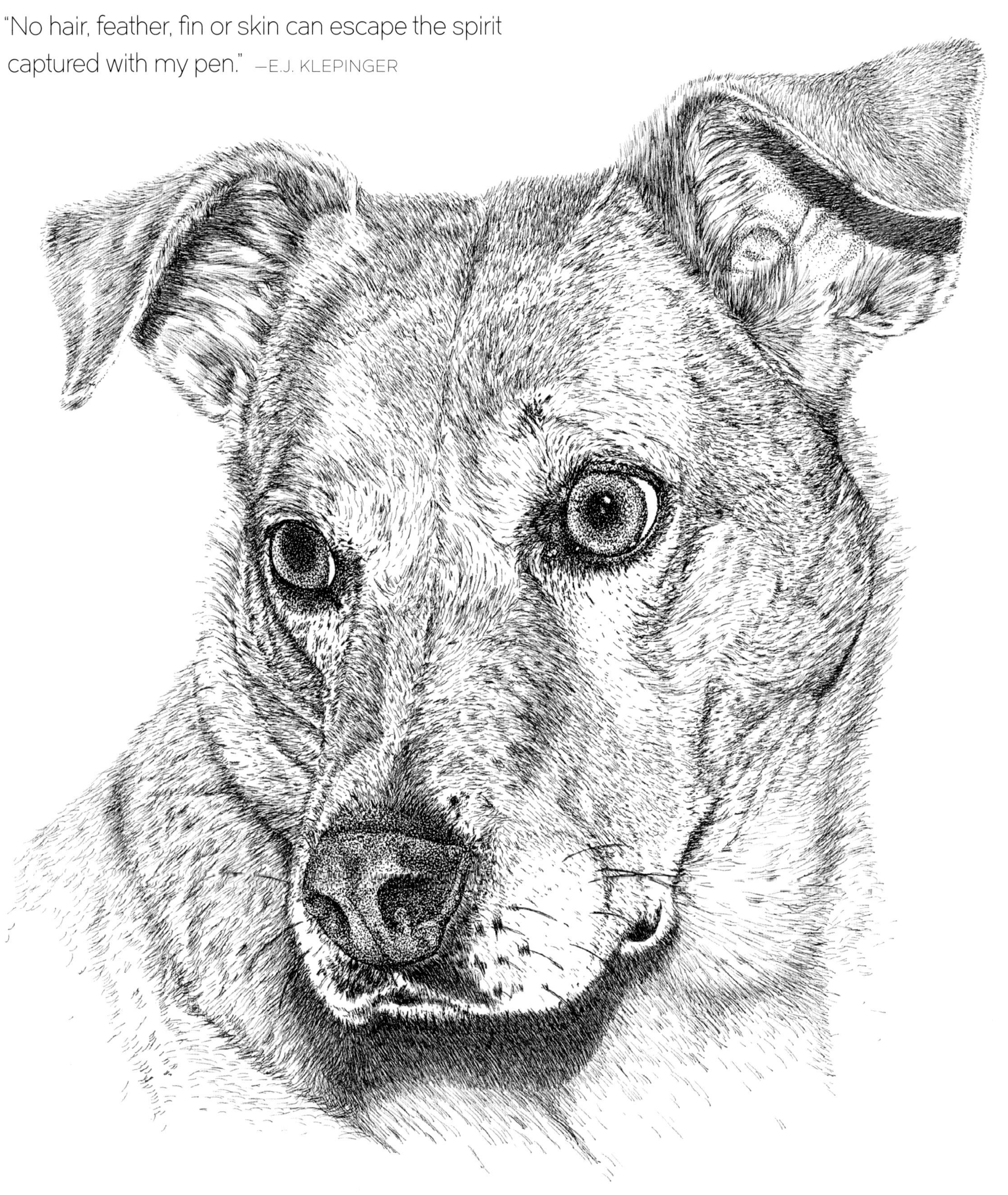

I use various techniques to capture the essence of a subject's physical attributes. Fur is easy as each stroke represents a hair, and the more strokes, the darker the area, thus creating color, depth and shadows. My solid dark areas are never washed in and are always built up by stippling, allowing me to control the varied gray tones. The more I truly see, the more realistic I can be.

▲ ROSIE
E.J. Klepinger
Rapidograph pen and black India ink on Borden
& Riley #234 Paris Paper for Pens
14" × 11" (36cm × 28cm)

Her feminine eyelashes along with the variety of texture, from the softness of the background fog to the roughness of the thistles, are what inspired me to draw *Doe Pretty*. To create the smooth textures of the nose and eyes I used a light hand to place individual pencil strokes as close to each other as possible. To create rougher textures, I spaced pencil strokes a bit farther apart and used shading techniques. The contrast of light and dark also helped to create the illusion of the coarser textures. I added the birch trees to frame *Doe Pretty* and to provide additional texture to the finished drawing.

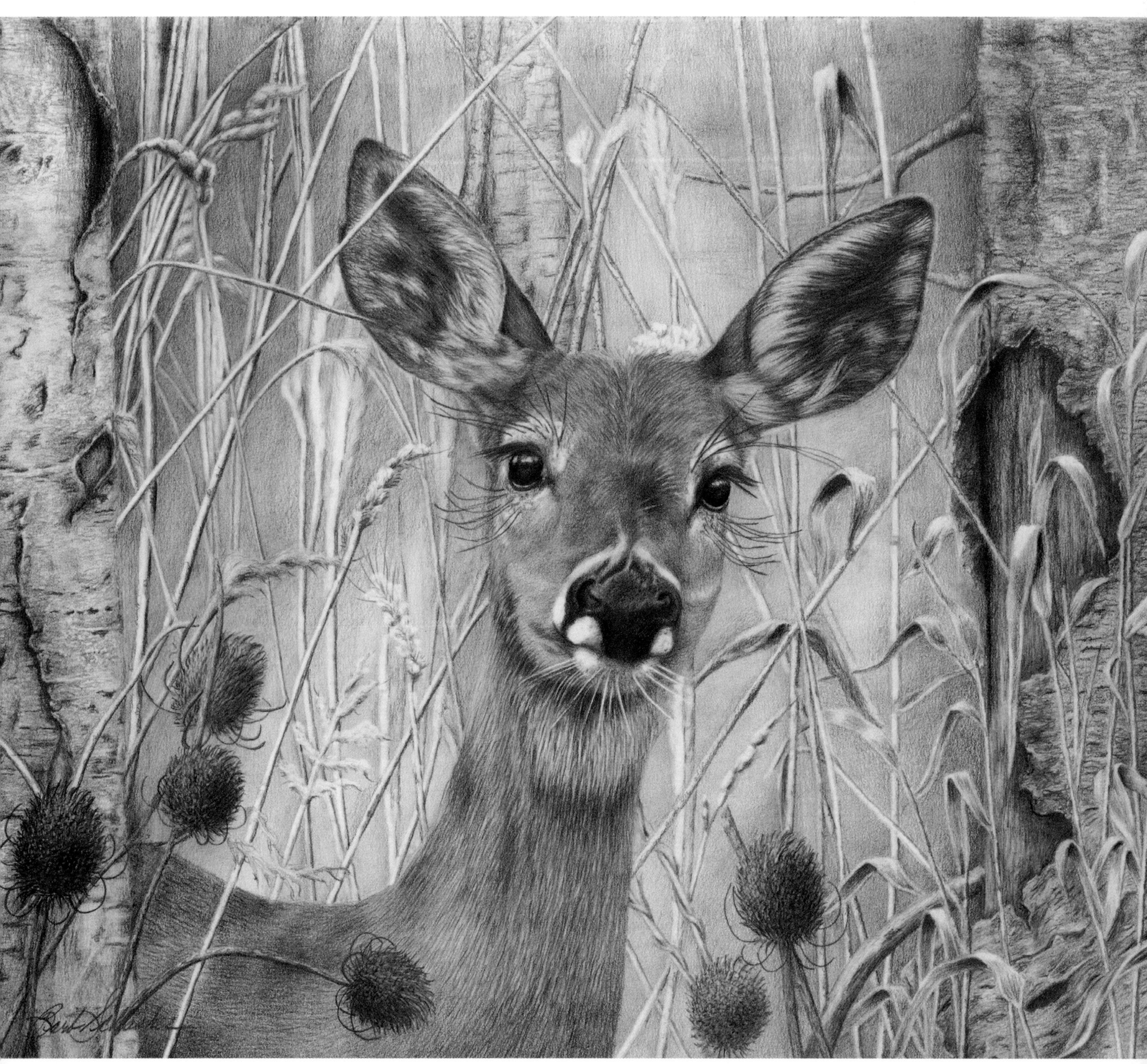

Elephantidae is part of an exhibition entitled *Periclitatus*, a word derived from the Latin word for endangered. Latin is considered to be an extinct language, a play on the symbolism behind this and each piece in the show, which was created to call attention to the pressing need to conserve endangered species. Black and white charcoal, one of the oldest drawing mediums, reminds us that animals have been surviving on earth for many years before us. The hyperrealistic style suggests how important species diversity is. *Elephantidae* took approximately 60 hours of studio time to complete and was created from a high-quality reference photo.

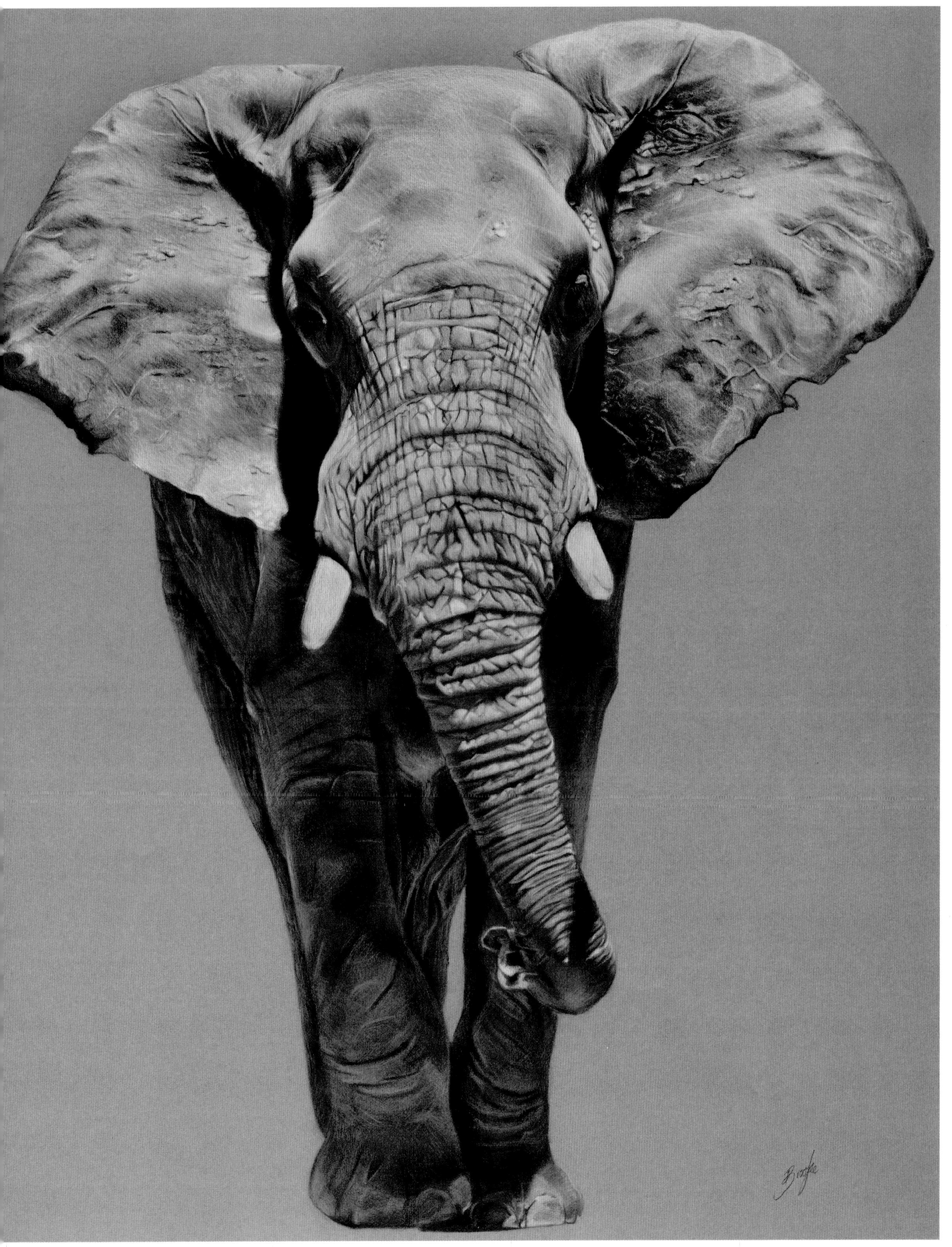

In *Waiting* there are two distinct worlds: inside and out. By lightly swirling graduating values of gray colored pencil over rag mat, I allowed texture to slowly build a muted effect throughout most of the piece, like dust floating in a closed room. In this atmosphere of stasis three pets wait along the back of a couch until their owners arrive home. In contrast, a fully saturated and heavy-handed full-color view of the outside world is seen through the window, marching along without them. This was painted with colored pencils and solvent. *Waiting* was created in my studio with its subjects at my feet.

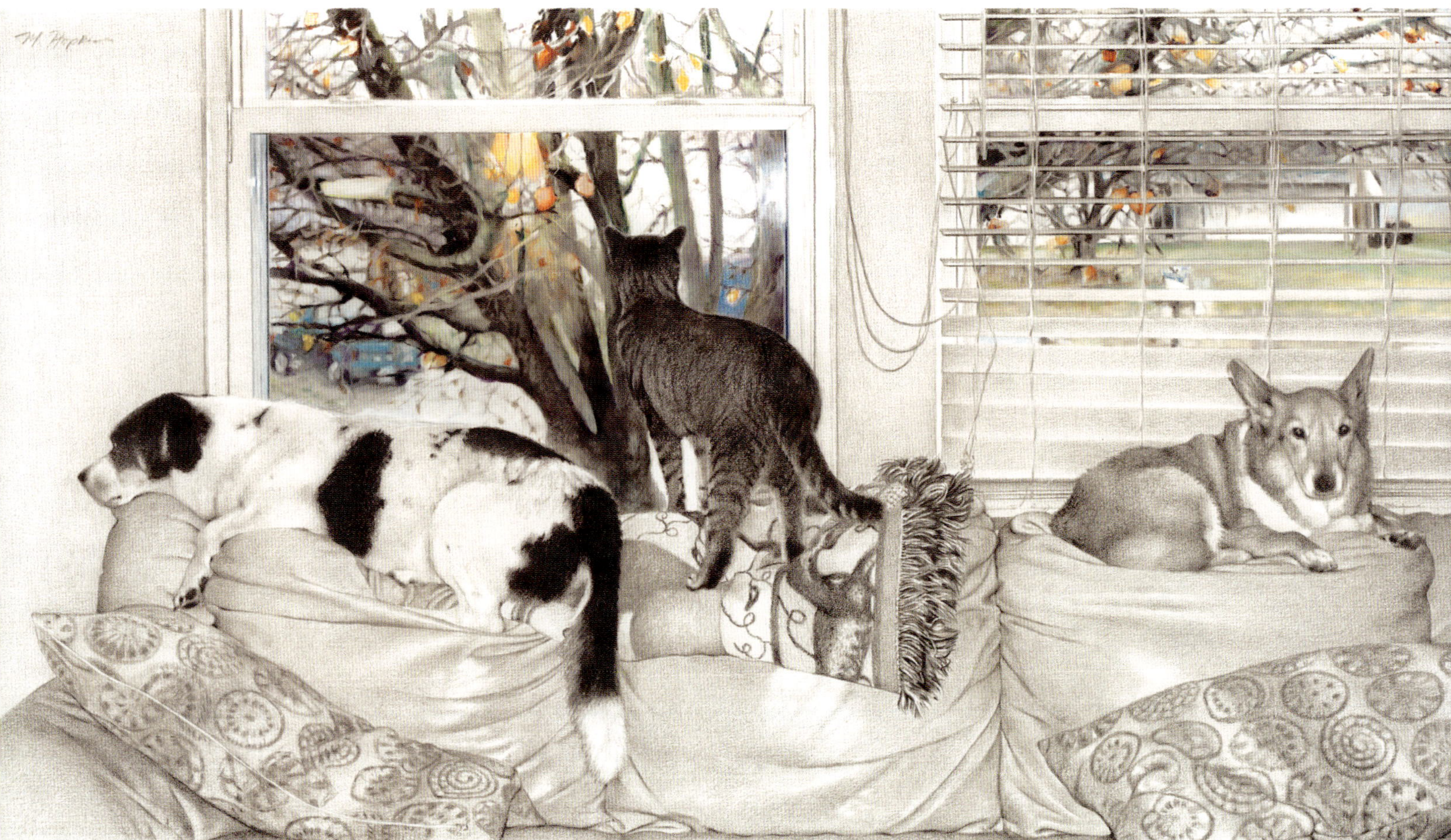

"A light touch on the appropriate surface, and texture will come alive." —MARGARET HOPKINS

I like to draw pets or children from either photo or life; I usually do an on-site quick sketch first, and then take six to seven photos as my reference. I started with the eyes since I think that is the most important area, but I spent a lot of time on the fur. I paid a lot of attention to the texture of the puppy fur, which had interesting ripples, variations and rhythms, making it exciting and aesthetically pleasing.

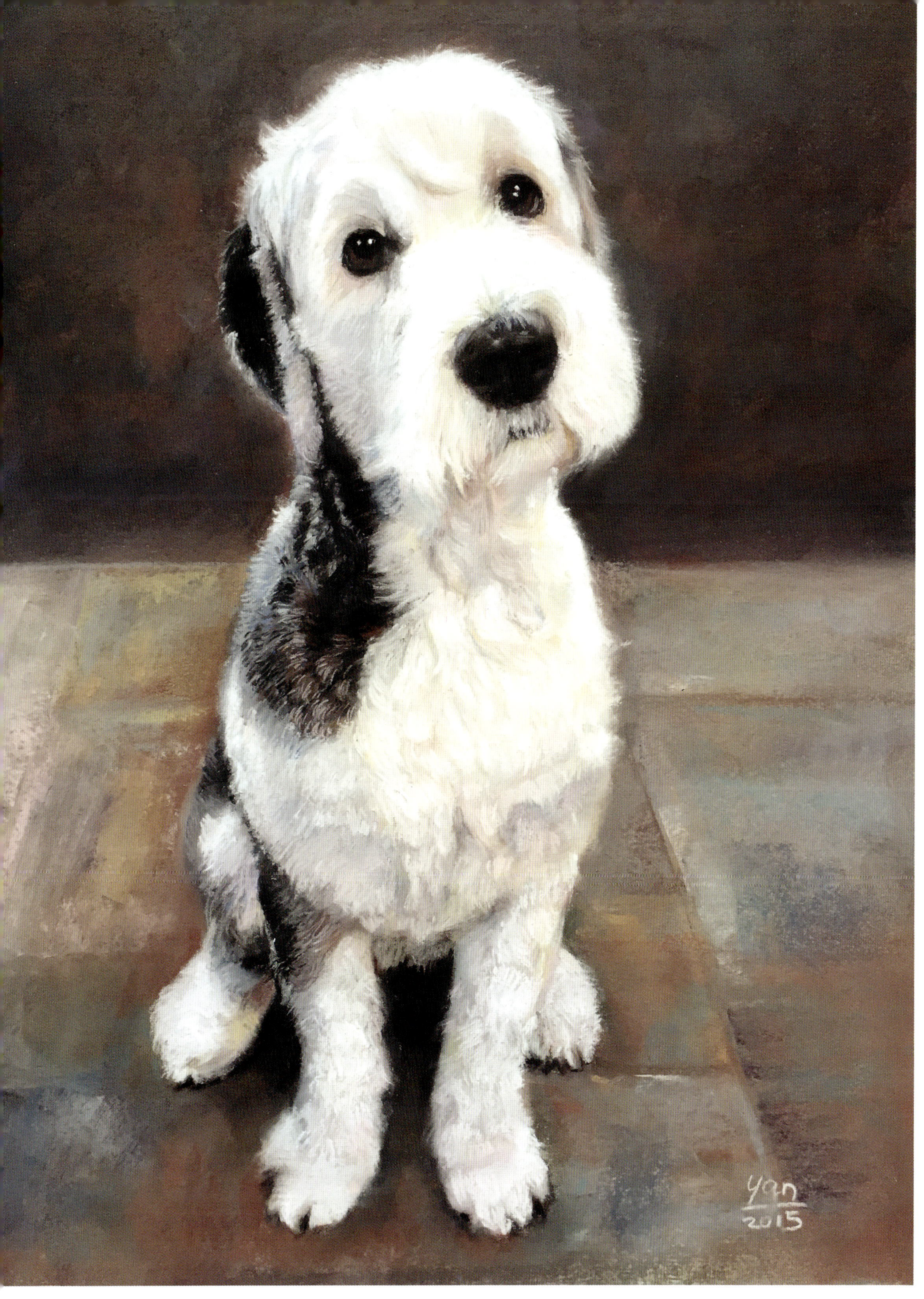

"Rich, varied texture is more attractive than monotonous and stiff texture." —WEI YAN

The setup for *Shadow* was a photograph provided to me by my client. For dry-brushed oil you remove the oil from the paint on the brush using paper towels before you drybrush it onto the watercolor paper. I add sewing machine oil to the paint to create darker blacks and erase lighter areas with a kneaded eraser. The realistic fur texture is achieved by a combination of the grain of the paper and the brush techniques; the slight grain of the Arches paper created a charcoal appearance. I used subtle color to give an extra pop of added realism to the glassy texture of the eyes and the softness of the nose.

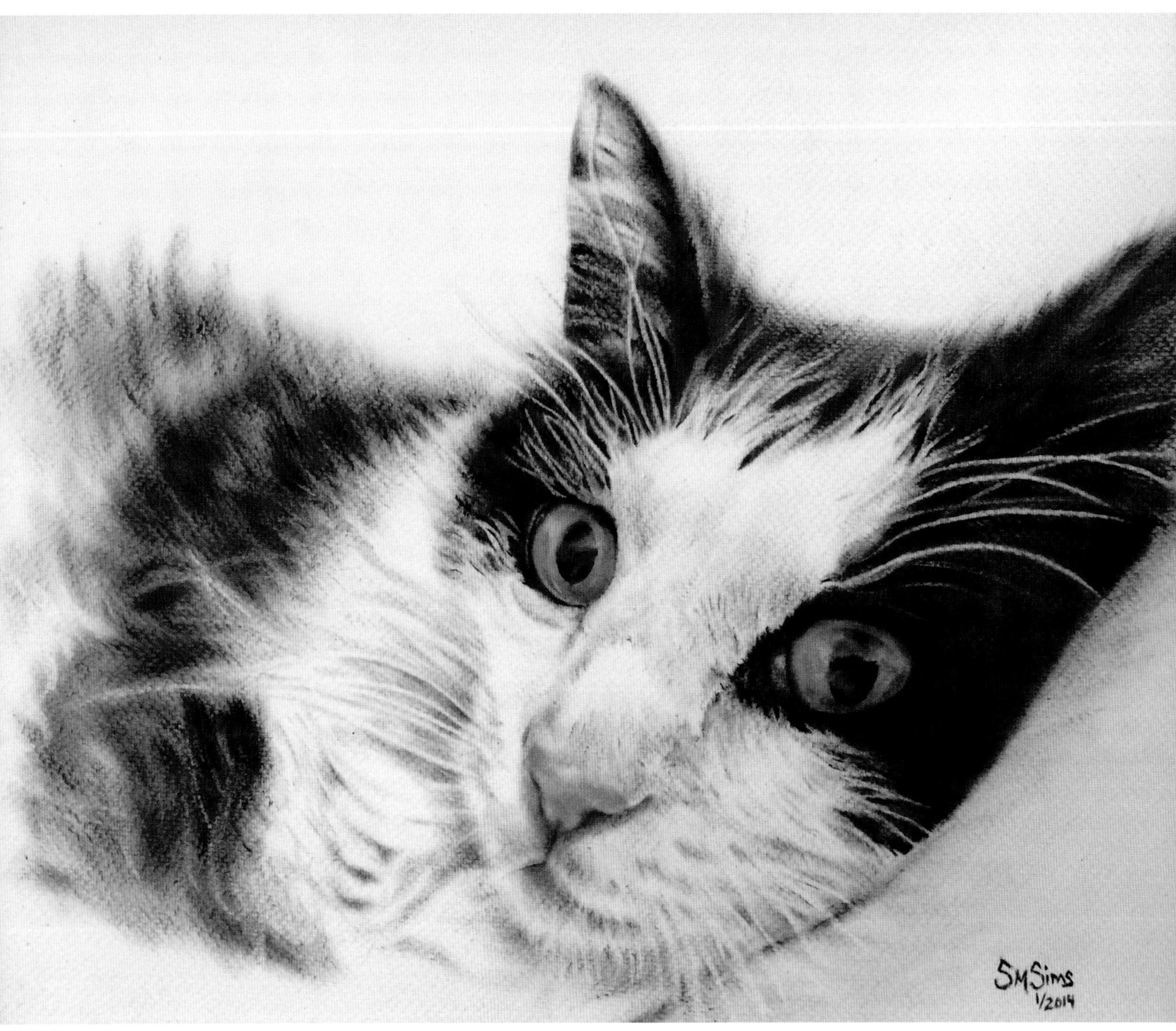

My mother and sister both worked in the movie industry painting backdrops and special effects. I, however, never really got involved in art until my best friend handed me a book called *Colored Pencil Portraits Step by Step*. *Dog in Light* started with a photograph of my friend's dog. I carefully applied many light layers of color over the dog and within the blades of grass, allowing the ridges and valleys of the white Stonehenge paper to reflect back through the colored pencil. This re-creates what we naturally see in life: color, light and texture.

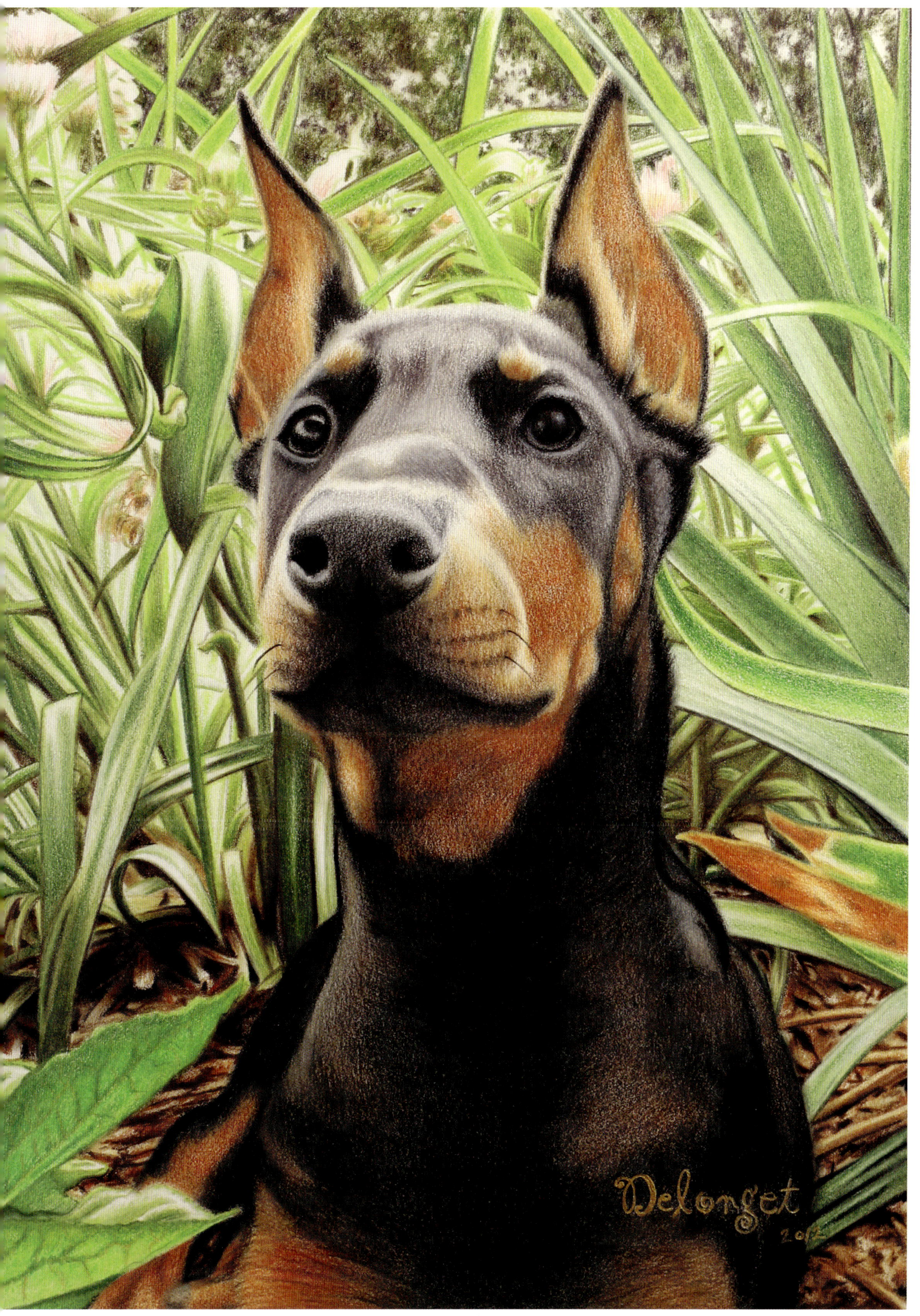
Delonget
2012

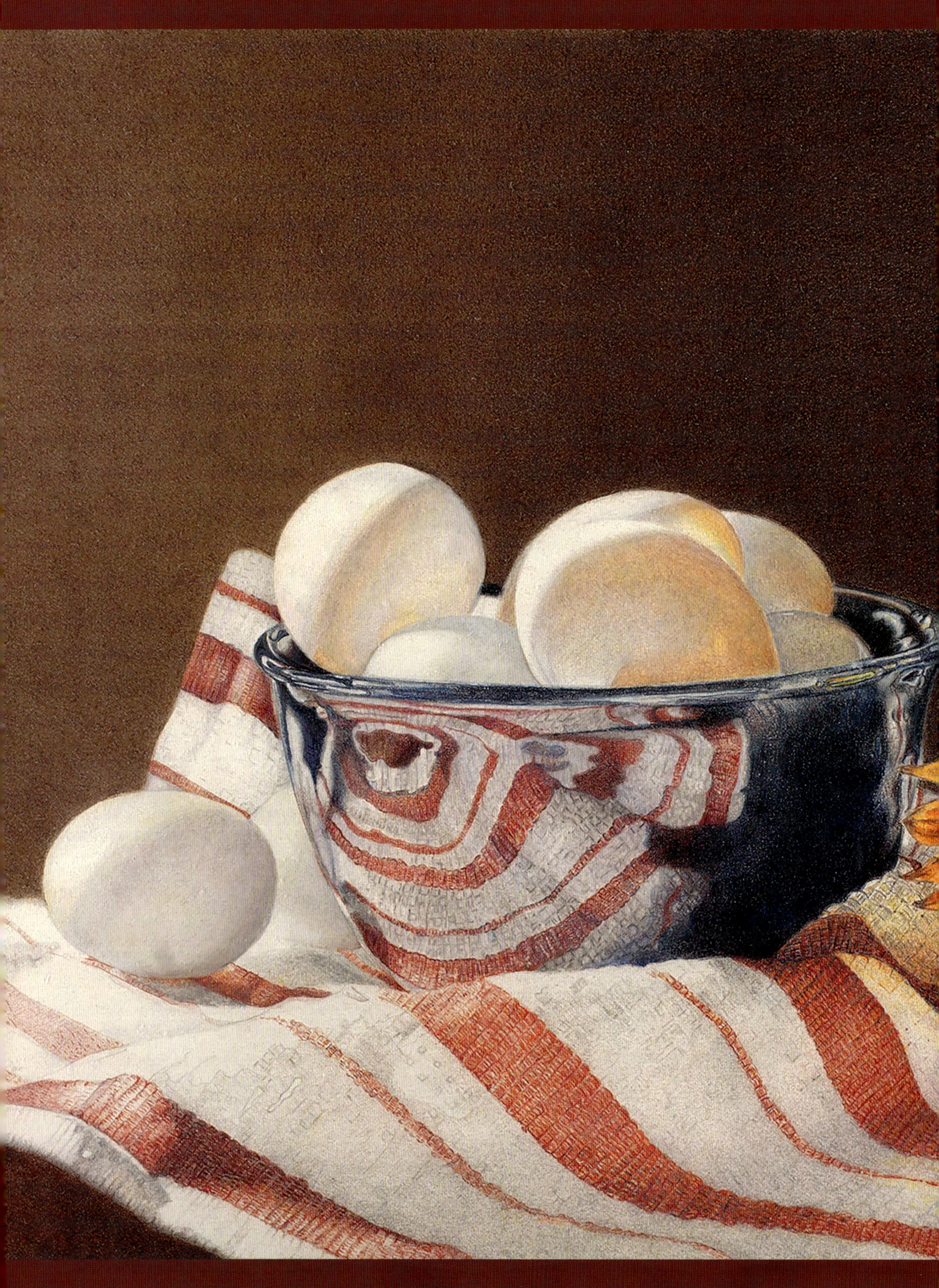

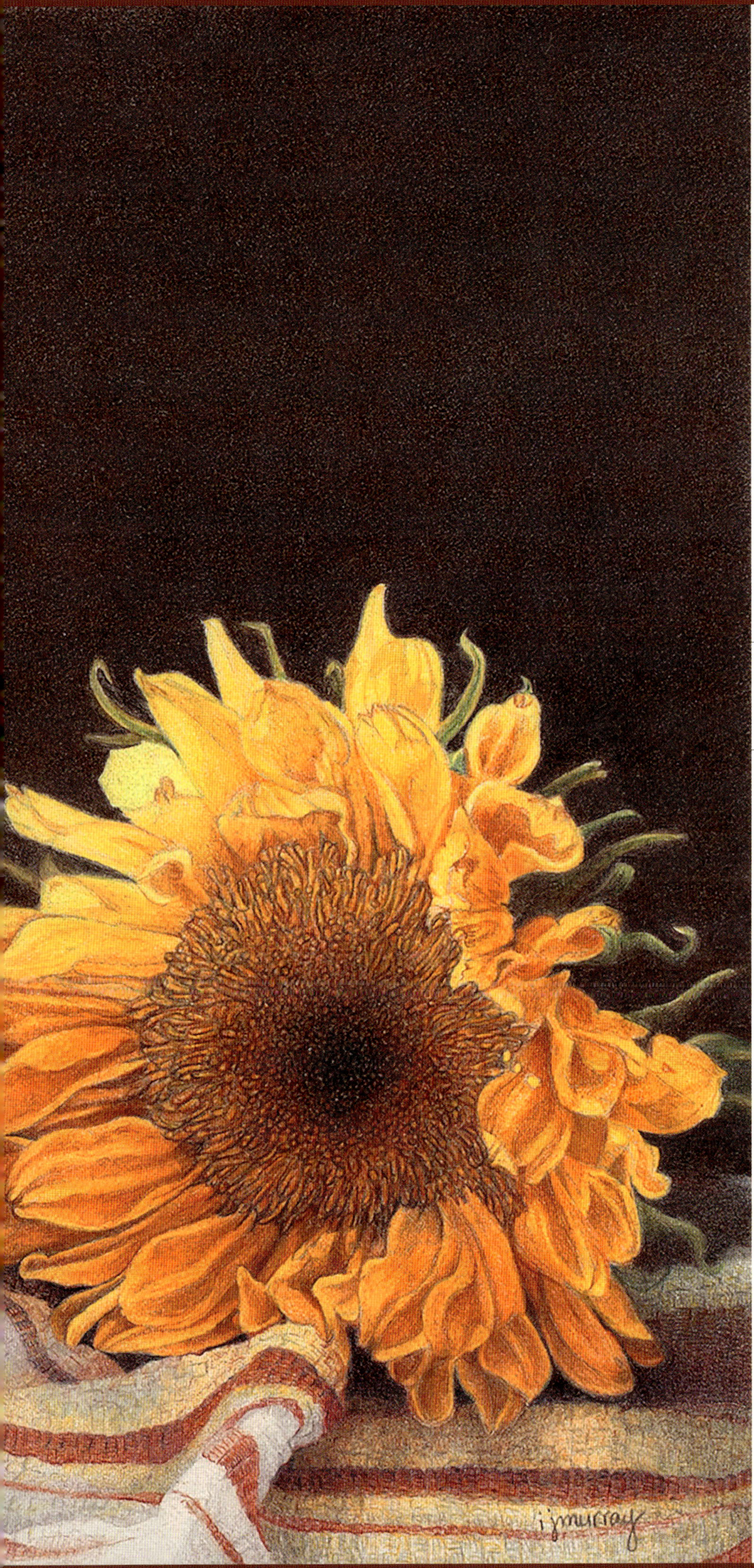

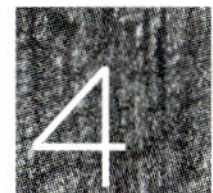

4

The Still Life

In the midst of difficult circumstances, the glorious morning sunlight streaming through my window inspired me to do something creative and positive with my day. I gathered a few favorite items from my kitchen for an impromptu photo shoot. My technical challenge in *Sunny Side Up* was to convincingly render the contrasting textures of the smooth reflective glass, the weave of the cotton towel and the translucence of the eggshells and flower petals. I slowly built up multiple layers of color beginning with the darkest areas.

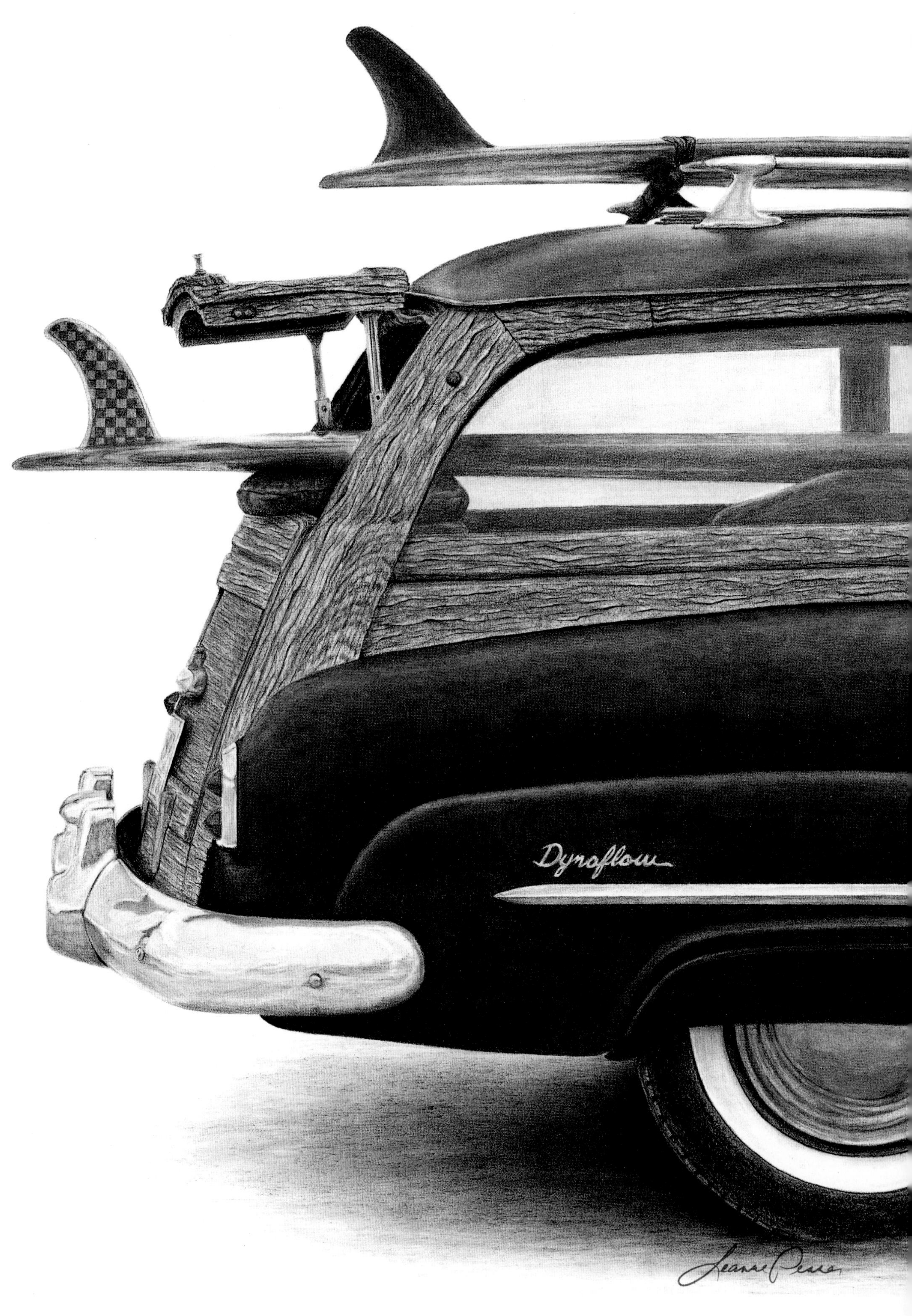
Dynaflow

It was a beautiful summer day; waves were crashing on the shore, a band was playing, people were dancing and cars were lined up on the beach. Many wonderful images from that day, but this summed up the feeling—beach, cars and fun. The contrasting textures called for a few different mediums. The body of the car was worn but smooth so PanPastel was a perfect choice with its silky texture. The wood grain was put in with a sharp charcoal pencil using small light lines, slowly adding more and more pressure to create the dried and cracked texture. Lastly, pencil was ideal for the reflective pieces.

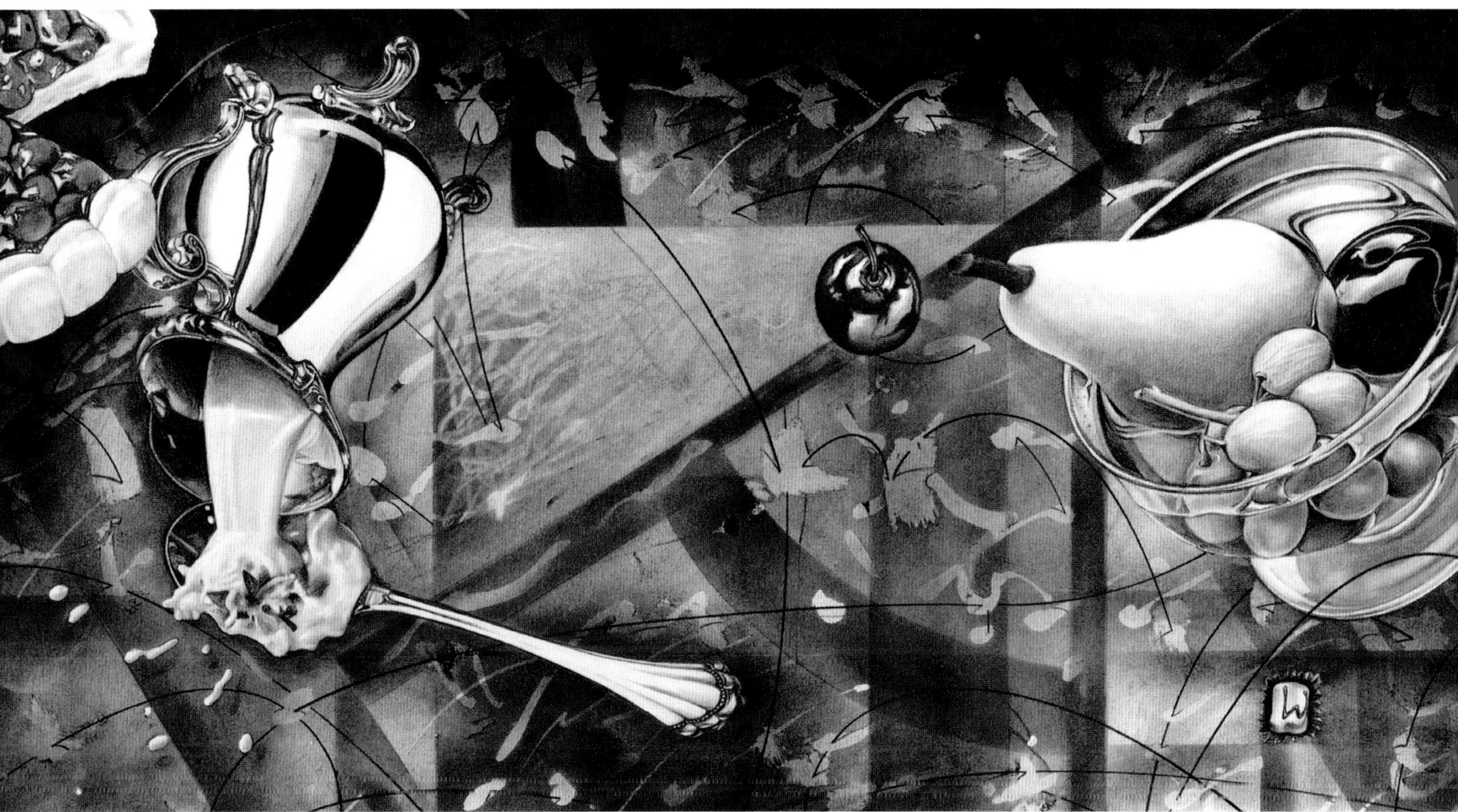

"Keep the main subject matter in the highest contrast areas to allow the eye a clear and clean read." —JERRY D. WERNER

I love drawings that combine realism and abstraction, balancing shapes, tone and volume. I started this drawing with a golden section, nonmodular grid; and then, drawing major elements on tangent points, I referenced photos and old ads and made up abstract shapes and textures. I wanted to see how far a pencil drawing could be pushed to contrast the texture and transparencies of fluids, such as milk, water and pie filling, with the hardness of glass and silver, all against abstract shapes in the background.

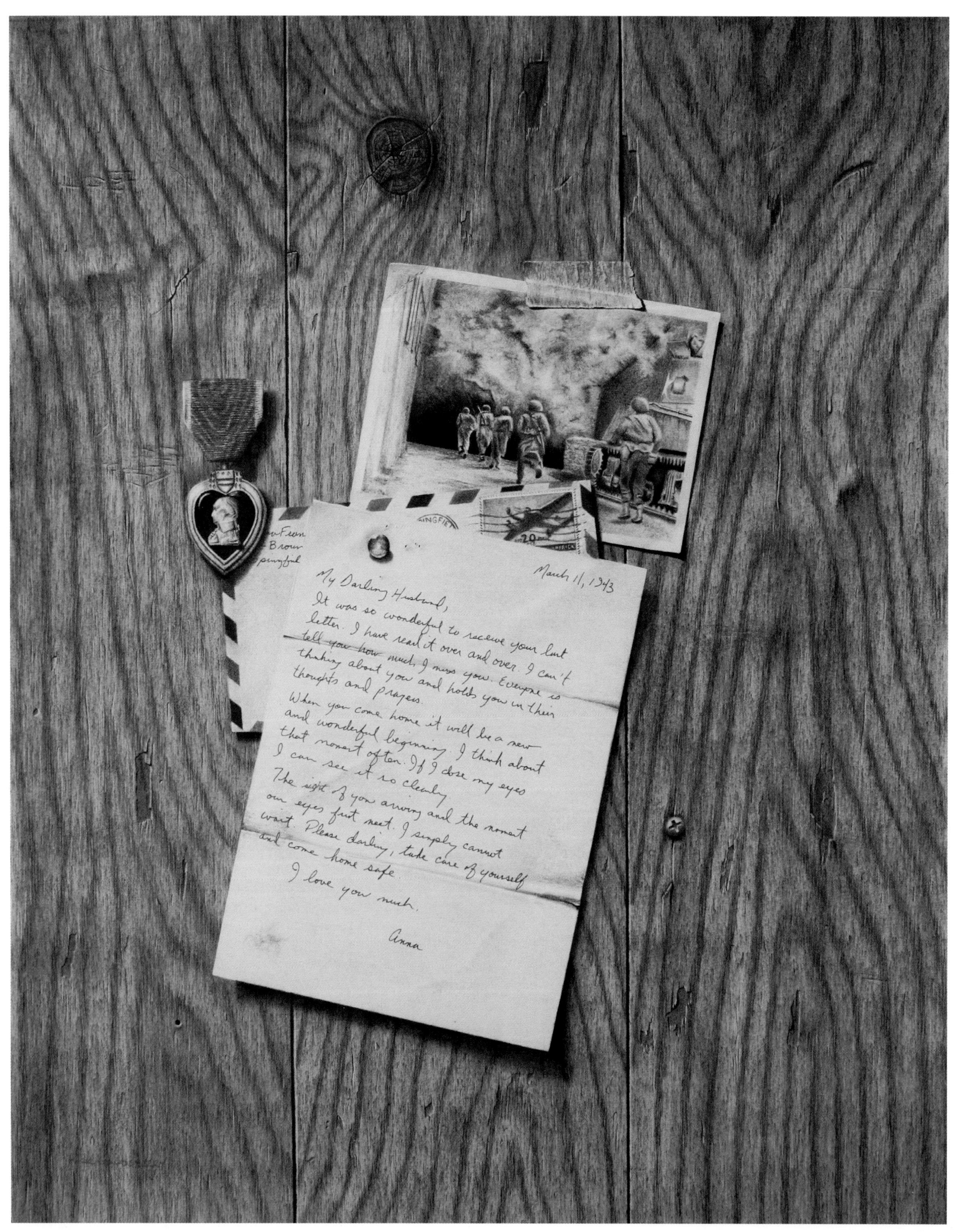

"Paper is critical for texture; I have had problems in the past when developing textures on a paper different from that used in the final drawing." —RICK GOLDSBERRY

◄ **REAL HEROES**
Rick Goldsberry
Charcoal, graphite, carbon and ink on
watercolor paper
20" × 16" (51cm × 41cm)

Real Heroes is my attempt to recognize both the soldier and the loved one back home as people performing heroic acts. Each role can test people's limits. The drawing has provoked a tremendous range of emotions from viewers. It was done in studio by carefully building a model of the components. I always spend more time creating the composition than the actual time spent drawing. The background is wholly invented. Most consider the main elements of a black-and-white drawing to be proportion, edges and tone. Texture is the fourth, and often overlooked, component of a realistic drawing. I save scraps of all my Arches watercolor paper to work textures out in advance.

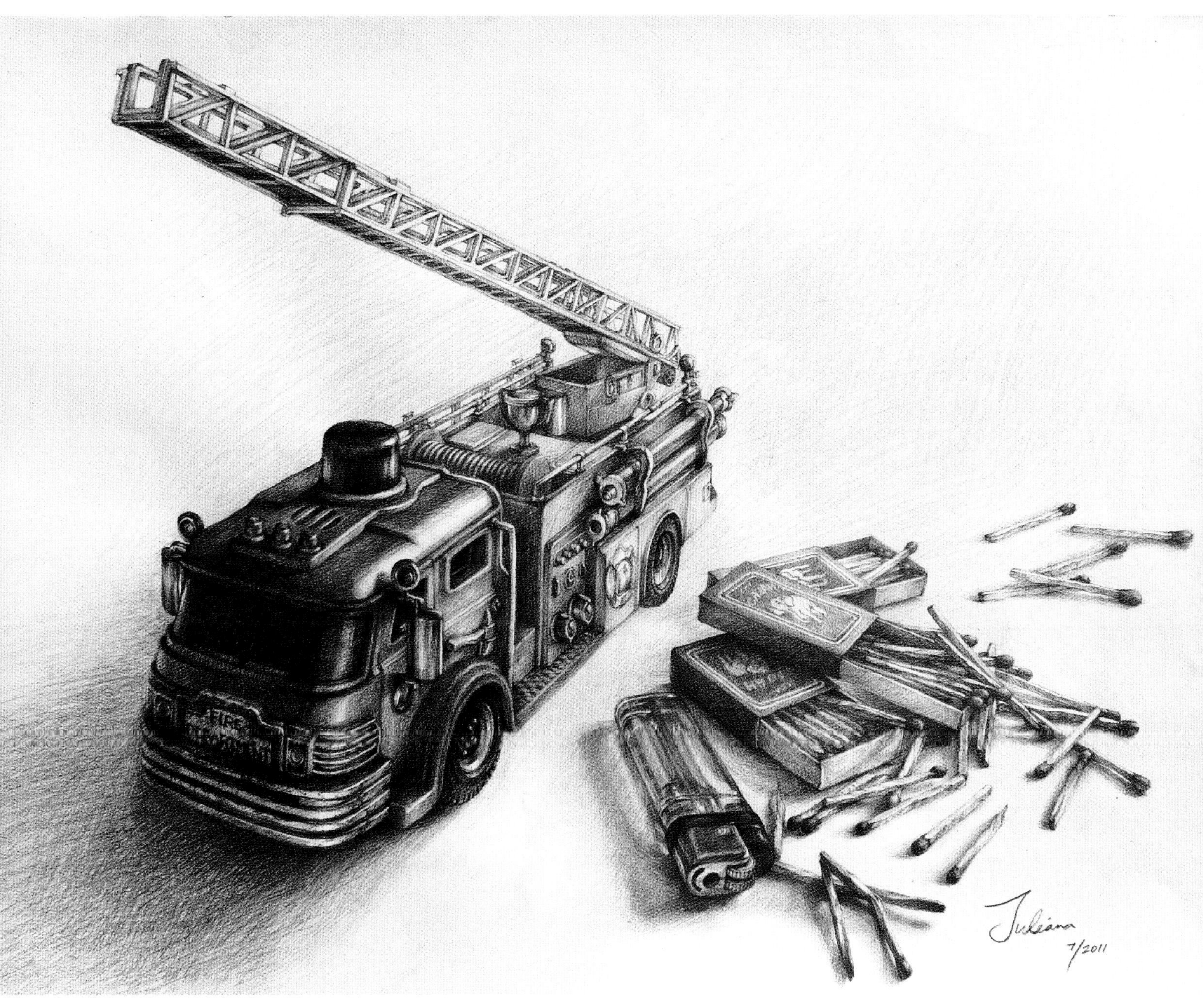

The rusty toy fire engine with the broken matchsticks symbolizes the traces of memories we carry. The rigidity of the toy giving way to the more relaxed spatial composition of the matchsticks represents the transitions of life. A child who is afraid of fire will eventually learn how to light up a match. The learning process involves gathering courage and taking the first step to let go. In maturing we learn to let go of rigidity, giving way to a more relaxed understanding. This is my philosophy both in life and in drawing. Varying the line strokes brings out the individual textural characteristics of the metal, plastic and wood. The fire engine, lighter and matchsticks also remind us that some "texture" (scars) caused by carelessness are not reversible.

▲ **YOUNG MEMORIES**
Chan Sok Yin Juliana
Graphite on cartridge paper
11" × 14" (28cm × 36cm)

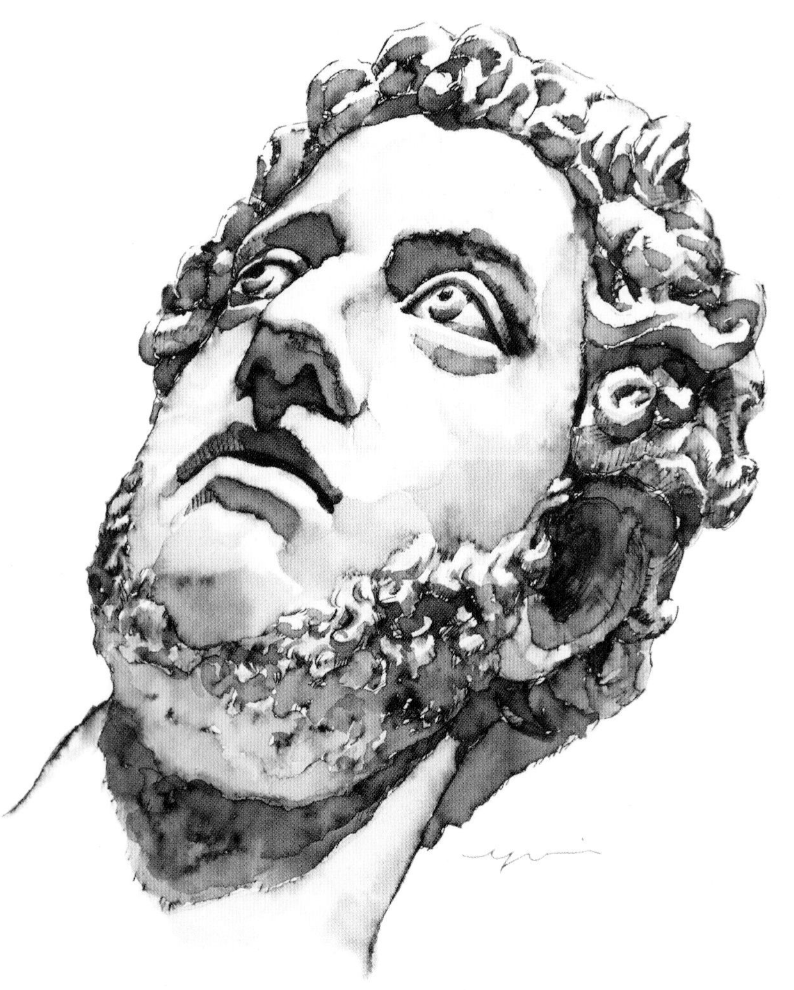

Many of my drawings are influenced by my
love of antiquity. After sketching and taking
pictures at a local museum, I began in pencil
to establish proportions and indicate value
masses. I then applied a hard-edged ink line
with a fountain pen to develop the features.
I completed the drawing with thin washes
of ink applied with a water brush pen. The
nonabsorbent surface of bristol paper allows
the water to soften the ink, creating a smooth
texture that seems to float on the paper.

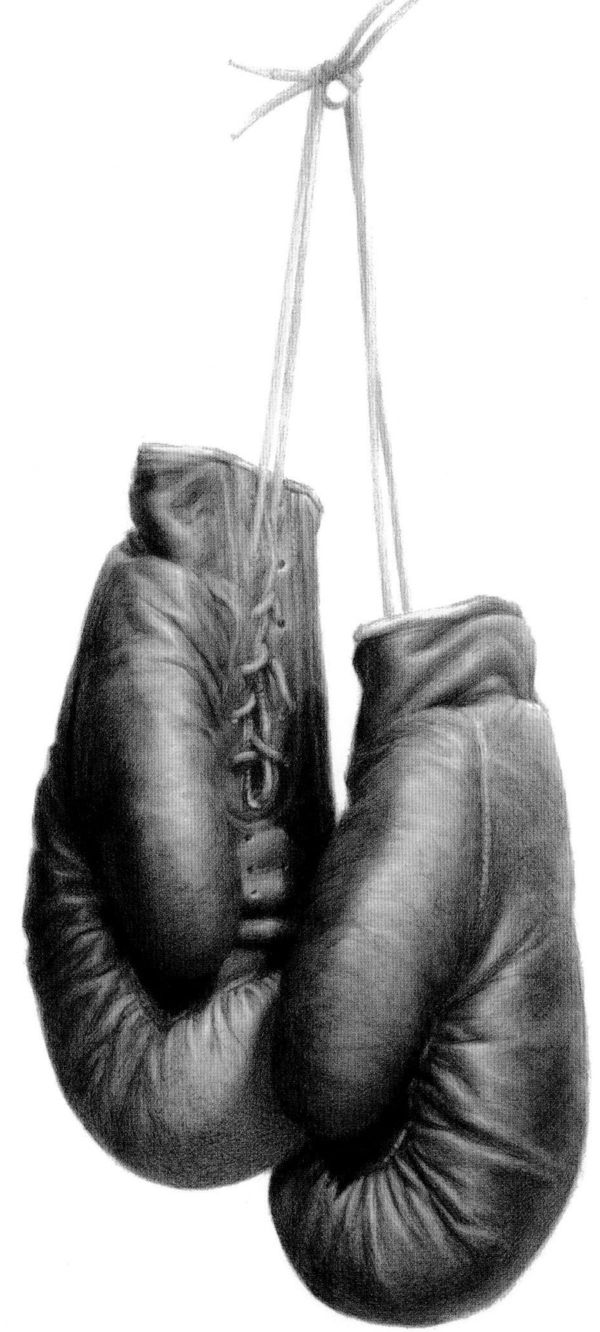

▶ BOXING GLOVES
Mandy Boursicot
Carbon pencil on Stonehenge paper
24" × 18" (61cm × 46cm)

Boxing Gloves was drawn from life in the
academic tradition with the aim to have the
drawing look exactly like the actual object and
to capture the beauty inherent in the object. It
was part of a series of drawings on vintage tools,
sporting items and toys. After drawing many flat
and geometric items, I was ready for something
more organic and complex, with volume and
rounded forms, as well as minute surface detail
like the cracked graininess of time-worn leather.
I like the idea that these old objects can enjoy a
second life as the subject of beautiful art.

"Texture is the finishing touch and the crowning
glory of excellent drawing." —MANDY BOURSICOT

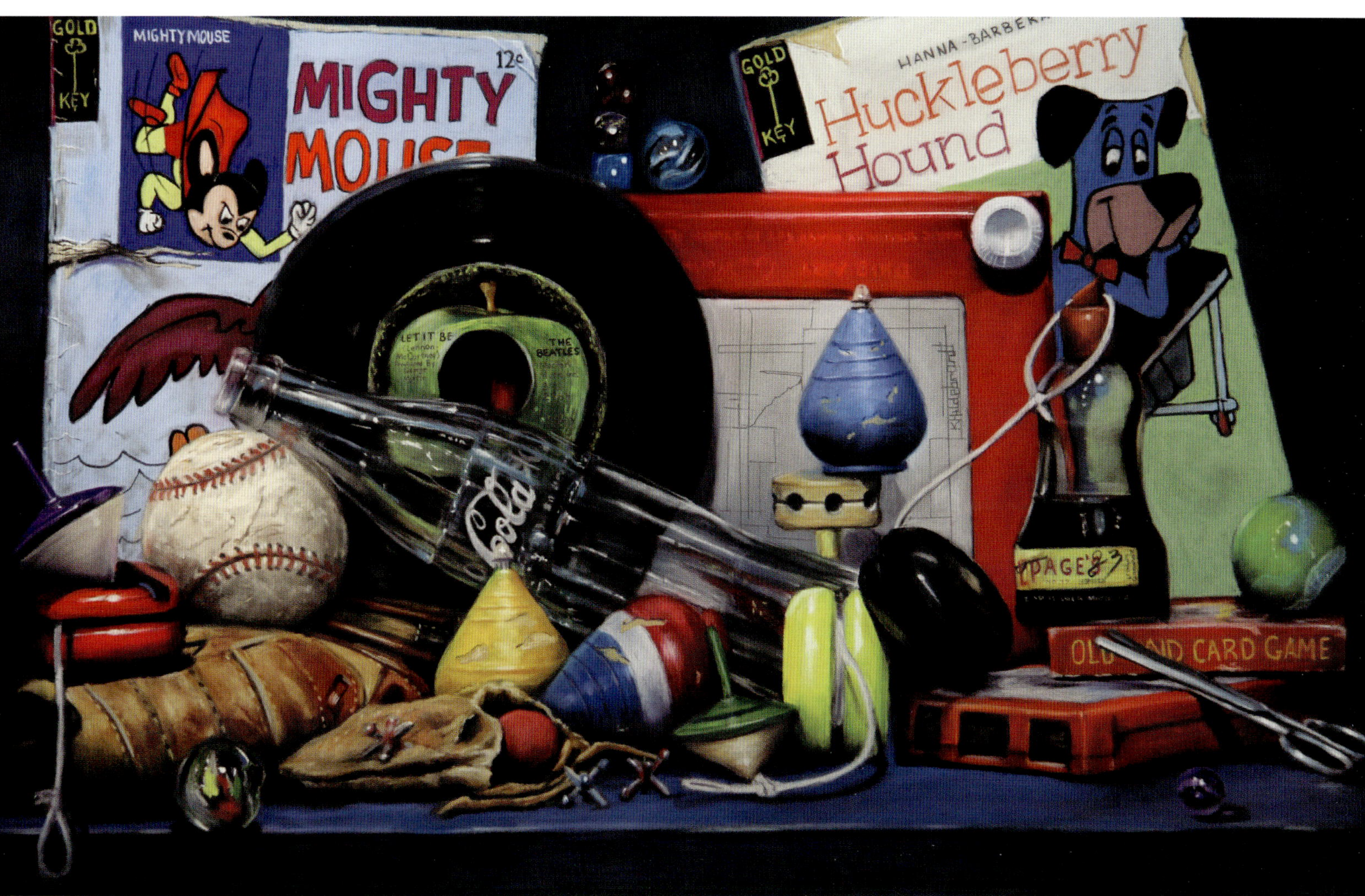

As I was setting up and arranging the composition for *Things Go Better With*, I knew that to create it convincingly was going to be a challenge due to all the contrasting textures. The paper, leather, wood, metal, plastic and glass all had to be approached differently. The transparency of the Coke bottle was partly achieved by distorting the objects seen through and behind it. The smooth, worn leather of the baseball glove had to be treated differently from the rough leather of the jack pouch. Some of the various techniques I used to create the illusion of these diverse textures are using the tip of a pastel versus the side, selecting a harder pastel or a soft stick, reaching for a pastel pencil, varying the pressure of the strokes.

▲ **THINGS GO BETTER WITH**
Kathy Hildebrandt
Pastel on PastelMat paper
16" x 27½" (41cm x 70cm)

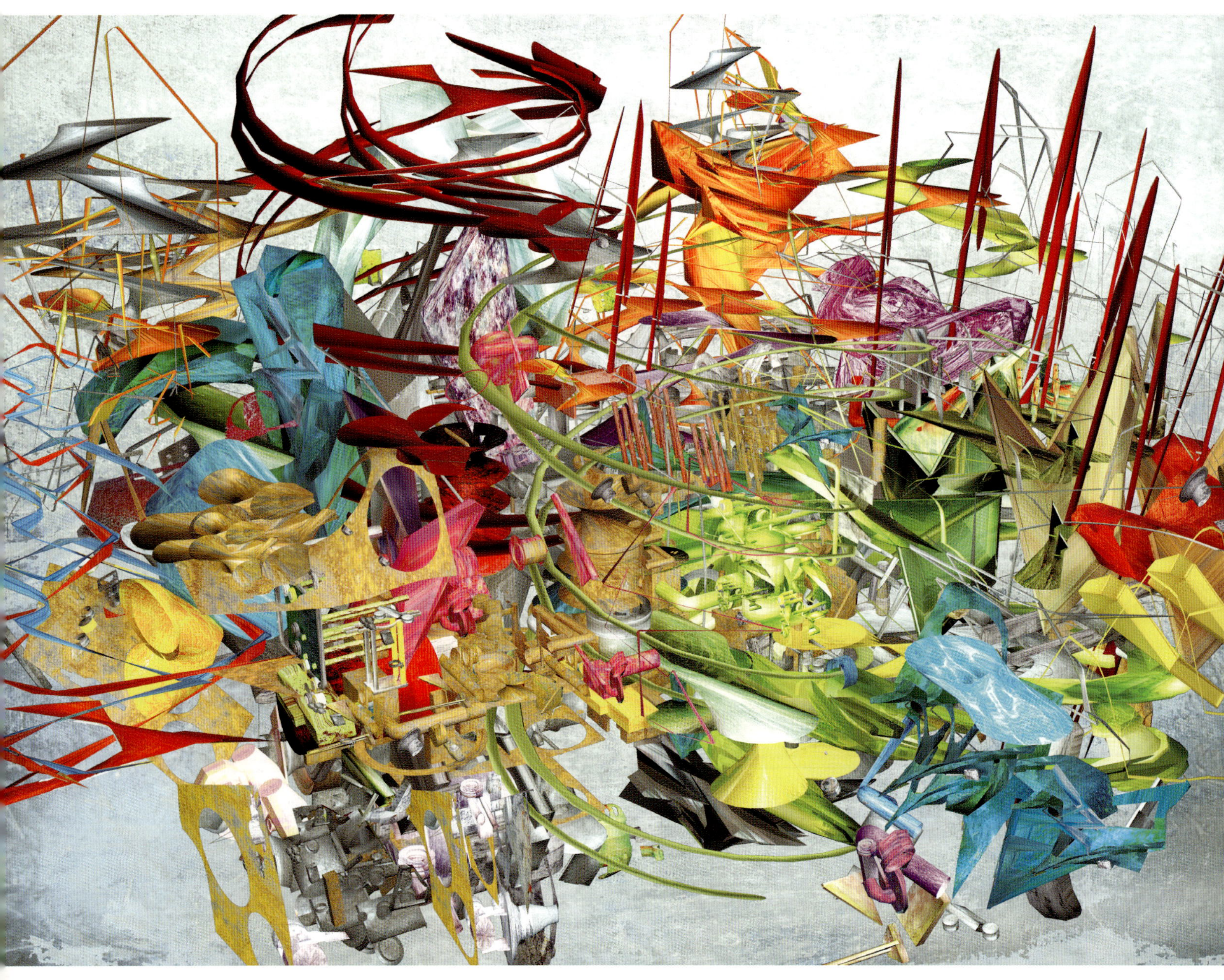

▲ THOSE WHO AFFIRM THE SPONTANEITY OF EVERY EVENT

Ryota Matsumoto

Mixed media on paper

33" × 47" (84cm × 119cm)

This is a hybrid drawing technique combining both traditional media (ink, acrylic and graphite) and digital media (algorithmic processing, scripting and image compositing with custom software). The intertwined texture is attained by the application of layers of tones, colors and translucent materials. The work explores the spatio-temporal conditions of our ever-evolving urban environments and acts as the catalyst for the speculative changes in notions of cities, societies and cultures.

Whatever medium I'm using I strive to develop texture in the application. Colored pencil can be a slow medium, so since there were fresh peaches in my setup, I took a photo taking care to create depth and drama with the lighting. Working on a sanded surface allows me to apply the pigment in a sketchy fashion, building up layers of color. This creates soft edges and allows for the pencil strokes to become more prominent on the last layers of the drawing—revealing not how I literally see my subject matter, but rather how I feel about it.

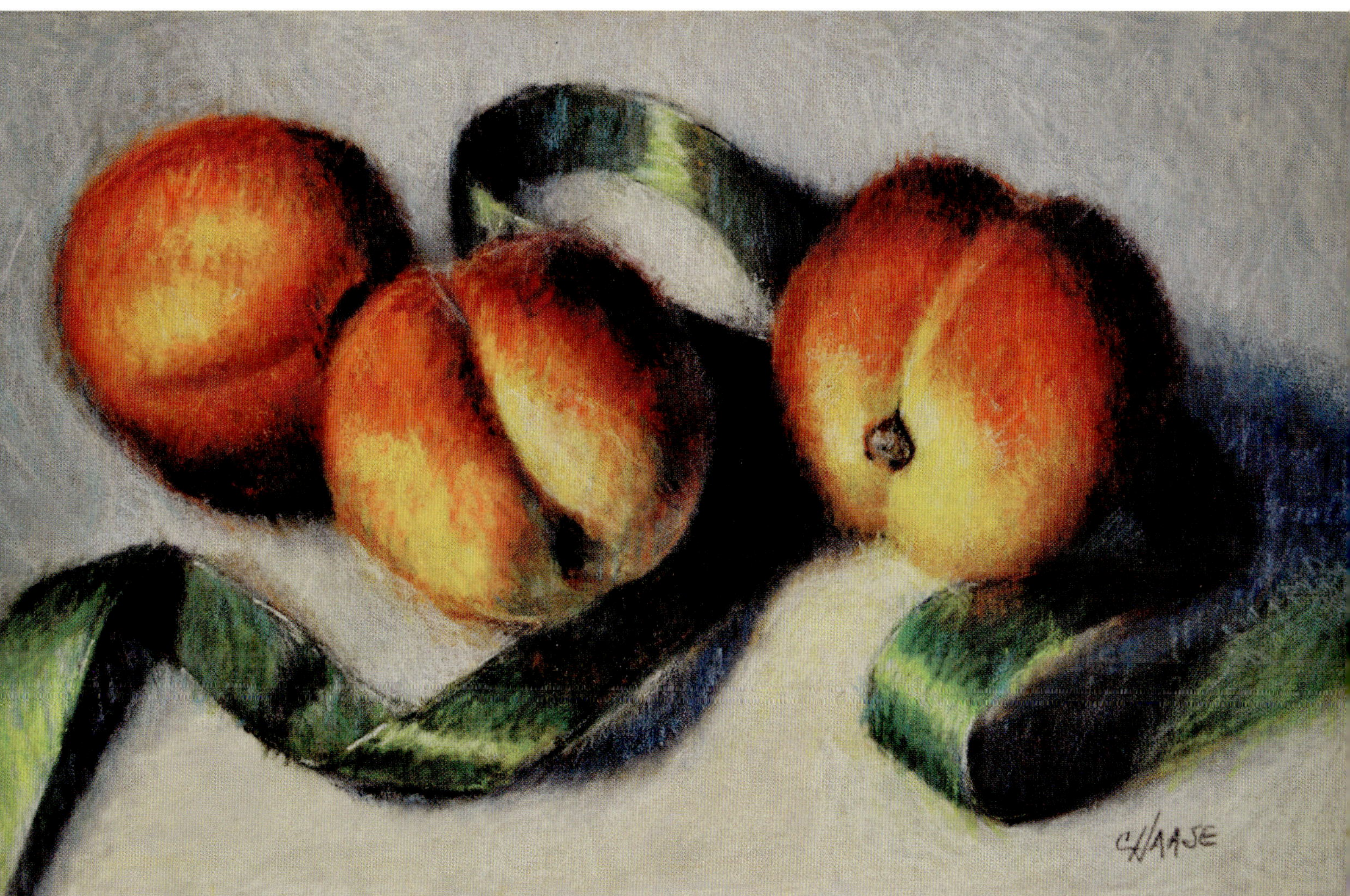

"Texture in a drawing shows me the hand of the artist." —CYNTHIA HAASE

My drawing was inspired by a tin I found on the South Fork of Long Island, New York. I loved its weathered look. To set up this nostalgic still life, I contrasted the tin and eggs with the dark background and table. I worked from both life and a reference photo. Using a heated Icarus drawing board for blending, I applied water-soluble wax crayons to the background and then used multiple layers of colored pencil throughout the rest of the drawing. To achieve the textures of the tin, I turned up the heat and was able to move the wax around, almost painting with it. Finally, turning the heat off, my drawing was completed by burnishing and adding additional highlights.

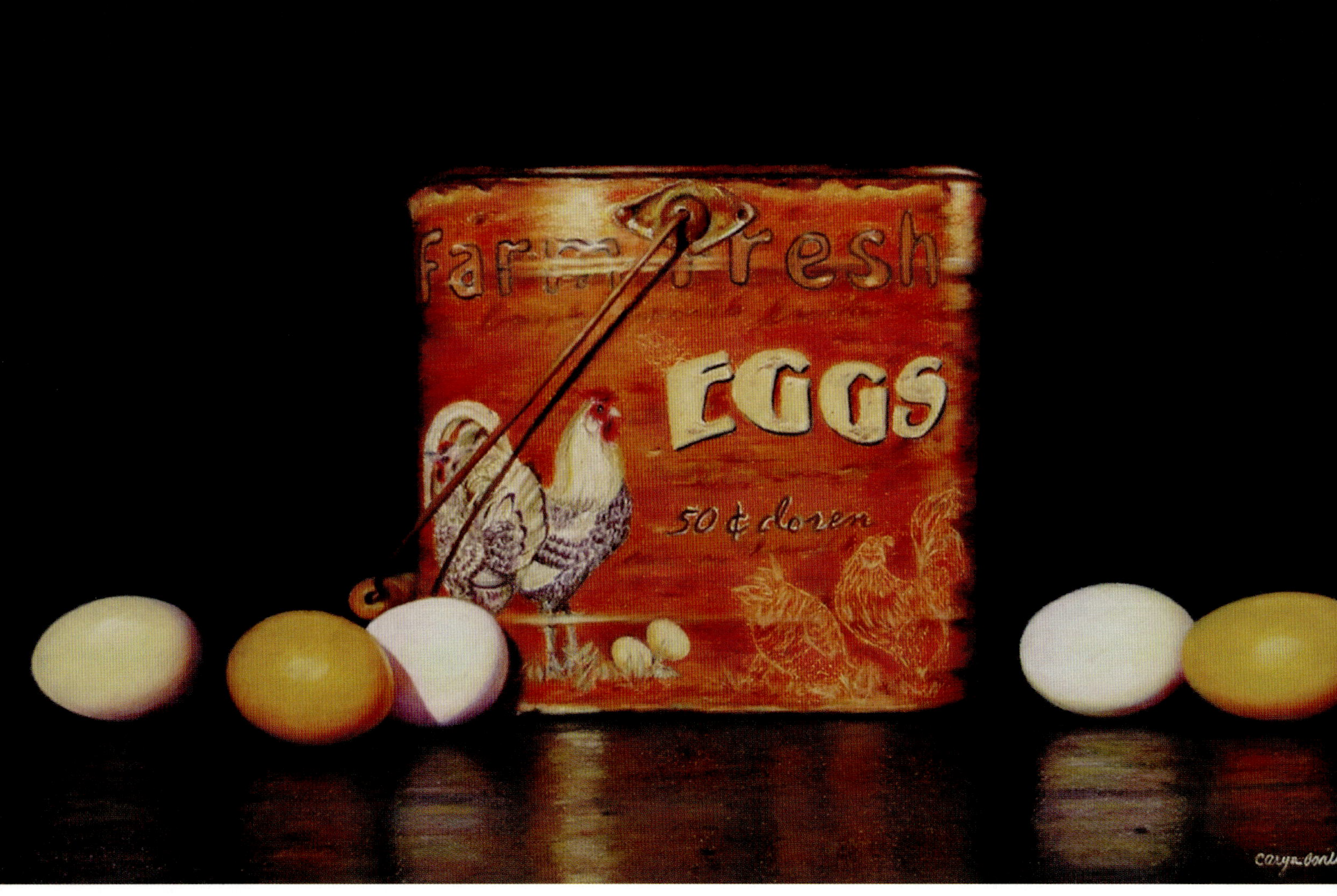

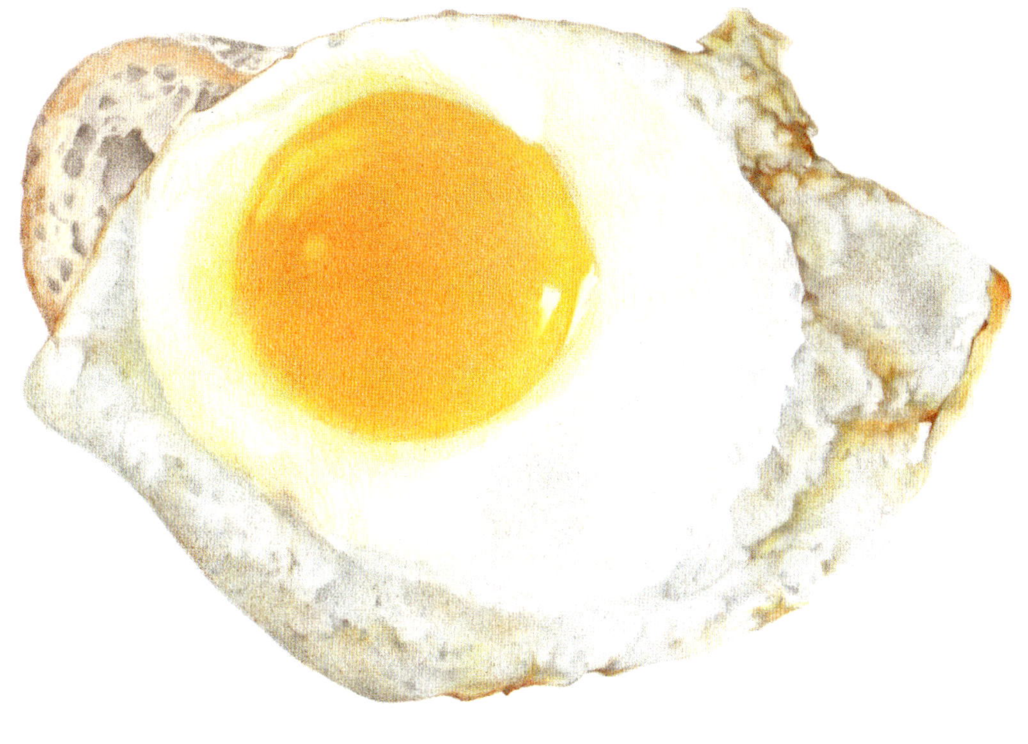

◄ **FRIED EGG ON SOURDOUGH TOAST**
Paula Pertile
Colored pencil on paper
17" × 11" (43cm × 28cm)

I love drawing food in an architectural way, showing the top, side and section views. The idea for this one came while I was contemplating lunch. I fried up the egg in some butter, toasted a thick slice of sourdough bread, plopped the egg on there and took some reference photos. I drew the whole piece with colored pencils on paper, without solvents or any special techniques. The textures in the sourdough were most challenging; the runny egg, most fun. It was also a delicious lunch.

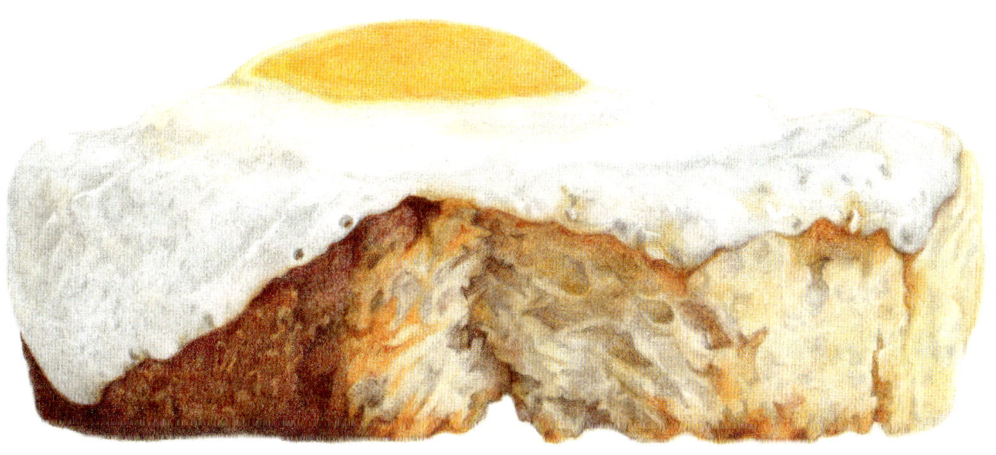

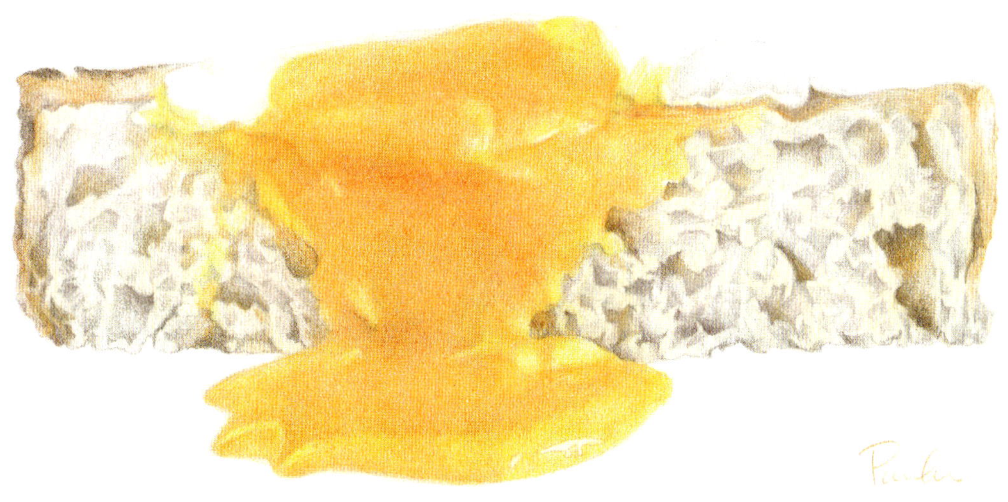

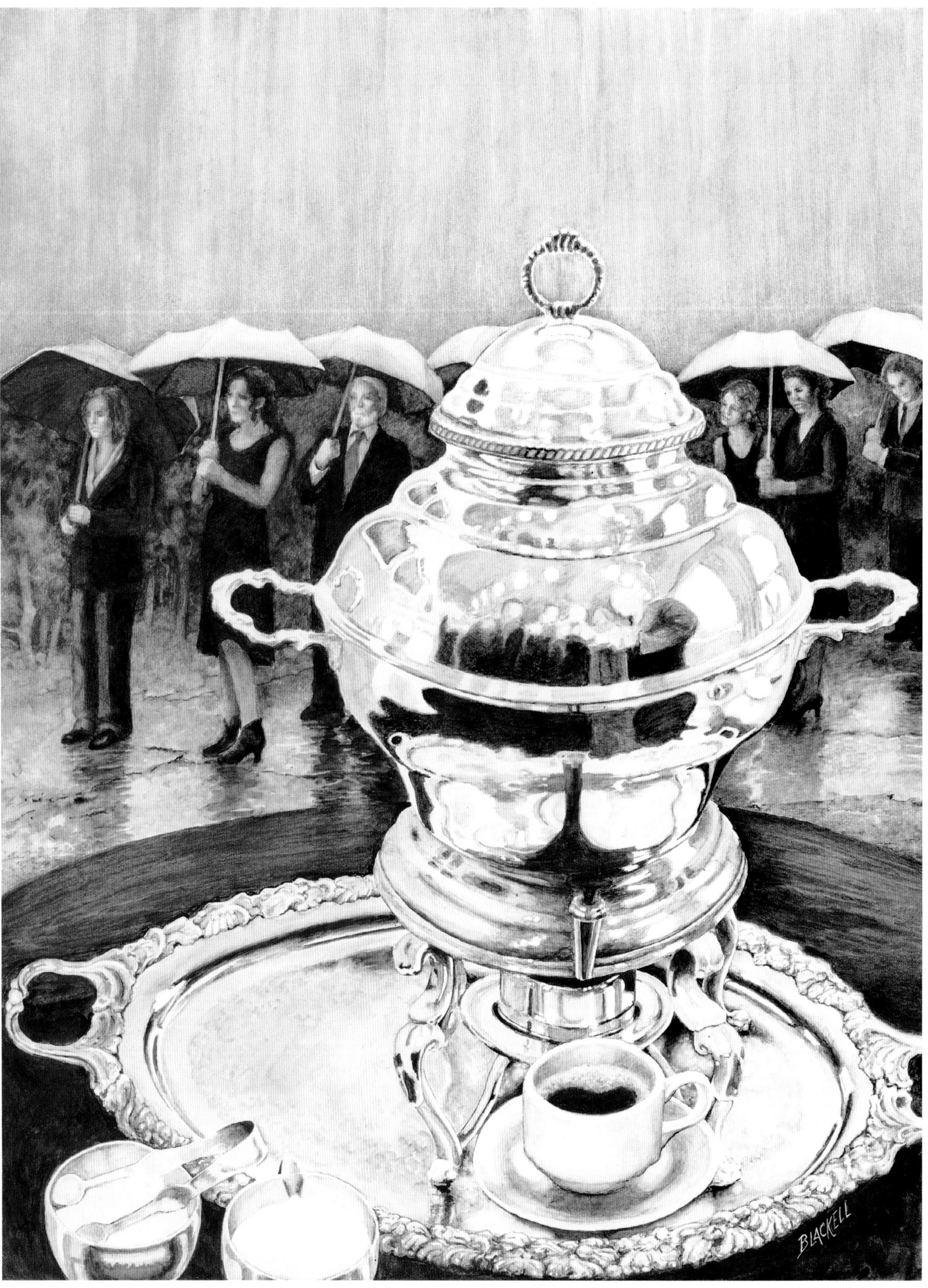
BLACKELL

◄ THE FUNERAL
Margo Blackell
Pencil and water-soluble graphite on 140-lb.
(300gsm) watercolor paper
24" × 18" (61cm × 46cm)

In order to do a drawing of this emotionally packed day, I found photographs that best summed up the experience. The coffee samovar offers an elegant antithesis to the weather outside. The two exist in the same space, as they do in my memory, rather than viewing the outdoor scene through a window, which was my original plan. The texture of the silver urn right next to the wet pavement emphasizes the contrast between the indoors and outdoors. The urn reflects the inside lights and the mourners gathered around for sharing of memories. On the outside, people stand alone with their own thoughts, physically separated by the perimeters of the umbrellas.

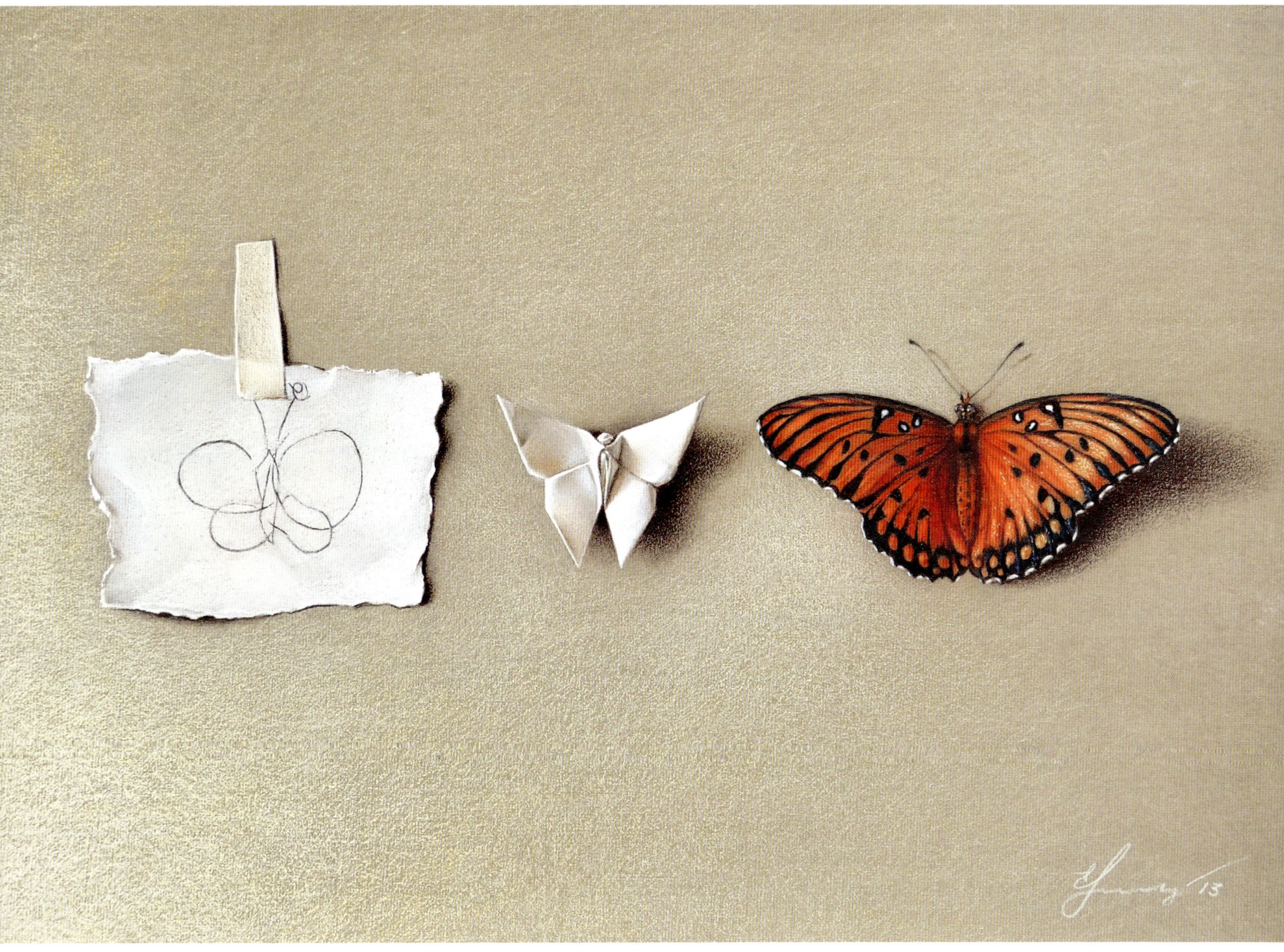

For this trompe l'oeil artwork I primed the beige mount board with clear fine-tooth Colourfix Primer to resemble a plastered wall. I constructed my idea on the board itself. The only thing I did not have was a real butterfly, so I made an imitation—which my cat tried to catch! I photographed the installation and worked mostly from the photo, referencing the installation for details. The concept is a statement of how human creativity—the ability to dream—combined with persistence and hard work can change the world around us. Dare to dream!

▲ PURSUIT OF A DREAM
Elena Kolotusha
Colored pencil on mount board
8" × 13" (20cm × 33cm)

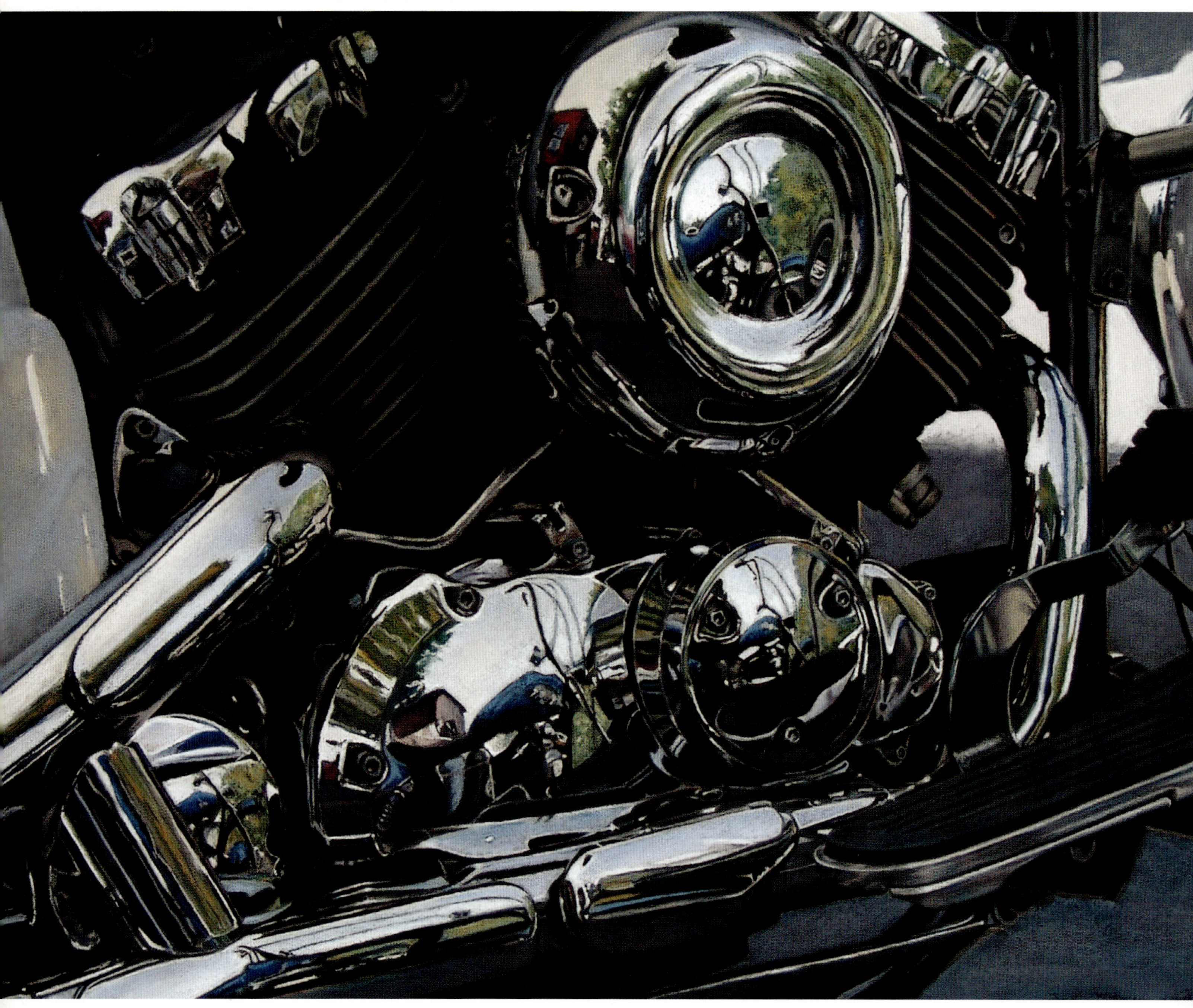

▲ **THE BLUE MOTORCYCLE**
J. Kay Gordon
Soft pastel on black Canson Mi-Teintes
18" × 24" (46cm × 61cm)

The underlying theme of this work is not the motorcycle we see first, but the blue one that is evident in a multitude of forms in the reflections. Those reflections can be as subtle as a narrow stripe or a blue haze. Texture is essential here for the eye to "see" the elements as chrome, plastic, unfinished steel, rubber and pavement. I am frequently asked, "How did you get the chrome to shine?" Or "Where did you find a silver pastel?" Of course, there is no shine or silver color here. The eye interprets the crispness of the reflections to be shiny chrome and decides it is silver. I worked on black paper, starting with a careful drawing and using white charcoal for the highlights. Before applying the pastels, the paper was the dark value of my sketch. The reference was a portion of a photo I took at a rally.

This charcoal drawing was done from life as a texture assignment for the atelier I attend. My goal was to precisely and accurately capture the variety of textures and personalities of the objects. I found I was able to represent a spectrum of textures by using a blending stump to manipulate the roughness of the watercolor paper. I drew this piece after I had recently been married. The objects in the right corner speak to my juvenile interests, and to the left is a photograph of my wife. The objects are crammed in the corner to represent my desire to "put away childish things" and move on to higher priorities. The wood grain in the background added an interesting unity and texture to the drawing.

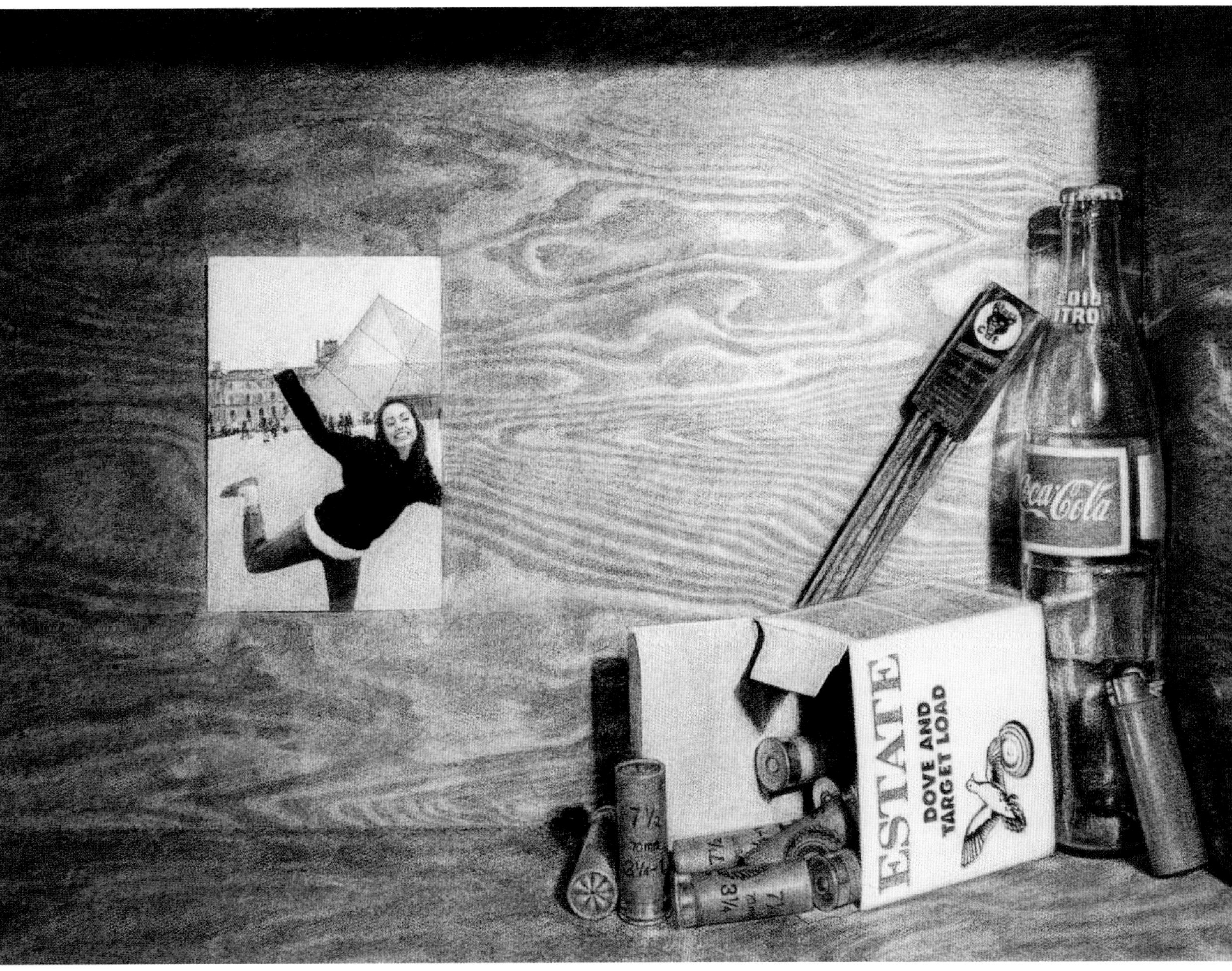

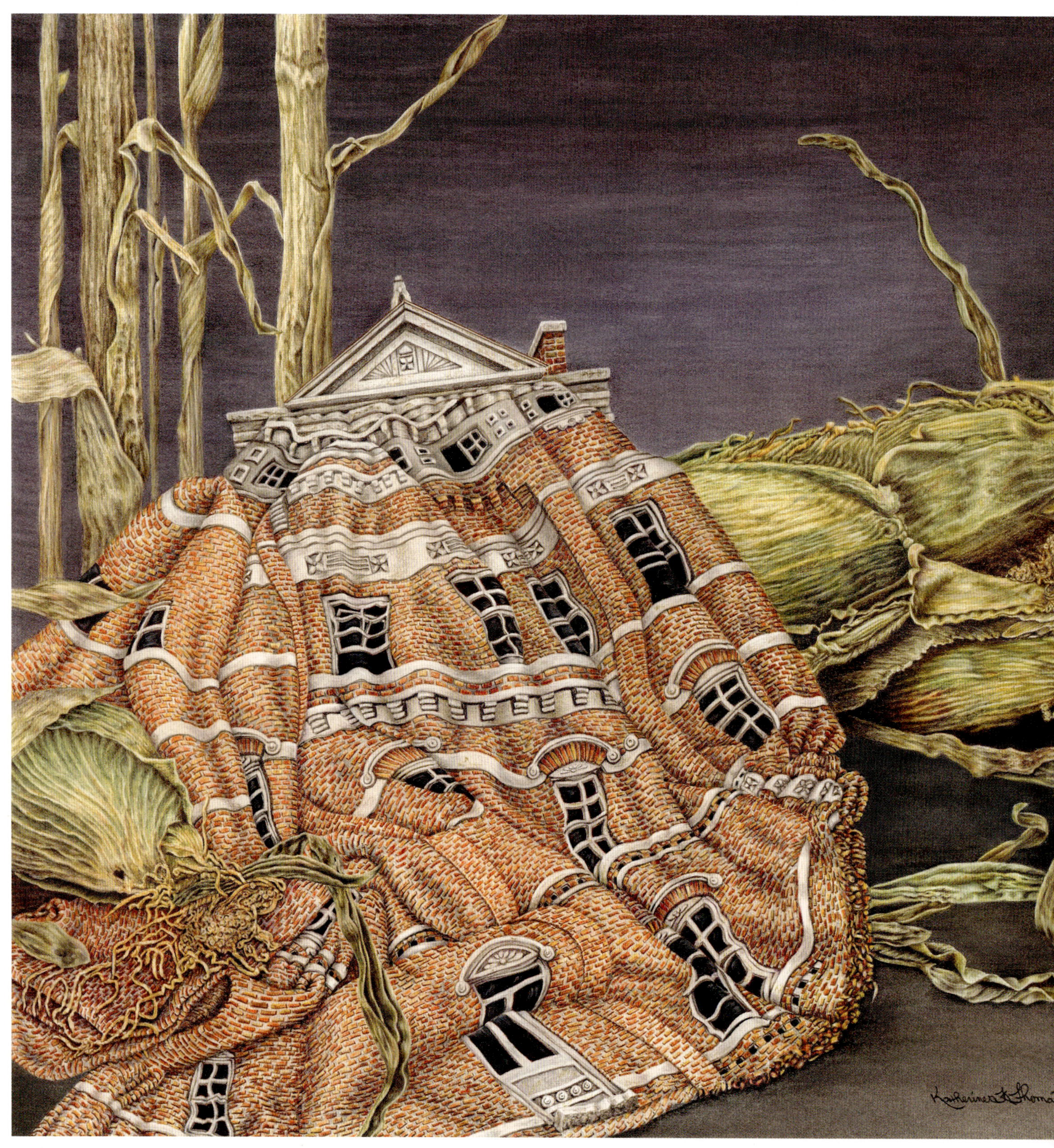

▲ OUT OF SEASON
Katherine Thomas
Colored pencil on hot-pressed Fabriano
18" × 18" (46cm × 46cm)

Out of Season is a reflection on the passage of time. The corn has begun to mellow, changing in color and texture. Similarly, the architecture and masonry of the brick house bow to the aging process. To achieve this transformation, I first set up a still life using the corn and a table napkin. I drew a complete graphite study, then transferred that drawing to the Fabriano paper for the colored pencil version. While drawing the house, I followed the contours of the fabric and used a ruler to correctly size the windows and bricks. To keep the perspective accurate, each window called for different vanishing points on the horizon as each was oriented on a different plane. The erosion of the house is metaphorical, reflecting on the way time inevitably affects all things.

In a local vintage shop I was taken by this distressed, worn chair, especially the balding velvet with the woven fabric backing peeking through. Everything from the chipped wood frame to the exposed stuffing and lining added to the character. Then I spotted the dirty broken doll and added it to my photo to enhance the story. I use unconventional tools such as cotton swabs and makeup applicators to blend the charcoal for detail. After the drawing was finished, I added a hint of color to the fabric and doll with chalk pastels to give texture and depth. My drawing symbolizes memories and how they deteriorate over time and become fractured, faded and dark.

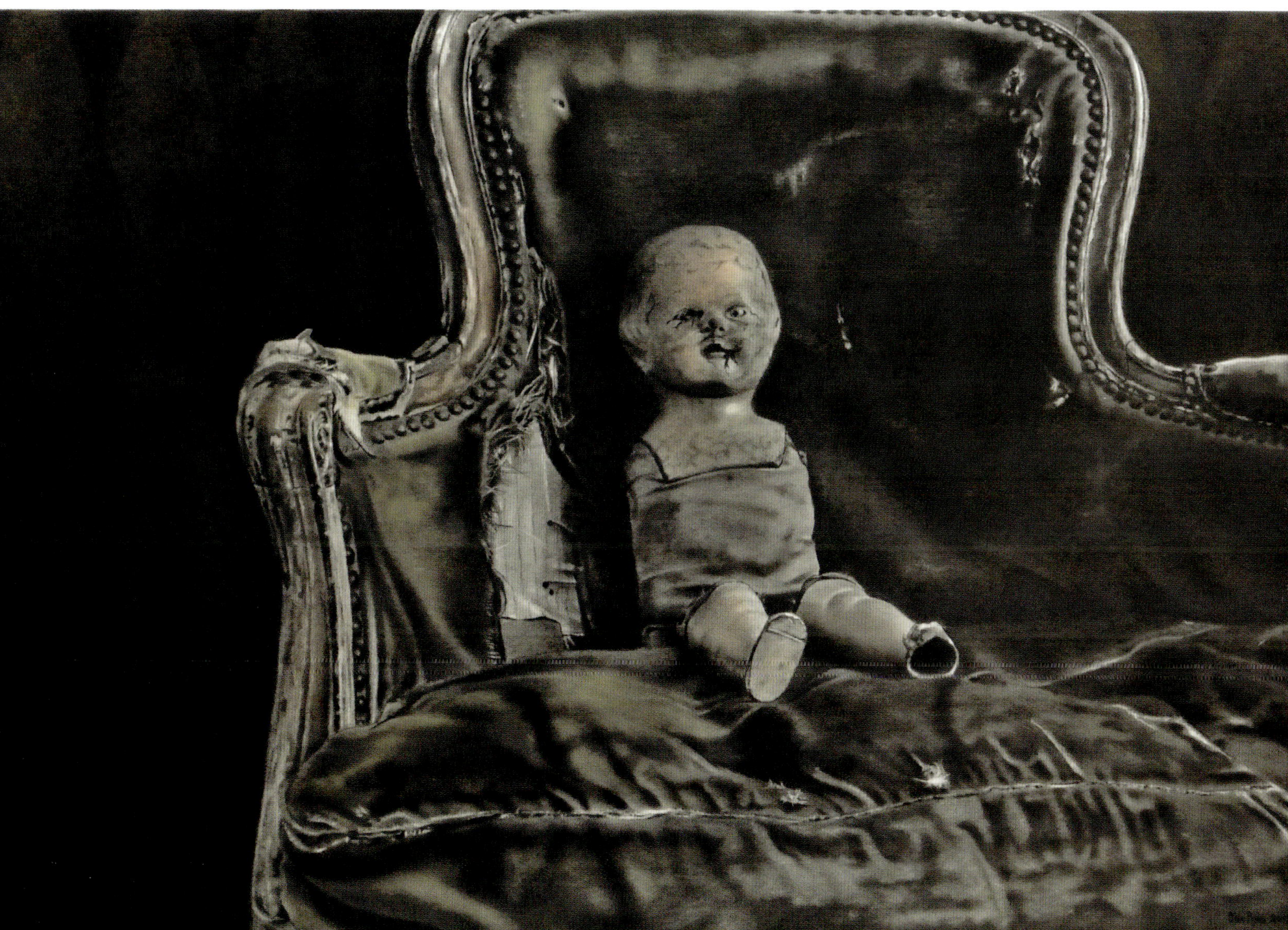

"Adding a hint of color to a dark charcoal drawing can give it life and depth, and add new dimension to the piece." —DAN PYLE

I love to transform everyday objects into luminous artworks. Capturing the transparency of glass objects is one of the most challenging aspects of the photorealistic still-life painting I enjoy doing. For this work I placed the bulbs on a colored surface, and with my digital camera I took many photos not using the flash. I made adjustments to color and lighting until I was satisfied. In this case I used a grid to accurately transfer the image to the surface. Then things are easy; I just paint what I see—and I see colors! I used Conté a Paris pastel pencils and Unison pastel sticks.

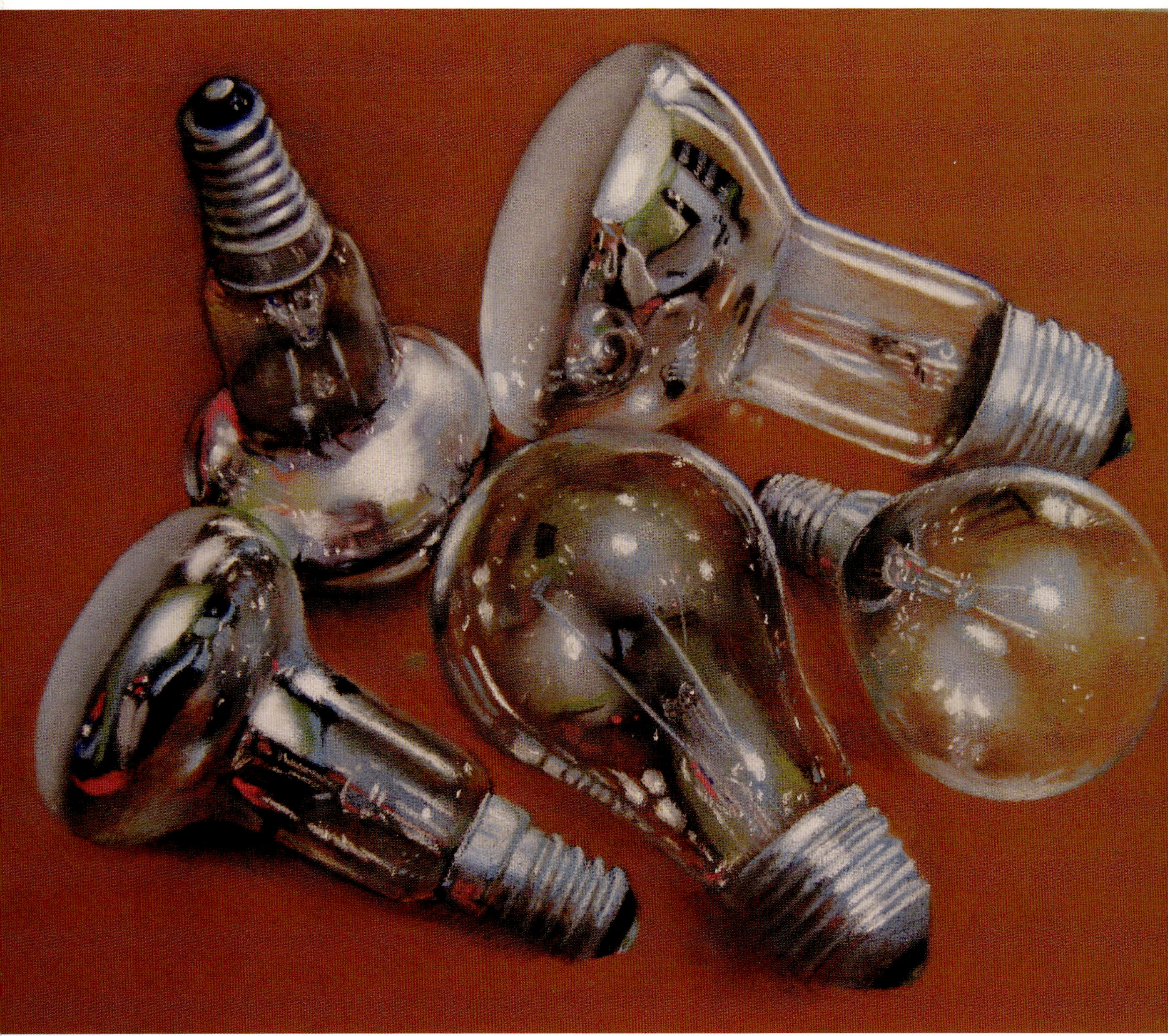

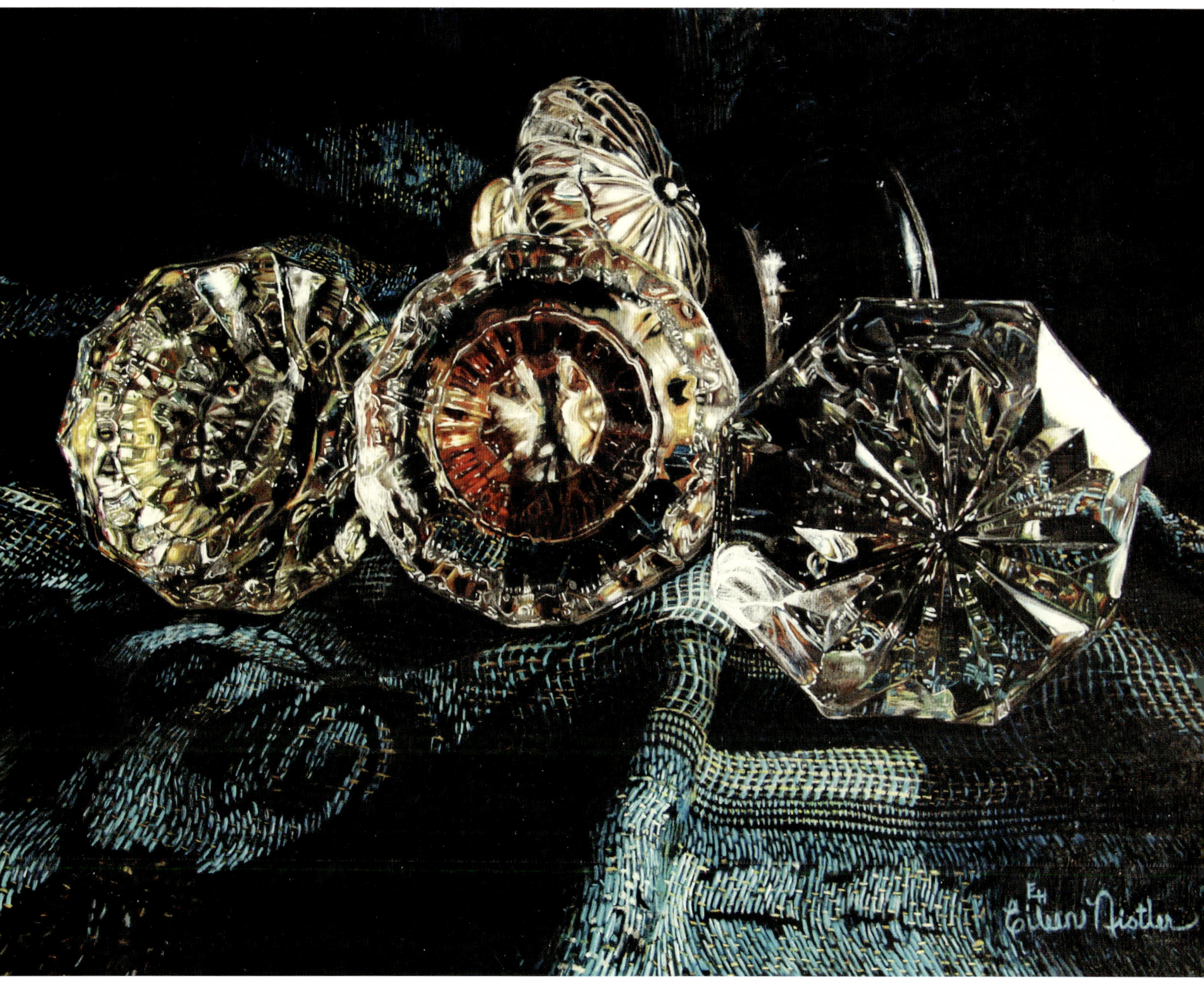

Doorknobs are objects of beauty! As a child I loved the television show *Bewitched*. Aunt Clara was the befuddled witch who stole doorknobs, and was known to often polish her collection. She was, however, sometimes on the wrong side of the door when she stole them. I too have a doorknob collection (though I never stole any of them). Some are from the homes that I grew up in. I used to think of them as exotic jewels or the magical crystal ball of a gypsy. In this painting I paired my crystal doorknobs with a richly textured piece of fabric that my daughter gave to me. I really enjoy drawing texture. And colored pencils are wonderful for little details.

▲ **AUNT CLARA'S COLLECTION III**
Eileen Nistler
Colored pencil on black 4-ply museum board
16" × 20" (41cm × 51cm)

"To reveal texture, look to where the light plays with the surface." —KIRA MENDEZ

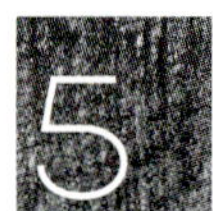

5

The Human Spirit

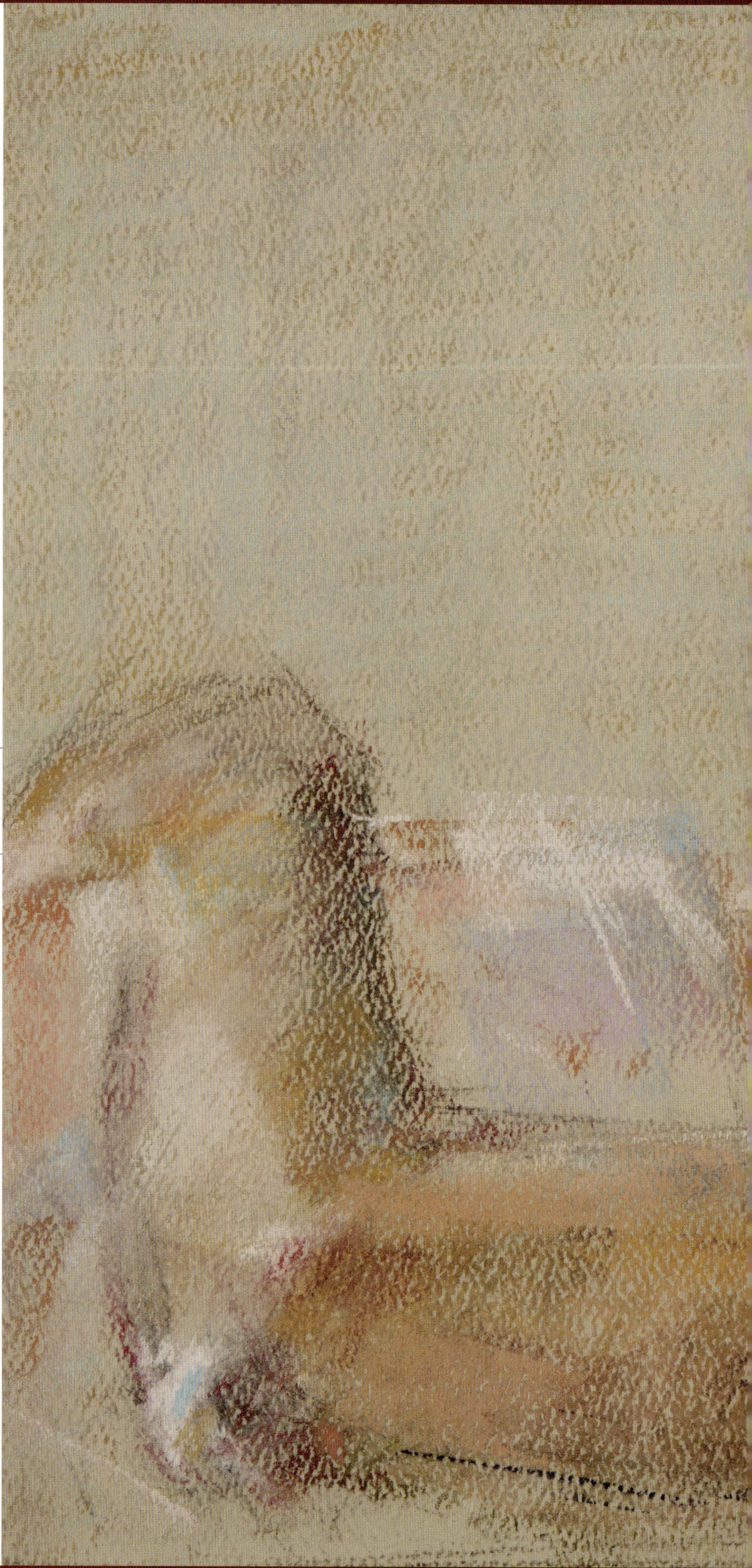

▶ **MORNING SUNLIGHT**
Kira Mendez
Pastel on paper
9" × 13" (23cm × 33cm)

Working from the live model during a morning session with wonderful natural light, I wanted to express the sense of being bathed and caressed by the light and to explore the light acting on the different surfaces. I chose a neutral paper that would blend with the skin tones and began with charcoal, drawing just enough to capture the gesture. I then laid in warm/cool undertones and shadows with hard pastel, using the side of the stick, switching to soft pastels to establish the form, tonal range and then final touches.

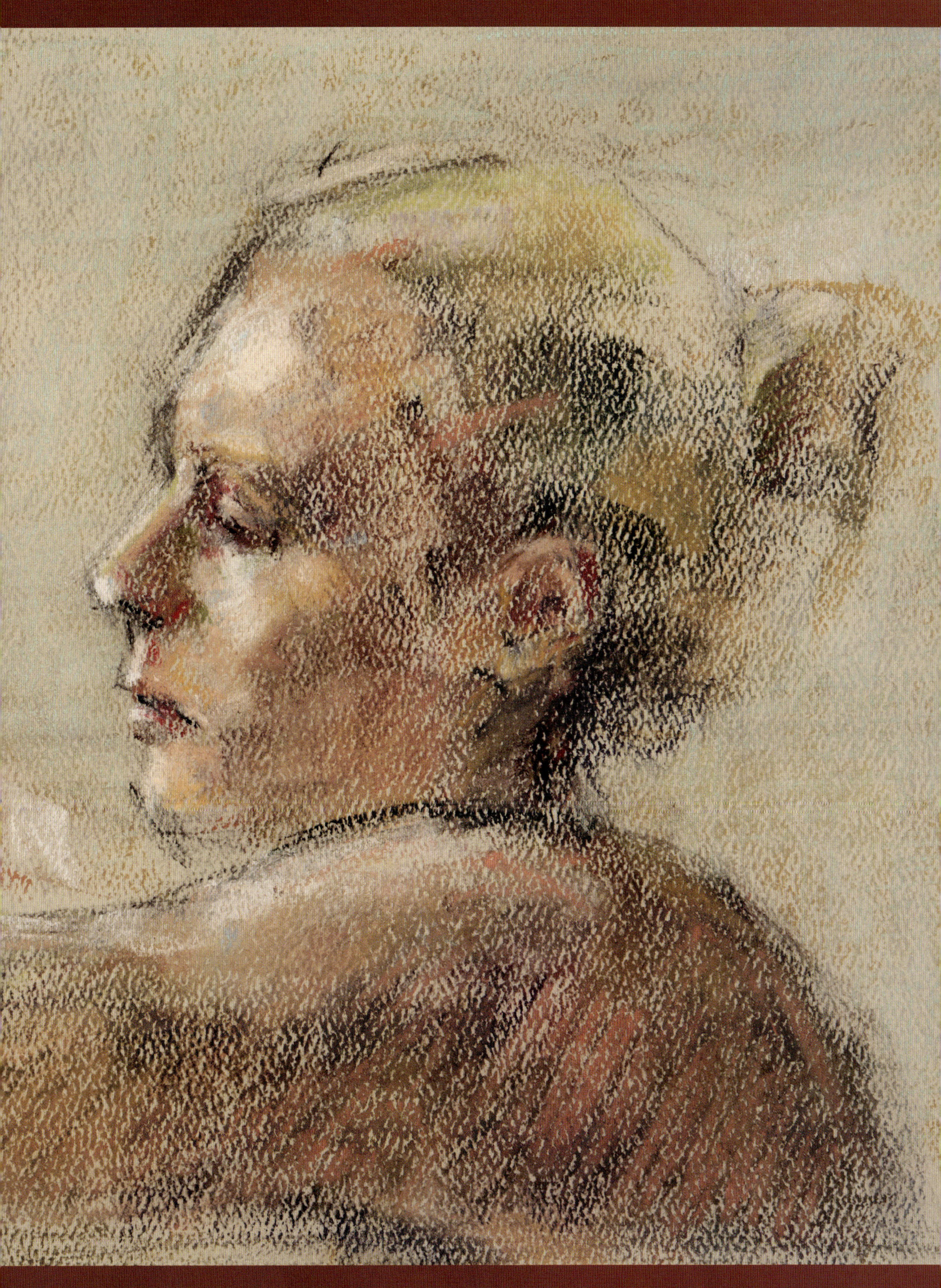

"If I find that I'm falling a little in love with the subject(s) of the piece,
I'm usually happy with it when I'm finished." —VICKIE DORSAM

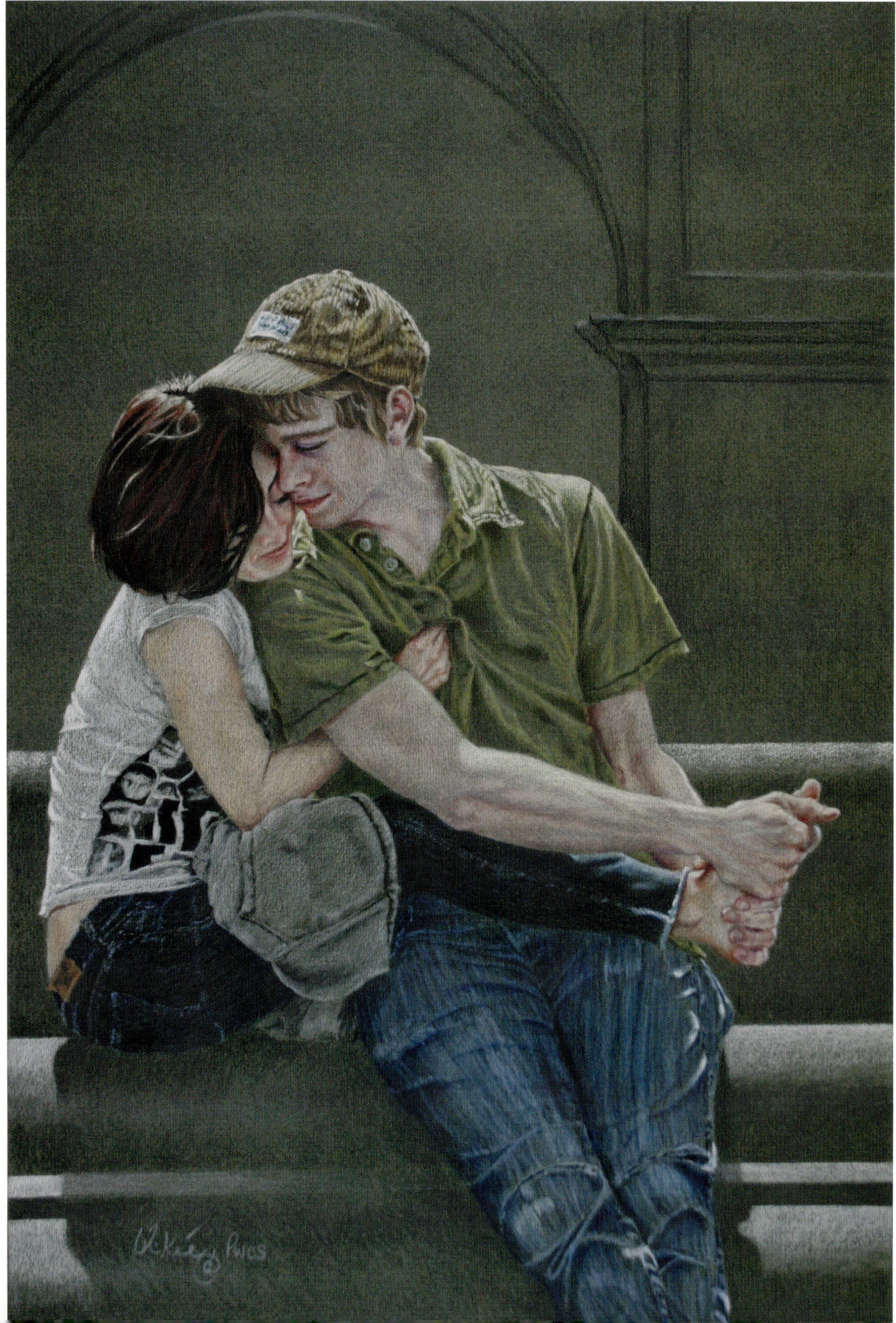

Love of drawing made working in colored pencil a joy from day one. I work in other mediums, but colored pencil can be more precise, intentional, detailed—and no worries about paint drying or hard edges! Working from two or more of my own photos, I layer colors slowly, careful not to fill the paper's tooth too soon. With my camera, I'm happiest in a place with people who are busy doing their thing in the sun. I don't try for a portrait but to re-create both facial expressions and body language. I sought to show his fair complexion entwined with her olive skin, showing their love with no boundaries.

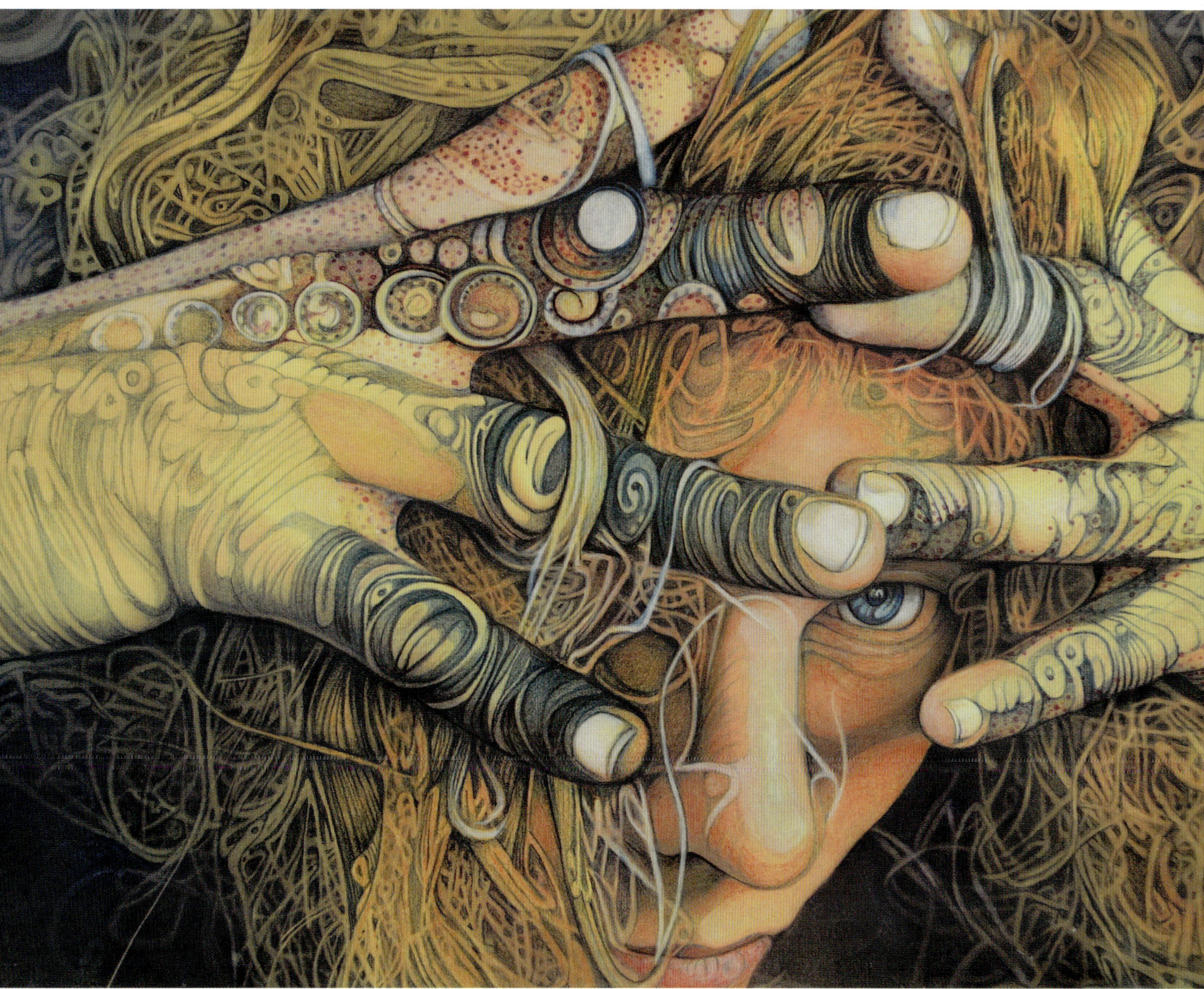

In this colored pencil self-portrait there are two dominant uses of texture: The first is the application of a texture on an area where it does not belong—octopus skin placed on a human hand. This incorrectness encourages the viewer to look again and to ask the question, "Why is that there?" Texture is also prominent in the meticulous designing of the hair, which takes on the look of delicately woven pasta. The intricate rendering of the hair also becomes a powerful vehicle for movement and illusional depth.

"To me, texture provides the opportunity for an artist to create works that are chunky, chewy and delicious."

—MARGARET MINARDI

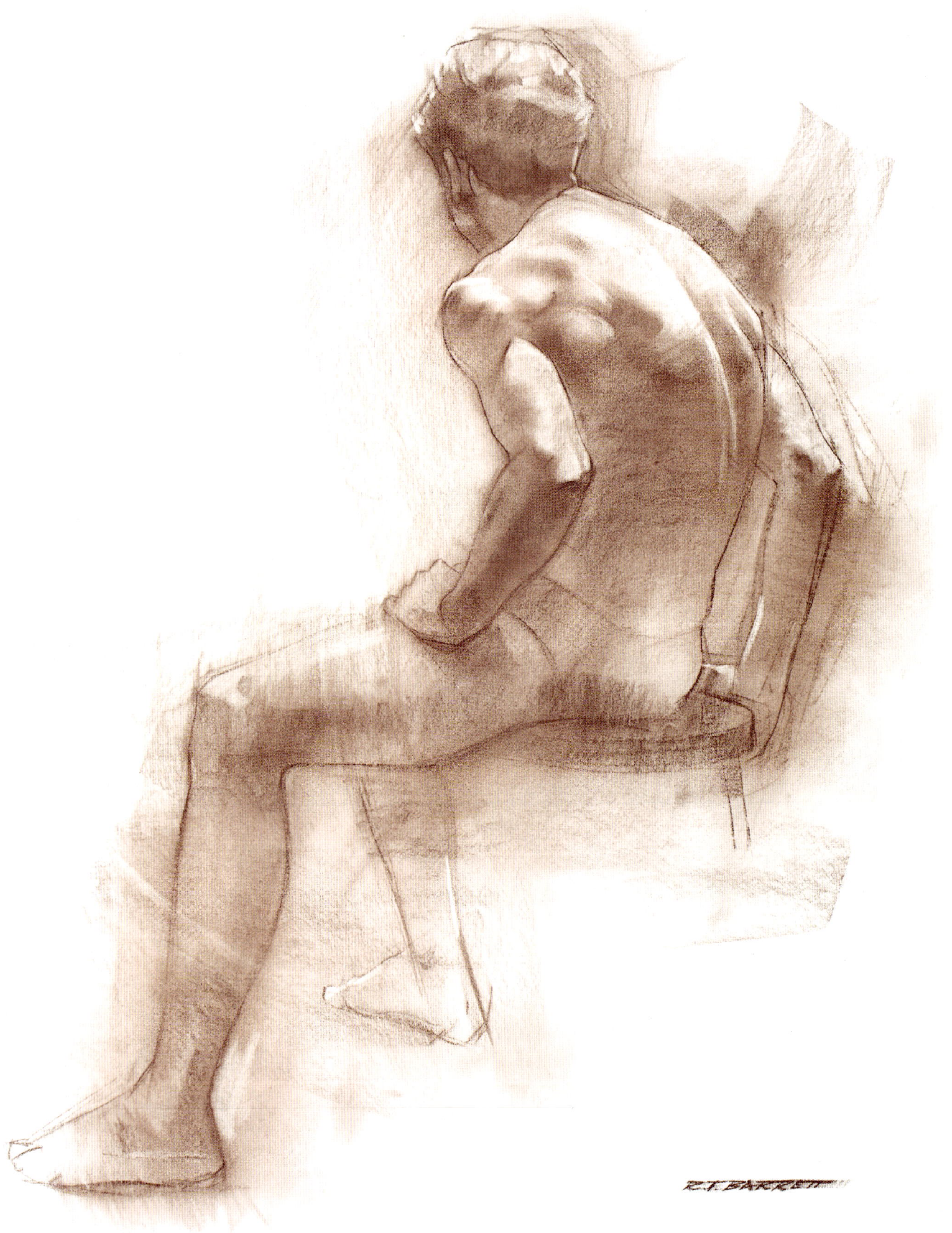

▲ SEATED MALE FIGURE
Robert T. Barrett
NuPastel (Indian Red) on vellum
29" × 23" (74cm × 58cm)

This figure was drawn from life using Indian Red NuPastel. I usually have a box full of the same color sticks so that I can use different ones for broad, more general shapes, and others that have been sharpened for finer detail. I also use my hand or a paper towel for blending edges. I work from more general aspects of the figure, including the overall silhouette, to the smaller details, leaving some parts of the drawing more ambiguous and others more developed. Much of the drawing is lightly toned, and I use a kneaded eraser to lift out the lightest lights.

This figure drawing was made using photo reference. I wanted to experiment with the painterly effect of vine charcoal on a medium-tooth paper. My main inspiration was the charcoal drawings of Russian master Nicolai Fetchin and contemporary artists such as Zhaoming Wu and Henry Yan. One can create beautiful textural effects using vine and compressed charcoal, and the medium gave me the opportunity to play with various contrasts: light and dark, rough texture against smudged/smoothed areas, tight rendering and loose painterly rendering. Finally I also wanted to achieve the effect of the figure emerging out of the page as if the viewer is looking through layers of atmosphere.

▼ FIGURE
Stephen Molyneaux
Vine charcoal and charcoal pencil on
Strathmore paper
23" × 16" (58cm × 41cm)

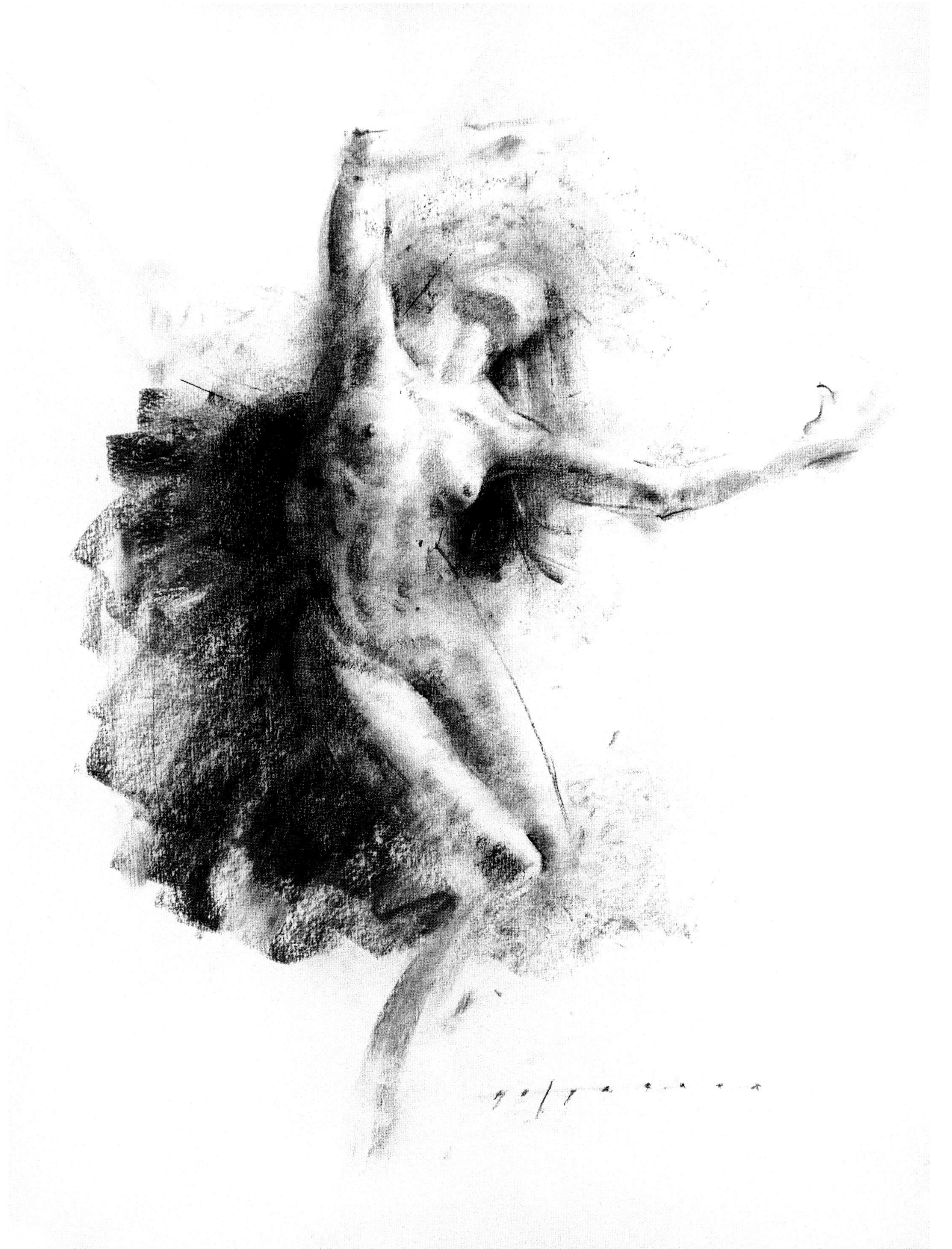

Waterlily evolved from a collection of photographs I have been taking of the water lilies that grow in my small garden fountain. I wanted to create a portrait that would capture the prism-like quality of the water on the pale smooth surface of the water lilies and skin. Not able to submerge a model in my tiny fountain, I held one of my foam life-cast heads under the water among the water lilies so I could capture the shadow placement and the reflective lighting patterns. I combined these images with photos of my model/daughter Abby submerged in the bathtub. One particular photo of Abby's face slightly immersed had that refracting rainbow effect I was looking for.

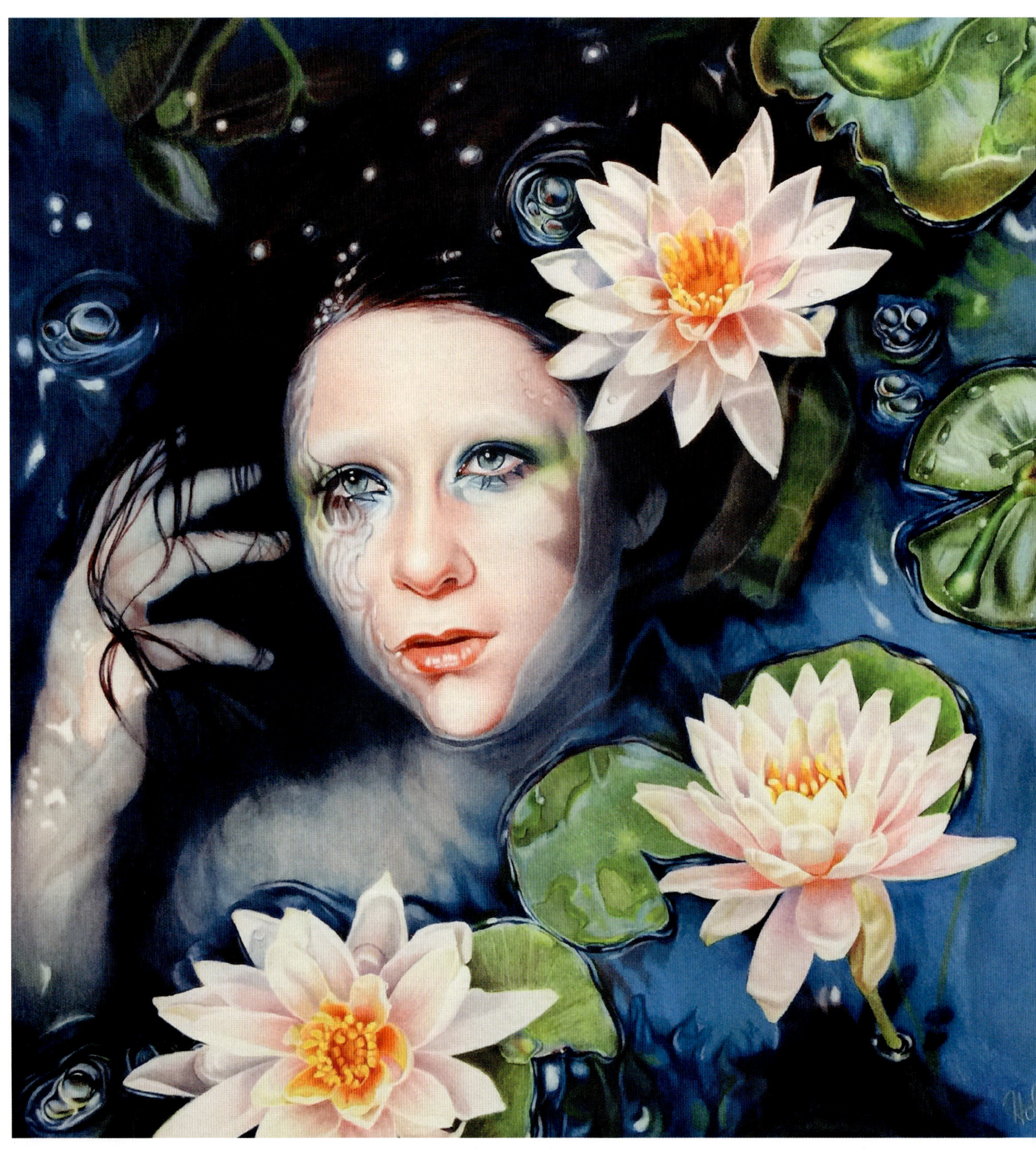

"Use an unexpected combination of media and tools. Juxtapose a smooth texture with a rough one for contrast." —SUZANNE VIGIL

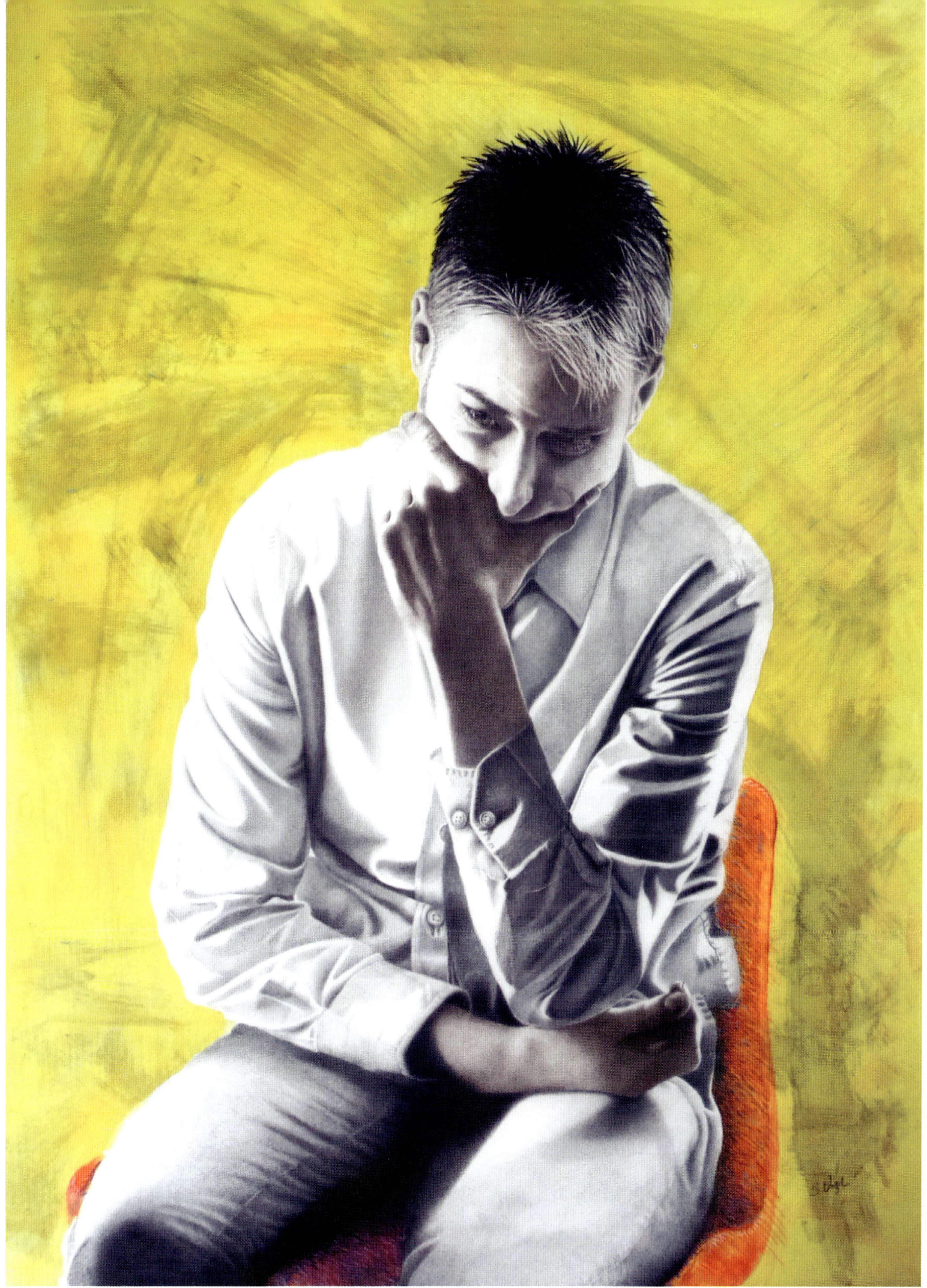

A bright light source shows texture. Use highly contrasting colors for eye-popping results. After the drawing was completed, I painted a background with yellow acrylic paint. Once it dried I used color sticks to suggest a chair. I then flipped the film over and wiped swaths of diluted black acrylic paint to add a subtle texture to the background. In addition, I pencilled areas I wanted to double in density when viewed from the front side.

▲ PENSIVE
Suzanne Vigil
Colored pencil and acrylic on front
and back of acetate
30" × 24" (76cm × 61cm)

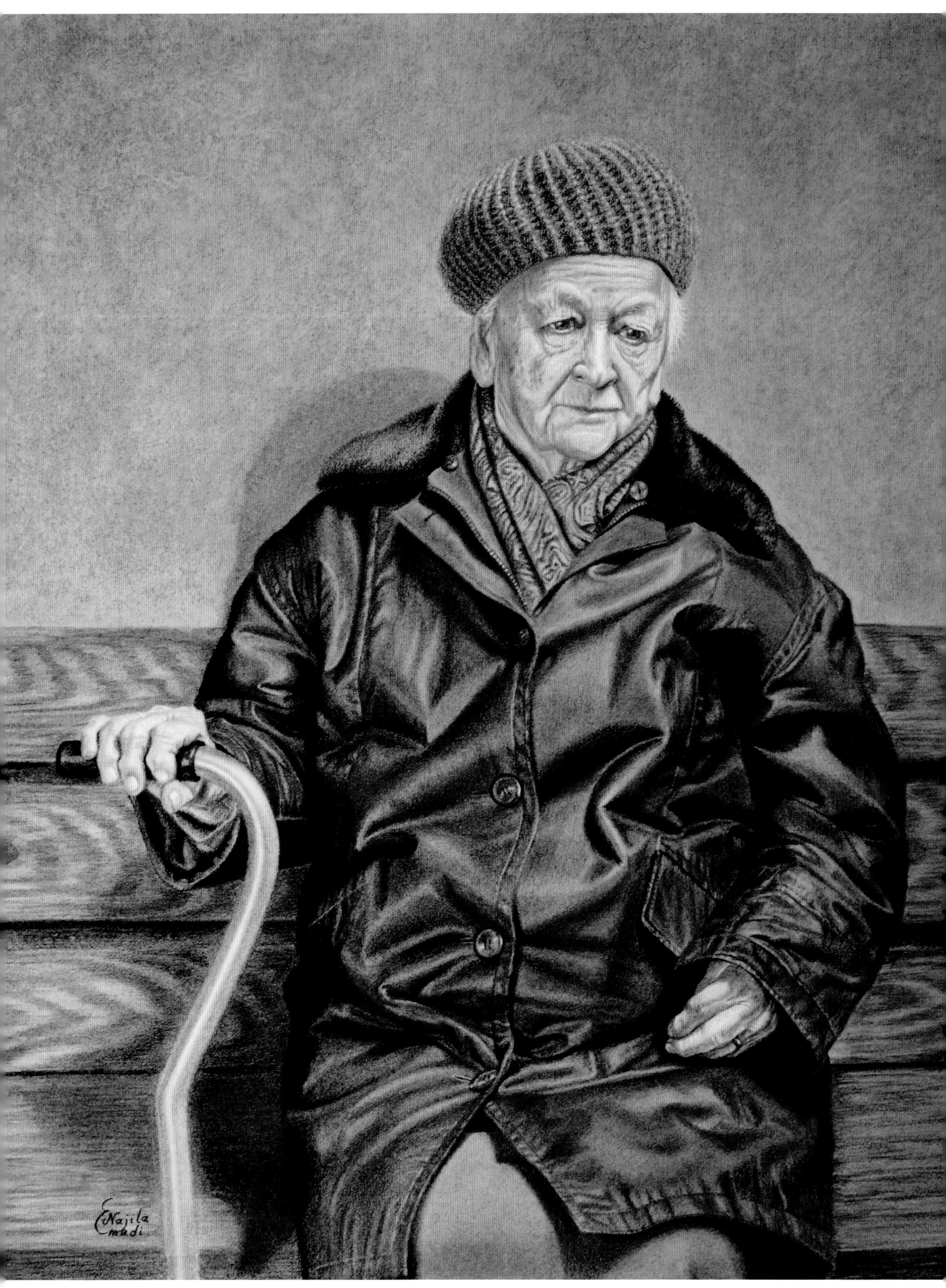

Najila
mhdi

Texture augments the story and character of the subject. The hat, scarf and fur around the coat convey the softness and delicacy of the human spirit, while the leather and the metal cane depict its resiliency. Working from my photo and from life, I used charcoal on midtoned pastel paper. After faintly drawing the large masses of the figure, I identified the darkest and lightest areas of the composition to establish the proper value range. Rendering and refining the piece as a whole, I made adjustments to the background and clothing to enhance the emotional expression.

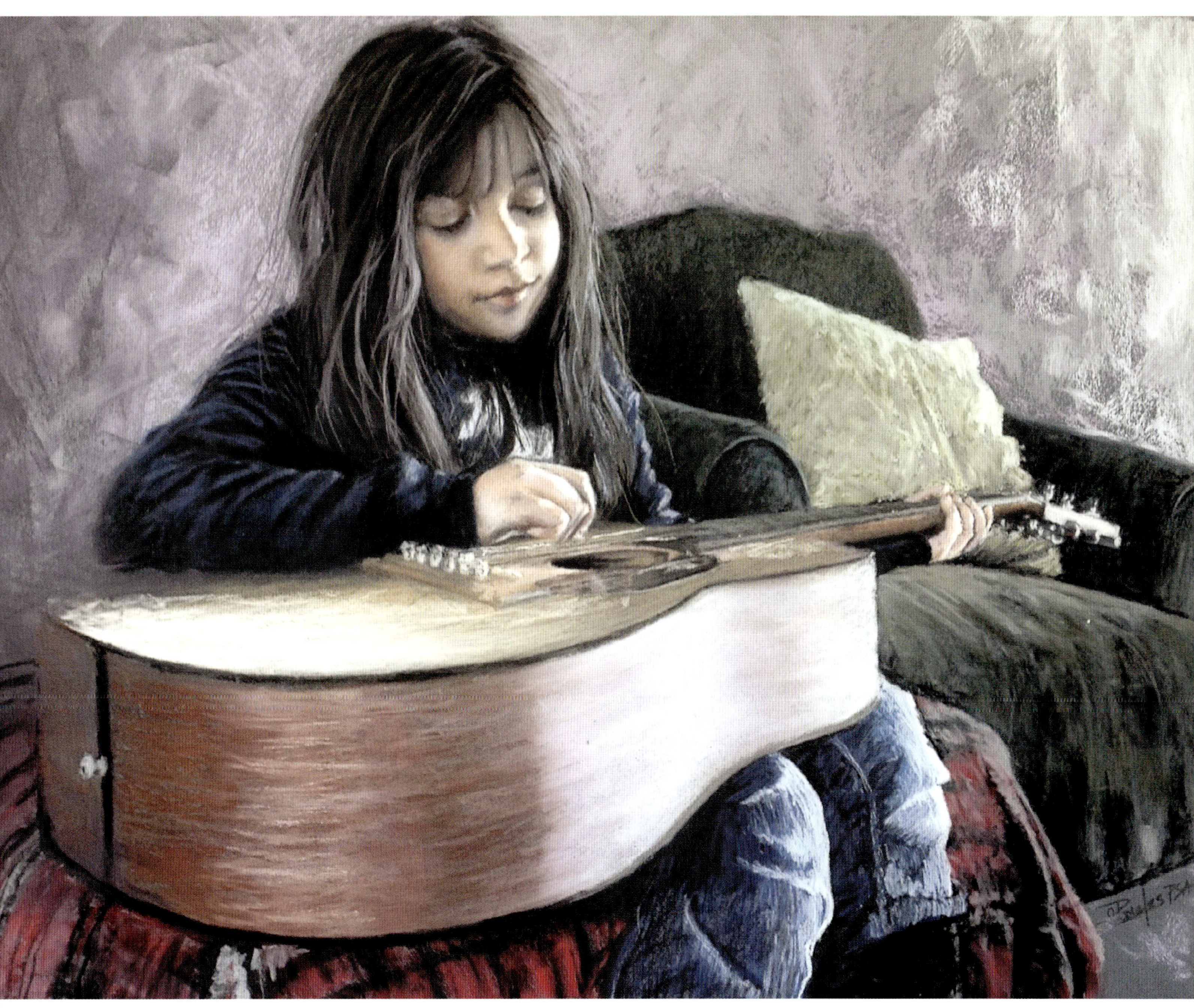

This image was first conceived the moment I saw my daughter trying to play her older brother's guitar. I asked her to pose for me, sketched her in different poses and took a few photos as reference. Then I chose to use pastel (I also work in oils) for its immediacy and luminosity. To create the variety of textures—loose hair, soft skin, clothing, the wood grain of the guitar, the weaves in the fabric of the chair and the pillow, and even the background—I used different strokes from short to long, wide to fine.

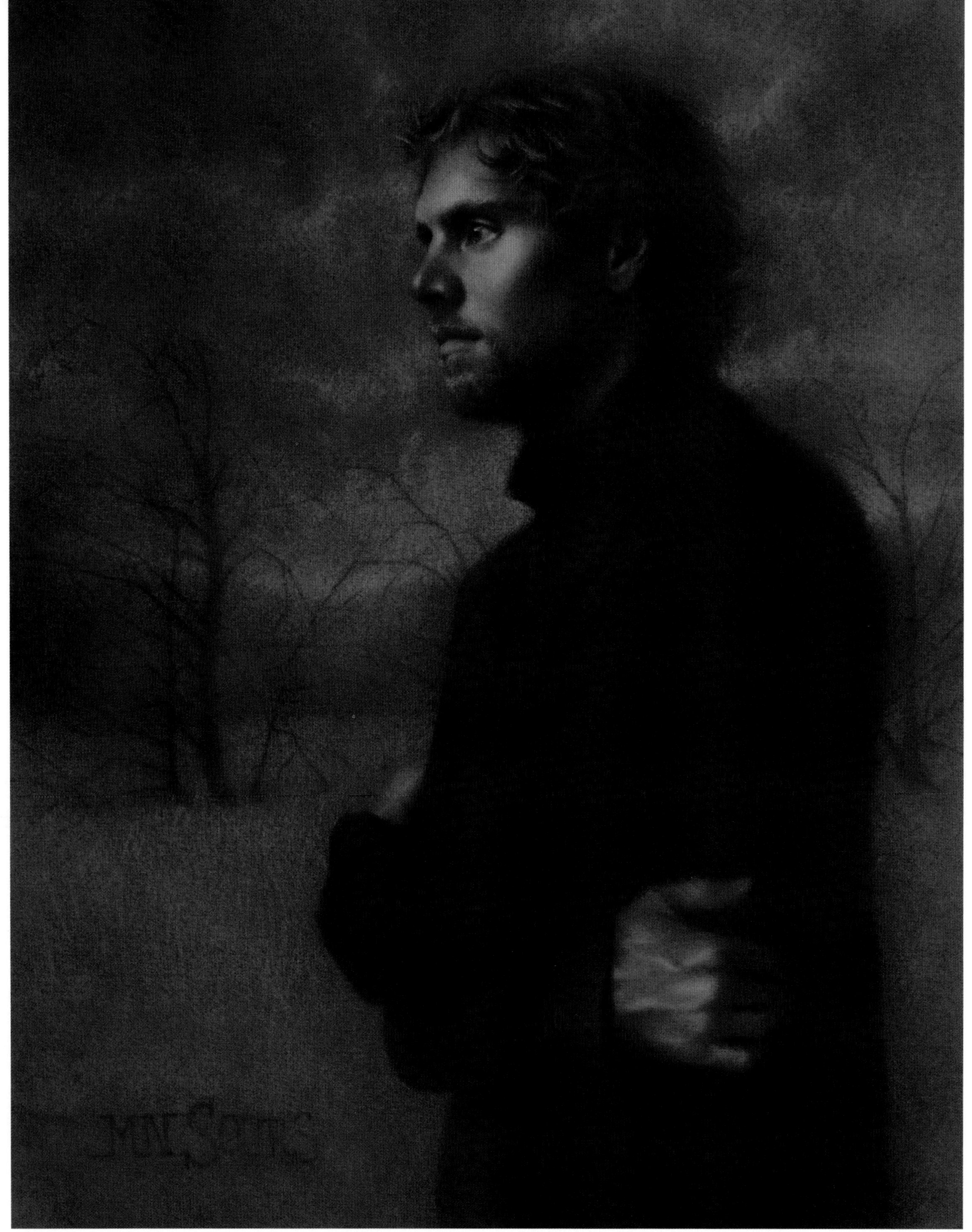

▲ **THE COLD EARTH SLEPT BELOW**
Meghan N. Sours
Charcoal and white chalk on paper with
some watercolor
16" × 12" (41cm × 30cm)

This drawing of my husband was rendered from both photographic reference and life studies. I roughly mapped out my composition with vine charcoal on toned paper. To focus on the portrait I spent most of my time pushing, not only accuracy and likeness, but capturing the character and spirit of my husband. I used layers of charcoal and white chalk to model the form and some soft watercolor with bristle brushes to create the variety of textures. I tend to over-soften my work, and my goal with this piece was to be looser and more expressive. This meant consciously letting go so as not to lose the tactile potency of both the figure and the landscape.

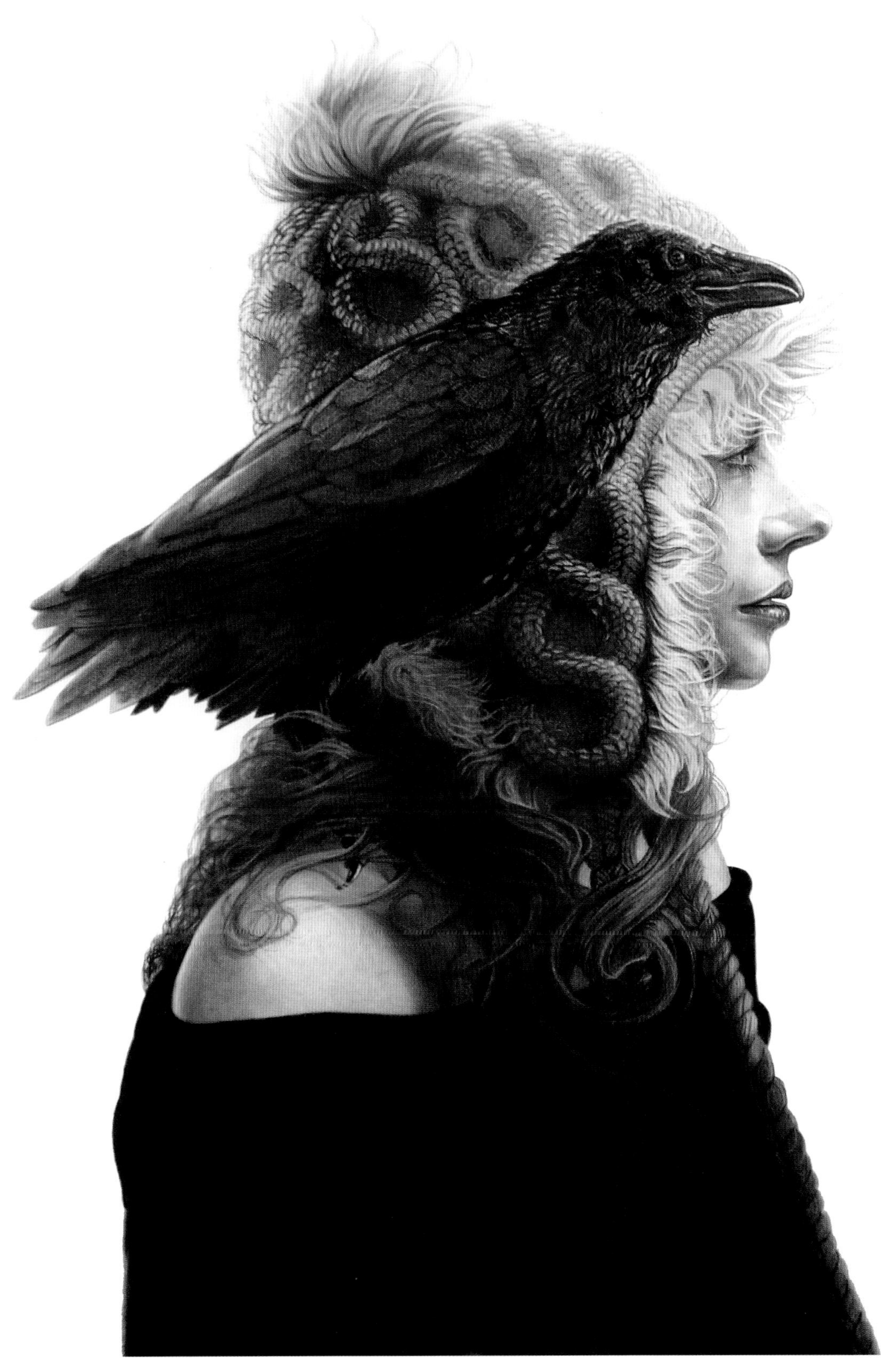

This is a straightforward graphite drawing starting with a rough block-in, building lines of a large variety and finishing with blending and reductive techniques. Charcoal is my usual go-to tool, but graphite is a friendly option when developing texture. *Sentinel* was produced in my studio from model Melissa and photos taken during a "getting reacquainted" meeting. *FlyingWomen* is my project that consists of portraits of local women on special creative paths. Melissa's art includes the creation of sculptural forms that build to experiential environments.

▲ **SENTINEL (MELISSA)**
Steven Rockwell
Graphite
29½" × 23" (75cm × 58cm)

I began drawing to pass the time while recovering from hip surgery a few years ago, but the hobby quickly became a mild obsession and a real blessing. The rehabilitation process is often long, and I was reminded of this upon seeing the worn-out padding and scratched-up stickers on my friend Lindsay's crutches. Thus, this drawing became something of an ode to what brought me to the pencils in the first place. The hair was done using a light layer of 2B, then patiently lifting out highlights with a shaped kneaded eraser, followed by darkening the shadows firmly with 2B, finally using 4H for the stray hairs. The well-used crutches, slightly disheveled hair, her exhausted look, the shadows betraying her slouched posture all capture the long and tiring nature of rehab.

▶ REHAB
Jim Little
Graphite pencil on Mellotex Brilliant White paper
12" × 7½" (30cm × 19cm)

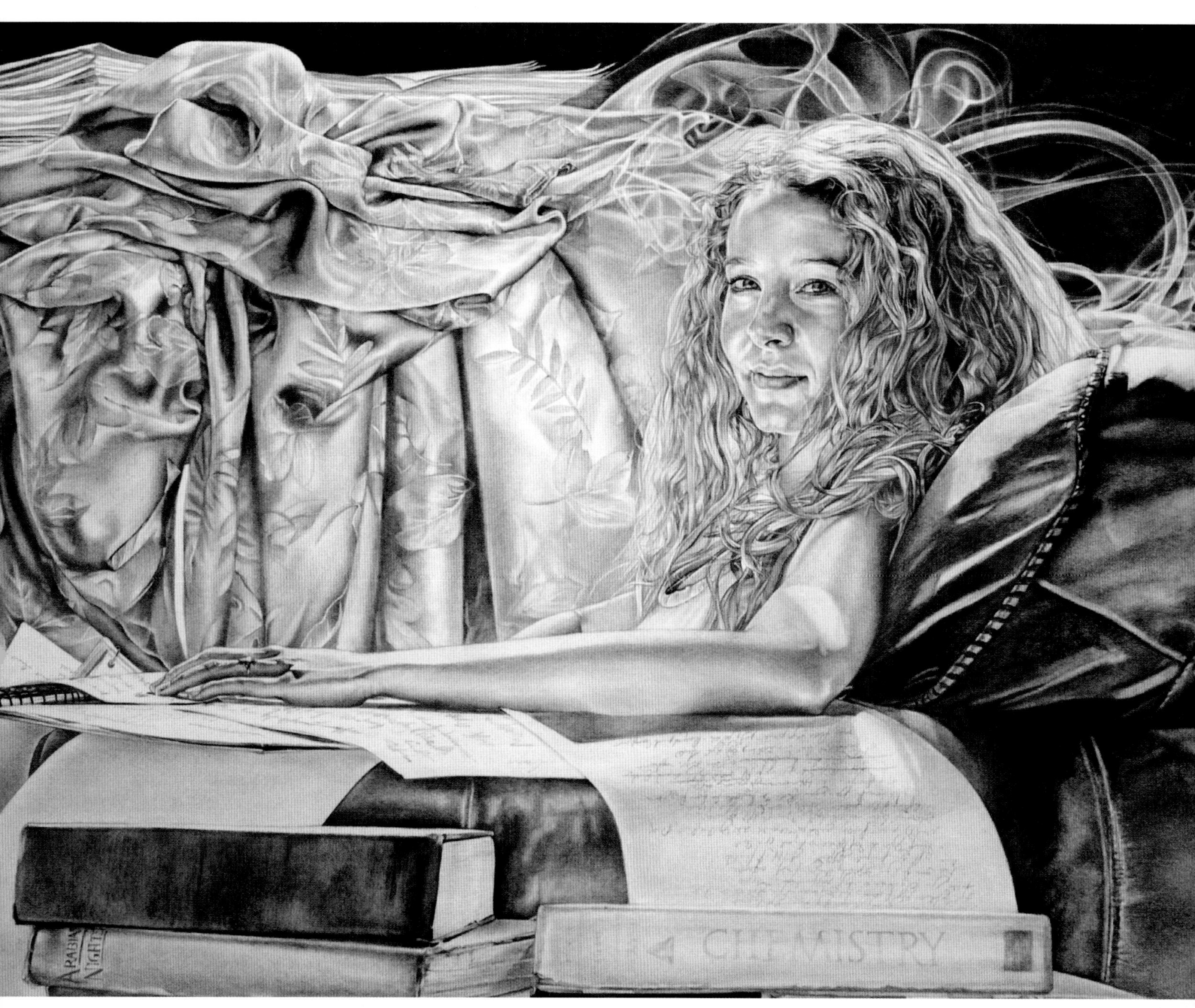

▲ THE MUSE
Cathryne A. Trachok
Graphite on Rives BFK
22" × 30" (56cm × 76cm)

In a way, *The Muse* began years ago when I had been borrowing my children's friends to be my models. These young adults were willing to sit for hours for me, and I started to think of them all as my muses. One thing led to another, and I am now working on a series of which this is the first. I work from sittings, photos and still-life setups. I like the Rives BFK papers because of the texture of the paper itself. It invites experimentation in both forms and ideas.

"Drawing is such a tactile experience, I find it impossible to not use texture as a major element." —CATHRYNE A. TRACHOK

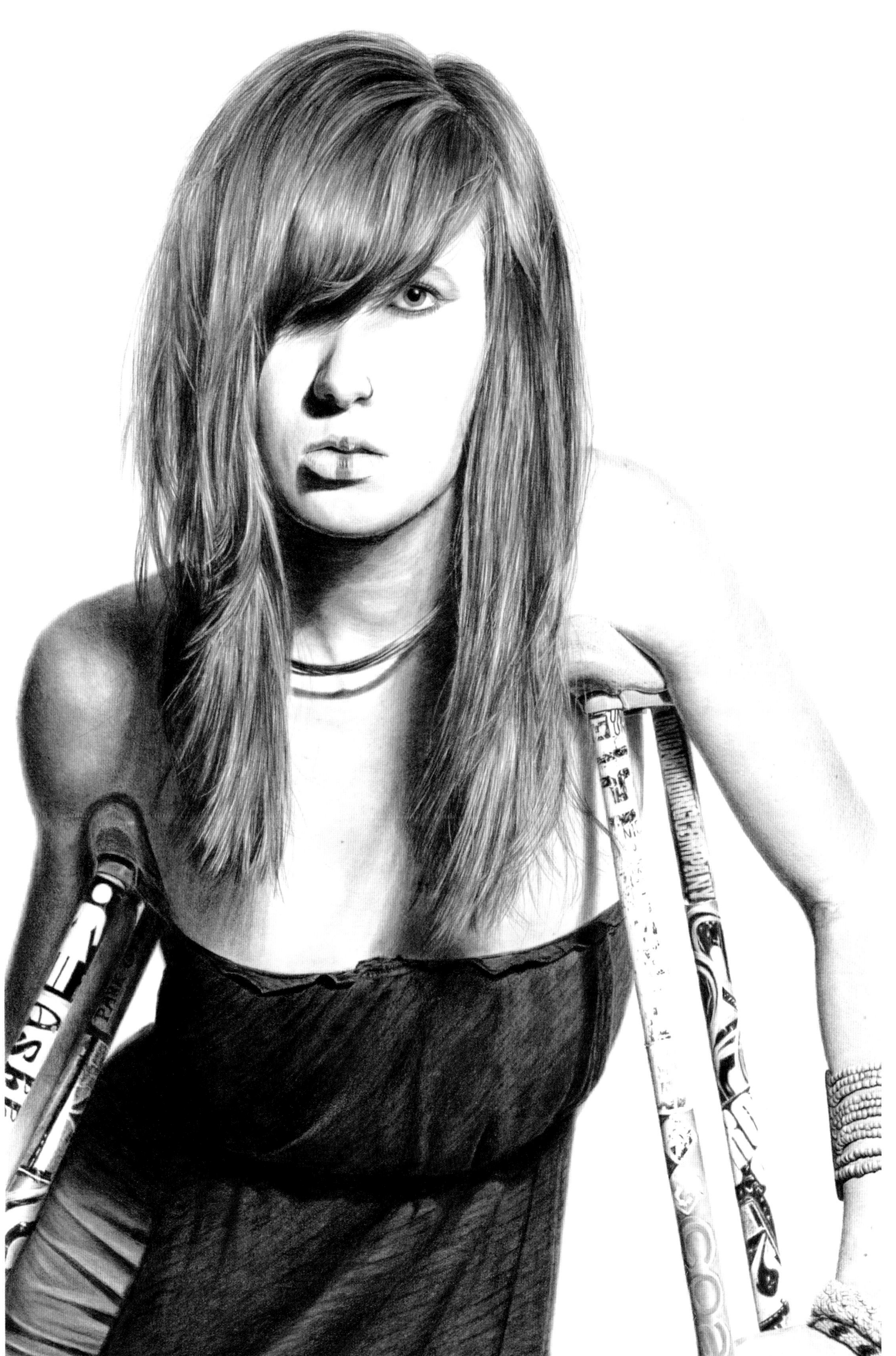

Sketching on-site at Art Walk in Marietta, Georgia, I was intrigued by Hillary's strong facial structure and tangled hair while she performed. I took a few photos and later began this work in vine charcoal, relying on light and dark patterns. Experimenting with lost and found edges, I created a disorganized maze of texture that became her hair. I hold my charcoal stick in various ways: upright, on its sharpest side, and sometimes I break it into small bits.

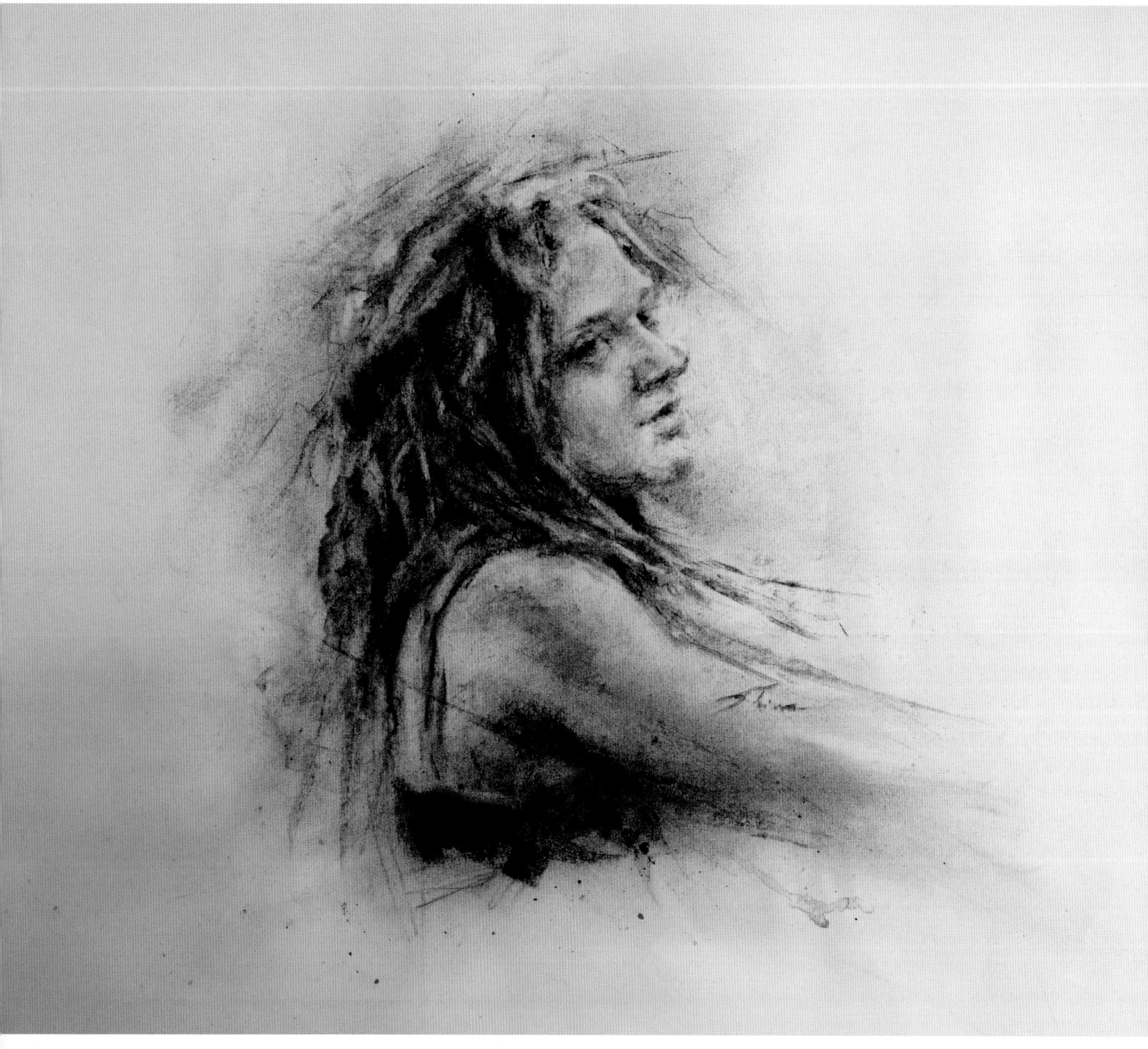

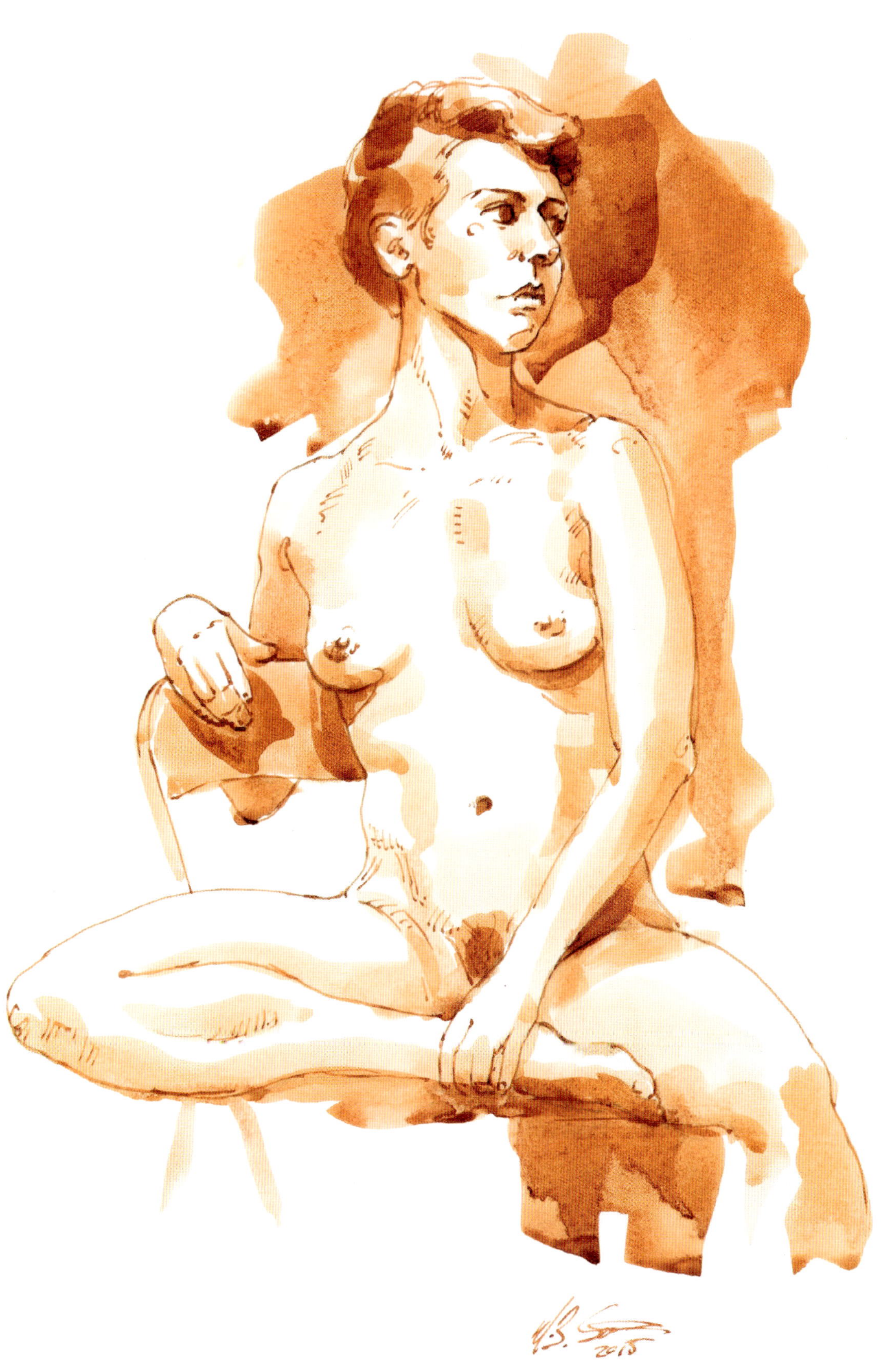

As I was drawing this young dancer from life, she seemed confident, strong and lost in her thoughts. I began with pencil lines. Once confident in the proportions, I began to use a fountain pen loaded with transparent Burnt Sienna acrylic ink. The lines capture the form in as few strokes as possible while also being expressive with shape and texture. The acrylic ink dries quickly and I'm able to apply washes of the same ink to the form, which exposes the texture of the paper.

▲ DREAMING OF DANCE
Mark Stephenson
Pen and acrylic ink on 100-lb. (210gsm) bristol
17" × 14" (43cm × 36cm)

My friend inspired me to create this collage. She enjoys posting selfies, and I found her facial features rather unique and interesting. Using her Facebook posts, I created a simple pencil sketch composition in three and a half hours.

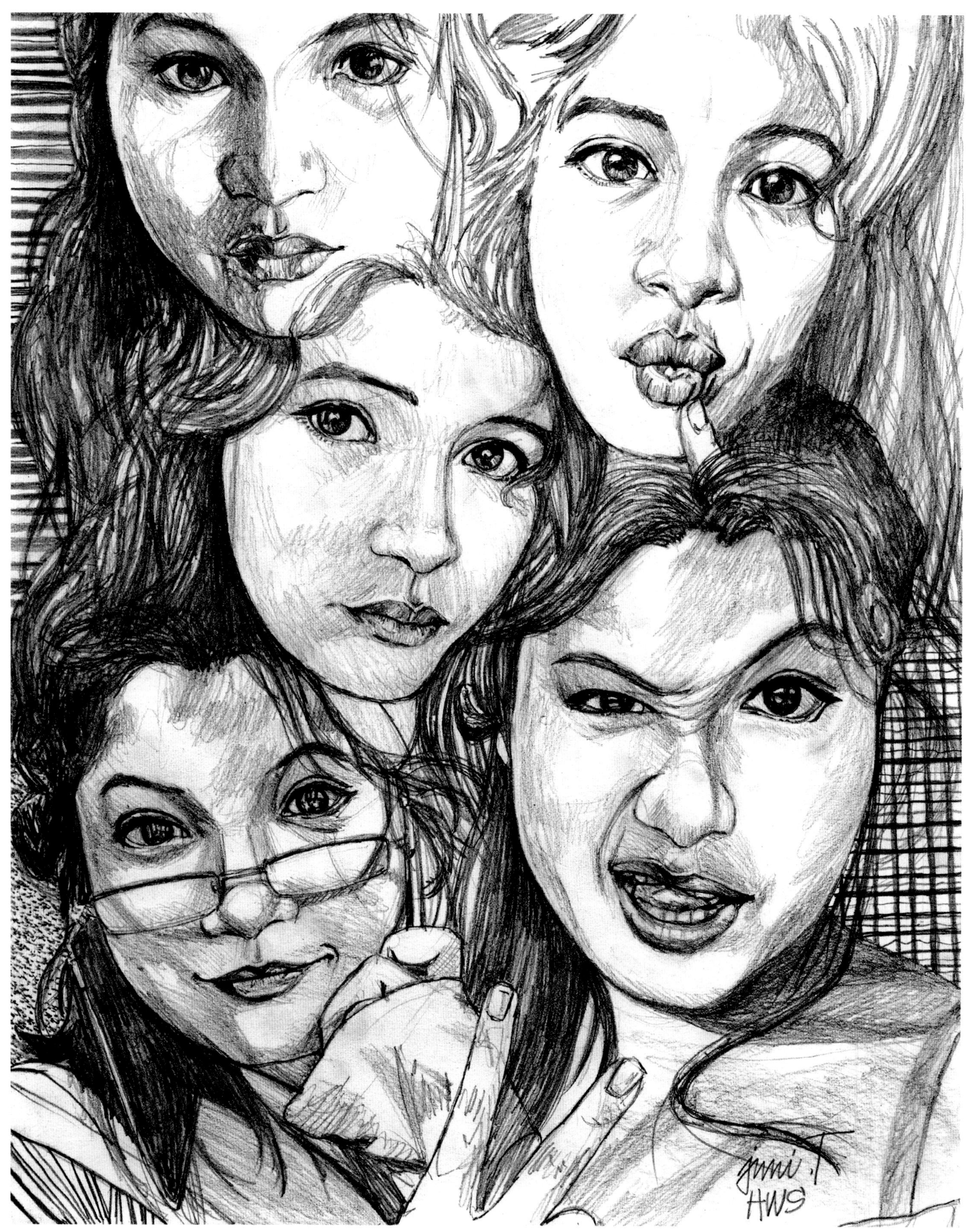

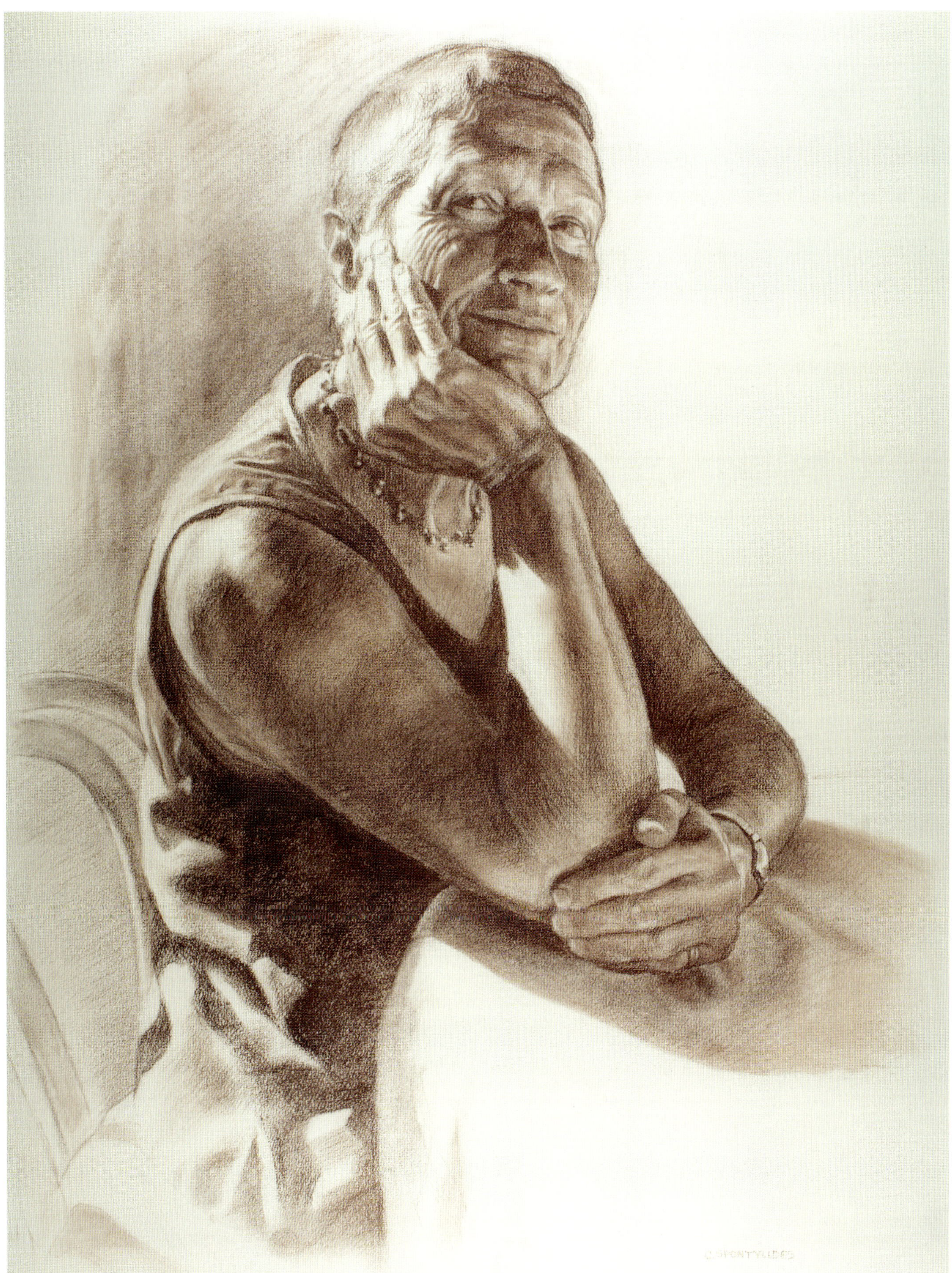

Having taken several photos of Dominique, this backlit pose in bright outdoor light seemed to reflect her individual and confident spirit. The strong light revealed otherwise unseen texture in her smooth skin, as in the wrinkles of her face, while the light bouncing into the shadows off the white table-cloth added surface texture to the shirt fabric. For the initial light values I applied the sepia chalk in powdered form with cotton pads. I then used solid sticks for hatching in deeper values. Some areas were rubbed into, while other areas were not. An eraser was used to pick out small areas of light.

▲ **DOMINIQUE**
Christos Spontylides
Sepia chalk on cream-colored pastel paper
25½" × 20" (65cm × 51cm)

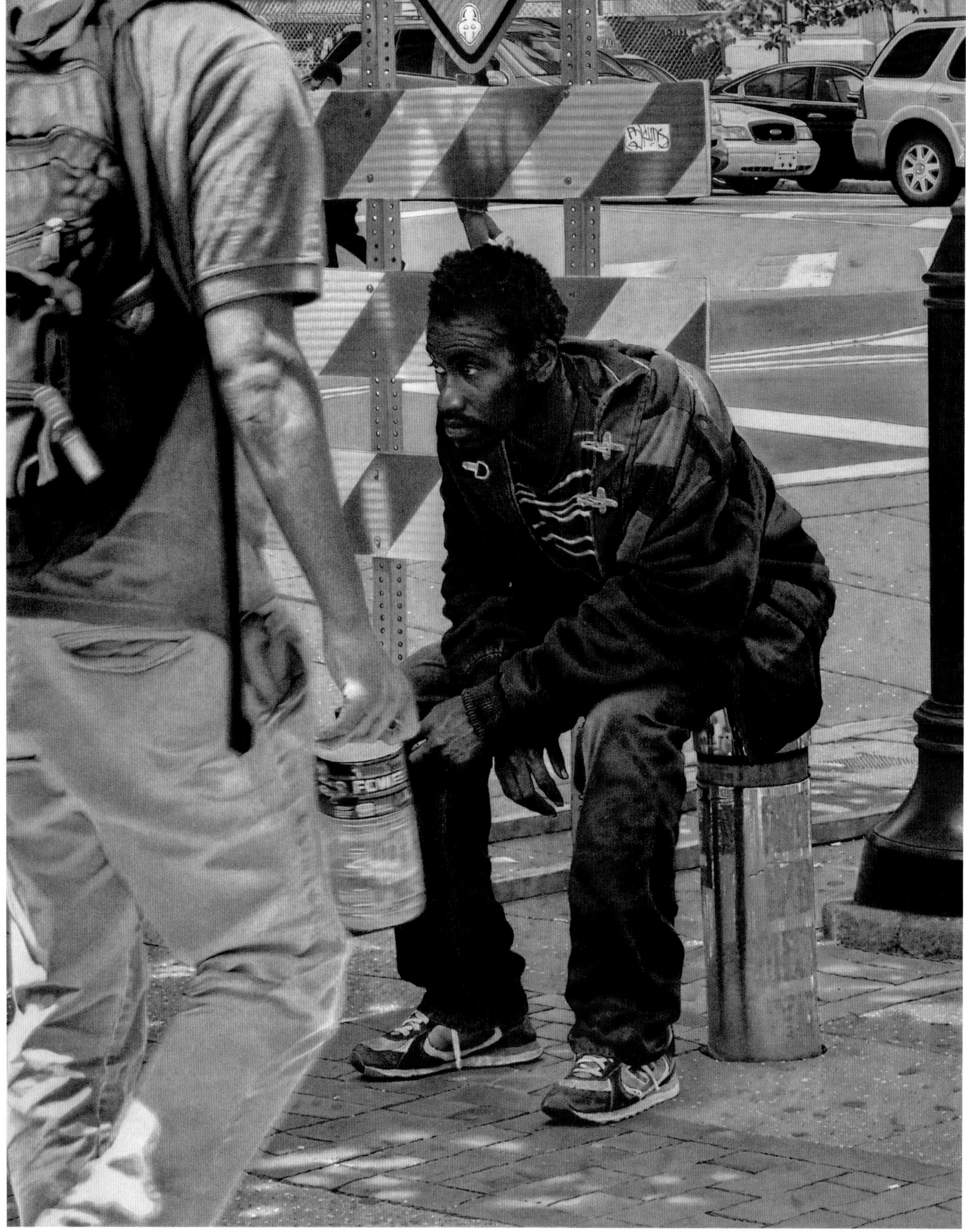

▲ POWER
Eva Csanyi-Hurskin
Graphite pencil on bristol vellum
20" × 16" (51cm × 41cm)

This is part of my *Living City Project*, a visual documentation of gritty street scenes, focusing on New York City, New Orleans, Philadelphia and Atlanta. I use my own reference photographs to create simple graphite drawings of the mundane and the unseen, elevating them to a level of significance. The same graphite used to express a man's hopelessness is applied to create the textures of the shiny chrome on which he sits. During the process I develop an intimacy with my subjects, hoping to give the viewer a new perspective on overlooked people and events hidden in plain view. The unremarkable or the disdained become the focal point, taking center stage!

A set of personal losses served as a catalyst for this artwork. Trying to predict or control the future is a futile exercise. My interests lie in the here and now as revealed in this self-portrait. Having studied nineteenth-century academic realism for over seven years, I am most intrigued by combining realism with imaginative elements as I believe that this demonstrates the highest form of personal expression. Of all of the techniques I have learned, rendering a drawing to a full finish using sharpened drawing tools (that better resemble needles than charcoal sticks) has been the key to my success. These fine points allow one to model with delicate certainty the values that are required for such subtly necessary details for realistic works.

▼ **THE FORTUNE TELLER**
Alexandrea Nicholas-Jennings
Charcoal on watercolor paper
9" × 13" (23cm × 33cm)

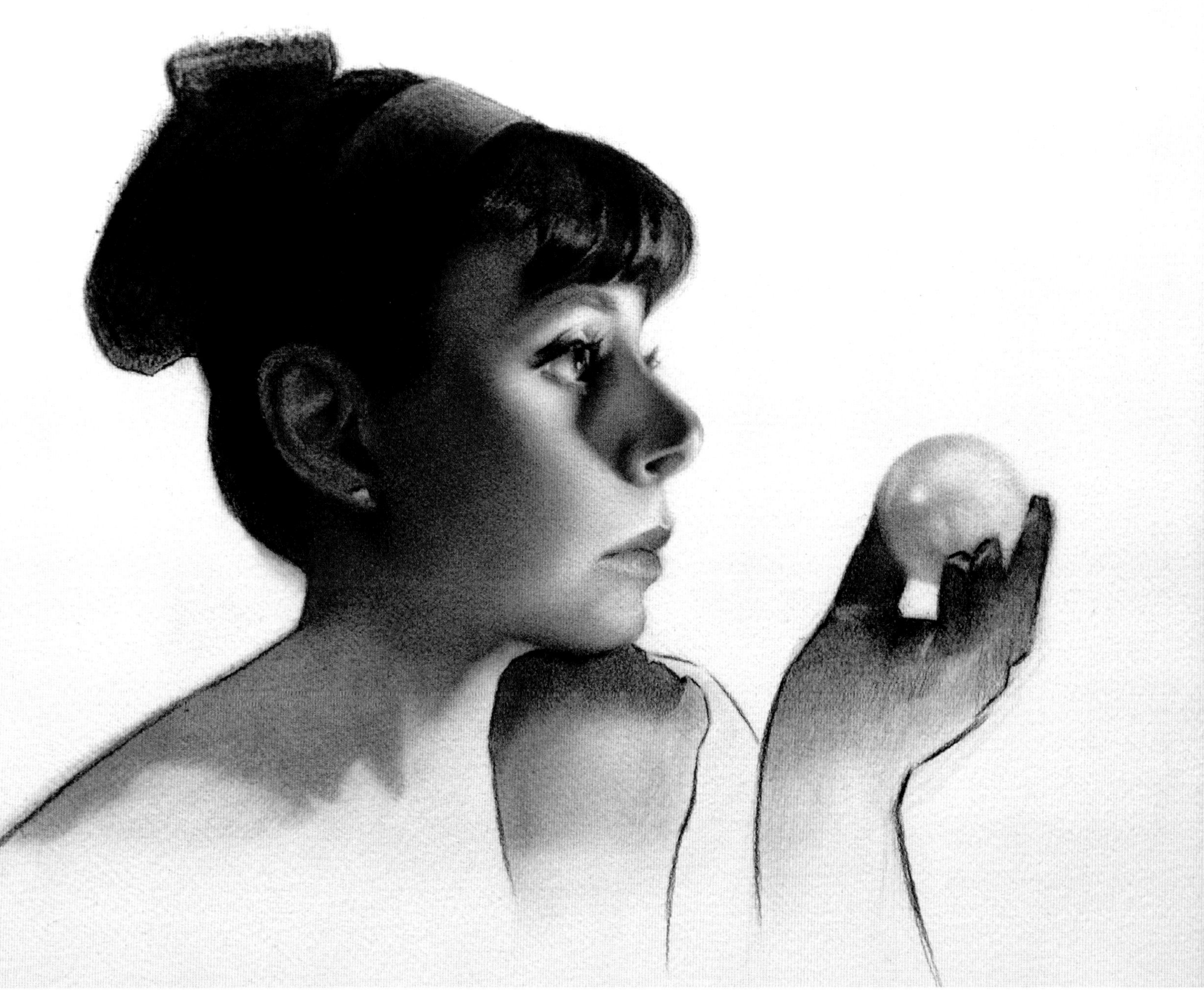

"Expressive texture comes from within—it is the fiber from which you are woven. Never compromise that for anything."

—ALEXANDREA NICHOLAS-JENNINGS

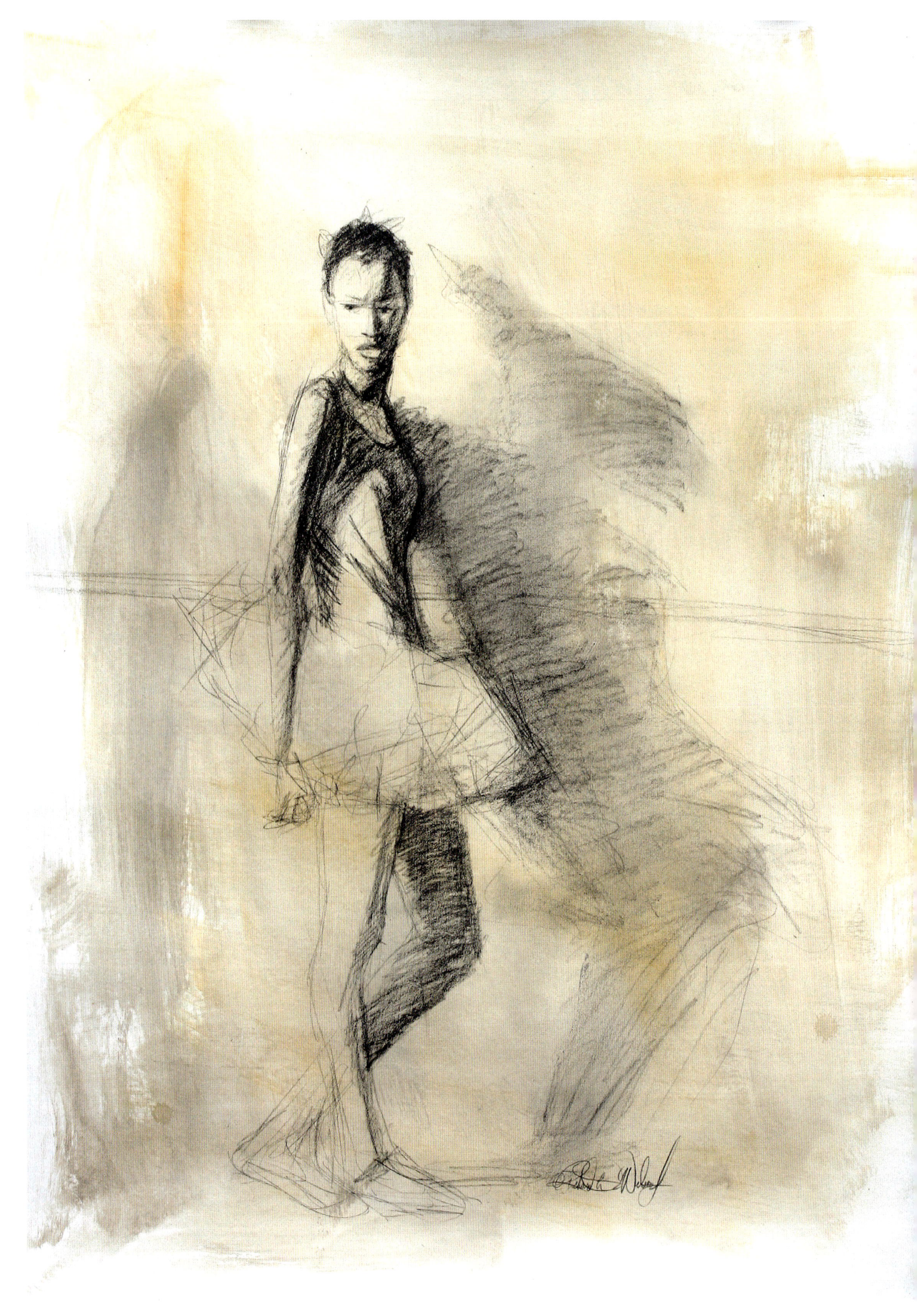

Dancing Shadow is a ten-minute quick sketch drawn from a photo of my daughter, Keona. I quickly layered my white watercolor paper with a Yellow Ochre wash. Then I used a 2B graphite pencil to loosely sketch the contour of my subject, gliding the pencil across the paper without lifting it off the surface. I worked very quickly to create energy using the elements of line and value in expressive gestural strokes applied to the model and the shadow. In the final minutes I went back in with a 4B graphite pencil to add detail and value contrast.

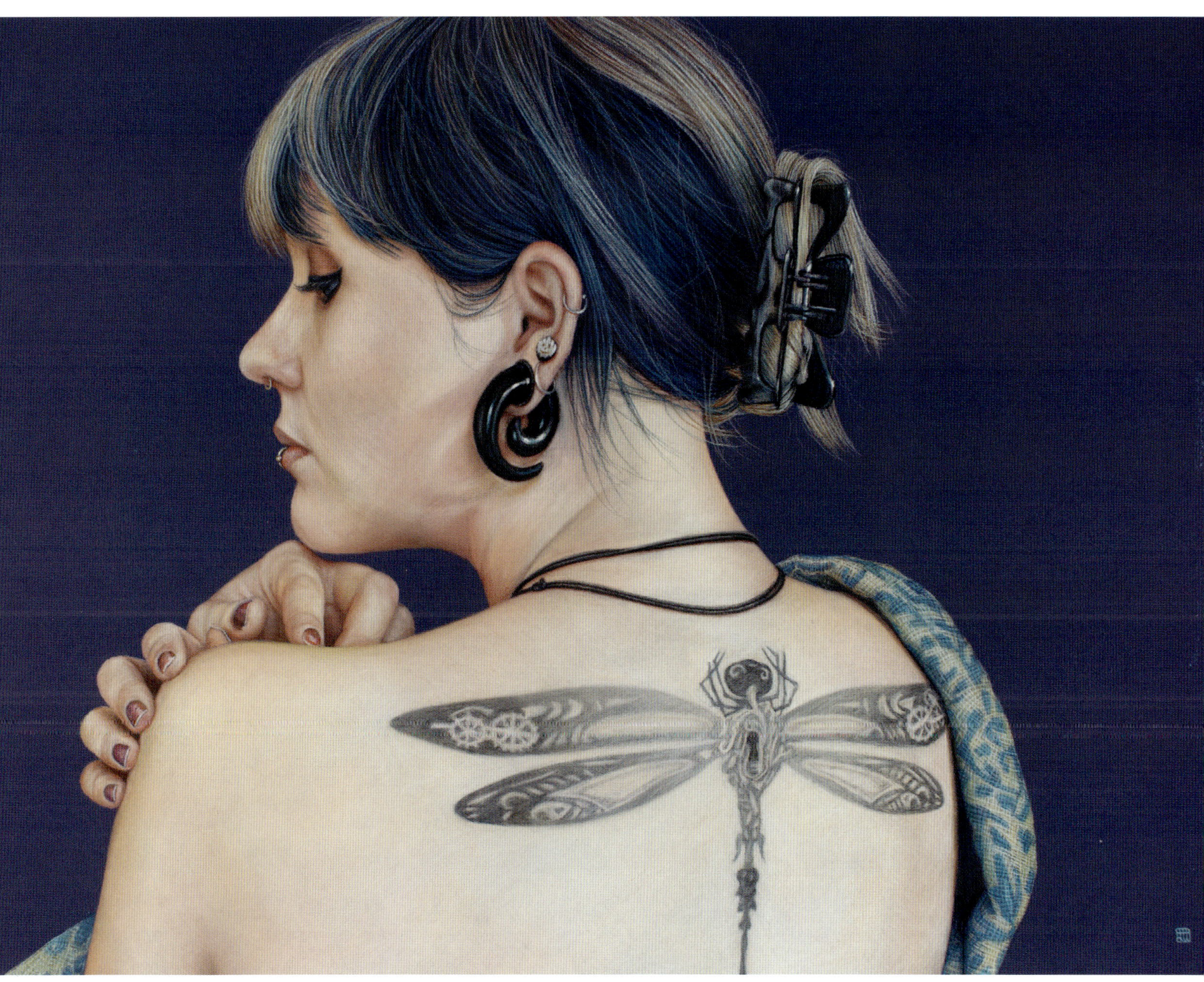

My portrait of Alex started with taking approximately 600 photos. I then made a handful of mono-chromatic sketches to clarify my ideas and composition. The pastel version was begun three times to allow a TV crew to film the work in progress at different stages. This helped me develop the art-work, but I'm not quite famous enough for that to be typical of my process. My technique includes soft pastels and pastel pencils, used in combination, to give me a lot of variation of marks. Texture is an essential element in my drawing; it can be contrasted or harmonized, exactly as color or tone. It is key to building the mood and feel of a piece.

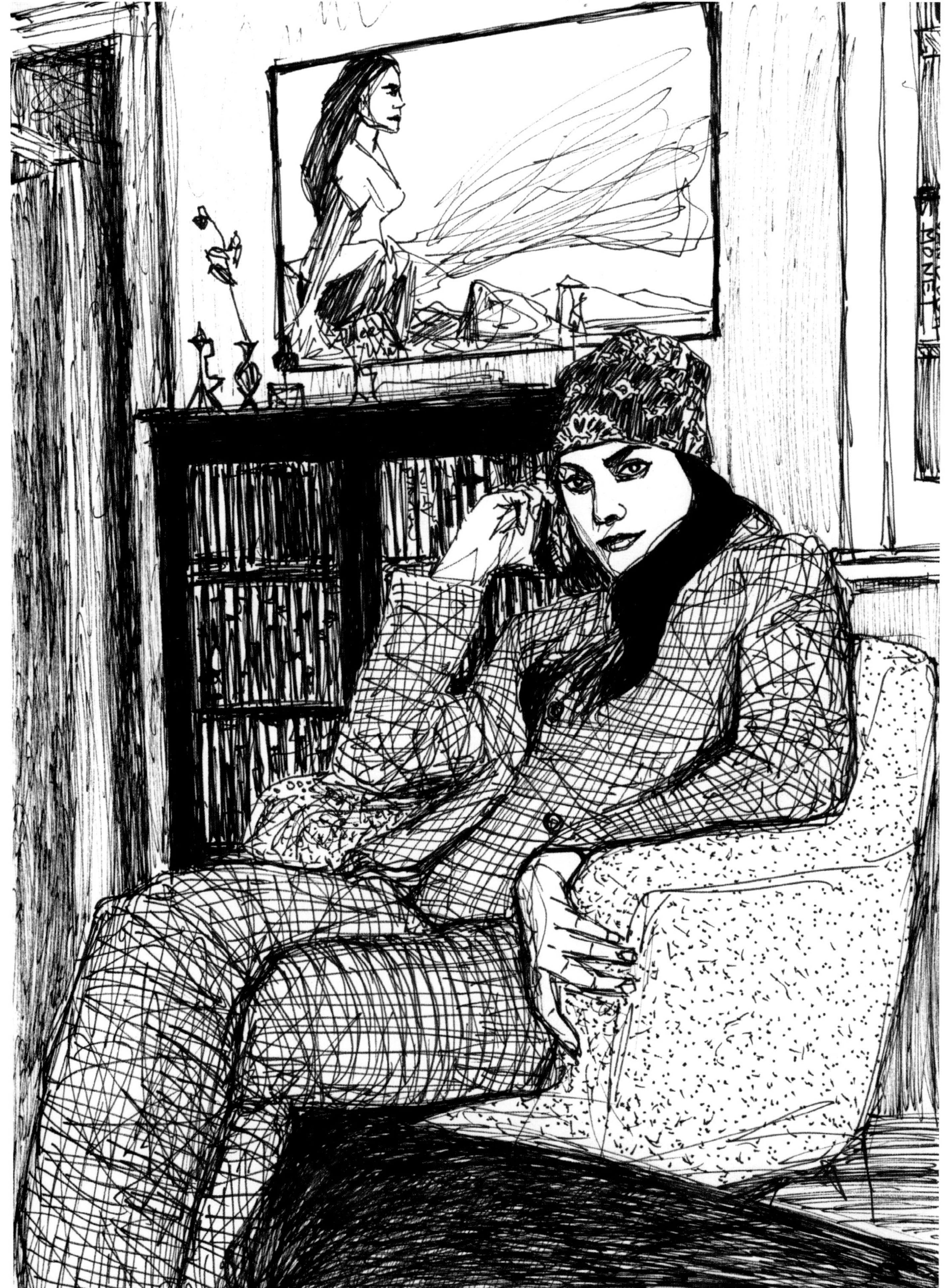

▼ **THE PHONE CALL**
Albert Wint
Pen on medium-weight, acid-free Sterling sketch-book paper
11" × 8½" (28cm × 22cm)

I used a photo I took of my good friend Alexis as a reference for this drawing. The painting hanging behind Alexis is one of my paintings of her; I've always liked pictures within pictures. For texture, I improvise a variety of marks as I go along. A bunch of dots can make you think you see stars if they are in the sky, but if they are on the side of a chair they look like upholstery fabric. Not being able to erase pen marks has forced me to pay particular attention to line quality. I try to combine loose and tight strokes to give each drawing a sense of energy even if the subject is sitting still.

I work with seniors with developmental disabilities. Many of my most recent artworks have been influenced by the issue of the aging of this population. People with Down syndrome live much longer than they used to. What happens to them? Or how about people with an autism spectrum disorder? Peggy, a lady who is moderate-functioning, lives at extremes of her emotions. Content while crafting, explosively happy with a balloon—and equally explosive if her balloon pops. I was lucky to catch a soft subtle moment and wanted to document it. She is a beautiful personality. I used watercolor and colored pencil, switching back and forth.

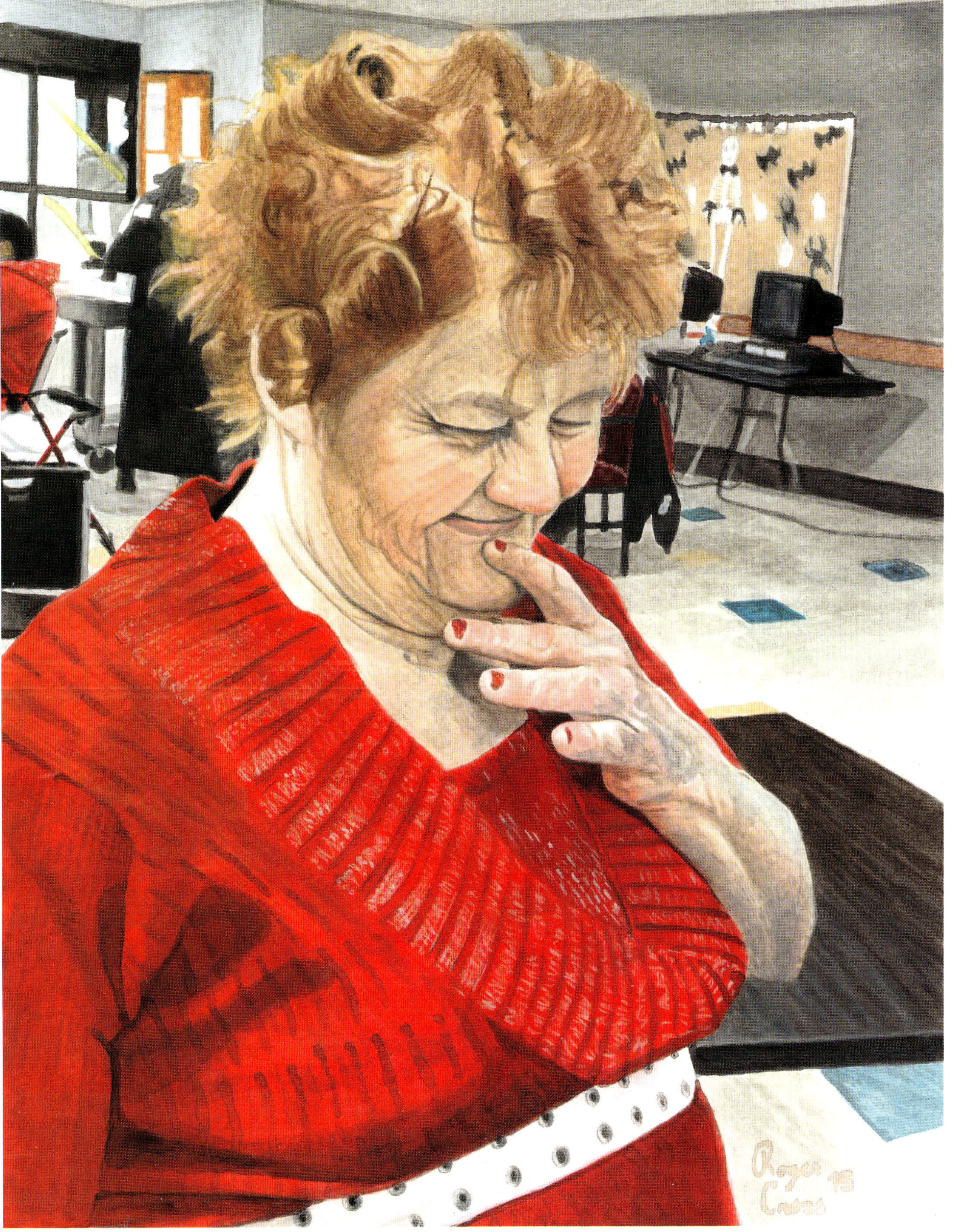

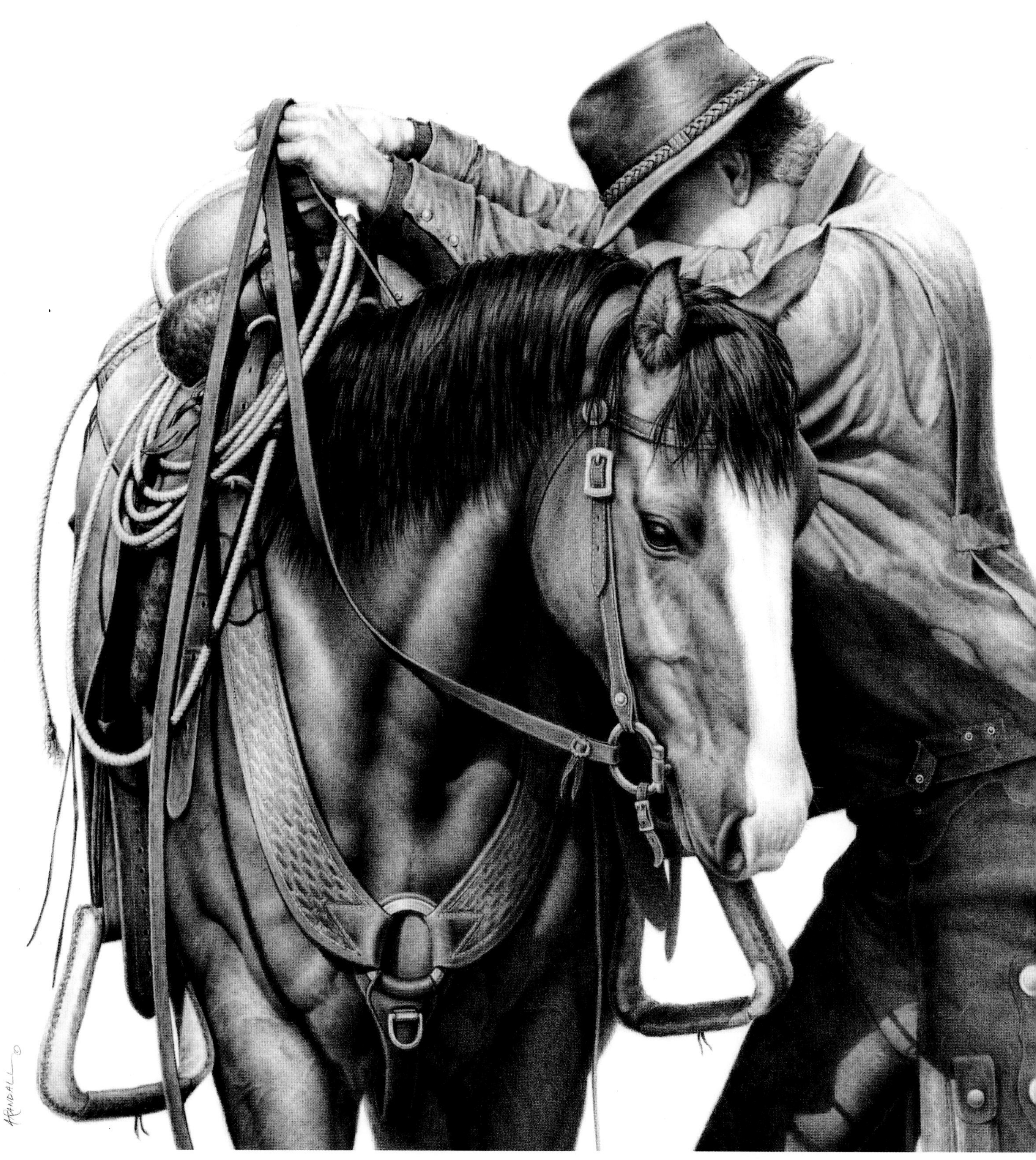

▲ LET'S GO HOME
Annette Randall
Graphite on bristol plate surface
16" × 16" (41cm × 41cm)

While photographing cowboys gathering and branding calves, I came across this worn-out cowboy getting ready to mount up and head back to the bunkhouse. The way the cowboy was positioned next to his horse was the impetus for creating the drawing. The natural texture of the horse's coat contrasts with the coarseness of the cowboy's canvas jacket and smooth leather chaps. Use texture to create form, as on the horse's ear. Paying attention to the play of light against dark can help create depth, such as where the white of the horse's blaze contrasts with the dark of the cowboy's jacket, projecting the horse's head forward. Choosing to leave the background white keeps the focus on the shapes and textures in the composition.

This piece was a first-year Illustration and Design project at Dawson College in Montreal. We were given the task of drawing a self-portrait with an unusual angle. I worked from photos, still-life reference and imagination. The piece was brought to life over the course of many hours and many layers of graphite, from 6H to 8B. The chosen imagery represents aspects of my life and my lifelong interest in myths, legends and world cultures, especially those of Native America, Japan and the many countries in Asia. The end result was a very dreamlike feel that I'm quite happy with.

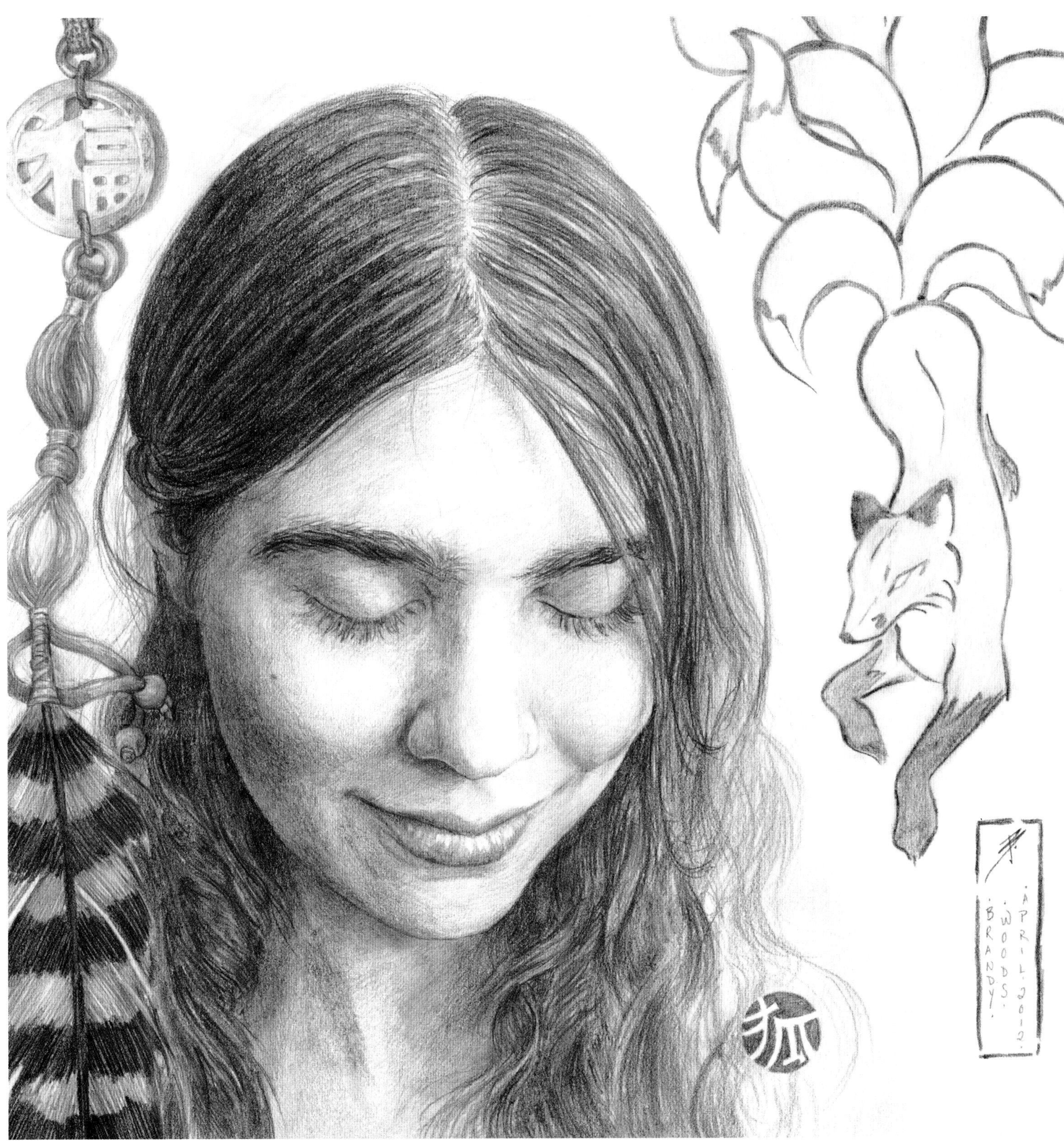

"Regardless of the subject matter, a little texture in the right place can breathe life into a drawing." —BRANDY WOODS

With *Braid* I wanted to convey mystery: the real and the surreal in one. I have always loved texture, and I knew it would be a key to bringing this drawing alive. Keeping my touch light, I built up the values slowly, using a kneaded eraser to pull out strands and highlights of hair and to soften lines and tones on the face. I had a very special model for my photo: my mother. She had arranged her hair in this braid for fun, but I had a powerful emotional reaction. I asked if I could make a portrait of her like that, and thankfully she agreed.

"Texture can be used to create a special intimacy with the viewer, inviting them to draw near."

—ERICA LINDSAY WALKER

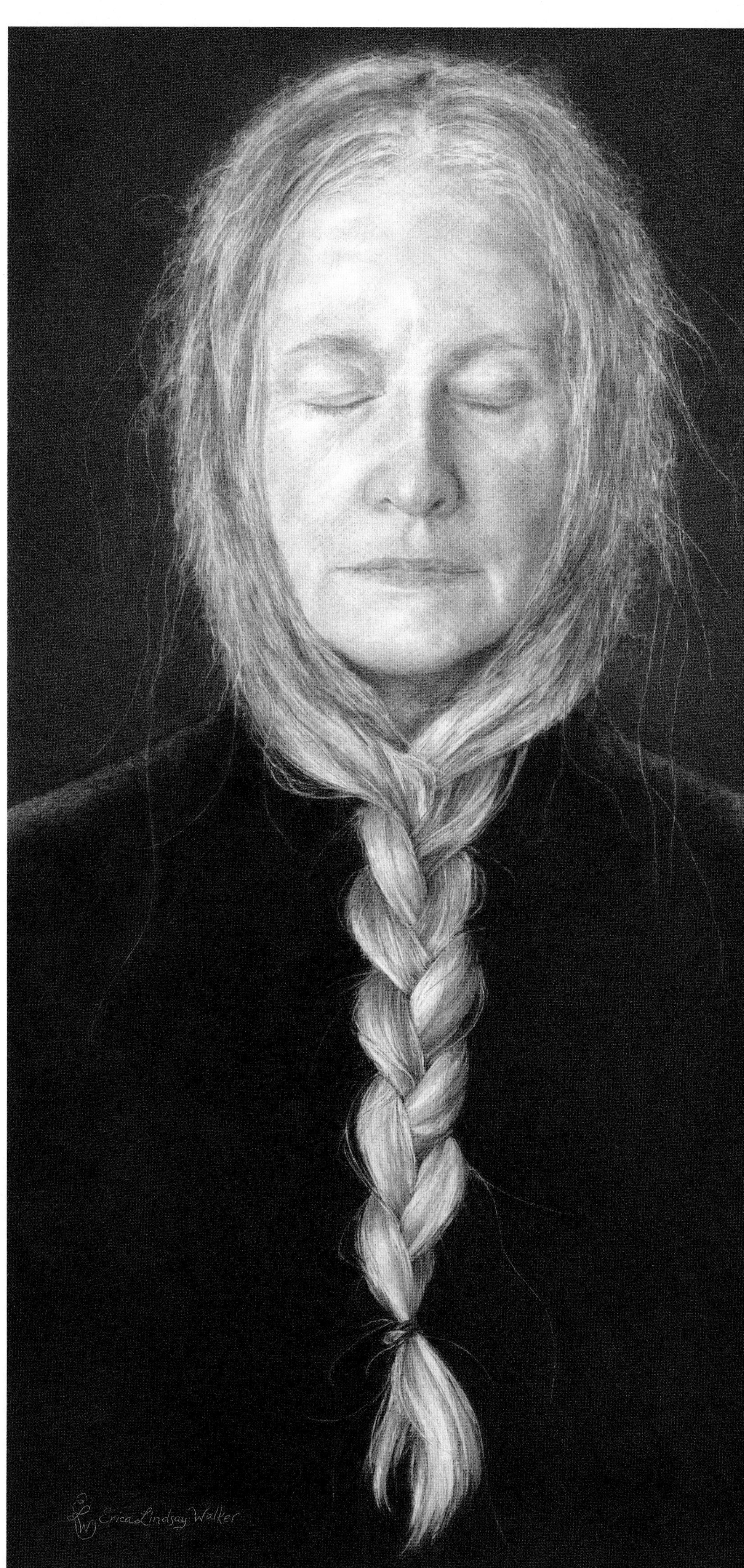

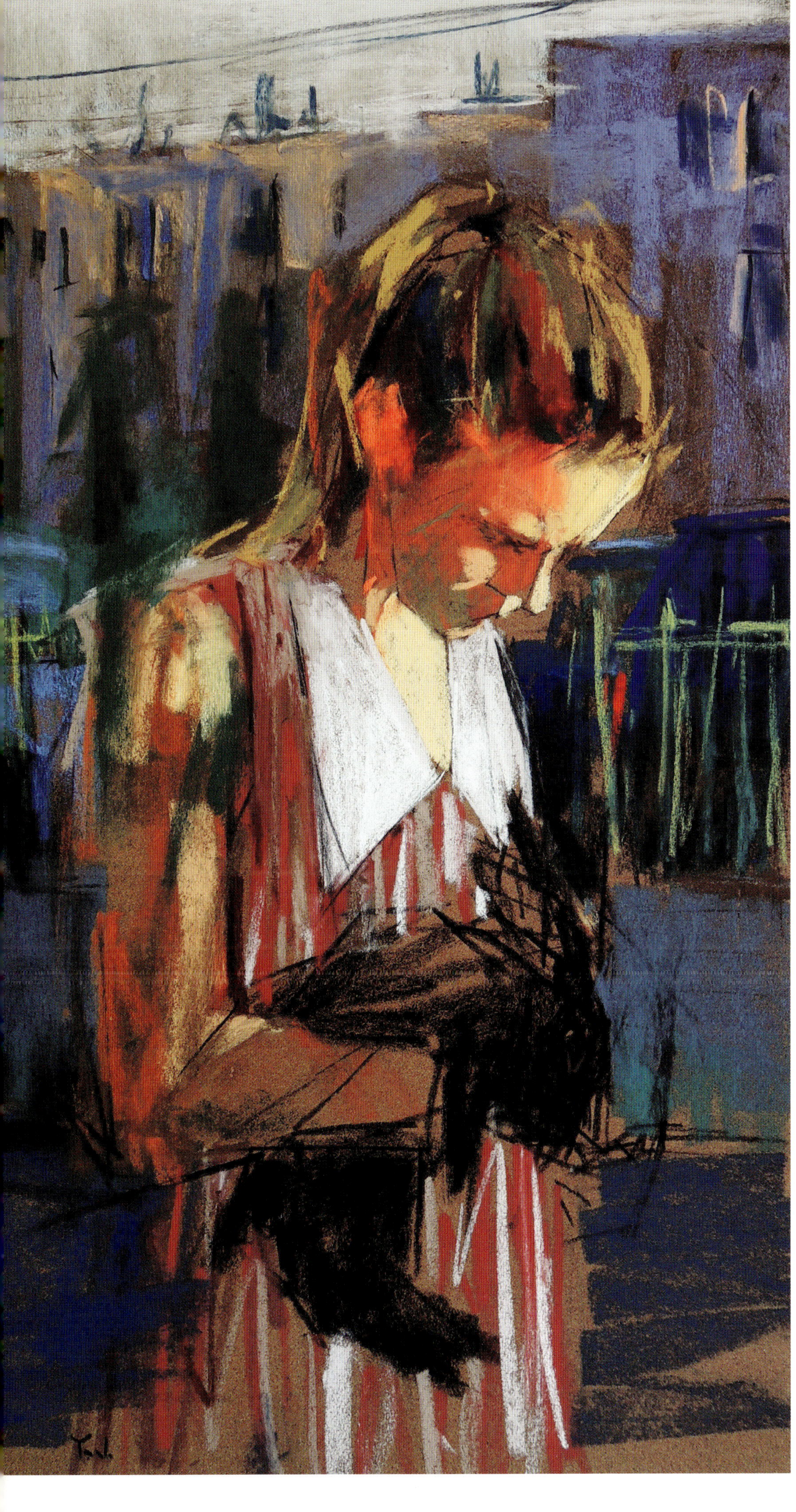

"Don't be afraid
to express your
emotions in color
and texture."

—YAEL MAIMON

◀ **ONE-WAY TICKET TO WONDERLAND #2**
Yael Maimon
Soft pastel and charcoal on
Sennelier La Carte
19½" × 11" (50cm × 28cm)

Inspired by Lewis Carroll's *Alice in Wonderland*, this portrays my version of Alice. In a chaotic reality, she feels lost and frustrated, yet she keeps going forward. This Alice's live rabbit companion is not a white rabbit but a black one. For its fur I used rough charcoal strokes with hard edges that express the feeling I was after. The marked absence of happiness and the sense of harsh times are enhanced by the strong contrasts and the visual rhythm of hard lines. For me Alice is a curious dreamer with fears to overcome; she is you and me when we want to escape from reality to Wonderland.

The original drawing of *Gulliver* is 4' × 32' (1.2m × 9.8m). Never having drawn on such a colossal scale, I was inspired by the idea of *Gulliver's Travels*. Like Gulliver, I was in a new world of discovery. While I have a passion for drawing portraits, I was pressed for time. This determined the degree of detail and texture that evolved, and a balance is struck between realism and fantasy.

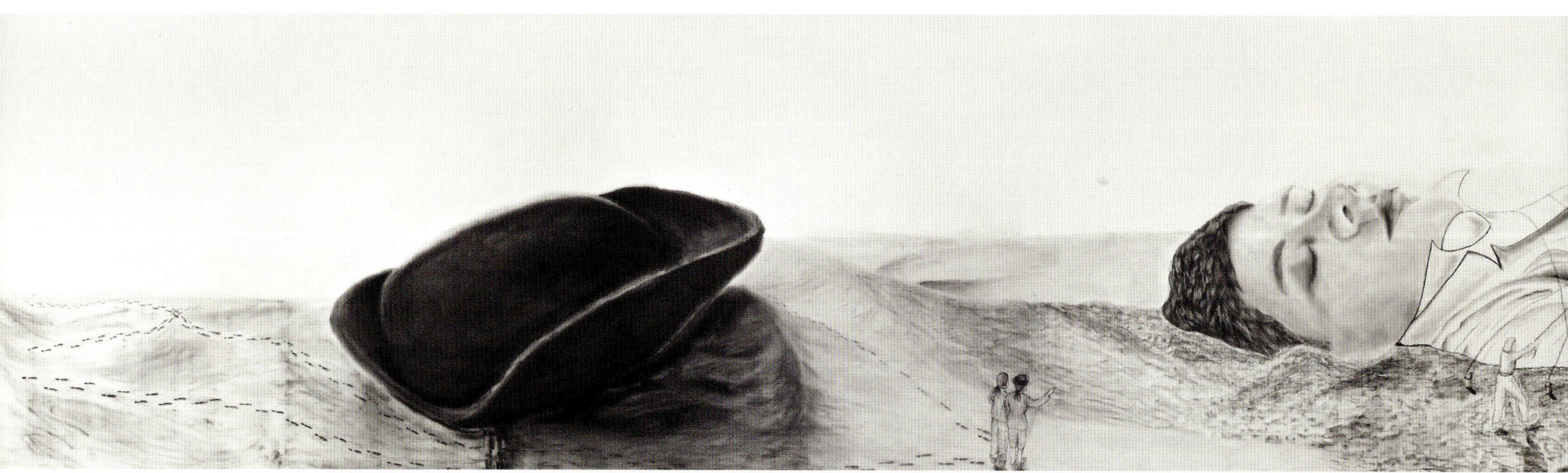

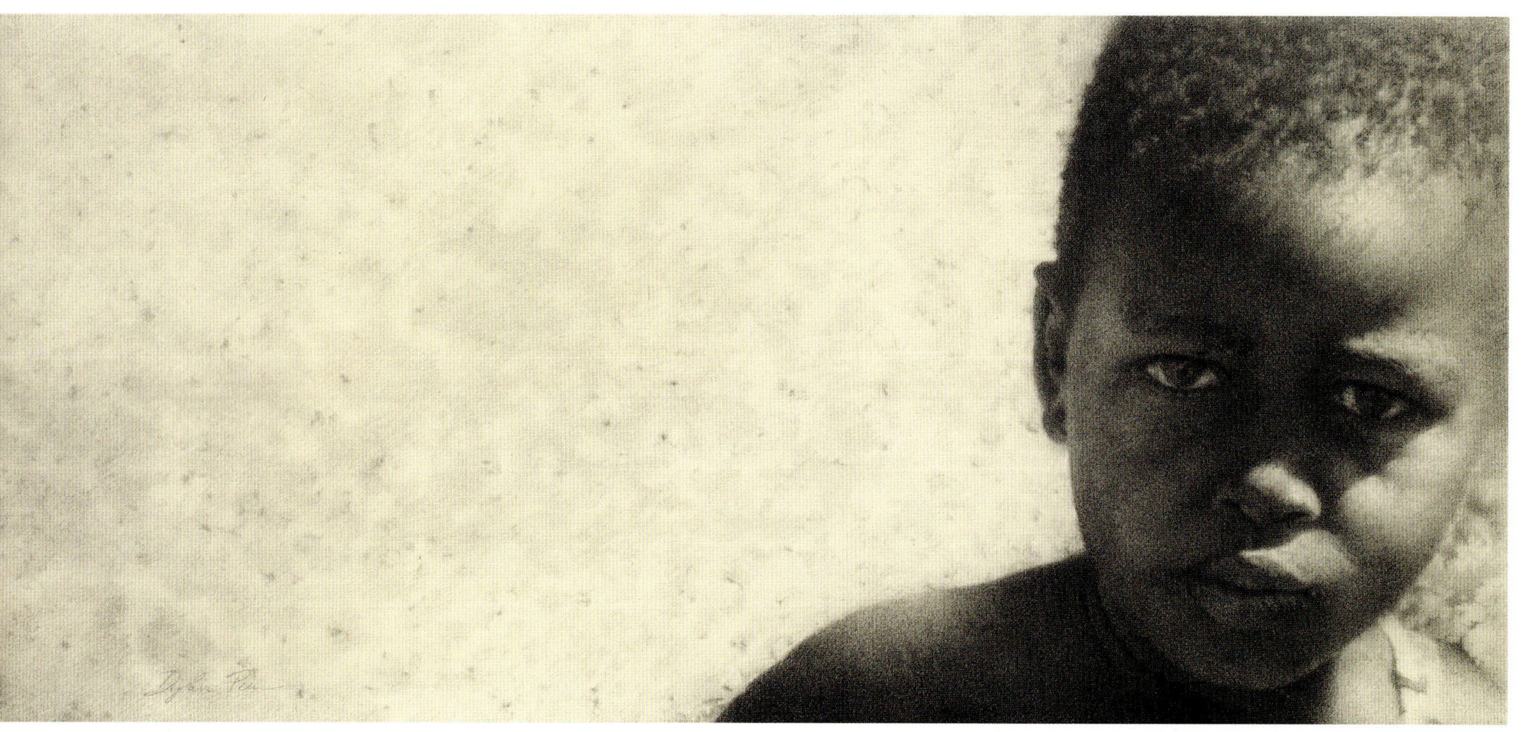

Drawn from a photo I took in Africa, this boy is learning to warm a closed heart. Turning his face toward the light and reaching out takes courage, especially when you're stagnant in your own shadow. The grainy texture in black and gray tones conveys the way the boy is seeing and feeling. The values were built up layer by layer using 3B, 6B and 8B pencils. The grain is partly from the paper and partly from looking at a grainy photo and mimicking the texture.

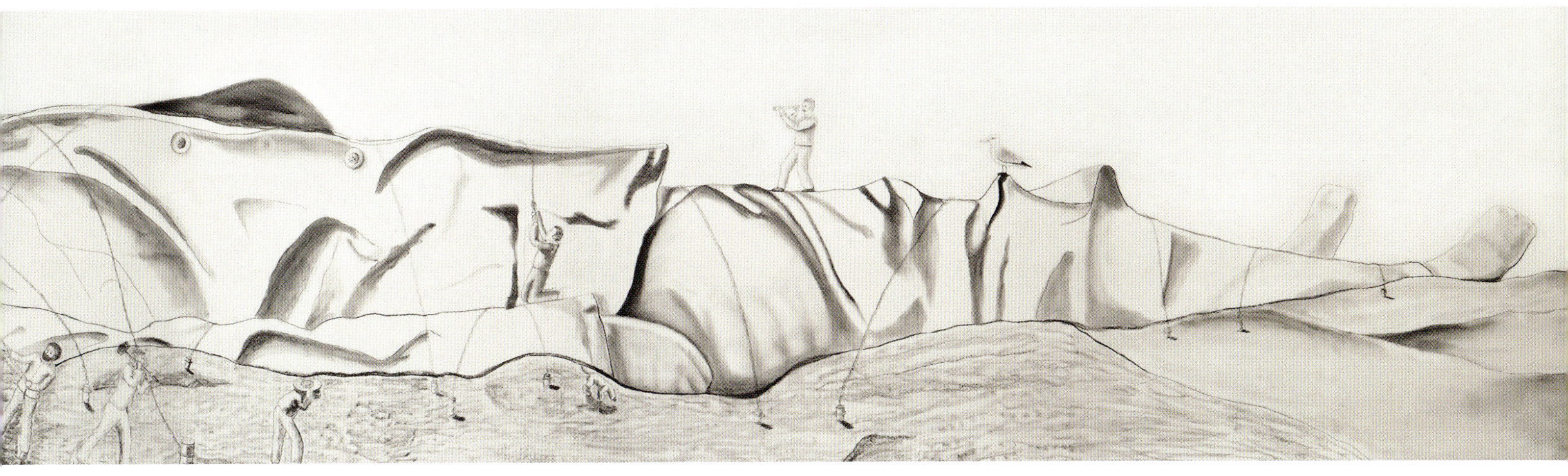

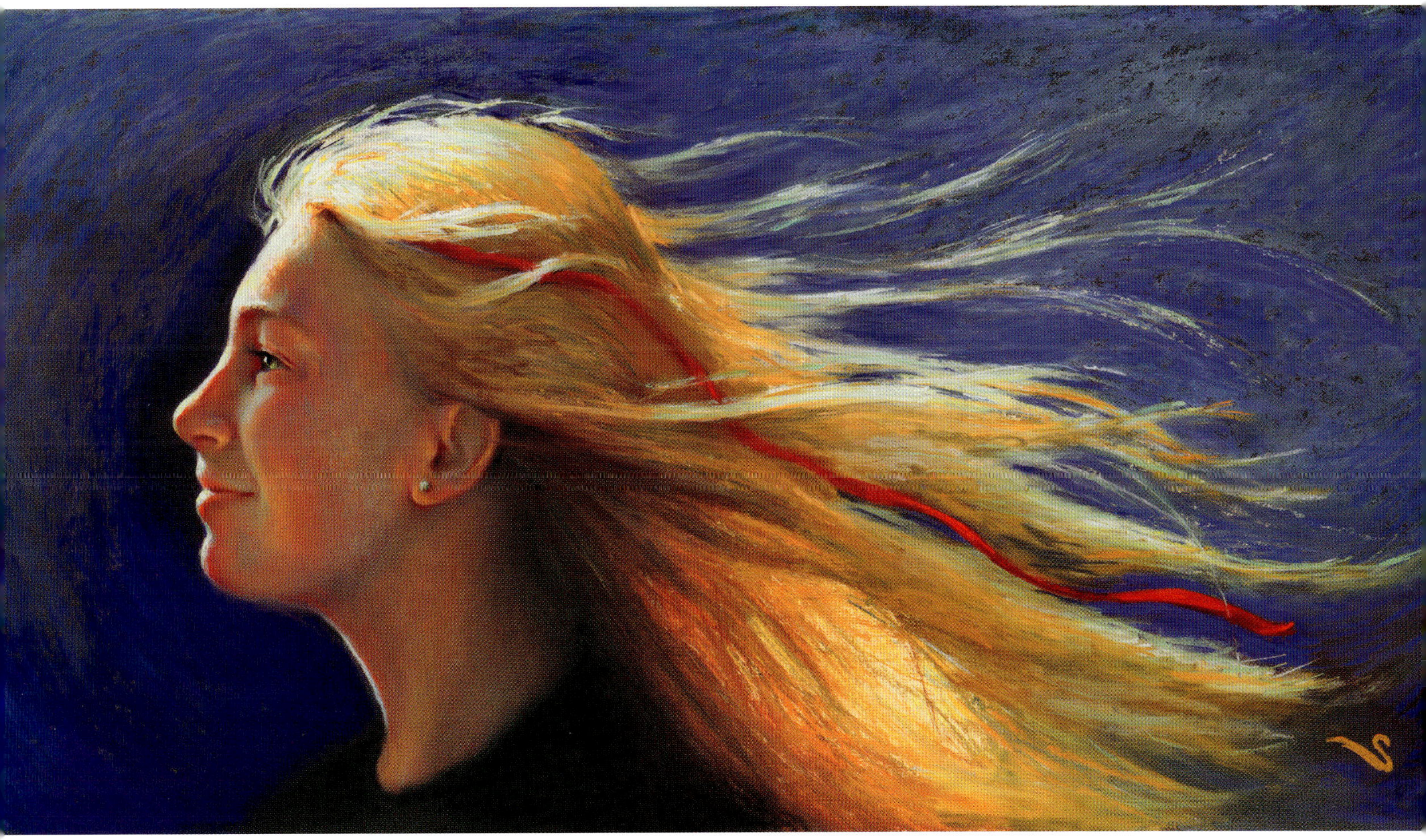

As a person goes through life they leave a trail behind them: words they speak, how they interact with others, even perfume. I imagined a bright red ribbon running through long hair to represent this trail. I did sketches first, then my daughter's friends posed while she operated a blow dryer and fan. This led to a lot of laughter! The hair represents the turmoil we go through in life: moving, unpredictable and yet beautiful. Soft, whispery strokes contrast strong, deliberate ones.

▲ TRAIL
Christine Swann
Pastel on UArt mounted on Gator board
15" × 28" (38cm × 71cm)

Contributors

NINA ASHRAF ASMI
AWA, Detroit Society of Women
Painters & Sculptors
ninaonline@gmail.com
ninaasmiart.com
p27 *Good Place for a Handout*

CRISTINA BALTAYIAN
American Society of Botanical
Artists, Botanical Artists Guild of
Southern California, Angeles Crest
Art Guild
Sierra Madre, CA
cristinabaltayian.com
p49 *Philodendron*

ROBERT T. BARRETT
Provo, UT
robert_barrett@byu.edu
roberttbarrett.com
p17 *Lizzie*
p112 *Seated Male Figure*

ANA BAYÓN
anabayon17@gmail.com
anabayon.com
p28 *Cristalle*

GLENN BEASLEY
International Guild of Realism,
PSA, Arkansas League of Artists
Sherwood, AR
gb1114@swbell.net
glennbeasley.fineartamerica.com
zhibit.org/glennbeasleyfineart
p10 *Emerging Young Artist*

CAROL N. BERNING
PSA, Oil Painters of America,
Women Painters of the Southeast
Lascassas, TN
berningcarol@gmail.com
carolberning.com
p30 *My Hubby, Vietnam Veteran*

MARGO BLACKELL
Ottawa, ON, Canada
margoblackell@bell.net
blackellart.ca
p100 *The Funeral*

MANDY BOURSICOT
PSA, Drawing Society of Canada
Vancouver, BC, Canada
mandyboursicot.com
p94 *Boxing Gloves*

CHRIS BREIER
Buffalo, NY
chrisbuffalony@gmail.com
cbreier.com
p36 *South Grand Island Bridge*
p37 *Basilica*

KEN BROWN
Edgewater, FL
artist@heritageartstudios.com
heritageartstudios.com
p61 *Cassie*

CYNTHIA BRUNK
Colored Pencil Society of
America, Cape Cod Art
Association, Flagler County
Art League
Flagler Beach, FL
brunkcm@gmail.com
cynthiabrunk.com
pp6–7 *Sophie*

AUGUST BURNS
PSA, Oil Painters of America,
National Association of
Women Artists
Middlesex, VT
augustburnsvt@gmail.com
augustburns.com
p31 *In Retrospect*

SVETLANA CAMERON
ASGFA
svetlanacameron.com
p33 *Daniel*

KAREN COLEMAN
CPSA, American Society of
Botanical Artists, Botanical Art
Society of the National Capital
Region
Round Hill, VA
kcoleman@rstarmail.com
p40 *Ornamental Grass*

CARYN COVILLE
caryncoville.com
p98 *Farm Fresh*

CATHERINE CREANEY
Northern Ireland
catherine_creaney@yahoo.co.uk
catherinecreaney.com
p20 *Thoughts*

ROGER CROSS
honeyrobison@hotmail.com
rogercross-art.com
p131 *Peggy*

EVA CSANYI-HURSKIN
Portrait Society of Atlanta
Atlanta, GA
info@evacsanyihurskin.com
evacsanyihurskin.com
p126 *Power*

JOHN DARLEY
Hein Academy of Art
johndarley801@gmail.com
p103 *Putting Away Childish
Things*

JEAN-MICHEL DELONGET
jdelonget@gmail.com
p87 *Dog in Light*

SUSAN K. DONLEY
International Society of
Scratchboard Artists, Pittsburgh
Society of Illustrators
Oakmont, PA
sue@susandonley.com
susandonley.com
petspictured.com
p76 *Goat Friends – Dolly and
Charley*

VICKIE DORSAM
PWCS
West Chester, PA
vickie.d.artist@gmail.com
p110 *More Than Words*

MICHAEL DUMAS
SAA, AFC, SWAN
Lakehurst, ON, Canada
natures.studio.inc@sympatico.ca
natureartists.com/dumasm.htm
p78 *Fox Sparrow Study*

NAJILA EMADI
najilae@yahoo.com
p116 *Life's Journey*

DAWN EMERSON
Pastel Society of America,
Pastel Society of the West Coast,
Oil Pastel Society
dawnemersonart@gmail.com
dawnemerson.com
p67 *April Fools*

MICHAEL J. FELBER
Guild of Natural Science
Illustrators, Colored Pencil
Society of America
Port Townsend, WA
michaelfelber@olympus.net
michaeljfelber.com
p63 *Grandfather*

ANDREA FENN
PSA, Connecticut Society of
Portrait Artists, Connecticut
Women Artists, Inc.
Farmington, CT
ajcfenn@sbcglobal.net
p16 *Andrea*

SUSAN FRECH-SIMS
Woodward, OK
ssims1870@sbcglobal.net
susanfrechsims.com
p86 *Shadow*

TANJA GANT
CPSA, CPX, PSA, Pencil Art
Society
tanjagantart@gmail.com
tanjagant.com
p27 *Sanctum*

IRENE GEORGOPOULOU
Athens, Greece
georgiren_art@yahoo.gr
igeorgopoulouart.blogspot.gr
p106 *Five Bulbs*

STUART GIVOT
San Mateo, CA
artiststu@yahoo.com
p39 *On the Tide II*

RICK GOLDSBERRY
Chillicothe Art League
Chillicothe, OH
rick@rickspencilart.com
rickspencilart.com
p92 *Real Heroes*

J. KAY GORDON
PSA, IAPS-MC, APS
Weaverville, NC
kgordon@main.nc.us
jkgordon.com
p102 *The Blue Motorcycle*

CHRISTY GREEN
Hartwell, GA
christygrn@hotmail.com
p13 *Breanna*

CLARK LOUIS GUSSIN
California Art Club, Art Renewal
Center – Living Artist
San Jose, CA
clark_gussin@yahoo.com
clarkgussinart.com
p12 *The Patriot*

CYNTHIA HAASE
CPSA, AIS
Arvada, CO
cynhaas@aol.com
cynthiahaase.com
p97 *Peaches and Green Ribbon*

MARK A. HANAVAN
Middletown, OH
mhanavan@aii.edu
markhanavan.org
p26 *Defense Mechanisms*

JENNA HESTEKIN
Independence, WI
indee.artist.jen88@hotmail.com
thecozyred.wordpress.com
p64 *Rooster*

KATHY HILDEBRANDT
AFCA, MPAC, PSA
Calgary, AB, Canada
khilde@shaw.ca
kathyhildebrandt.com
p95 *Things Go Better With*

STEVEN R. HILL
Northwest Pastel Society,
American Impressionist Society,
American Society of Marine Artists
Lopez Island, WA
steve@windsweptstudios.com
windsweptstudios.com
p56 *Kittitas Valley*

DEB HOEFFNER
Doylestown, PA
deb@debhoeffner.com
debhoeffner.com
facebook: debhoeffnerillustration
pp74–75 *In the Henhouse*

MARGARET HOPKINS
CPSA, Signature Member, SAA/A
Batavia, OH
margi@pepperportraits.com
pepperportraits.com
p84 *Waiting*

DENISE J. HOWARD
CPSA, UKCPS, MPAS
Santa Clara, CA
info@denisejhowardart.com
denisejhowardart.com
p53 *Tree of Character*

BUENA G. JOHNSON
CPSA, Culver City Art Group,
Black Artists in Los Angeles
buenavisionart@gmail.com
buenaartist.com
p51 *How 'Eye' Wonder*

MARY JO JOHNSON
Bradenton, FL
maryjojohnson.com
p23 *Madonna and Child*

SONJA JOHNSON
CPSA
Idaho Falls, ID
sonjamjohnson11@gmail.com
sonjajohnsonsart.webnode.com
p77 *Bedroom Eyes*

CHAN SOK YIN JULIANA
Artists Society of Singapore
Singapore
nchanstudio@hotmail.com
nschanstudio.com
p93 *Young Memories*

KELLY JUST
Traralgon, VIC, Australia
artist@kellyjust.com.au
kellyjust.com.au
p9 *The Old Gentleman*

HELEN KLECZYNSKI
Pastel Society of America,
Signature Member;
International Association of
Pastel Societies/Master Circle;
Great Lakes Pastel Society
Vicksburg, MI
helenkleczynski@yahoo.com
helenkleczynski.com
p45 *Porch Light*

E.J. KLEPINGER
Duluth, MN
eric@ejklepinger.com
ejklepinger.com
p81 *Rosie*

MIKE BARRET KOLASINSKI
PSA, Signature Member;
International Association of Pastel
Societies/Master Circle; Chicago
Pastel Painters, Master
Chicago, IL
mbkolasinski@earthlink.net
mikebarretkolasinski.com
p25 *Ady*

ELENA KOLOTUSHA
yelena-bella@hotmail.com
elenakolotusha.com
p101 *Pursuit of a Dream*

AARON A. LADE
Colorado Springs, CO
musket@musketmedia.com
musketmedia.com
p68 *Christmas King*

ZE ZE LAI
Yuen Long, Hong Kong
zex2@live.com
zezelai.com
p80 *Give a Hug*

MARGARET LARLHAM
Pastel Society of San Diego, San
Diego Museum of Art Artists Guild
larlham@mac.com
margaretlarlham.com
p50 *The Drive Home*

WENDY LAYNE
CPSA, PAS, VAA
wendy@wendylayne.com
wendylayne.com
p24 *Hard Times*

SANGHWAN LEE
Seoul, South Korea
35830@jisedu.or.id
p46 *The Pump*

MARY BETH LESKO
Freeland, PA
mbl4cp@outlook.com
p62 *Hog Day Afternoon*

CATHERINE LIDDEN
Fullerton, NSW, Australia
cjlidden@yahoo.com.au
catherinelidden.com
p66 *Reading the Menu*

JIM LITTLE
info@drawingswithoutborders.org
drawingswithoutborders.org
p121 *Rehab*

YAEL MAIMON
Ashkelon, Israel
yaelmaimon.com
p72 *Deer, Golden Meadow*
p135 *One-Way Ticket to
Wonderland #2*

DOUGLAS MALONE
douglasmalone.com
p21 *Stalwart*

CAROL E. MALTBY
CPSA, Buffalo Society of Artists,
Allied Artists of America
Hamburg, NY
cemaltby@roadrunner.com
cemaltby.fineartstudioonline.com
p14 *The Straw Hat*

PETE MARSHALL
Artists for Conservation,
Australian Guild of Realist Artists,
Australian Society of Coloured
Pencil Artists
Whittlesea, VIC, Australia
pete@ecoart.com.au
ecoart.com.au
p68 *A Bunch of Galahs*

JORY MASON
Pastel Painters Society of Cape
Cod, North River Arts Society,
Plymouth Center for the Arts
Halifax, MA
jorysm@sprintmail.com
jorymasonfineart.com
p54 *Lots a Color*

RYOTA MATSUMOTO
ryotamatsumotostudio.
blogspot.com
p96 *Those Who Affirm the
Spontaneity of Every Event*

KATHLEEN MCDONNELL
PSA, Pastel Painters Society of
Cape Cod, Pastel Society of the
West Coast
Glenwood, NY
kathymcd10@aol.com
kathymcdonnell.com
pp34–35 *Silence #2*

LYNDA L. MCMORRIS
Portrait Society of Atlanta
mcmorrisl@msn.com
lyndamcmorris.com
p60 *Westie I: 'Soooo … What's
Up?'*

KIRA MENDEZ
kiracmendez@gmail.com
kiramendezart.com
pp108–109 *Morning Sunlight*

STUART MEYER-PLATH
Sculptors Queensland
Burpengary, QLD, Australia
stuart.meyer-plath@hotmail.com
stuartmeyer-plath.wix.com/stuart-
meyer-plath
pp48–49 *Brooklyn Bridge, New
York, USA*

TERRY MILLER
Takoma Park, MD
terrymillerstudio.com
pp48–49 *Good Friday Spell*

MARGARET MINARDI
NAWA, NYSATA
Ft. Salonga, NY
margaretminardi@yahoo.com
p111 *Octopus*

CAROL MODERY-KILKEARY
p80 *Two Little Stinkers*

STEPHEN MOLYNEAUX
UK
stevemolyneaux@hotmail.com
stephenmolyneauxart.com
old-boy82.blogspot.com
p113 *Figure*

IRMA MURRAY
CPSA, Visual Art League of
Lewisville, Cross Timbers
Artists' Guild
Lewisville, TX
ijmurray@verizon.net
irmamurrayart.com
pp88–89 *Sunny Side Up*

KAREN NEAL
International Society of
Scratchboard Artists, Master
Scratchboard Artist
Rarangi, New Zealand
karen@wild-impressions.co.nz
wild-impressions.co.nz
p4 *Do My Stripes Look Big in
This?*

ALEXANDREA NICHOLAS-
JENNINGS
Academy of Realist Art – Toronto;
PSA, Alumni Member
Oshawa, ON, Canada
artaholic@hotmail.com
facebook: alexandreaartist
p127 *The Fortune Teller*

OLGA NIELSEN
National Sculpture Society,
Elected Member; PSA, Signature
Member; Fellowship of the
Pennsylvania Academy of the
Fine Arts
Wilmington, DE
olganielsenart.com
p11 *No Excuses*

EILEEN NISTLER
CPSA, APA, AWA
Upton, WY
eileennistler@netscape.net
eileennistler.com
p107 *Aunt Clara's Collection III*

KARIE O'DONNELL
Society of Animal Artists
Brant Rock, MA
kariejean88@msn.com
karieodonnell.com
p75 *Sergeant Study*

CHRIS PAGE
docpage@sbcglobal.net
chrispageart.com
nyoverheard.com
p19 *Kevin*

SARAH PARKS
Oil Painters of America, Portrait
Society of America
Chesapeake, VA
sarahparksartist@gmail.com
sarahparksartist.com
p41 *Sunflowers*

LEANNE ELKOW PENNER
Sechelt, BC, Canada
leannepennermail@gmail.com
leannepenner.com
p90 *Surf's Up*

PAULA PERTILE
CPSA
paulapertile.com
p99 *Fried Egg on Sourdough
Toast*

DYLAN SCOTT PIERCE
dylanpierce.com
p136 *Hiding in Shadow*

JAN PINI
PSA, Pittsburgh Society of Artists,
Pittsburgh Watercolor Society
Venetia, PA
janpini@verizon.net
janpini.com
p70 *Shake It Off*

SHARON POMALES
Portrait Society of America; Pastel
Society of America, Signature
Member; National Oil and Acrylic
Painters' Society
sharonpomalesart@yahoo.com
sharonpomales.com
p117 *Little Girl with a Big Guitar*

DAN PYLE
dan@danpyleartist.com
danpyleartist.com
p105 *Portrait of a Memory*

ALBERT RAMOS CORTES
albertramosart@gmail.com
albertramos.com
p38 *Minotaur (Part 1)*

ANNETTE RANDALL
info@annetterandall.com
annetterandall.com
p132 *Let's Go Home*

DAVID RANKIN
Ohio Watercolor Society,
Society of Animal Artists,
Artists for Conservation
University Heights, OH
davidrankinwatercolors@gmail.com
davidrankinwatercolors.com
facebook: davidrankinwatercolors
p41 *Woodpecker in Saguaro*
p65 *Greylag Goose Study –
Kashmir, India*
p65 *Stretching Tiger –
Bandhavgarh, India*

ROBERT M. RICHARD
Barrie, ON, Canada
rmrconnect@outlook.com
p32 *Flower Girl*

STEVEN ROCKWELL
North Little Rock, AR
laughingbirdarts@mac.com
p119 *Sentinel (Melissa)*

BARBARA ROGERS
CPSA, OPA, CAC
pyehouse6@yahoo.com
barbararogersfineart.com
p55 *Timeless*

JENNIFER ROWE
PSA, Associate Member; Pastel
Society of the West Coast,
Distinguished Pastelist; Sierra
Pastel Society, Signature Member
jenniferrowestudio@gmail.com
jenniferrowestudio.com
p18 *Out of the Blue*

LESLEY RYAN
Lennox Head, NSW, Australia
lesleyryanart@hotmail.com
facebook: lesleyryanart51
p73 *The Gift*

DAVID SANDELL
UK Coloured Pencil Society,
Portrait Society of America
david.sandell@triad.uk.com
davidsandell.com
p15 *Wileman*

BARB SCHACHER
Women Artists of the West,
Pencil Art Society,
Northwest Pastel Society
Newport, WA
barb@barbswesternart.com
barbswesternart.com
p82 *Doe Pretty*

THOMAS W. SCHALLER
AWS, NWWS, CAC
Marina del Rey, CA
thomaswschaller@gmail.com
thomaswschaller.com
p57 *French Cottage*

DONNA SHIVER
Woodstock, GA
donna-s62@yahoo.com
donnashiver.com
p122 *Hillary*

BILL SHOEMAKER
Colored Pencil Society of
America, Signature Member; St.
Augustine Art Association; Flagler
County Art League
Palm Coast, FL
keshoe1031@bellsouth.net
billshoemakercpsa.com
pp58–59 *Lady in Pink*
p71 *Did You Floss Today?*

HOLLY SINISCAL
CPSA
Henderson, NV
hollyarts1@aol.com
hollyarts1.com
p114 *Water Lily*

JOHN P. SMOLKO
CPSA
Kent, OH
jpsmolko@aol.com
smolkoart.com
p29 *Fran (Artist)*

DIANNA WALLACE SOISSON
CPSA, International Guild of
Realism, Chelsea Painters of
Michigan
Saline, MI
dwsoisson@gmail.com
diannasartcorner.com
p44 *Beyond All Boundaries*

MEGHAN N. SOURS
Orem, UT
meghan@meghansours.com
meghansours.com
p118 *The Cold Earth Slept Below*

CHRISTOS SPONTYLIDES
Etna, CA
cspon@sisqtel.net
mesart.com/cspon
p125 *Dominique*

MARK STEPHENSON
Ottawa, ON, Canada
mark.b.stephenson@gmail.com
markbstephenson.com
p123 *Dreaming of Dance*

CHRISTINE SWANN
PWS, IAPS/MC
Baden, PA
christine@swannportraits.com
swannportraits.com
p137 *Trail*

JIMMY TABLANTE
HWS, NWWS
Honolulu, HI
jtdesignsonline@gmail.com
p124 *Three and Half Hour Sketch*

KATHERINE THOMAS
Liberty Township, OH
katherinet@live.com
katherinethomasart.com
p104 *Out of Season*

JAC TILTON
Dubuque, IA
jac@jactilton.com
jactilton.com
p42 *Cosmic Irrelevance*

LYUDMILA TOMOVA
NWS, Watercolor Society of
North Carolina, Southwestern
Watercolor Society
Cary, NC
ltomova@nc.rr.com
tomovafineart.com
p43 *Careless Nation*

CATHRYNE A. TRACHOK
AWA, OPA, IGOR
Napa, CA
catrachok@sbcglobal.net
catrachokstudios.com
p120 *The Muse*

NYNKE VAN ZWOL
NABK PRO (Dutch Association
of Professional Artists), BOK
(Dutch Artist Society)
Purmerend, The Netherlands
info@nynkevanzwol.com
nynkevanzwol.com
p69 *Micro Desire II (Antarctic
Krill)*

FRANCES VELLA
fvella@nyc.rr.com
musekisses.com
pp136–137 *Gulliver – New World
of Discovery*

SUZANNE VIGIL
CPSA, Signature Member
Alexandria, VA
mikesuzvigil@aol.com
suzannevigil.com
p115 *Pensive*

JAMES W VOSHELL
Parkton, MD
jamesvoshell@hotmail.com
jameswvoshell.com
p74 *Snake Skin*

BROOKE WALKER
South Australia
brooke@brookewalker.com.au
brookewalker.com.au
p83 *Elephantidae*

ERICA LINDSAY WALKER
ericalindsaywalker.com
p134 *Braid*

SANDRA WEINER
Trumbull, CT
sandraweinerart@gmail.com
p1 *Strength at Rest*
p79 *Vigilance*

DAVID WELLS
davidthebrush@gmail.com
modernlifeform.com
p129 *Alexandria*

JERRY D. WERNER
Bend, OR
jw4art2go@bendcable.com
wernergraphics.com
p91 *Spatial Ambiguity with
Desserts*

MARNIE WHITE
marniewhite.org
p22 *Laurie in Profile*

STEVE WILDA
Allied Artists of America,
Academic Artists Association,
National Society of Painters in
Casein and Acrylics
Hadley, MA
stevewildaart@gmail.com
stevewilda.com
p47 *Brutes*

RICHARD D. WILSON JR.
PSA
Greenville, NC
richart71@aol.com
richardwilsonart.com
p128 *Dancing Shadow*

ALBERT WINT
Society of Illustrators
of Los Angeles
albertwint@hotmail.com
albertwint.net
p130 *The Phone Call*

VERONICA WINTERS
Naples, FL
nika@veronicasart.com
veronicasart.com
p8 *Adolescence*

BRANDY WOODS
Montreal, QC, Canada
mail@brandywoods.com
brandywoods.com
etsy.com/shop/brandywoods
p133 *Memory of Me*

DIANE WRIGHT
Mitchellville, IA
diane@dianewrightfineart.com
dianewrightfineart.com
p52 *Indiana Barn*

WEI YAN
Portrait Society of Canada,
Portrait Society of America
yuran527@yahoo.ca
p85 *A Puppy*

YUMI YASUMURA
Oil Painters of America, Portrait
Society of America
yumiyasumura.com
p94 *Vision*

Index

Abrading, 42
Acetate, 115
Acrylic, 26, 96, 115
Acrylic gesso, 78–79
Alcohol, 54
Artistic license, 51

Baby oil, 49
Background, 6–7
Blending, 13, 49, 105, 112, 119
Bristol board, 6–7, 12–14, 48–49, 79
Brushes, 44
Brushstrokes, 80
Burnishing, 52, 72–73, 98

Canvas, 78–79
Carbon, 42
Chalk
    red, 10
    sepia, 10, 125
    white, 10, 82–83, 118
Charcoal, 16, 22, 26, 31, 42, 82–83,
        90–91, 103, 105, 108–109,
        116–117, 135–136
    compressed, 113
    nitram, 30
    vine, 17, 30, 113, 122
    white, 102
Charcoal powder, 12–13
Charcoal sticks, 30
Colored pencil(s), 8–9, 14–15, 24,
        28–29, 32, 40, 51–53, 55,
        62, 68–69, 72–73, 76–77, 84,
        88–89, 98–99, 101, 104, 107,
        115, 131
    black and white, 60
    Caran d'Ache, 8, 14, 49, 58, 71
    Derwent, 63
    Prismacolor, 8, 44, 49, 58, 69, 71,
        86, 110–111, 114
Crayons
    Conté, 27, 33
    wax, 98
Crosshatching, 13, 43, 76

Digital media, 96
Drawing tools, sharpened, 127
Dry-brushed oil, 86
Drybrushing, 36–37

Edges, 21, 30, 97, 122
Engraving, 76
Erasers and erasing, 42, 125
    eraser sticks, 20
    ink eraser knife, 39

kneaded, 30, 86, 112, 120–121,
        134
    Magic Eraser, 14, 18
    putty rubber, 20
    stick, 61

Fixative, 31

Gator board, 50, 137
Gouache, 72–73
Graphite, 6–7, 10, 16, 23, 27–28,
        41, 47–49, 52, 56–57, 61,
        75, 78–80, 93, 96, 119–120,
        128–129, 132, 134, 136
Graphite powder, 38–39
Grids, 13, 74, 91, 106

Hatching, 41, 48
Heated drawing board, 44, 98
Hyperrealism, 82–83

Illustration board, 47, 105
Imprimatura, 50
Incising, 42
Ink, 36–37, 39, 80, 96
    India, 8–9, 68, 76, 81
    Sumi, 67
    walnut, 39

Layers and Layering, 21, 44–45, 72,
        86–89, 133, 136
Lighting, reflective, 114
Line drawing, 28–29
Linework, 36, 42, 48
Live sketching, 65

Mark making, 28–29
Mixed media, 50, 96
    Museum board, 28–29, 51, 55,
        107

Negative space, 46–47

Palette
    limited, 34–35
    monochromatic, 19
    warm, 24–25
Paper
    Bellotex Brilliant White, 120–121
    black sanded, 24–25, 62
    Borden & Riley Paris, 81
    bristol, 27, 32, 61, 64, 80, 82,
        94, 131
    Canson Mi-Teintes, 11, 19, 21,
        33, 40, 60, 66, 76–77, 102,
        110–111, 129

cartridge, 48, 93
    clay-coated, 23
    coquille, 63
    Colourfix, 66, 68–69
    Fabriano, 20, 75, 90–91
    gessoed, 30
    gray, 19, 21, 33, 60, 76, 82–83
    hot-pressed, 58, 72–73, 104,
        128–129, 133
    Mellotex, 52
    pastel, 8, 84–85, 116–117, 125
    rice paper, 68
    sanded paper, 24–25, 44–45,
        54, 70
    Saunders waterford, 80
    Sennelier La Carte, 72, 135
        sketchbook, 41, 65, 130
    Stonehenge, 24, 44, 52–53,
        86–89, 94, 98, 114
    Strathmore, 10, 16, 19, 27, 61,
        64, 113, 134
    textured, 56–57
    tinted/toned, 10, 17, 19, 39
    UArt, 44, 54, 137
    watercolor, 36, 56–58, 72–73,
        86, 69, 100–101, 103–104,
        127–129, 133
    See also Surfaces
Pastel(s), 11, 18, 21–22, 33–35,
        50, 84–85, 95, 105–106,
        108–109, 117, 137
    NuPastel, 112
    PanPastel, 19, 90–91
    soft, 20, 24–25, 44–45, 54, 70,
        72, 102, 108–109, 129, 135
    white, 17, 20, 33
PastelMat, 14–15, 66, 95
Pen(s), 48, 130
    ballpoint, 56
    dip, 36
    fountain, 94
    micron, 64
    rapidograph, 81
    water brush, 94
Pen and ink, 43, 46–47, 64, 123
Pencil(s), 13, 90–91, 100–101, 124
    carbon, 94
    charcoal, 12–13, 17, 19, 113
    graphite, 38–39, 74–75, 82,
        120–121, 126, 133
    Mars, 12–13
    pastel, 20, 66, 129
    woodless graphite, 41, 65
    See also Colored pencil(s)

Reductive techniques, 119

Sanding, 78–79, 97
Scratchboard, 4–5, 76
Scribbling, 43
Scumbling, 54
Shading, 8, 13, 36, 82
Silverpoint etching, 23, 56
Sketching, 43, 65
Smudging, 42, 75
Solvent, 44
Stippling, 48, 64, 81
Stumps, 12–13
Surfaces
Textural effects, 56
Textural strokes, 27
Texture(s), 5, 17–18, 28–29, 31, 39,
        42, 62, 66, 82, 115–118, 129
    in black-and-white drawings,
        92–93
    botanical, 40, 48–49
    contrasting, 32, 48–49, 60, 72,
        91, 95, 113
    fabric, 13, 104, 117
    of feathers, 64, 75, 68–69, 72–73
    of fur, 60–61, 66, 70, 80–81,
        84–86, 132
    of glass, 88–89, 91, 106–107
    gritty surface, 78–79
    of hair, 8, 20, 23, 111, 117, 122
    layers of, 43, 75
    liquids and water, 55, 91
    metal, 91, 98, 102, 126
    of rocks, 38–39, 48–49
    of skin, 6–7, 8, 11, 14–15, 20–21,
        111, 117
    of snake skin, 74
    of snow, 34–35
    of surfaces, 8, 10, 22, 36–37, 41,
        56–57, 103, 120, 123, 136
    urban, 126
    weathered, 44, 47, 50 51
    of wood, 38–39, 48–49, 52–53,
        66, 79, 103, 117
Tortillions, 12–13

Underdrawing, 20–21
Underpainting, 54

Value contrast, 13, 128–129
Values, 41, 84
Vellum, 49, 112, 126

Washes, 36, 39, 94, 128–129
Watercolor, 63, 68–69, 80, 118, 131

Strokes of Genius 8: Expressive Texture. Copyright © 2016 by F+W Media, Inc. Manufactured in China. All rights reserved. No part of this book may be reproduced in any form or by any electronic or mechanical means including information storage and retrieval systems without permission in writing from the publisher, except by a reviewer who may quote brief passages in a review. Published by North Light Books, an imprint of F+W Media, Inc., 10151 Carver Road, Suite 200, Blue Ash, Ohio, 45242. (800) 289-0963. First Edition.

Other fine North Light Books are available from your favorite bookstore, art supply store or online supplier. Visit our website at fwcommunity.com.

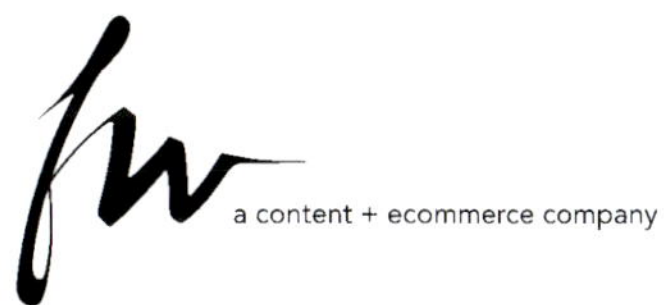

20 19 18 17 16   5 4 3 2 1

DISTRIBUTED IN CANADA BY FRASER DIRECT
100 Armstrong Avenue
Georgetown, ON, Canada L7G 5S4
Tel: (905) 877-4411

DISTRIBUTED IN THE U.K. AND EUROPE
BY F&W MEDIA INTERNATIONAL LTD
Brunel House, Forde Close, Newton Abbot, TQ12 4PU, UK
Tel: (+44) 1626 323200, Fax: (+44) 1626 323319
Email: enquiries@fwmedia.com

ISBN 13: 978-1-4403-4276-9

Production edited by Sarah Laichas
Designed by Clare Finney
Production coordinated by Jennifer Bass

Front cover image: Ken Brown | *Cassie* | p61
Back cover image: Denise J. Howard | *Tree of Character* | p53

Art page 1:

STRENGTH AT REST
Sandra Weiner
Graphite on bristol board
8" × 10" (25cm × 20cm)

I spend a lot of time with a graphite drawing, so I choose my photo references carefully (here, a photo by Paul Sherman). I was attracted to the contrast in the intensity of the leopard's eyes and the relaxed posture of his body, all in sharp focus.

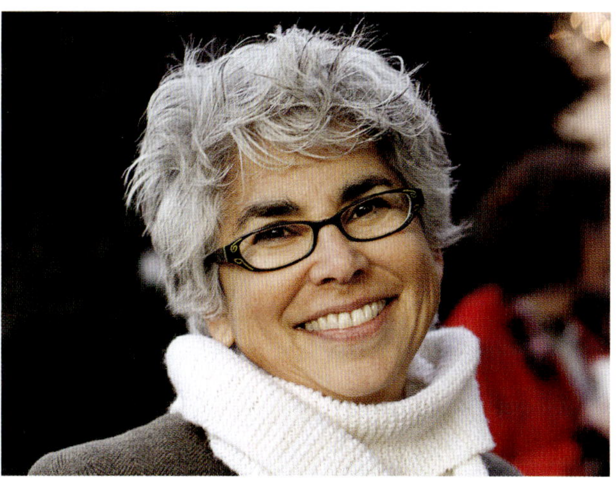

About the Editor

Rachel Rubin Wolf is a freelance editor and artist. She has edited and written many fine art books for North Light Books including *Watercolor Secrets*; the *Splash: Best of Watercolor* series; the *Strokes of Genius: Best of Drawing* series; *The Best of Wildlife Art* (editions 1 and 2); *The Best of Portrait Painting*; *Best of Flower Painting 2*; *The Acrylic Painter's Book of Styles and Techniques*; *Painting Ships, Shores and the Sea*; and *Painting the Many Moods of Light*. She also has acquired numerous fine art book projects for North Light Books and has contributed to magazines such as *Fine Art Connoisseur* and *Wildlife Art*.

Acknowledgments

Continuing thanks to my terrific *Strokes of Genius* partner, production editor Sarah Laichas, who collects and organizes material for me and takes care of the digital artwork among many other things. Thanks also to designer Clare Finney and to Tara Johnson who navigates the technical ins and outs of our online entries as well as the other editors, designers and staff at North Light Books. It takes a village to turn artwork and a manuscript into this beautiful finished book.

My gratitude to all of the artists who contribute so much texture to our lives! Each *Strokes* artist shares their work with much generosity of spirit. Your artwork and thoughts are inspiring to so many of us. Thank you also for getting the properly formatted digital photos to us in a timely manner, and for your vision that enables you to create these beautiful drawings.

Ideas. Instruction. Inspiration.

Receive FREE downloadable bonus materials when you sign up for our free newsletter at artistsnetwork.com/newsletter_thanks.

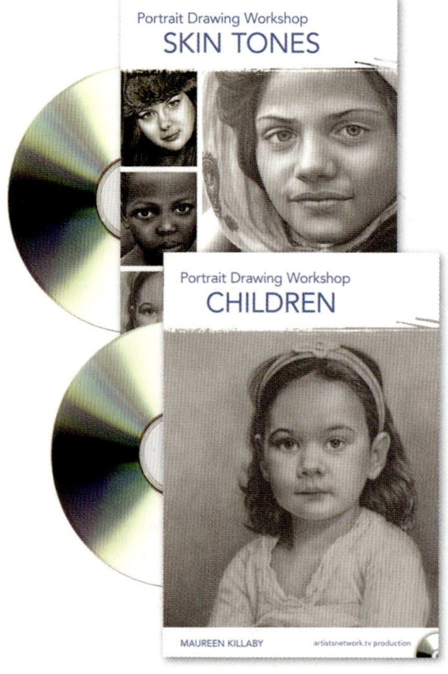

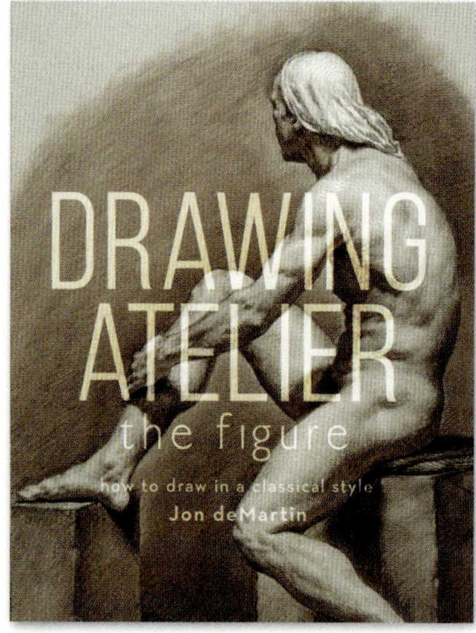

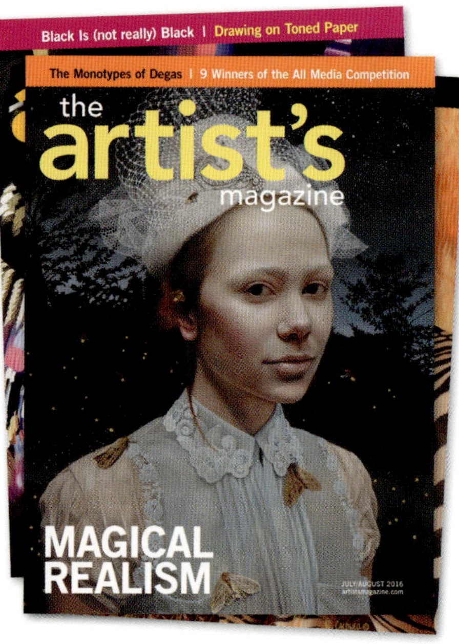

Find the latest issues of *The Artist's Magazine* on newsstands or visit artistsnetwork.com.

These and other fine North Light products are available at your favorite art & craft retailer, bookstore or online supplier. Visit our websites at artistsnetwork.com and artistsnetwork.tv.

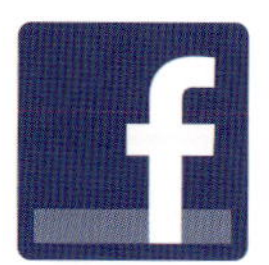

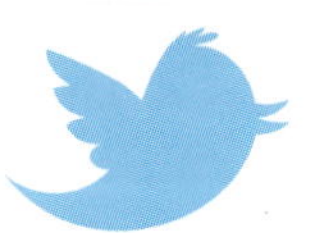

Follow Artist's Network for the latest news, free wallpapers, free demos and chances to win FREE BOOKS!

@artistsnetwork

Get your art in print!

Visit artistsnetwork.com/competitions for up-to-date information on *Strokes of Genius* and other North Light competitions.

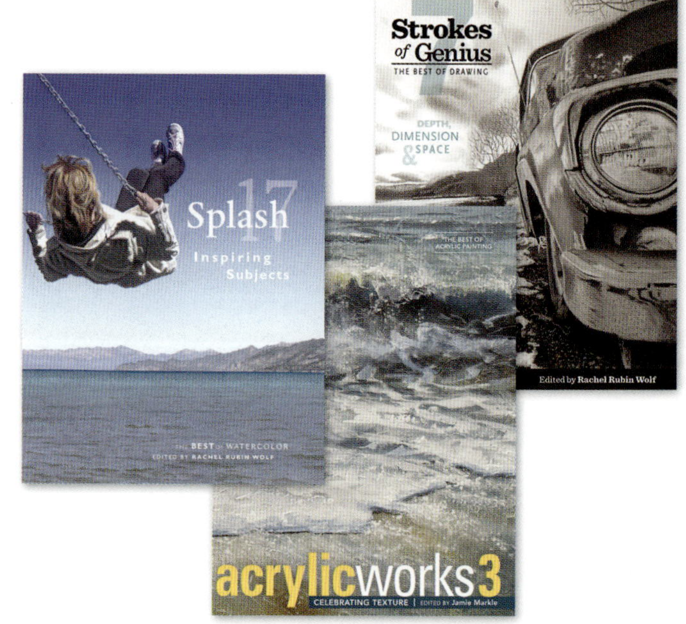